Nothing Is Lost

Nothing Is Lost

Selected Essays of Ingrid Sischy

Edited by Sandra Brant

Alfred A. Knopf

New York

2018

THIS IS A BORZOI BOOK PUBLISHED BY ALFRED A. KNOPF

Copyright © 2018 by Ingrid Sischy Estate

All rights reserved. Published in the United States by Alfred A. Knopf, a division of Penguin Random House LLC, New York, and distributed in Canada by Random House of Canada, a division of Penguin Random House Canada Limited, Toronto.

www.aaknopf.com

Knopf, Borzoi Books, and the colophon are registered trademarks of Penguin Random House LLC.

Library of Congress Cataloging-in-Publication Data
Names: Sischy, Ingrid, author. | Brant, Sandra, editor.
Title: Nothing is lost : selected essays of Ingrid Sischy / Ingrid Sischy ; edited by Sandra Brant.
Description: First edition. | New York : Alfred A. Knopf, 2018. | "This is a Borzoi book." |
    Includes index.
Identifiers: LCCN 2017047884 | ISBN 9781524732035 (hardcover)
Subjects: LCSH: Art. | Fashion.
Classification: LCC N7445.2 .S56 2018 | DDC 700—dc23
    LC record available at https://lccn.loc.gov/2017047884

Jacket design by Carol Devine Carson
Book design by Sam Shahid and Matthew Kraus

Manufactured in Germany
First Edition

For Ingrid

Try to be one of the people on whom nothing is lost.
—Henry James, *The Art of Fiction,* 1884

Contents

Foreword

By Laurie Anderson

I'm thinking of a summer evening in Venice in 1982. The Biennale was on, and Ingrid and I were standing outside a palazzo where there was a loud party in full swing. Ingrid was expected at the party and so we walked over to the girls with the clipboards standing at the door. Slicked-back ponytails, pale and sleek in identical black dresses, they had perfected the "Do-I-know-you?" look.

They were checking off the names on the guest list. Ingrid said, "Hi. I'm Ingrid Sischy, editor of *Artforum.*"

They raised their eyebrows. "Oh? And do you have ID?"

She did not and since she looked approximately nine years old it was hard to imagine she was an editor of an art magazine or that she even knew what an art magazine was. Ingrid said, "That's okay." Her eyes lit up, followed by a quick sideways glance and half smile. Her friends had seen this sequence many times—her eyes darting back and forth as if she were rapidly scanning the pros and cons of something she was about to say or do, running the alternatives and consequences. Laptop fast. We were familiar with this because Ingrid was one of the rare people who allowed you to see her think.

"Okay!" she said. "Let's go around the back and climb in the window." So we went around the back of the villa, pried open a first-story window, and jumped into the party we didn't really even want to be at. Once inside, Ingrid did some brisk and intense networking. She stood right in front of the people she was talking to, leaning toward them and giving them her complete attention. We left by the front door, which was pretty much the way she did a whole lot of things—coming in the back way and leaving by the front.

Ingrid was so many things: an editor, a critic, a writer who was interested in the political and cultural, and a sometime curator. *Nothing Is Lost* is a collection of essays and articles she wrote for a few books and such publications as *Vanity Fair, The New Yorker, Artforum,* and *The New York Times Magazine,* and they are intimate, warm, funny, and brilliant, like Ingrid. From the late seventies to the mid-teens, she wrote about and defined some of the most colorful and pivotal moments in the worlds of art and fashion.

Ingrid was also an insightful social critic, and her portraits of people were detailed, full of life, and never predictable. Reading this collection is like taking a walk through many different scenes, eras, and places: the East Village, Paris, Milan, and New York galleries, clubs and bars, as well as her days at *Artforum,* the AIDS crisis, and morphing cultural scenes. It's also a portrait of New York City, her hometown, as it constantly transforms itself with new images, trends, and ideas. When she describes Grandmaster Flash getting new sounds from scratching vinyl, she writes, "The result was the sound of a different city, deep inside the old."

She meets and talks with artists of all kinds—painters, photographers, designers, thinkers. We encounter her friends and subjects in new and intimate ways. And she talks about herself as well, telling us personal stories, quoting her favorite authors, voicing her opinions about trends and social and political developments. Throughout, I feel her sense of morality, justice, empathy, and social conscience.

As I read her words in 2018 her work seems especially relevant and I'm struck by her prescient comments on America, conformity, consumerism, and the social contract. Writing about the photographers William Eggleston, Robert Frank, and Garry Winogrand, she said they had "an ability to tap into our nation's psyche and the changes that are in the air." This could easily be said about Ingrid.

Or her haunting words in 2001 in "Triumph of the Still": "While the climate in recent years has never been better for art photography, fashion photography, and celebrity photography, socially concerned photojournalism has been marginalized. America by the end of the twentieth century had become like a country living in a bubble. It wanted to know very little about the injustices going on inside its borders and even less about those in the rest of the world."

Ingrid was a realist, a rebel, and a human rights champion working and writing in the rarefied and often elitist of worlds of culture and fashion. In 1989, describing the shifting social fabric, she noted, "It is about people being beaten down and psychologically bruised by the corporate machine." She watched and described consumerism taking shape on many levels. Thinking about making the country great by buying things and looking at pictures of people who were high on the new is especially relevant now. How did we get this way?

Whether they were angels or "terrible jerks," she wrote of the subjects in a photography exhibition, "most of them really seem to have believed that the work they were doing and the things they were buying were going to make their country great and their lives 'happy.'" She continues, noting that Martin Luther King, Jr., and his wife, Coretta Scott King, and their baby are also in the exhibition: "They do more than stand out; they remind us of a different dream."

Her descriptions of the Americans in these pictures begin to give us a sense of who we are now. Sometimes she looked back to daily life in the fifties and her descriptions are dead on. "A good number of the males in these photographs resemble Feds as they have been imagined by Hollywood—in boxy suits and fedoras. . . . The women (except for the showgirls) look neat and uptight. The children look worried." These people are on the go and in love with the new. "A rather handsome man holds a meeting in his Bel Air home, in a room that seems to be a combination of tree house, boardroom, and appliance store." And they show us the origins of some of what our self-obsessed culture has since become. "Yes, there are photographs that bring out the snake-oil aspect of advertising, and photographs that display people at their most self-important. And there's proof of how tight the door to the new Paradise was."

Throughout her work Ingrid was clear about her role as a critic: "The notion that art speaks for itself is appealing but unrealistic. To get into circulation and to achieve some kind of status, art needs believers, defenders, interpreters, dealers, collectors, and museums." She herself was a deep believer, consummate defender, and brilliant interpreter.

I learned so many things from her insights and sometimes sidelong observations. She writes that Bob Richardson's photographs "conveyed some essential qualities of the sixties: the drugginess, the sexual freedom, the growing gulf between men and women." Reading about this gulf was exhilarating, not something I saw very clearly, if at all, at the time.

Nothing Is Lost highlights Ingrid's mix of savvy erudition and playful archaic slang like "hoi polloi," "bombshell allure," and "the big kahuna." She had an ear for the expressions of her artist and designer subjects, and always let them speak for themselves. She notes that the late painter James Rosenquist "still says, 'You dig?'" and that when he's listing his dead artist friends he asks her, "Who do I go to for stuff like 'How do you make rabbit-skin glue again?'" She doesn't have an answer for him, but she does go on to explain to her readers that rabbit-skin glue was used in a traditional method of coating canvas to increase the sense of depth in a painting.

Ingrid often used comparisons that put unlikely artists together, such as the photographers Minor White and Robert Mapplethorpe. The link between their work is love, she says and writes damningly of White, "There's very little warmth or humor in the bulk of White's work. . . . He makes all the discoveries, and the viewer's job is to respond to what he found." She also looked behind the images and used them to talk about things like doubt and honesty. "One way to avoid pedagogy is to be human, to show doubt by acknowledging that life brings more questions than answers. But to do that requires an honest look at oneself—exactly what White felt he couldn't afford in his public pictures."

Comparing Clementina, Lady Hawarden, and Cindy Sherman, she called them "soul sisters separated by more than a century." We meet Hawarden, who played dress up with her daughters and then photographed them, photographs that were admired by Charles Dodgson. Seeing Lady Hawarden's and Cindy Sherman's work in the same article makes both women's work even more vivid, intuitive, and inventive. Always expanding on her themes, Ingrid goes on to describe Marilyn Monroe as a person consumed by her own image, another mirror. As a critic of photography, she would sometimes pose philosophical questions like What is a picture and how does it relate to our experience of reality?: "[Dan] Weiner's photographs look more like images from TV and the movies than like photographs of real people doing real things."

Ingrid was fascinated by the complicated relationship between stars and fans and wrote about it as "a form of cannibalism" amid the growing certainty for the last several decades that famous people's lives are "*our* business." For some writers name-dropping validates their stories but Ingrid did the opposite, dropping the names out of the story and focusing on the person behind it. As a writer, critic and editor she had been an essential part of every scene for decades in downtown Manhattan, and she knew hundreds of artists, many as close friends. When she describes having dinner at Da Silvano with Mapplethorpe or having Christmas dinner with Sam Wagstaff she writes with the confidence that her readers won't see this as name-dropping but as her own storytelling.

Ingrid takes us in. She puts herself in her pieces. She wrote about her childhood in South Africa in "A Picture of One's Own" when she described what it felt like not to have photographs of a man who worked for her family. One of the leitmotifs in the collection is a gray corduroy skirt she wore briefly in 1977. When Ingrid was told she had gotten a job in the public affairs office of an important New York cultural institution, and not to report to work wearing pants, she went to Bloomingdale's and bought a gray corduroy skirt. Once freed from that job, she went to the banks along the West Side Highway and threw the skirt into the Hudson River; she would not need it for her next job, a photography fellowship at MoMA, which had no dress code. Her friend Versace loved the story. She bridged her interest in art and fashion with passion, styling her own liberation. Writing about Miuccia Prada's clothes triggered an emotional response:

> *. . . The clothes had an answer for problems that are rarely faced in fashion: "It's okay if you've made mistakes, if you're scared, if you're aggressive, if you're fat, if you're beautiful, if you're ugly, if you feel crazy, defensive, happy," the collection seemed to say. "Come into my arms." I watched it, entranced. Especially the dresses. It was the first time in twenty years that I'd been able to picture myself wearing one.*

And talking about her own way of dressing, Ingrid cited her friend k.d. lang, who she said didn't wear the clothes she did to be associated with men or because she wanted to come off as a man but because "it's just that there were no other kinds of clothes that had to do with confidence and authority instead of vulnerability and stereotypical sexiness." Until, that is, by chance k.d. tried on that Prada jacket. Once in a while Ingrid enters the story as herself. By the way, she explains, "I bat on Gertrude Stein's team, and love my partner."

Ingrid was able to create touching pictures of artists and these pictures become indelible. There's Jeff Koons's mother serving him milk and cookies, Calvin Klein's mother sewing the labels into his first batch of clothes, and Keith Haring's father dropping him off in New York City for school and just leaving him there. "*Where was I?*—dumping him in the middle of New York City, putting him on the sidewalk with his boxes of belongings. I couldn't even go in with him."

She slips in such details as that Francesco Clemente played the hypnotist in a Gus Van Sant movie and that his wife, Alba Clemente, and Helen Marden used to go to Bar Pitti. As Marden said, "We'll bitch about Francesco and Brice for hours. . . . When we're finished with lunch, we always say, 'Well, they're really wonderful.' But we've spent the preceding hour and a half totally complaining about how they talk about themselves all the time."

Ingrid wrote extensively about AIDS and its effects on the art world. She could write in a clear-eyed but passionate way about danger and loss. She wanted to know what people cared about, what drove them to work. She was persistent and talked to her subjects many times as she drew their portraits. In the middle of the interview process Francesco Clemente said, "You have to remember that I am from a country where artists were once the equivalent of the prostitute or the drug dealer," but she kept asking questions until she finally asked what was his "deepest reason" for becoming an artist. Clemente replied, "Because I am heartbroken."

During an interview she often questions herself and makes the reader part of her process. She described how she had been writing about the "explicit" Mapplethorpe photographs and the Corcoran Gallery's cancellation of the show and then suddenly found herself sitting in Jeff Koons's studio looking at images of Koons and porn star/politician Cicciolina engaged in various positions. She described her confusion and ambivalence about the lines she had drawn between sex, art, and pornography. She also notes her complicated reactions to Lee Friedlander's nudes, asking and then unasking questions, asking herself why she's asking questions, why "he's been dressed in a room while his subject has been naked." She talks about how her antennae go up and then traces the picturing of the female nude through history.

Ingrid was a historian and traced the history of images. She identified the links between sign painting and art as she described the young Rosenquist out with the rest of the sign painters, many of whom were ex-cons, "whooping it up" across the Midwest painting billboards, grain silos, and gasoline tanks. Suddenly the connection between sign painting—Phillips 66 and Coca-Cola—and art comes into focus, and Jasper Johns makes a new kind of sense. "How can I use this method to show the emptiness and numbness of all this?" she quotes Rosenquist.

What comes between me and my Calvins? Nothing! Ingrid connects fashion to art in her writing about the famous Calvin Klein underwear images shot by Bruce Weber. She's also interested in the mechanics and nuts and bolts of photography. She quotes Friedlander: "Flash renders everything. And everybody knows when you've taken the picture. It's not a secret. It's not a quiet moment." Her observations about photography range from the technical to the cultural phenomenal and are often about how these are linked. "Cameras have become as available as candy, with millions of people trying to be their own Ansel Adams."

She wrote of 9/11, "the days immediately following the tragedy marked the first time that more people logged on to news sites than pornography," and noted that photography became more accessible. During September 11 and its immediate aftermath many Magnum photographers happened to be in New York and shot at the Trade Center site, but the interns were also there and ended up sharing space on the Magnum website with their famous members.

"I think of September 11 as the day photography got back one of its most important jobs, the day it regained its potential. Now let's watch it go to work as we try to stop the world from blowing up," she wrote at the time, optimistically.

She was unafraid of covering controversy and took on issues relating to institutions navigating politics and art and government suppression of imagery, as in her story of the Smithsonian's treatment of Subhankar Banerjee's photos. The show opened at the time of a debate about the oil exploration bill in the Arctic, "so the timing couldn't have been worse." She continues, "The Smithsonian's capitulation, whatever the reason, reminds me of another wasteland, the one T. S. Eliot spoke of in 1921 when he wrote this: *The awful daring of a moment's surrender / Which an age of prudence can never retract.*"

She often expressed her gratitude to people she worked with and people who helped her, especially to her mentor John Szarkowski, who, in turn, had championed Diane Arbus and Garry Winogrand. But she didn't shy away from describing disagreements such as the one with Szarkowski about how he occasionally missed in his analysis of the differences between photography and art. In a unique choice of dramatization, she described this argument with him in third person and watched herself having a heated discussion with him in a restaurant.

Ingrid was passionate and empathetic and unafraid of emotion. Writing about John Szarkowski's nostalgia for the past as he describes his adventures working on his book *The Idea of Louis Sullivan,* she quotes him, "I think Americans were more interesting then. It makes me want to cry to say it." "Looking at his photographs created over the last fifty years makes me want to weep myself. They are truly American pictures; one feels his desire to show not just what America was but what it still can be." Ingrid's words about Szarkowski's reactions to Louis Sullivan take us on a journey back in time as she shows us chain reactions and how ideas and feelings are passed down.

Her empathetic profile of John Galliano after his career-wrecking anti-Semitic comments went viral was full of research about addiction and self-destructive behavior. She didn't just speculate but talked to experts in psychology and addiction about how that could have happened. She brought herself into the story when she explained she hadn't gone to the first Galliano show following his disgraceful departure because her brother Mark, a brilliant judge who was also an alcoholic, had died, and she had to attend the stone setting in a cemetery in Edinburgh.

Ingrid was never afraid to mix her admiration for artists with acerbic, often hilarious comments. Jeff Koons reminds her of Darrin, the "very courteous husband in the sixties TV show *Bewitched*." Of her friend Rene Ricard she wrote, "Rene's charisma was not lost on Andy Warhol, who cast him in *Kitchen* and *Chelsea Girls,* among other films. For my money, though, this poet, critic, painter, was born to play a thief and a priest." Of pictures in her friend Robert Mapplethorpe's exhibition, she adds, "And even among the controversial photographs there are affected examples—such as *Joe* (1978), a man in head-to-toe rubber—that are just silly; the image is all outfit with nowhere to go."

The pretentiousness of museums did not escape her notice, as when the director of exhibitions at MoMA approached John Szarkowski, the man who eventually became her mentor, with the oblique "It has occurred to us that you might like to talk with us about our future and possibly yours"—an invitation "so courteous and so vague and so pregnant with the belief that the museum was the center of the universe, it really is a hoot." And she was a sharp critic when controversy was involved. On the Corcoran Gallery's cancellation of the Mapplethorpe show she writes, "Often, though, it is the people in charge of these museums who have the closed minds; and the audience, as Mapplethorpe's crowds prove, is fully capable of dealing with the controversial material."

Ingrid understood and appreciated fame and its pitfalls and pleasures. She lovingly described Catherine Opie photographing Elizabeth Taylor's house, and using the decor in the elegant Parisian apartment of the mysterious Mr. H., she creates a portrait as she is hypnotized by listening to him talk about decorating as "ghost chasing," and then she segues into how fantasies of dream places are created and how association works. Part of the pleasure of reading Ingrid's writing is the way she relates ideas and art forms. She compares Mr. H. to Pip in *Great Expectations.* After Pip's first sight of Miss Havisham's he was never the same. She quotes Dickens, "Pause you who read this, and think for a moment of the long chain of iron or gold, of thorns or flowers, that would never have bound you, but for the formation of the first link on one memorable day."

For me, reading her words is also hearing her voice, hearing her laugh, feeling the pleasure of sharing secrets and in-jokes. She often addresses her readers. In an aside after telling an anecdote about Jean Pigozzi's father cleaning himself all over with alcohol, even his penis, she leans in and says, "And you thought you were going to read about just another rich guy."

She got to know her subjects and sometimes wrote about that process using art or photography terms. Quoting the war photographer Robert Capa, "If your pictures aren't good enough, you're not close enough." She herself was always zooming in on facts, getting closer to her subjects. Of Lee Friedlander's nudes she wrote, "With the nudes you can almost feel the seconds passing. You can just about see these bodies breathing."

When she was working on a piece she was tenacious about getting the backstories. She had a great interest and compassion for people in trouble and knew how to put it into words, such as when she wrote about the English historian who tracked down the photographer Bob Richardson—one of the missing-in-action drug casualties—to an SRO hotel in California. Or for a Jeff Koons piece, she followed the trail of Koons's missing wife Cicciolina to South America, where she was doing her porn shows.

Ingrid was always part of the scene and often got to watch artists working. She ran into Lee Friedlander taking photos on the street. She went to watch Karl Lagerfeld photograph. She knew so many people and introduced them without name-dropping, using them instead to make a bigger picture or cut to the heart. She quoted Elizabeth Taylor, who wrote in her biography, "I believe that people are like rocks, formed by the weather. We're formed by experience, by heartache, by grief, by mistakes, by guilt, by shame. I'm glad that in my life I have never cut short my emotions. The most awful thing of all is to be numb."

Talking with Ingrid was always exhilarating for me. She would remember the last conversation we had—what we were celebrating or worried about or making fun of. Our friendship was one long animated conversation punctuated by the work and travel we both did. But she always knew how to make people feel like her best friend and she talked wholeheartedly as if nothing else mattered.

My only regret in our friendship is that I didn't see more of her. She was often lost in her work, "closing a story," "holed up in the city writing," but was always ready to help. "Give a bell if there is anything, and I mean anything, I can help with," she wrote. Her selflessness and her determination were integral to most of her friendships, and she was always generous and specific in sharing all sorts of advice and information, making sure to note things like "Oh and here's her cell phone, and don't forget she's off on Tuesdays." Her enthusiasm morphed seamlessly into hard work. Once she decided to put one of my songs, "Let x = x," into *Artforum* as a flexidisc. When she decided to do something she got it done and then just went on.

Ingrid and my husband, Lou Reed, shared a birthday, March 2, and I think they felt that this bond, this twin number, magically linked them. The other things that linked them were their antennae and their absolute trust in their intuition. Ingrid had the greatest antennae for the real story, for the spin. Both of them deeply trusted and expressed their emotions.

Through the eighties until her death in 2015, we were often meeting by chance at art openings, shows, concerts, and events. She also invited us to operas, plays, and to join the group of her artist friends on the east end of Long Island. On special occasions she and her partner, Sandy, often sent presents from Paris or Bilbao. For Lou's seventieth birthday, seventy small and delicate vases, each with a flower, arrived precisely on March 2.

In my house now I keep Ingrid's picture in my hallway next to one of Lou. I see her when I come in and go out. She inspires me every day with her radicalism, her truthfulness, her work ethic, and her love of life. I know you will love her ideas and her writing as much as I do.

—Laurie Anderson, February 2018

Nothing Is Lost

Let's Pretend

How many artists have passed through the world without being noticed? How many got a flash of attention, and that was it? Over and over, we hear about the same artists, but what about all the others—the unknown, uncelebrated ones, who far outnumber those whose work has stayed visible and valued? Among the uncelebrated ones, how many never had a chance, just because luck wasn't with them—because they weren't in the right place at the right moment, or they weren't the "right" sex or the "right" race? You don't have to be hyperconscious of cultural biases to realize that art history can involve more than judgments about the good, the bad, and the ugly.

The notion that art speaks for itself is appealing but unrealistic. To get into circulation and to achieve some kind of status, art needs believers, defenders, interpreters, dealers, collectors, and museums. If an artist lacks such support, he or she has one basic hope: that some time in the future the work will be recognized and honored. For that to happen, though, it has to survive. There is no guaranteed system of protection for art. Anything can affect its fate. Age, say, can destroy it. It can be in a city that is bombed, it can be in a house that is burned. The vicissitudes of taste can come into play, and art that was once treasured can be abandoned. It can be deaccessioned by a museum, or it can be put into storage and become as good as lost. But disappearing for a while can also serve art well; being ignored can be a form of accidental preservation until its time has come. That is what happened to the photography of Clementina, Lady Hawarden.

Hawarden's entire body of work was made in eight years, from 1857 to 1865, when she died, at the age of forty-two. Soon after her death, except

Clementina, Lady Hawarden, *Clementina & Isabella Grace Maude,* ca. 1863–1864

for a few photographs that she herself had sold or given to friends and that eventually ended up in private and public collections, her work was out of public sight. Her photography turned into a secret because almost all of it was passed down within her family. But even after Hawarden's granddaughter Lady Clementina Tottenham gave the family pictures to London's Victoria and Albert Museum, in 1939, the work remained in obscurity. This gift was a windfall, but by then no one remembered Hawarden, and there was no demand for what she had accomplished. Back in the 1860s, for a season or two, her prints had been singled out when they appeared in group exhibitions, winning her compliments and silver medals, but in 1939 she had been dead for almost seventy-five years, and her reputation had been buried with her. The photographs were stashed away.

People compare museums to shrines, and that comparison seems appropriate for the rooms one usually gets to see. Behind the scenes, though, many museums are more like a crowded attic; there's usually an accretion of stuff, some of it valuable, some of it junk. These unfeatured objects have an especially touching aura. It's as if they were waiting in the wings, ready understudies. Will they get a chance to appear? Sometimes the big break happens, as with Hawarden. Fifty years after her photographs got to the V & A, a group of them was selected for an exhibition there—the first all-Hawarden show ever. Now, that's what one calls waiting for recognition.

Being sequestered as private property and then landing in museum storage are only two of the reasons that Hawarden's photography was almost lost to history. Another factor was a lack of interest in her *kind* of work, which must be why the museum shelved her photographs in the first place. Mostly, Hawarden took photographs of her daughters in fancy dress. Perhaps if she'd used famous people as her models the interest in her work would have been greater, but she didn't; hers are family photographs, a genre that has historically been thought unworthy of serious attention. Nevertheless, they're wonderful. And they were born of one of the few things in life in which women have traditionally been granted more opportunity for self-expression than men—dressing up.

When Mark Haworth-Booth, curator of photography at the V & A, assigned a graduate student, Virginia Dodier, to go through the museum's Hawarden material, she had an art historian's dream job. Almost nothing was known about the eight hundred or so Hawarden pictures, or the woman who took them. It was Dodier's detective work that eventually led to a catalogue raisonné and to Lady Hawarden's first exhibition, which then traveled in smaller versions to the Musée d'Orsay, in Paris; the Museum of Modern Art, in New York; and, finally, the J. Paul Getty Museum, in Malibu. It's unlikely that the pictures will soon be let out on the road again: The darkness that enveloped them all those years turns out to have been healthy in terms of their physical protection. Like most photographs made in the early days, they don't like light.

At first, Hawarden's photographs are shocks, and for a number of reasons. Not only do they seem otherworldly in their beauty, but they are peopled almost exclusively by women. (You can find men in her work, but their roles are minor—they function merely as tokens of the life that surrounded these flights of fancy.) One is not used to such subliminally charged pictures, and certainly not ones that cross back and forth between purity and sensuality as these do. Nor does one usually see at exhibitions photographs whose corners and edges have been dramatically torn, giving them idiosyncratic shapes. (This occurred when they were ripped out of the family albums in which they once sat—apparently before they got to the Victoria and Albert.) The baroque shapes add to the works' mystery, by reinforcing their similarity to pieces of a puzzle. With their cuttlefish hues, their feeling of age, and their deformed state, many of the photographs appear so fragile that they seem to float, and their content enhances their sense of weightlessness. There's something dreamily luxurious about them. And, like dreams, they're imbued with a mysterious sexuality.

Hawarden's body of work simply couldn't have happened if everyone hadn't put in long hours. Since her daughters were her models, one wonders what she would do today. Would the girls sit endlessly for her, as they did then? Would they be willing to put on all that cumbersome fancy dress? Or would they be out and about in London—at university, at jobs, watching *Twin Peaks*? If the girls should prove too busy for her, there is someone in New York she could call on who would understand her: Cindy Sherman.

No exhibition has yet been mounted at which we could view photographs by Lady Hawarden and Cindy Sherman side by side, but both of them have several images reproduced in a recent book by Constance Sullivan, *Women Photographers,* published by Abrams. Sherman provides the final image, one of the ugliest photographs ever made. Bugs crawl through a tacky, knotted-up pinky-blond wig that all but covers Sherman's face—strangles it, really. One eye is visible. You could say that that eye is patriotic—it's red, white, and blue. (The eyeball is blue, and it would take a six-pack of Visine to clear up the surrounding redness.) Sherman's nutty self-portrait is at the opposite pole from Hawarden's work when it comes to aesthetics; Sherman has indulged herself in an orgy of aggression against beauty and self-control, while Hawarden's portraits eagerly accommodate Victorian society's expectations of how women should look. Hawarden's and Sherman's portraits in *Women Photographers* beg for comparison: They're like images you find in "before" and "after" narratives—in this case, the narrative of women before and after they publicly took the matter of their lives into their own hands. However, the fact that Hawarden and Sherman appear to be opposites is not what makes them an interesting couple. Cindy Sherman and Clementina, Lady Hawarden—two women whose names sound as different as a ringing telephone and a church chime, and whose pictures have equally contrasting contexts—are soul sisters separated by more than a century. There's a tie between their photographs that connects them as surely as an umbilical cord.

With these two, what you're looking at is home entertainment that doesn't require stereos, TVs, or prepackaged games. Both artists are involved in building fantasies, and that does require other players, though, or at least the illusion of other players. Hawarden found her stars in her own house; her daughters were not only her leading ladies but occasionally her Romeos, too. There's no family nucleus in Sherman's imagery. The stamp of a Sherman, so far, has been that she is her own model—her own woman, man, et cetera. (You can't always count on finding Sherman in her photographs nowadays, but her absences are a relatively new development in a fourteen-year career.) The references and the vocabularies of Hawarden and Sherman are clearly products of different eras. For instance, painting, literature, and a sense of faraway places inform Hawarden's work; the movies and magazines are what inspired Sherman's first tableaux, and later, when she moved on to spoof painting, her photographic twists on art history were decidedly contemporary. But, again, these differences are less interesting than what the two women have in common.

Hundreds and hundreds of photographs prove how central to their art dressing up and pretending have been. Just an atmospheric setting, an assortment of outfits, and a camera: That's all these two artists need. Of course, there's something else they bring—imagination. Hawarden and Sherman are examples of giving in to fantasy wholeheartedly. And not only for the sake of art. It's public knowledge that Sherman started dressing herself up as someone else before she began doing it for her pictures—that she continued this typical childhood game into adulthood. In an interview that appeared last year in *W* she explained, "I guess whenever I would get moody or depressed, I would spend a couple of hours turning myself into somebody else with makeup or clothes. . . . It was a cathartic thing that I needed to do. In Buffalo"—she went to college there—"when I would go and watch TV with people, I'd be dressed up like Lucille Ball. Or there'd be an opening, and I'd go as a pregnant woman or something."

People who have seen Sherman's wild pictures seem to be surprised when they meet her for the first time. "But she's the girl-next-door type," they say.

Well, who but someone who's been there could conjure up what Sherman does with such authority? In the *W* interview she provides another memory— one that qualifies as a collective refrain, it's so widely shared: "I could remember putting on a girdle, putting myself through torture at 13, when I certainly didn't need a girdle, because I thought, 'This is what beauty is.' . . . I can remember waking up before going to school and spending 45 minutes putting on makeup because you never know who might be at the door—Mr. Right might be there—remember him?"

Over the years, Sherman's technique has grown highly sophisticated, but there's something especially compelling about her earlier, rougher work. You can see a mass of it in *Untitled Film Stills,* which Rizzoli published last October. The book reproduces forty of more than eighty eight-by-ten-inch photographs that Sherman made between 1977 and 1980. The photographs have the look of movie publicity stills, hence their title. Talk about striking oil quickly! At this experimental stage of her career, Sherman found her voice as an artist, precisely because she didn't try anything fancy; she simply started recording what she was already up to—getting dressed up as somebody else—and that's why this work is so authentic and convincing. Much of what has followed is technically cleverer and visually richer, but these earlier images have something particularly magnetic about them. The pictures are so spontaneous that it's almost as if she were fooling around with a friend, not making art with a capital *A.* Her approach to the medium is still amateur, which gives these pictures the sense of freedom that can occur when people do things they think nobody's paying any attention to.

When Sherman made "Untitled Film Stills," she had no money to speak of. During part of that time, she supported herself by working as a receptionist at Artists Space, one of many "alternative spaces" created in the seventies by groups of artists who felt that museums and commercial galleries weren't responsive enough to what was happening in contemporary art. Sherman didn't always show up for work looking as one might expect her to. Not that a receptionist has a particular outfit, but unless you're in a doctor's or a dentist's office you usually don't find the person at the front desk in a nurse's uniform—clothing that Sherman once wore to the job, we are informed in Arthur Danto's introduction to the Rizzoli book. Danto correctly links Sherman's cameos to the performance art that was burgeoning then, but the odds are that she would have got herself up in nurse drag all on her own.

Sherman's stills are generic more than specific; mostly, they recall images of women that one might find in movies or magazines of the fifties and sixties. Since the stills were made before the fashions of those years came back into vogue, her out-of-date wardrobe was cheap. She could find plenty of outfits and props in thrift shops and flea markets, and her ingenuity is a lesson in making something on a small budget. Again and again, her imagination saved the day. Beyond her visual resolutions, there's her talent as a chameleon. Whether or not Sherman's skills at role-playing would translate onto the stage or the screen I don't know, but in her own photography she's a real Sarah Bernhardt. She plays sex kitten, ingénue, anxious lover, fallen woman, gal about town, victim, vixen, virgin, lonely girl, rich girl, the girl everyone wants—all right in key. Her settings and costumes have a genuine B-movie touch.

The shot that always gets to me is one that might have fallen out of *Bus Stop*. In it, Sherman stands on a country road, her back to the viewer. She has put on a ponytailed platinum wig, a loose white shirt, a checked skirt, white ankle socks, and "girls' sneakers." A suitcase is on the ground next to her. She's looking up the road, as if waiting for a bus or a car to round the bend. Years ago, interviewing Sherman, I asked her about that photograph. She said that her father had taken it. It had happened when she and her parents were motoring through Arizona, and Sherman, who was sitting in the backseat, noticed that the view they were about to drive into promised a photo opportunity. The family was used to her routine. The car stopped. The trunk was opened. She put on her costume, set up the shot with her suitcase, and then ran into the scene.

Her well-trained father snapped the picture. This story tells a lot about Sherman's approach to photography. She isn't bothered that it's a medium anyone can handle. She takes advantage of its mechanical properties: Sometimes she's had someone else press the button. She's just the type to have appreciated those roadside billboards that used to alert drivers, PICTURE AHEAD! KODAK AS YOU GO.

It's more than a decade since Sherman finished the "Untitled Film Stills" series. With time, the images have settled into place as classics, the foundation for all that came after, and, like anything repeated too often, they could have turned into a rut. But Sherman moved on to make all sorts of different images of herself, among them pictures that suggest brutality, and funny images, too, that are full of grotesquerie, foulness, and campiness. Then her over-the-top expressions of hideousness gave way to witty, technically impressive photographic parodies of Renaissance paintings, in which, as usual, she used herself as the model, whether male or female, gross or thin, gorgeous or unappealing. These large-scale pictures are a kind of climax to what she began with the film stills, and from the moment they were shown they were smash hits. Who doesn't want a Renaissance masterpiece in his or her apartment—an au courant one at that, since Sherman's gender-bending in these works seems to call for the joke that they're really Ms. Pieces?

Right from the start, Sherman has been held up as a paradigm of feminist photography, and as a "postmodern" example of artists who appropriate images already in the world and redo them in a way that somehow throws the spotlight on their metameaning in our culture. She has come to embody all this, but I don't believe it's how she began—there's been so much more to her constructions than image deconstruction. At the time she started out, wearing lipstick, heels, and short skirts didn't exactly earn you merit points in the women's liberation movement. As Sherman herself says, she was self-conscious about how "silly" dressing up was. When you ask her about her work, she's noticeably untheoretical and tentative. Listening to her, you'd think it all came about by accident, but looking at the work itself you can clearly see that it was motivated by pleasure and desire.

Given Sherman's apparent freedom to move in and out of different situations, even different eras, the consistency of time and place that one sees in Lady Hawarden's photographs of her daughters is an obvious point of contrast. The architectural details and the decorative elements in the photographs leave no doubt that the female Hawardens are almost always shown in the same few rooms, and it is the repetition of these environments that gives Hawarden's images their cloistered atmosphere. But that doesn't mean that these girls didn't go anywhere. You don't have to leave a place physically to take journeys of the imagination, and that they certainly did, along with their mother and what must have seemed a magical vehicle: her camera. The camera in the late 1850s was a fashionable recent invention, an exciting addition to a moneyed household. As we can see in Hawarden's work, the camera could transport the already beloved parlor games of the time into a new dimension. The daughters seem so taken up with posing for it that their interest in collaboration must have gone beyond indulging Mama.

Many questions about Lady Hawarden remain unanswered, and since nothing has yet been found that documents what she intended by her pictures it's up to us to make of them what we can. Usually, art historical information restricts one's interpretations like a leash, and it is easy to forget that such information is often the product of assumptions. With Lady Hawarden, the mystery is out in the open, and one can dive in freely and respond subjectively, stimulated by the minimal yet evocative facts.

She was a Scot who ended up in London, but her mother, Catalina Paulina Alessandro, was Spanish. The Mediterranean background doesn't come through in Hawarden's maiden name, Clementina Elphinstone Fleeming; it's as Scottish as high tea. Still, you can detect traces of the grandmother's

Cindy Sherman, *Untitled Film Still #48,* 1979

heritage in Hawarden's daughters, and it may have influenced Clementina's un-Victorian sense of elegance. In other ways, she fitted the norm. As was customary for women then, she spent her entire adult life having children. There were ten in all, over a span of eighteen years; the first child was born the year after she got married, the last the year before she died, of pneumonia. Eight lived—seven girls and one boy. Clementina came from money and she married money—Cornwallis Maude, who eventually succeeded to the title Viscount Hawarden. The family's wealth is evident in her pictures: The costumes, the homes, and the bearing of the girls themselves suggest that one is looking at people of some social status.

From the Getty show (which included forty-two prints) it appears that three of Hawarden's daughters—the older girls—were her principal models. There's something intensely rarefied about her presentation of the girls; they're like hothouse prizes. You can't stop being aware of their appearance, or of what they're doing physically. One of Virginia Dodier's captions told us that Clementina, the second daughter, was her mother's favorite subject, but Isabella Grace, the eldest, and Florence Elizabeth, the third, had major roles in this exhibition, too. At the Getty, I regretted the absence of a picture of the much younger Elphinstone Agnes (called Eppy) that had been included in MoMA's show. That photograph is a charmer. Little, and a bit chubby, Eppy has a naughty look. Standing in her bare feet, in her summer dress, she's got to be a kick.

Hawarden's photographs, and her daughters, caught the eye of a fellow amateur photographer, Charles Dodgson, and it's not a surprise. Dodgson expressed his admiration in his diary, and he also bought five Hawarden prints. What with his reputation for being—shall we say—focused on young girls, and not just the one he sent down the rabbit hole, one could ascribe his pleasure in the portraits to his own very particular tastes. But many other people take Hawarden's work to be suggestive, especially when they first come upon it without the knowledge that all the girls are her daughters.

This is understandable. Sensuality oozes from many of these pictures. Hawarden liked to pair her daughters, either by posing them together in tableaux or by using mirrors, which gave her an intimate double image, and some of these scenes are ripe for being taken as erotically charged love scenes. They may well be; it was the Victorian age, after all—a puritanical time that produced a lot of titillating imagery, and on the whole the girls themselves were at an age where everything's primed for falling in love. But ultimately Hawarden's pictures are about moods and thoughts; and who knows who, or what, was actually going through the minds of the girls? Many of the photographs thrive on a sense of ambiguity; drive them too hard to conclusions or interpretations and they lose their lovely state of suspension. Hawarden didn't title her pictures, perhaps because she and the family knew what each one was about, or perhaps because she intended the mystery—the pictures were taken while the family was playing games of make-believe. At any rate, when she displayed her photographs at public events—such as one Dodgson referred to in his diary as a "bazaar for the benefit of Female Artists"—she listed them as "Studies from Life" and "Photographic Studies." This was a typical way of establishing that the photographs were to be considered as art.

The Getty title for the Hawarden exhibition was "Domestic Idylls," and that suits the content of Hawarden's imagery. You can visualize how it all came about. Together much of the day, the mother and the daughters found a never-ending source of amusement—each other. And they had material that would never run dry: their lives, their favorite stories, beloved characters, exquisite dresses to put on and dream in—costumes that could transport them to other times, other cultures, other narratives. For example, at the Getty one could see Clementina acting a biblical part, or one could find her as a male figure, in breeches, down on the proverbial knee, at her sister Isabella's side. There were instances of the Hawardens' use of Oriental costumes and peasant dress, and obvious nods to the fad of the day, Pre-Raphaelite painting. And there were homages to that heroine of heroines for the Scots, their Queen Mary. But ultimately these more illustrational pictures aren't as mesmerizing as Hawarden's simplest photographs—her shots of the girls at dressing tables or looking out of windows.

It's lucky that Hawarden's themes lent themselves to all that head drooping and holding on to drapery, walls, mirrors, and windows—between the dressing and the posing, the girls must have been exhausted. And Mother had to do far more than "press the button." It's evident from her angles (and, one supposes, her choreography of the girls) what a grand compensator Hawarden was in terms of solving the difficulties of her medium—for example, the strain on a human being who had to hold still for as long as the camera required. And it's clear from her solutions concerning light—most obviously in the pictures that involve mirrors and windows—what a grasp she had of the problems that characterized photography then. The mirrors and windows had more than one function: They were technical as well as narrative devices. This is decades before flash; natural light was obligatory.

Hawarden's most original decisions may be harder to discern than her technical control, because they're about what she didn't do. She didn't jam her images with all the material stuff that was such a feature of Victorian decoration and fills typical photographs of the era. Maybe it was the Scot in her that kept things so sparse; maybe her appreciation of empty space came from the Mediterranean influence of her mother, or from a trip she made to Rome. (That she made such a trip is one of the few things we know about her besides her marriage, children, and death.) In any case, this aesthetic led her to place her models in near-empty settings, thereby filling the pictures with atmosphere, emotion, and the excitement of stories instead of with possessions. There's something very modern about it all. Hawarden was a Victorian Minimalist. Often her pictures are set against simple backdrops—a piece of fabric, say, or a wall (sometimes wallpapered with stars)—and they include only the odd chair, table, dressing table, mirror. Other photographers of her time didn't go in this less-is-more direction, and their photographs are much less poetic than Hawarden's. Her use of curtains alone is enough to put you in a romantic mood.

She was also a marvelous balancer, capturing with breathtaking grace the sweep of pattern, the folds and fall of cloth, the shimmers and shafts of light, the meetings of planes and of gestures and of eyes. There isn't a lick of pretentiousness in her compositions. You can sense the delight she took in her work from a photograph that is all about the challenge of balance and the joy of the leap. It's a shot of a stylishly clipped poodle balancing with forepaws on one chair back and hind paws on another—an acrobatic stunt that must have taken great timing on the part of all involved, and probably much practice. When the picture worked, it must surely have had everyone clapping.

Who knows what involvement Lord Hawarden had in his wife's work? According to the biography that accompanied the show at the Getty, they had been married for twelve years when she took her first pictures—in 1857, at Dundrum, the family estate in County Tipperary, Ireland, which he had inherited the year before. How she got her first camera is unknown. According to various articles by Dodier, Hawarden began with a stereoscopic camera, which was all the vogue then. It was a machine particularly conducive to taking landscape views, to capturing the breadth and bounty of nature—all of which the Hawardens had in abundance at Dundrum. "Domestic Idylls" did not include examples of Hawarden's stereoscopic pictures, but there were a couple of albumen prints in which Lord Hawarden is seen, together with one or more of his daughters.

So her husband definitely joined in on occasion—a fact that's also apparent in the only book on Hawarden. (This book, titled *Clementina, Lady Hawarden,* was published by Academy Editions/St. Martin's Press in 1974, and it remained as much of a specialized secret as its subject. With good reason: It is a reminder of how bad printing can be. The reproductions are like coffee when it's mud at the bottom of your cup. The curlicue edges of the prints have been cropped, and the cropping kills the poetry of what happened to them. A short, unsigned introduction feels as if it had too many words in it, although, reading it, I felt starved for information.) However, when the basic cast of players gets diluted, when the father or servants or friends appear, the pictures lose that sense of locked-away, carried-away concentration that makes Lady Hawarden's photography so special. Her most unforgettable images are like views you might spy through a keyhole.

Although these photographs rank, in their way, with the great, rich painted depictions of interiors of rooms, it is their power to induce understanding of another kind of interior that makes you fall under the spell of their magic: the interior lives of the girls. These cocoonlike photographs, formed of light and of silks and laces and other fabrics from a dressing-up box, and starring women grown-up enough to look like women but not yet old enough to leave home, have at their core the promise of a narrative that sucks you in the way certain novels do that are dedicated to the souls of their characters. Your imagination can have a field day with the narrative's construction and its unraveling, for, while the Hawardens must have had their own goals for each of the pictures, 130 years after they were taken the images have the subjective possibilities of Rorschach blots. Yet they're also grounded by place, period, and relationships; these are not strangers but sisters, whose photographer wasn't just any photographer but their mother.

Hawarden didn't merely take a few mementos, so that one day the grandchildren and the great-grandchildren might have a sense of their ancestors. She took eight hundred photographs in less than eight years, which, given what each of them took to create, goes well beyond casual documentation. These were not albums filled with birthdays, holidays, graduations, balls, and weddings but objects that were meant to display the art of photography. We know of Lady Hawarden's art ambitions because she entered her pictures in exhibitions. Just the names of her acquaintances, mentioned in Dodier's pamphlet, which accompanied the exhibition, place her smack in the middle of the art world of her day. There was her friend Sir Francis Seymour Haden, an eminent surgeon and a successful etcher; there was Sir Henry Cole, the director of the South Kensington Museum, which eventually became the Victoria and Albert; and there was Oscar Gustav Rejlander, who was as influential then as a photographer could become. But all this traveling in the right circles didn't mean that there were no barriers for Lady Hawarden and her work; it's no accident that until recently she didn't turn up in the art history books. There is the fact that she was expressing herself with photography, a medium that had just begun its struggle to be respected as an art form. And, of course, that is not the only bias that Hawarden experienced.

Would a eulogy to a man comment, as Rejlander did of Lady Hawarden, that the photography community had lost "a member as useful as a clasp and bright as a diamond"? We know the answer, just as we know that Lady Hawarden and her daughters—no matter what privileges they enjoyed as the rich and beautiful people of their time—were born into lives with set patterns to which there was really only one acceptable answer: "I do." That is what makes these photographs so familiar and so moving. If these aren't women's photographs, what are? They were taken before the daughters' marriages, while their future was still outside that window, and when their sense of pleasure in each other drew them together and held them in the room for hours. There they put on costumes, enacted roles, and probably laughed like crazy, teased each other, and bucked when they had to freeze for an uncomfortable amount of time. From certain expressions on their faces one gets the feeling that they did their fair share of "Come on, Mom, I can't hold this pose forever!"

One can only imagine how precious Hawarden's photographs became to her family after she died: pictures to trigger the grief at what was now gone; reminders of the pleasure that once was. Each person in the Hawarden clan must have had an individual response to these idyllic views. To the child who was only a year old when Hawarden died, they surely meant something different from what they meant to the older girls, who were there in that room, and who became part of her art. When the photographs left the family and went to a museum, they lost their precise history, but they took on a new openendedness, which fits right in with their capacity for suggesting stories.

Unfortunately, it's clear why they had to wait so long before being taken seriously enough to be put on exhibition. Everything about them projects that gender, "feminine," and that place, "home." There has been plenty of room in art history for works that depict interiors, and they often include families and pets, but it's rare to see such works in a museum if the perspective is that of the wife, mother, and overseer of the household. And the official history of photography is even more empty of domestic pictures by women than the history of painting is. Until recently, in most of the history books there was only Julia Margaret Cameron—like Mary Cassatt, an accomplished artist who became a token.

While Lady Hawarden's work stands out through its beauty and originality, too much should not be made of the notion that she was working with a camera so soon after photography was invented. By her day, photography had become a fad—the *carte de visite* business was booming. And the camera was not just a professional tool but a device that was being seized upon by amateurs, many of them wealthy. For women of a certain class, photography was a genteel hobby just as it was for men. You can see how many women were using cameras by the end of the century in a recent book called *The Story of Kodak,* which is chock-full of information.

The Story of Kodak has a long, at times fascinating, text by Douglas Collins, and many wonderful pictures. This book, published by Abrams, doesn't feel nearly as heavily curated as art historical photography books. It's not a connoisseur's book; although it does include famous images and famous names, many of the pictures have a homey quality to them. This domestic tone is in keeping with the company's oldest pitch for Kodak cameras: Anybody can use them. And how was the point made that using a Kodak was as easy as pie? In part, with that old stereotype of unmechanical beings—women.

As is obvious from the early ads for Kodak reproduced in the book, the company's founder, George Eastman, knew how to use a woman to sell his product. Eventually, his brilliant marketing strategy of "the Kodak Girl" led to campaigns that make today's lifestyle packages look restrained. There was a "Vanity Kodak ensemble," for example, which included a color-coordinated camera, lipstick holder, compact, mirror, and change purse. Earlier ads weren't so tightly plugged in to the accessories market, but they, too, were fashion-conscious. The book includes a reproduction of an ad from 1889 that shows a woman dressed to the nines. Her camera case is as chic as a Chanel bag. The caption explains:

> *The fashionable woman of the late nineteenth century, this 1889 advertising photo suggests, could carry a Kodak camera without the least bit of bother or embarrassment. With its leather carrying case strung over the shoulder, the Kodak camera was stylish, portable, and conveniently available whenever the occasion called for a picture.*

From the perspective of today, these ads, and also a number of the book's snapshots and other illustrations, take on a peculiar twist. They could be reissued as feminist memorabilia. Just the fact that each of them depicts a different woman photographer places this book in a separate category from art historical surveys of nineteenth-century photography; from most of these surveys you'd infer that a woman photographer in those days was as rare as the Hope Diamond.

Although women and photography is only a side topic of *The Story of Kodak*, it emerges on a number of levels. We're shown a pinup photo of Marilyn Monroe with an inscription to a Kodak employee that reads, "Dear Daan— Please remember me in your emulsions. love, Marilyn." And we're told about another autographed pinup, to a Kodak researcher, on which Monroe thanks him and the company with "All I am I owe to Kodak and you." Monroe's off-the-cuff acknowledgments are revealing about photography's relationship to illusion. If ever there was a subject who illustrated the term *photogenic,* it was Monroe. She knew how to use the camera as a tool for her self-inventions, but she got swallowed by an even bigger machine—Hollywood—and she has come to symbolize the tragedy of a person losing herself to her image. But, more than that, she is the symbol of what it means to be a sex object. For Monroe, clothes and cosmetics were a kind of mold. What she put on for the movies and for photographs always fitted her era's idea of a sexpot so well that her image became analogous to sex, though not the kind of sex that good girls then were supposed to know about. Monroe became an icon of sizzling, adulterous, uninhibited sex, the good-girl-gone-wrong type, an object of fantasy, not reality. Everything about her image reinforced this pinup idea of eros, from the way her lips were painted to the way her clothes so often revealed her body rather than covered it. If it weren't for people like Monroe, works such as Sherman's wouldn't have the same meaning.

While Sherman can "do" Monroe, she's the opposite of a Monroe. There's never any question that when it comes to Sherman's images, it's she who's in charge. She's the director, the producer, the set designer, and the costume mistress, and the star as well. She casts herself; decides when she should smile, when she should frown; decides whether she'll look ridiculous or not. In her hands, images aren't straitjackets but vehicles to show the infinite possibilities of who she could be. For Sherman, clothes and makeup are the fixings with which she cooks up her various personae; they're the tools she has used to change her identity so convincingly that she has built a career out of the idea of transformation. Her work resonates for her audience because of what it embodies: It's hip suffragette art, pro-choice imagery. Here is someone who chooses who she's going to be, someone inventing herself in public. And although there's a lot of idealism to all this, Sherman's work isn't weighed down by a sense of agenda. She's a parodist at large, having fun with the world of appearances. We've seen her spoofing fashion, Hollywood, art history, even Christmas—she took a portrait of herself as Mrs. Claus for *The New York Times Magazine.*

Sherman's never impersonated Madonna, though, and no wonder. Madonna herself is always changing so fast it's hard to get a fix on her, which is part of her appeal, just as it is Sherman's. But there's a difference in what each has accomplished with the constant reinventing of her image. Madonna is about power; about being both a brilliant businesswoman and a sex goddess. She's trying to be Superwoman. Sherman's on a much humbler path. Her work isn't about projecting herself as bigger than others; the real Cindy Sherman remains anonymous. In fact, people are so used to seeing Sherman in disguise that when they run into her just as she is they often don't recognize her. In a way, she's more in disguise when she's not dressed up than she is when she's costumed as somebody else. Not dressed up, she melts into a crowd—just an ordinary woman in her thirties, in stretch pants, an innocuous top, hardly any makeup, simple-to-maintain hair. Hers is that contemporary unfussy look you see on so many women today. Call it invisible style, stylish no style—easy does it, not corsets and curlers.

Sherman's work has become so well known that certain photographs made years before she was born look like hers, and not the other way around. Recently, Keith de Lellis, a private photography dealer, told me he had picked up at auction some work from the 1920s that looked just like Cindy Sherman's pictures. He was right: This curious group of photographs, signed Mesdames Morter, is eerily Sherman-like. From the writing on the prints and from the documentation accompanying them, it's apparent that the Morters were two sisters who lived and worked in London. And their genre? One of them photographed the other in costume, playing out various themes. Penned descriptions at the bottom or on the back of their pictures tell us what's going on. The model holds up a feather duster, her face a caricature of industriousness; the inscription reads "The Modern Housemaid," and below there's a parenthetical addition, "Found in the coalcellar." Other photographs have such labels as "Unseemly Mirth," "Love's Hand," "Embarrassment," "The Squire's Daughter." There's a photograph in which the subject looks as if she had just seen an apparition. She's dressed in gypsy clothes, and she's acting very spooked. In this image, which is titled "Autumn Defying Winter," and in some of the others as well, there's a tone so similar to the feeling in some of Sherman's photographs that it's uncanny.

The Morters' pictures have much in common with Hawarden's, too: Here again are sisters immersed in dressing up, fantasy, and photography. Like Hawarden, the Morters won prizes in their day. Like Hawarden, their renown was brief the first time around. Who knows what else we're going to discover about them in the future? The Morters' photographs aren't as perfect-looking as Hawarden's, and they're too eccentric to be moving in the way hers are. And, despite the Morters' use of old-fashioned subjects, it's clear that modern life has begun. Still, the same romanticism that is so seductive in Hawarden's work pervades theirs, too. In one photograph, the posing sister holds a letter to her heart, and underneath the image is written, "Why! Oh! Why?" You can't say that Sherman's photographs are romantic; too much has happened for them to be that. They were made after a sexual revolution that affected the sense of identity women and men had lived with for so long that it seems forever.

Until I saw Lady Hawarden's show, I took Sherman's use of costume for granted. Dressing up was just part of her style, and it's not so surprising a tactic: Many artists use costume as an element of their work. But the similarities between the photography of Sherman and Hawarden raised questions. Is it the dressing up that makes the pictures by both these women so powerful? Is that what's so haunting about what they do? And in the idea of dressing up is there something especially meaningful to women?

I'd like the answer to the last question to be no, because generalizations about women and men are what got us into trouble in the first place. But to take away the specificity of what Sherman and Hawarden have created with dressing up is to drain their work of its impact, and to miss what is perhaps the most meaningful implication of their connection. Together, they suggest how dressing up could be used as a thread to weave in and out of the history of photography in order to help find what has been missing: the presence of women.

This is not to say that male artists don't do their share of dressing up, or that men don't know what role-playing's all about. Today, there are plenty of examples of male artists who employ costume. There are Gilbert and George, who dress like prisspots; there are Peter McGough and David McDermott, who go about accoutred as late-nineteenth-century gentlemen; there's James Lee Byars, who parades around in all-gold or all-black ensembles, with top hat to match. And it could be said that the most famous work of the century to involve dressing up is by a man, Marcel Duchamp: his presentation of himself in drag as Rrose Sélavy (*Eros c'est la vie*). Yes, dressing up, dressing down, and going in drag are subjects that relate to both sexes, go way back in time, and have different histories in different cultures. In our culture, whether you embrace dress codes or rebel against them, they're there—so much there that each person's relationship to clothes becomes a personal statement. If you could track the wealth of imagery that has been produced in art and photography in which people use costume to express themselves, it would be a spectacle of self-assertion and of cultural revelation. And, of course, it would reaffirm our knowledge that there are men who go in for fancy dress, too. But let's remember: From the minute they're out of diapers, women have to deal with the world of appearances in a more inexorably pressured way than men do. That's what makes this a subject on which women are expert witnesses: all women—not only Clementina, Lady Hawarden, and Cindy Sherman.

The New Yorker, May 6, 1991

The
Hands
of
Time

The apartment is in an elegant section of Paris, not in the bleak English marsh country of *Great Expectations,* and the clocks have not stopped at twenty to nine as they did at Miss Havisham's, yet when people talk about this house, they bring up Dickens's haunted setting. So with a nod toward the other side of the Channel let's call the owner Mr. H. It is only to be expected that a man who has cut the labels out of his articles of clothing would also prefer to have his identity cut out of a magazine article about his house. You might think he'd object to the idea that his remarkable two-level apartment reminds people of a place Dickens described as a cobwebby, sun-deprived ruin, but on the contrary I suspect Mr. H. is the one who started this ironic comparison. It's a shorthand way of emphasizing atmosphere, mood, and history over price and status and fads, none of which impress him. Things work the other way around. He influences.

Mr. H., who spends most of his time in New York, comes from the school that believes in downplaying one's possessions. He calls his place a "junk pick-er's apartment," but in fact it's filled with amazing finds. Most of the contents would make curators in both the decorative and the fine arts kick themselves for missing what he discovered at his favorite secondhand shops. He says he prefers shops to museums. One of his chief delights used to be Comoglio's on the rue Jacob, now sadly gone but once a sort of antiquarian's heaven—or, as John Richardson put it, "that moth-eaten place of wonders." Since almost everything in the apartment comes from one antiques shop or another and since I know that Mr. H.'s occupation keeps him busy day and night, I was curious about how he found the time to amass all these treasures. He clearly had to comb many a jumbled-up joint. When I asked if he did it by just walking from shop to shop to shop, he corrected me: "I *raced*. All this stuff was col-lected between appointments for more important things—you know, work. I got it by dashing in and dashing out of flea markets. I'd say it was decorated by accident and instinct." And by the radar that only the true collector possesses.

Mr. H.'s extrasensory antennae have led him to some extra special prizes. In his apartment you come across furniture and objects and paintings that are not only marvelous period pieces but almost magical because of where they've been, whom they've seen, what they've heard—in other words, because of their provenance. Hanging above a set of Italian Empire consoles and lit by a pair of alabaster urns Mr. H. transformed into lamps is a turn-of-the-century gem—a carved bat that once belonged to Comte Robert de Montesquiou, the epit-ome of Belle Epoque aestheticism. Montesquiou's bat doesn't just conjure the spookiness and jeweled creepy-crawly creatures of the arts of the fin de siècle; it brings on a whole parade of associations. One thinks of Proust's *Remembrance of Things Past* (Proust modeled the Baron de Charlus in large part after Mon-tesquiou) and of Whistler, that snob who painted the portrait of Montesquiou

Jean Kallina, *Apartment, Paris,* 1989

in the Frick Collection—a picture that exudes such a sniffing superiority it clearly records a perfect match between artist and subject. As Philippe Jullian tells us in his biography of Montesquiou, Whistler would address the count in letters as "Dear Bat" and refer to himself as "the butterfly."

Mr. H. has seen his own share of social butterflies. He also has a great appreciation for what conformists call "battiness." He has a history of being the first on the block to recognize a visionary. He's a great believer in imagination and fantasy, and he has used plenty of both to create his Paris interiors. "I'll make up whole stories about a room when I'm doing a place," he says, "about the people who lived there." He is especially fond of literary types. He had lots of material to work with here—the apartment's previous owner was Violet Trefusis. Although she may be remembered as a third-rate writer, Trefusis played a major role in the literary romances of her era—namely as one of Vita Sackville-West's lovers (and as the nemesis of Sackville-West's husband, Harold Nicolson)—no doubt spicing the apartment's allure for Mr. H. As he tells of his sense that she haunts the place, he smiles and elaborates: "When I first saw the apartment, all her things were still around, including some old pictures of Edward VII, who they say was her father—a detail she enjoyed promoting."

By the time he bought the apartment in 1973, it had fallen into disrepair. The rooms needed quite a bit of gutting and construction as well as delicate restoration—the filling in of broken paneling and molding, for example. In addition, Mr. H. made changes—such as making all the doorways taller— that now look so right you'd never know they were alterations. This talent for arranging things as though they belong in a room is rare, but Mr. H. has it to spare. He's not stiff about placement; he goes at it loosely, as though he's doing a dance with the furniture, the "hokeypokey," as he calls it. "You get a hunch, you move the piece around, you shake it all about." And he doesn't spoil a room's choreography with too many steps. "Knowing when to stop is the trick," he says, lamenting all the artists who "would have come so close if only they had known when to stop."

Listening to Mr. H. talk about his place and the eras and people that haunt it is a hypnotic experience. He is so full of knowledge and so undry about it all; in fact, he's very wry. About a piece of sculpture he muses, "That's from Molière's garden. I usually keep the top of her head on, or do I take it off? I don't remember." A set of Louis XVI–style chairs that Mr. H. says "look like strange widows" take us back to *Great Expectations,* to the first time Pip comes home from Miss Havisham's—that monument to forsaken brides—and his sister and uncle cross-question him about what he's seen. Convinced that no one would understand any of it if he told the truth, Pip says, "She was sitting in a black velvet coach." Mr. H.'s chairs have little gold feet, not wheels, and the eighteenth-century-style dustcovers that shroud them are velvet, but not black. The chairs once belonged to Misia Sert, and their original covers were made out of dress fabric around 1931 by Coco Chanel. But, even for Mr. H., these covers were approaching the limit of the desirably worn-away, so he had replacements stitched together from a velvet negligée fabric he found in China. He is pleased that they're finally acquiring a worn look. There are actual Louis XVI pieces, such as a mammoth Jacob sofa over seven feet long, above which hang two large paintings attributed to Girodet-Trioson, the classically trained Romantic artist who worked for the royal court. In the middle of all this pedigreed furniture there are some mutts, too. The centerpiece of the living room is a nineteenth-century *borne,* a round sofa Mr. H. found in New York and refers to as "corny hotel deluxe." It looks like a wedding cake. One of the bedrooms has a shocking-pink bed inspired by Schiaparelli and designed—or, as he says, "cooked up"—by Mr. H. himself.

Everyone who sees Mr. H.'s apartment says it seems like a place in their dreams. So memorable a place can unearth your deepest feelings. This happened to Pip in *Great Expectations,* too. After that first sight of Miss Havisham's he was never the same. Dickens expressed it for Pip—and for us—perfectly: "Pause you who read this, and think for a moment of the long chain of iron or gold, of thorns or flowers, that would never have bound you, but for the formation of the first link on one memorable day." Mr. H.'s first links came from houses that intrigued him because of how they were decorated, a great-aunt's house, for example, and places in Texas that he knows very well, and later the magnificent rooms in the Château de Fontainebleau, and rooms full of personal style and extraordinary art in Paris, New York, and elsewhere. It's hard to imagine Mr. H. doing up his flat in France without all these views to the past. He has always been attracted to what he calls "ghost chasing," a decorating style he says disappeared in the 1960s when everything went minimal. Although Mr. H. is as American as a cowboy, it is impossible to conceive of his paradise for biographers as being anywhere but the country it is in. As he says, "It's very French. It's a literary place in the spirit of Violet, who was an old Francophile." Like Mr. H.

House & Garden, July 1989

Julian Schnabel, *Portrait of Fred Hughes,* 1987

White and Black

When photography is about love, the picture usually crops up in someone's wallet, or perhaps on a desktop, but rarely on a museum's walls. Yet love is at the core of the two most resonant photography exhibitions of the year—Minor White's and Robert Mapplethorpe's. White lived much longer than Mapplethorpe, and White's work has been in the public eye for almost half a century, yet only now, with this new exhibition, can we see so many of the photographs that show his heart on their sleeves. While the Mapplethorpe exhibition, "The Perfect Moment," has caused enormous debate, "Minor White: The Eye That Shapes" has barely been noticed. The Mapplethorpe show carries a warning that it contains strong material, a reference to the sexual explicitness that has made Mapplethorpe's photography so controversial. The White exhibition should warn visitors that they might be bored. But there's something instructive to be found in it anyway.

In one respect, "The Eye That Shapes" is no different from other projects dedicated to White's work: It's filled with eye-glazers. White—who has been acclaimed as one of America's most important photographers, and who was undoubtedly an influential teacher, writer, and editor—started out as a botany major, and his beginnings show. In picture after picture, he kept zooming in on nature, all too often arriving at results as scintillating as laboratory slides. These photographs have the same anesthetized and out-of-context quality as cross sections. (A few of them look like stills of fluids in lit-up lava lamps when the goop is swirling.) In White's other work, too, context is often ruptured to the point where it's hard to know what you're looking at, and the mystification seems suspiciously like an easy way of announcing "Art."

Most people associate White's photography with austerity. Typical White nature scenes look as squeaky clean as Ansel Adams's landscapes. You don't see empty Tab cans on any rocks he photographed. Snow always looks clean and crisp, not grimy and slushy. He did photograph graffiti, but on walls, not knifed into trees. The very asceticism of so many of his well-known photographs contrasts starkly with the standard definition of modern living: that we are ruled by fashion, artifice, instant gratification—the vanities. In the context of that embarrassing description of our collective personality, White's photographs of stones and pebbles on unpolluted beaches, of whiter-than-white icicles, could provide an oasis for the eyes. They do the trick for some. But White's work never released any magic for me. It's hard to care about images if there's nothing in them to suggest that their maker saw deeper or more than others have seen: We don't need Minor White to help us appreciate the fact that snow crystals have patterns. However, White is a crucial figure when it comes to another kind of pattern—a pattern of response to the arts when they seem to threaten some societal notion of what's proper. Because White's photography has a long history of being received as perfectly respectable, it's difficult to imagine its being slammed as "dirty." But in fact, as the current exhibition demonstrates, this respectability is the result of careful decisions that White made about his photographs to keep them from frightening the horses.

The spectacle we witnessed this summer surrounding Mapplethorpe's photographs involved the very responses that White tried so hard to avoid—shock, disgust, hate. Despite a taste for the occult, White was a conventional man, who obeyed the conventions of his time, and one of them was that if you were unfortunate enough to love your own sex—which he did—you controlled that information, and certainly didn't advertise it in your work. Almost from the start, White held back those pictures of his that gave too much away about his personal life. His solution to the split between what supposedly belongs in public and what supposedly belongs in private was to develop an alternate, acceptable pictorial language that he thought could express what he wanted to express in ways that wouldn't offend. Abstraction played a large part in his attempt to make images that "passed" but that also communicated, as did his use of sequences. This interest in abstraction and sequences went beyond the need to disguise imagery, but if ever there was a photographer who made pictures that need to be "read between the lines," it is White.

He wasn't flush with alternatives. Here was a guy who in the forties and fifties began to try to make a name for himself in American photography. He wasn't a Beat, he wasn't a bohemian, he wasn't rich, he wasn't worldly. This wasn't Paris in the twenties. This was a culture that was phobic about differences. It's no coincidence that Edward Steichen's 1955 show "The Family of Man" was such a crowd-pleaser. Steichen's exhibition fit the mood of postwar America. It echoed the era's obsession with the nuclear family. Its sentimental theme of the world's disparate people as one big family was a sweet idea, but it swallowed up realities, trying to wish away the fact of cultural and economic difference by showing that everyone everywhere still laughed, cried, and had babies. Although White wasn't included in Steichen's blockbuster, he was by then a part of the inner family of the photography community. It hadn't taken him very long to find his way in.

Right after he was discharged from the army, in 1945, with a Bronze Star, White headed for New York, where he aimed straight for the top—the most important duo in photography—Beaumont Newhall, the curator of photography at the Museum of Modern Art, and his wife, Nancy, a major force in the field in her own right. They were receptive; at once, White got a job at the museum, making copy prints of works in its collection, and through the Newhalls he met many of the figures in photography who were, or would become, the powers in the medium, among them Ansel Adams, Edward Steichen, and Edward Weston, whose gorgeous landscapes and nudes had an everlasting influence on White.

On his own, White met Alfred Stieglitz. The self-taught White had come to New York to learn more, and what better person to seek out than the man who had been claiming, for half a century, to have the answers to what photography was all about? If there was one area in which White had no conflict, it was his attraction to people with answers. The way White remembered it, much of the conversation during their first meeting—in Stieglitz's legendary gallery—sounds like your usual modern-art chat:

> *Sitting on the radiator in the little back room of An American Place six months after World War II, we talked about how* to make *photographs, spoke about the* Equivalent. *Stieglitz said something or other about photography that makes visible the invisible, and something else about true things being able to talk to each other. His talk itself was a kind of equivalent; that is, his words were not related to the sense he was making.*

Their professional talk, as professional talk often does, turned personal. White's version of the story ends with Stieglitz asking a question and also giving an answer: "Have you ever been in love? . . . Then you can photograph." That dot dot dot we have to fill in for ourselves.

This version of White's version of his talk with Stieglitz comes from "A Living Remembrance"—the homage to White that made up a 1984 issue of *Aperture*. In another account of that conversation, White says yes, he has been in love, but he doesn't volunteer any details. It's easy to imagine him protecting himself by not revealing with whom. The walls around the subject of homosexuality were so fortresslike that most people would have hidden behind them in order not to be branded, let alone not to make a bad career move—even in the company of a bohemian like Stieglitz, whose own life wasn't exactly a shining example of commitment to hearth and home. With all Stieglitz's talk about *Equivalents,* White probably decided to let it be assumed that his experience was equivalent to Stieglitz's.

It is obvious why White often referred to that encounter with Stieglitz as crucial to his life. To be told that an emotion that has caused so much guilt—

the guilt permeates White's writing—is at the heart of one's ability to create is not a tip likely to be forgotten. On top of that, Stieglitz offered White a systematic approach to photography. As is clear from all the other systems White eventually followed—Zen, the teachings of Gurdjieff, Catholicism, Ansel Adams's zone system, the *I Ching*, and astrology, to name his major guideposts—he was system-happy. Even before the two men met, Stieglitz's series of symbolic photographs, called "Equivalents," had impressed White, and, indeed, was one of the reasons he had sought out the older photographer. The concept behind these "Equivalents"—that metaphor, since it goes further than the literal, is the most creative form of expression—wasn't just aesthetically useful to White; it was a godsend in terms of White's problems with subject matter. It was the notion of equivalents that gave him a way to

photograph his various difficult subjects. For beyond the forbidden one, there was the impossible one—faith. Many painters have taken on the spiritual as a theme, but White is one of the few photographers to have tried to make prints of the ineffable. He once explained that if he kept going, he would "give proof that this instrument can carry out the work of God." Here, too, Stieglitz's "Equivalents" were a model. To some, they were evidence of the Almighty—an assessment that Stieglitz didn't contradict. "I'm most curious to see what the 'Clouds' will do to you . . ." he wrote to Hart Crane. "Several people feel I have photographed God. Maybe."

The year after White met Stieglitz, something happened that must have confirmed White's fear of being direct in his imagery. An exhibition of his work was canceled on grounds of taste. He had shot a sequence titled "Amputations," to be shown at the California Palace of the Legion of Honor, in San Francisco. According to Peter Bunnell, who curated "The Eye That Shapes" and wrote the accompanying book—which I have relied on for most of my biographical information about the photographer—there were two problems that White had to confront. A text he had written to go along with the pictures was attacked for being too long and of poor quality. And, more significant, White's focus on the human cost of war seems to have provoked the accusation that "Amputations" was unpatriotic. Some of the images from the sequence are included in "The Eye That Shapes." One of them, *Double Navel,* a detail of a rock that has the same contours as a human torso, comes in close on the gashes, holes, and scoria of a rock's surface, and the analogy White was making with the wounds of war is hard to miss. The sequence also offers examples of the way White exploited the talent of trees for symbolizing tortuousness. Still, from the perspective of today it is almost unbelievable that any-

Minor White, *Earle Curtis, Vicinity of La Grande, Oregon,* summer 1941

one could have confused White's poetic attempt to get at the horrors of war with a lack of patriotism. No wonder honesty about other subjects, ones that were even more explosive, seemed like career suicide to so many people then.

"The Eye That Shapes" is the result of a career spent avoiding calling a spade a spade, and the show includes a narrative photograph that suggests the spade that was taboo. In this photograph, as usual, White told his story with codes, and so some detective work is necessary. (Bunnell is the Sherlock Holmes who uncovered the clues in it.) Made in 1950, and titled *Market Street, San Francisco,* this picture features a sailor and a woman in semiembrace at the corner of a busy street. One of her arms reaches behind them, her fingers pointing like arrows to a traffic light that spells out STOP. Just beyond, you can make out the word *Camera* above a store.

Camera STOP? You don't have to stretch metaphor very far to get what's being illustrated: the social and pictorial rules about sex that White was confronting. In *Market Street,* White used an acceptable couple—a man and a woman—to suggest the bind he was in. The bind itself appears in public for the first time in "The Eye That Shapes." Displayed next to this very forties image of a sailor and his girl is *Ernest Stones and Robert Bright* (1949). In this simple photograph, it is two young men who are in semiembrace. They're indoors, not out on the street, where they might be seen by others, but they're nevertheless very presentable—both of them in white shirts and ties, both with regular-Joe crew cuts. There's nothing else in the picture, just the two men. There's no subtext of signs; nothing's interfering with their intimacy. Because of what we're used to seeing, or not seeing, this calm portrait of men loving each other with all their buttons buttoned is a jolt—actually a double jolt, because it's by White, whose work has always seemed so empty of human interaction.

Minor White, *Ernest Stones and Robert Bright, San Francisco,* 1949

"The Eye That Shapes" is not the first time White's homosexuality has been acknowledged, but it is the first opportunity we've had to see the photographs on exhibit that once seemed so much like dynamite they were kept out of public sight. These images are Bunnell's big scoop, and they are very welcome for the way they humanize White. There has always been something unconvincing about his work's opacity; no one seems at home behind many of the pictures. By unveiling previously unexhibited work, Bunnell gives us the raw material that lay beneath some of the shapes that caught White's eye. Bunnell's show and book demonstrate how White recast imagery so that it could go safely out into the world.

Among the photographs that White shelved are male nudes. A few of these images could have been made by George Platt Lynes, given their theatrical use of light and shadow to highlight men's bodies in arty, cheesecake poses. And then there are models who could slip right into Calvin Klein's ad campaign for underwear, except that White's models are lower on beefcake and no one is wearing those come-and-get-it briefs. But "The Eye That Shapes" also includes nudes that are personal. White made these in the late forties, and they belong to a sequence titled "The Temptation of Saint Anthony Is Mirrors." The body of his model, Tom Murphy, has a grace that satisfied White's ambition to make sensitive pictures. Even in shots where White added touches of the kind a bad art director brings to commercial photography—such as a rose placed near Murphy's penis, an arrangement with all the subtlety of a boulder—this sequence has a fleshy reality, and two of the shots are actually unpretentious. When White resisted the frills—when there is no self-conscious lighting, no coy hiding of (or decorating) the genitals—what a difference! These photographs give us a chance to see what White was capable of without all the shticky overlay.

When I first saw the exhibition at the Modern last spring, this different side of White made it seem as though someone else's pictures had been shoe-horned into his. Yet, despite the fact that the unknown photographs looked like aliens, the installation of the exhibition made it clear that they were very much a planned part of the event. Every decision about how to hang them appeared to be the result of careful, serious thought—too much thought. The sequence of images on the walls almost exactly paralleled the sequencing in the accompanying book—an unusual correspondence, since even though most curators start out with a plan, they add, drop, and move works around until all the art seems comfortable in the allotted space. Here there was no sense of spontaneity. I wonder how much of this rigidity was due to the fact that White's image was being changed—and with a kind of photography rare at the Modern, whose walls, like those of most art institutions, have been basically genital-free. That same art decorum that inhibited White has kept most figurative art from getting too detailed or graphic (and, of course, the ruling modern style, abstraction, solved the problem of the need for a fig leaf). In addition, at the Modern, as at almost all other museums, homosexuality has not been a deliberate theme, however understated. Peter Bunnell was breaking ground, and his desire to serve White's work yet preserve his reputation surely dictated some of his moves.

The White show will travel around the country for almost the next two years. Its contents will not vary much from stop to stop, and the plan is to install it as closely as possible to the way it was displayed at the Modern (and the way the photographs are ordered in the book). It's not that Bunnell pulls punches when it comes to White's unknown work: He sets up the show by clumping together, near the beginning, enough nudes to cue visitors that they are going to see a White they've never seen before. And Bunnell's text is very open about White's homosexuality. The problem is more a matter of too much editorializing. In his effort to reveal correspondences among certain photographs, Bunnell separates others that would have been better kept together. Splitting apart the "Temptation of Saint Anthony Is Mirrors" photographs is particularly odd, since they were made as a sequence. The way Bunnell spots these pictures around, they are as unnerving as a flasher popping out from behind a tree. Inserted between two abstract photographs that look like peeling walls, an image of the unpeeled Murphy is startling; when it's considered with the other pictures in the sequence the surprise dulls. Bunnell's arrangement reflects the split that divided White's work into public and private imagery, but as a result the "Saint Anthony" pictures haven't really surfaced. Bunnell's half-showing them is tantamount to asking you to come into the closet with them rather than bringing them out.

A side effect of this peekaboo installation is the intensification of an already charged atmosphere. Bunnell clearly wants us to catch every sexual metaphor.

His juxtapositions spell out (and perhaps induce) the resemblances between, say, Murphy's member and an icicle. But even without this curatorial help, one can grasp how White developed his own system of equivalents. He wasn't subtle. He treated rocks as stand-ins for people, producing some images that give new meaning to the term "nature lovers." Using geology as a substitute for anatomy, White employed close-ups and cropping to express what he couldn't show directly. Once you get the point that a stone's cracks and orifices are references to the entrances and exits that come with a body, no stone remains unturned into a potential double meaning.

Rarely did White's use of equivalents avoid gimmickry. Whether the allusion is to the body or to the Bible, metaphor failed to enrich his photography. His biblical references are utterly unconvincing. A photograph called *Burning Bush,* made the year he met Stieglitz, is typical of White in its apocalyptic mood and its flashy use of light and shadow. In this picture, a starburst of light brightens up a scraggly tree and a couple of bushes. It has the look of a special effect in a low-budget movie.

White's pursuit of the spiritual took him in more esoteric directions as well. For example, he titled a photograph after the most famous Zen koan, "the sound of one hand clapping." The subject, an Oriental-looking bowl, is as good an answer as any for a riddle that's not supposed to have an answer, but it really doesn't do much to encourage a Zen attitude. Zen is about attention, and this dull gray object against a darker gray background doesn't invite attention for long. A seascape titled *Shore Acres, Oregon* does draw attention, but not for the reason White intended. Above the Sturm und Drang of crashing waves, a lone bird picturesquely draws the eyes skyward; a streak of pure white light divides the heavens from the ruckus of the sea. The whole shebang is clearly meant to inspire awe, but the bird is so small and is photographed at such an ambiguous angle that initially it's hard to tell whether it's a gull or only a splotch of grime on the print.

. . .

There's very little warmth or humor in the bulk of White's work. What there is mostly is pointing. The exhibition includes a small selection of color photographs. The color injects a little oomph into the images, but it also underlines White's superficial grasp of design. He was hooked on colors that went together or matched: a red faucet handle, say, must have caught his eye because it was on a barrel with a red patch. His propensity for interior-decorating an image led him to take photographs of landscapes that look arranged, rather than found by his camera. His street pictures have some life—he was obviously trying to connect with city energy—but he stiffened the action instead of snapping it, the way a Bill Klein or a Garry Winogrand did. In their photographs, all the different elements cook together; in White's, the potential hubbub of a street picture has been strained out, so that you can't miss what he wants you to focus on. He spoon-feeds the viewer. He makes all the discoveries, and the viewer's job is to respond to what he found, rather than to join him in a process of discovery. Whether the photographs are pointing to nature, pointing to colors, pointing to sex, pointing to God, or pointing to art, they're didactic. One way to avoid pedagogy is to be human, to show doubt by acknowledging that life brings more questions than answers. But to do that requires an honest look at oneself—exactly what White felt he couldn't afford in his public pictures. This fear of exposure is painfully clear in the letters of his that are reprinted in Bunnell's book.

What is striking in these letters is the mysterious absence of any mention of love or romance—that whole department. These letters were written to the people he felt closest to, and they're full of his ideas about work, photography, and spiritual matters. Yet there's only one person, Isabel Kane Bradley, in whom he confides any emotions or experiences having to do with his homosexuality. For more about White's personal life, one has to go to his poems and to his private journal, which carries the name "Memorable Fancies." (Some of this material is included in the book.) In "Memorable Fancies," White attempted to get to the bottom of what made him tick, of what made him ashamed: His entries reveal that he was trying to understand the relationship between his personality and the stigma of homosexuality. A comment he wrote on March 10, 1960, reads, "I have often said that for anyone who likes self pity—homosexuality is a grand source . . . I recall from [my work in] Sequence 13 the statement 'By a law of yourself you are condemned to live in fear of those that will love you.' What LAW? What and why Law?"

Too bad White didn't harness this ability to dig below the surface when he was actually making photographs. At "The Eye That Shapes" you can see the effect of imposed rules and formulas on an artist's work. You can see how silly a subject can get if it can't be expressed directly. You can watch what happens as life is edited out. And in the book you can read how White advised others to stick to propriety. A letter written in 1962 to an unidentified photographer who had sent his sexually revelatory work to White indicates just how slavish he was to a recipe of what should and shouldn't go into art. "These prints outline for me a rather tragic story of a man's life," White wrote. "Your photographs are still mirrors of yourself. In other words your images are raw, the emotions naked. To present these to others they need appropriate clothes. These are private images not public ones."

White recognized that the other photographer had created images that were "very real" and very affecting, yet White was telling him to cover up the elements that conveyed such meaning. White's insistence that the photographer dress up his story to enable it to pass as a reflection of Mankind was presented in the name of the standard notion that art should be universalized—the concept that makes White's own photography so hollow. Despite all his talk of mirrors, he didn't seem to understand that there can be no such thing as common experience if there are no specific selves to reflect it.

Looking at much of White's photography is like listening to a sermon from someone who is unable to communicate to you because he doesn't acknowledge what life is really like. White's diaries and his letters to Bradley suggest that he knew about the struggle to have faith, to find intimacy, to accept himself, and to be accepted by others, but you cannot tell it from the bulk of his work. He squeezed conflict from his art, leaving it mechanical. Bunnell's substructure in "The Eye That Shapes" reinforces the sermonizing quality that so many of White's pictures have. Pompous titles introduced each section at the Modern—"Possession," "Observation," and "Revelation"—and the final portion of the show gave us a dose of White's preachiest photographs of crosses, cross forms, and beams of light.

White's isn't the only faith on view in "The Eye That Shapes." Bunnell's faith in White is almost palpable in this carefully plotted production. I wasn't at the lecture Bunnell gave at the Modern in conjunction with the opening of the show, but I heard a tape of it later. In it you can hear his emotion and his devotion to White. His intention is obviously to provide such a wide overview of White's biography and the development of his pictorial vocabulary that the viewer can come away with an understanding of the man and a method of reading White's codes and substitutional devices. He succeeds—and, as a result, viewers can understand more easily what went wrong.

White is not unusual in having two bodies of work—the pictures he showed to the world and those he didn't. But although the hidden pictures have been referred to as private imagery, they were actually treated as secret imagery—and there's a big difference between privacy and secrecy. Privacy is a choice; it's about living your life the way you want to. Secrecy is usually a form of protection, but the safety it affords has the same relationship to freedom as being locked in an isolation chamber. Many of White's photographs show what it's like to be inside that room. They're like messages sent by someone trapped, who has to disguise or code what is being transmitted so that it gets through; once you break White's codes, you simply apply them where appropriate. The rest of the time you're seeing standard pictures within standardized genres, be they religion, landscape, architecture, or abstraction. Often the results are perfectly fine, but "fine" doesn't have much to do with being moved or captured by pictures.

It can't be assumed that if White had been able to express himself more openly, he would have been a more imaginative photographer. Even with those early nudes, some preconceived notion of artistic presentation—of lighting or pose or prop—tends to drain the images of life. But those are the photographs of a young artist looking for a style, a way to give his pictures his own stamp; their self-consciousness is typical of a beginner's work. Who knows what he could have done if he hadn't been so deeply involved with developing covert and acceptable ways to communicate his experience?

There are early pictures by White—especially the intimate ones of people—that have a real pictorial "voice." *Ernest Stones and Robert Bright* is a gem, made all the more precious because you know that these two men couldn't show their feelings for each other out in the world. And the "Saint Anthony Is Mirrors" sequence is rich enough to hint at the possibility that if White had directly approached what he was struggling with in his life he might have produced vital work. These photographs expose the source of White's conflict between his religious beliefs and his desires. You can't unravel the two subjects in these images; they are knotted together here the way they were in White's mind. It is the tension one feels between them that gives the photographs force. When there is no figure in his spiritual work, the pictures lose passion and become hokey and stripped flat; the voice gets lost. The photograph that sums it all up is a self-portrait he made in 1957. It's completely abstract, a white surface with black streaks. You can't have a more blatant image than this of a missing person—or an emptier use of abstraction.

White wasn't the kind of artist who did great work either despite or because of taboos. We like to remember those individuals who broke through the social and moral codes of their day, or who found ingenious ways around them. However, there aren't many with Genet's sense of nothing to lose, or with Proust's scope. What about those who are crippled, rather than inspired, by repression? Isn't it likely that White's defensive reflexes put so many brakes on his imagination that his picture making froze?

Today, the images that White had to keep locked up cause no outrage. When his exhibition was at the Museum of Modern Art last spring, it drew some coverage but not much excitement. Although it will be seen in many distinguished institutions, it will not go to Washington. The show was packed in crates all summer, because it wasn't scheduled for an appearance until September, when it opened at the Oregon Art Institute, in Portland. When the Corcoran Gallery, in Washington, canceled Robert Mapplethorpe's show, it filled the space with a show that had been scheduled for the fall, but actually White would have been a cleverer solution. In the White exhibition the Corcoran would have got the same basic subjects that are represented in the Mapplethorpe show—nature, portraits, and male nudes—plus some extras, such as landscapes and street pictures. It would not have received any photographs comparable in shock value to Mapplethorpe's sex pictures, yet it would still have had homosexuality as a theme, so no one could have accused it of being homophobic. There are other touchy issues that the Corcoran could have avoided by using White as Mapplethorpe's understudy, such as who's footing the bill. Although government money helps keep the doors of almost every art institution in America open, the White show itself comes courtesy of Merrill Lynch & Co. Backed by big business, the White package can't be accused of using taxpayers' money to support monkey business.

White's career is the well-behaved precursor of Mapplethorpe's. White is not so loaded, because he fits a stereotype that many people are comfortable with—the homosexual artist who feels rotten about his sexuality and agrees not to thrust it in people's faces. White did what Mapplethorpe wouldn't do: He censored himself. Mapplethorpe left the censoring to others, and the Corcoran obliged. It would have none of Mapplethorpe's show rather than some of it, the Corcoran announced, explaining that it did not want to have to censor parts of it. But no one had asked it to. It claimed that it wanted to keep the heat off the National Endowment for the Arts for giving a grant to the University of Pennsylvania's Institute of Contemporary Art, the institution that originated "The Perfect Moment." With help like that, the NEA doesn't need enemies—nor do any of the institutions that have shown Mapplethorpe's work and could be tagged as irresponsible because of the Corcoran's action.

Just like White, Mapplethorpe was ambitious, but he was not a follower of systems. He worked with what he saw around him and took cues from his own responses. You could write his biography on the basis of his photographs, without needing any secondary material, so many of the people he was involved with are right there in the pictures. And you can follow Mapplethorpe's sexual history through his work. There are early cutouts from pornography magazines. Then there are the portraits of Patti Smith, the S & M pictures, Sam Wagstaff, the men who followed—the story of his life. Like White, Mapplethorpe, a Catholic, often made work that included the iconography of the cross. Unlike White, Mapplethorpe leaped on the sex taboo in art as though it were the last frontier to explore. Instead of circling around homosexuality, Mapplethorpe made it an unavoidable subject for anyone looking at or talking about his pictures. Instead of being afraid that homosexuality would ruin his career, Mapplethorpe used it to forward his reputation. Instead of photographing rocks to suggest sex, Mapplethorpe made pictures of men having sex. But that does not mean that Mapplethorpe wasn't initially as

Robert Mapplethorpe, *Self-Portrait,* 1980

freaked out as the next man about being a homosexual. He, too, had to deal with the question "What am I?" Much of the time, he used his work to try to answer that question. His self-portraits are an inventory of identities: himself as a woman, as a gangster, as a devilish imp, as a gentleman, as a toughie, as nothing special.

He was a photographer who took advantage of all the taboos and mysteries surrounding sex and homosexuality. They were his keys to doing something that would be noticed. Of course, the subject matter of his photographs wasn't

new; what was different was that he was presenting explicit images that he wanted to show aboveground, not underground. The content of his most controversial work has an informational usefulness, too. These pictures provide views of sexual activities that are a puzzle to many people. He makes up for the sex education most of us didn't get. Because he broke through the usual secrecy that surrounds homosexuality, homosexuality became the frame through which his photographs are seen. But many of his pictures—including many that are sexual—have nothing in them that makes them inherently

about homosexuality. A man with his penis hanging out of his fly—which is what we see in Mapplethorpe's wryest image of all—is a joke on the way everything that has to do with sex is supposed to be zipped up. Many of his "naughty" photographs are like this one, in which Mapplethorpe was having fun shocking. Others are displays of his virtuosity with form. What better way to get people to look at your ability to compose photographs that are technically and formally sophisticated than to show off with a shape—a penis, a bottom, a nipple, a belly button—that you know has box-office draw? So many photographers who care about composition forget about our boredom, or maybe don't respect it; they give us formally clever pictures, and we yawn. Mapplethorpe wanted to grab our attention, and he did, with that which had grabbed his own attention.

On the subject of sex, it's as though Mapplethorpe had picked up a shovel, not a camera, and dug up what was buried. His most infamous imagery—the all-male S & M pictures—has angered many, including homosexuals who believe that these dark scenarios weaken the argument that homosexuality is as healthy as heterosexuality (and who remind us that sadism and masochism are not unknown in the heterosexual world). But Mapplethorpe wasn't following any party line; he wasn't into messages. Nor was he a moralizer. And he clearly wasn't trying to be ingratiating. He took the photographs because he and the men who engaged in these blendings of punishment and pleasure had seen and experienced something they felt should be made visible. These photographs are different from other works that have S & M as a subject, many of which glamorize what goes on, or titillate. Mapplethorpe's S & M imagery is unvarnished. It's the real thing—so real that some people call it dangerous and outrageous material, not art. The pictures are inarguably upsetting, but upsetting is no reason for banishment. The shouts of "Scandal!" are aimed in the wrong direc-

Robert Mapplethorpe, *Larry and Bobby Kissing,* 1979

tion. If there's a crime, it is that the individuals in his pictures are driven to see themselves as people who need to be punished in the context of sex, or to have so much anger about sex that they have to thrash others. When these images first appeared, ten years ago, there were those who couldn't believe what they were seeing. And then, as the years went on, Mapplethorpe's portraits, flowers, and nudes took front stage, and the S & M pictures were integrated into the history of his work—always there as a kind of invisible influence on the way people read his other imagery.

Although Mapplethorpe made very few S & M images, they would have to be included in any serious retrospective of his photography, as would examples of his non–S & M sexual imagery. Of all his subjects, sex is the one that most clearly reveals his intuition and his cleverness. In fact, only a small proportion of his work is on this topic, but this is where his contribution to photography stands out. His boldness, his cropping, and his frequent wit make other people's photographs of similar subject matter seem diluted or somehow off base. The rest of Mapplethorpe's photography is not all so original. His stylization can appear forced. And even among the controversial photographs there are affected examples—such as *Joe* (1978), a man in head-to-toe rubber—that are just silly; the image is all outfit with nowhere to go. Mapplethorpe did best with simplicity. He was street-smart, and when he used his canniness he hit his target. No other photographer has shown a black head and a white head up against each other with more effect: Mapplethorpe's image is tight with both tension and harmony. No other photographer has given us a kiss between two men that has made the word *queer* seem so obsolete. No one else has tapped the drama of closed eyelids so knowingly.

Mapplethorpe's flowers can have a riveting beauty that derives from a sense of their short life. Some are at such a peak you want to smell them. A lot of painters and photographers have worked with flowers, and often these pictures are said to be sexual. Mapplethorpe's flowers can certainly be erotic, as

Georgia O'Keeffe's can, but that's due to the nature of flowers. Mapplethorpe certainly didn't need to use flowers as vehicles of sexual allusion, because he worked with sex directly. Besides, when his flower photographs are at their best it is because he saw some quality—prickliness, say, or purity—that he had to catch before it passed. But Mapplethorpe also treated flowers cursorily or used them as a prop. In those instances, his flowers are forgettable. His last flowers are not forgettable. It is as though all the life and color that were being drained from him were being sucked into the petals, the stems, and even the backgrounds that he used.

As for his portraits, some of them hit and some miss. It's not that any of them are flops—they're all elegant—but the ones that are less imbued with his personal interest can be like head shots off the eight-by-ten-glossies rack. Not the stark portrait of Doris Saatchi, all enigmatic and floaty, with the strict contrasts between white and black that are his signature. Mapplethorpe's portrait of de Kooning is strong also; in fact, it is wrenching. The begging in de Kooning's eyes turns the image into the opposite of a commemoration of greatness. The photograph is a portrait of dependency and loneliness, and it makes de Kooning's overalls seem more like a kid's bib than like a painter's dress. De Kooning obviously touched Mapplethorpe. When Mapplethorpe wasn't moved or interested in a person, his portraits became merely workman-like, a way to make a buck, too stock Steichen. His nudes also vary in quality. Like White, he could be derivative of Weston, but he extended what Weston did, creating some nudes that have no counterpart in their sense of physical intimacy and their luscious depiction of the texture of skin. When Mapple-thorpe let himself be tempted by too broad a theatricality, the pictures get gift-boxy. He was strongest when he exerted his minimal aesthetic, and when he was at his most provocative.

"The Perfect Moment," which was curated by Janet Kardon, offers a sensible cross section of Mapplethorpe's work. The images that are said to have caused the blowup in Washington belong to three portfolios of prints cleverly titled *X, Y,* and *Z.* As the exhibition travels, the portfolios (which also include flowers, portraits, and texts) are always installed in a Mapplethorpe-designed slanting cabinet at counter height. They are avoidable; by just looking at what's on the walls, one could go through the show without seeing them. But to miss this tougher aspect of his work is to miss what gives Robert Mapplethorpe his place in photographic history.

That place is becoming clearer and clearer after a summer and a fall in which Robert Mapplethorpe, the Corcoran, and its director, Christina Orr-Cahall, had almost daily attention in the papers. There's irony in Mapplethorpe's becoming such a political cause célèbre. He may have been political in terms of whom to talk to at a dinner party, but he didn't give a hoot about real politics. Still, real politics found him when his work was about to appear in the capital. The reason he's controversial now is that he touched on all those territorial questions about the body that are once again such a vivid part of American politics. But whereas it's life—the life of the fetus—that is at the core of the abortion debate, it's the specter of death that is hanging over Mapplethorpe's pictures. Mapplethorpe didn't disappear into a hole when he became ill and his illness was diagnosed as AIDS. He didn't blame himself; he was a logical man. He didn't consider his condition God's punishment. He understood it for what it was—a virus, not a sign that he had sinned. He had no shame about having AIDS. This, in combination with his reputation as a homosexual who photographed homosexuals, made him a magnet for the media. Some articles even benefited from the panache of an accompanying Mapplethorpe self-portrait, done after his AIDS started showing. He took several such pictures of himself. In one that has now become famous, because it has been reproduced so often, he's holding a cane that has a skull knob and looking us straight in the eye. These self-portraits enabled everybody to witness him getting thinner, the sockets of his eyes getting more dramatic, his skin changing, his exhaustion visible. In addition, paparazzi constantly snapped him when he went out; they had a market for pictures of Robert Mapplethorpe with AIDS.

The brew of Mapplethorpe's artistic history, his personal openness, and then his openness about his medical condition has made him an icon of the age of AIDS—a rival to Rock Hudson as the most famous person to have had the disease. The press coverage of the Corcoran's cancellation made it clear just how glued together Mapplethorpe and AIDS have become. Practically every time his name was mentioned, AIDS was mentioned, too, as his ID. This isn't surprising. Reporters so often have to hold back on the word *AIDS* when people with AIDS have died that it seems writers can't string together the words "Robert Mapplethorpe, the photographer, who died of AIDS" often enough. There are those who use his AIDS in obviously manipulative ways. For example, in the public debates that have gone on—and on—about the Corcoran's cancellation, the information that Mapplethorpe died of AIDS is also always available, perhaps more often than his correct name. He's been referred to as Mapplewood, Mappleton, and Mapplesex, these "slips" usually coming from politicians excoriating his photography as part of their platform of decency and taxpayers' rights. (One supposes that their inability to retain the correct name of the man who made the so-called dirty pictures is a symbol of their righteousness.)

In fact, AIDS has a lot to do with what has happened lately with Mapplethorpe's work. In 1988, when it became widely known that he had AIDS, the Mapplethorpe business boomed; there was a rush to buy prints he had personally overseen and signed, and there was a flurry of retrospectives. After he died, the boom intensified, but we also got to see how his having had AIDS could be used to fuel an assault against his photography. The outcome of the Corcoran's cancellation of Mapplethorpe's show has been a debate in which his photographs have been treated by some as though they were a virus that curators have to be careful about exposing the public to. The stigma that his death carries has made his image and his work much more vulnerable to misrepresentation and projection. Now the physical sickness that the man endured is being used to confirm ideas that the work itself is sick.

The woman who brought Mapplethorpe back from the dead, Christina Orr-Cahall, is not immune to the criticism that she, too, approached Mapplethorpe's work as if it were contaminated. Who, other than someone very anxious, cancels a show so late in the schedule that the invitations have already been mailed out? Granted, there were rumblings and grumblings on the Hill. Granted, Orr-Cahall appears to have been uninformed about Mapplethorpe's work—a rather unusual position, to say the least, for someone in the art profession. (Mapplethorpe's been famous for a decade, and "The Perfect Moment" had already been in two museums.) Still, above and beyond Orr-Cahall's faux or real ignorance about the content of the show, she simply didn't give the pictures proper professional regard. Everything about her process before, during, and since the cancellation has had the aroma of panic, and, more serious, could suggest museological misconduct. For example, Orr-Cahall made the decision to cancel the show on the basis of photocopies of Mapplethorpe's pictures, which, according to *The Washington Post*, she had dispatched three scouts to Philadelphia to obtain. Apparently, it was on the basis of her descriptions of these photocopies that the Corcoran board confirmed her decision—at a thinly attended special meeting for which no agenda had been announced. (I rarely wish I were a fly, but to have been one on the wall on this occasion would be worth putting up with a lifetime of leftovers.) Whatever was said at this meeting, what resulted was a substitute show—and some important questions. For example: How could the Corcoran's director have allowed her museum to respond to political rather than cultural imperatives? How could she have allowed an artist's work to be rejected on the basis of photocopies, when so much of this photography's message depends on the feeling and scale of the actual prints?

When it turned out that the Corcoran's cancellation had alarmed many people in the arts, among them artists and dealers who said they would not participate in future exhibitions at that institution, the museum was forced to issue a statement of regret. But the tenor of its statement was rather sad proof that the institution's leader really doesn't understand what the problem is. It was hopelessly political in the bureaucratic sense—a transparent PR move—and it didn't work: "By withdrawing from the Mapplethorpe exhibition, we, the board of trustees and the director, have inadvertently offended many members of the arts community, which we deeply regret." If only they weren't so worried about offending people, the higher-ups at the Corcoran would be able to see the issues with more clarity. It is nice that Orr-Cahall personally passed on the Corcoran's regrets by calling, say, Donald Lipski and Annette Lemieux, two artists whom they were counting on for upcoming exhibits, but what about Mapplethorpe's family, who have had to live through all the Mapplethorpe bashing that resulted from the Corcoran's implicit agreement that his photographs are something to fear? To this day, the Corcoran has not written to or called those responsible for the Mapplethorpe estate, which owns the majority of the pictures in the exhibition. Usually a prime lender is treated with kid gloves. Here it's as though the Mapplethorpe estate was getting the rubber-glove treatment— avoidance. When the Corcoran pulled out, it did so through the press. When Orr-Cahall "apologized," it wasn't to anyone who had anything directly to do with Mapplethorpe or his work—it wasn't to the people he chose to be the caretakers of his pictures after he was gone. Meanwhile, Jane Livingston, the curator who was responsible for bringing "The Perfect Moment" to the Corcoran, has resigned. The gallery has lost 10 percent of its membership. What a mess. But it has exorcised so much.

From the beginning, the latest drama over NEA funding was reminiscent of one of Mapplethorpe's sadomasochistic scenes. A few members of the House and a few senators were holding the whip, and the two institutions that received NEA money to support Mapplethorpe's show and that of the other artist, Andres Serrano, who has been accused of photographic evildoing were said to have committed crimes for which they must suffer. (Although Serrano's picture *Piss Christ* is utterly innocuous, the sound of its title alone could distress people and be used as a tool by the same group who tried to shut down Martin Scorsese's *The Last Temptation of Christ.* Over the last few months, when Serrano's photograph has been labeled "blasphemous," his defenders have explained that the artist's intention was to call attention to the vulgarization and the commercialization of sacred imagery, but this does not seem to have impressed any of those who feel the work belongs in an incinerator, whether or not they've seen any of it.) While the punishment that had been suggested—no more money for five years—was voted down in the House, what was voted in isn't much better. Now the Endowment has to notify Congress thirty days prior to the giving of any grant money to either place, the Institute of Contemporary Art at the University of Pennsylvania and the Southeastern Center for Contemporary Art in Winston-Salem. In other words, these institutions are being treated like criminals on probation. They're not on their knees, or in chains, or hanging, the way some of Mapplethorpe's men are, but they, too, are victims of notions of sin that not everyone accepts. In addition, $45,000 was chopped from the NEA's allotment—the amount of money given out for Mapplethorpe and Serrano. These two decisions alone are alarming, because they uphold the notion that the institutions involved have done something wrong.

This is not a climate in which politicians are careful about how they slander artists. About a picture in which a little girl has her dress hiked up and no underwear on, Senator Helms told a *New York Times* reporter, "I'm embarrassed to even talk to you about this. I'm embarrassed to talk to my wife." Here, Helms was pushing yet another false image of Mapplethorpe—that he exploited children. I spoke to one of the subjects who has been cited as a victim of Mapplethorpe's abuse—Jesse McBride. His mother and Mapplethorpe were close friends. In Mapplethorpe's photograph, McBride is naked and he has leaped onto the back of a chair. "I must have been four or five then," he said (he's eighteen now). "I remember jumping around and laughing. I'm not as free-minded now. In those days, I'd just take off my clothes and start jumping on the chair. It was fun—Robert snapping away, and my mom laughing. When I got older, up to when I was twelve, I was embarrassed by the picture. I turned it toward the wall when my friends came over. I didn't want them to see my private parts. I didn't mind the adults' seeing me naked, but when you're that age you're easily embarrassed by friends. Now when I look at the photograph I think it's a really beautiful picture. I think back to when I was so young and innocent. I look particularly angelic." As Pat Steir, a painter, pointed out to me, this image echoes almost exactly a 1506 drawing of a young boy by Dürer, which he made as a study for his painting *Madonna with the Goldfinch.*

Still, some people accept as truth the fabrication that Mapplethorpe exploited or abused children. After the staff of the Washington Project for the Arts stepped in and took over Mapplethorpe's show in Washington, they received many letters. Congratulations were almost unanimous, but a few people wanted to go on record as being offended. A man from Kansas wrote the following letter to the staff: "I heard on the radio today that you have opened an 'Art' exhibit that depicts the exploitation of children. One that exposes male and female children's genitalia. That's disgusting! I also understand that this 'artist' is/was a homosextual [*sic*] and depicts other works with men in strange positions and environments. An exhibit of this sort would never be shown here in Kansas because we do not believe that our tax dollars should support such blatant, disgusting material. If Washington is supposed to lead the country in being an example, I'll stay in Kansas. I intend to notify my Reps and Senators that this is appalling to us here in the plains. Shame on you!" Taxes, dollars: That's the hook being used to get into the NEA's pocket. It has been said that taxpayers shouldn't have to support work that is offensive to community standards. But nobody yet has defined which taxpayers, or who or what is meant by "community."

In fact, the community that wants to see Mapplethorpe's work is enormous. Viewers come in numbers that make his shows blockbusters. The Whitney reported that his retrospective there in 1988 was one of the most highly attended events in its history. And the record crowds that have attended "The Perfect Moment" at each of its first four stops are not unusual for his work. After the Mapplethorpe show left Washington, the next venue was the Wadsworth Atheneum in Hartford. Andrea Miller-Keller, its curator of contemporary art, told me that there has been some community distress over the notion that the museum is exhibiting the work of a man who exploited children, and the afternoon I was there, on opening day, demonstrators carrying anti-abortion signs were gathered outside the museum. Nevertheless, the Mapplethorpe exhibition has had the most successful first week in the history of the Wadsworth. And Mapplethorpe's catalogue and book sales indicate a readership that's much broader than the usual art-book market. One assumes that all the people who are seeking out his work are taxpayers, too. Detractors are bound to argue that the huge audience that Mapplethorpe attracts is merely responding to his notoriety. Actually, ever since his pictures first appeared he has had devoted viewers. Nowadays it's fair to assume that some people go to view his work because of the publicity, but it says something that they want to see it for themselves—that they aren't scared of what will happen to them if they look at these supposedly contaminated images. And it says something, too, that there have been no more than three or four complaints from viewers at each of the American museums where Mapplethorpe's most graphic imagery has been included. Even so, his photography is said to be inappropriate for public expenditure and public consumption.

Can we, the public, handle direct images of sex? That, not taxes, is the real question. (If we're really going to be in control of our tax money, let each of us be given a checklist on the IRS form each year showing all the items our taxes are to be spent on, so that we can indicate exactly how we want our money to be used. On the stealth bomber? Aid to the Contras?) As for whether or not Mapplethorpe's graphic imagery belongs in a public institution, perhaps the best answer is to describe what goes on when it's shown. At the Wadsworth, in the gallery where the S & M pictures were on view, I saw a long line of people waiting to see what was in the cabinet. Around that display there was a hush, not a riot. The night the Mapplethorpe exhibition opened at the Washington Project was another good example of reality versus projection when it comes to the way people respond to Mapplethorpe's work. It was an evening that was obviously at high pitch, because of all that had gone on about the exhibition in Washington. There was the busyness of reporters scribbling, taping, filming, and swarming that one finds at phenomenal events; here, too, those on assignment depended on the impressions of eyewitnesses. The event had the feeling more of an ethnological-research project than of an art opening. Cameras focused on people viewing the photographs, and studied their reactions as if they were a tribe confronting artifacts from another world. Surprise! No one fainted at the sight of a black or white penis. Many viewers looked as if they'd seen one before.

Some commentators who are concerned about the impact of Mapplethorpe's most explicit photography feel that viewers have to be protected because we don't know what we're going to see when we walk into a museum. But people who go to museums or galleries don't run into art by mistake. Sometimes we know about the work and sometimes we don't, but when we don't, we go because we want to look at what someone has decided was important enough to put on the walls. Then, there is the question "But what about the children?" One answer came from Barbara Jakobson, a collector and an active member of the art community. She said, "Young children shouldn't be wandering around museums. At most shows they don't have a good time anyway, and their unhappiness ruins the experience for everyone else." (Her theory sounds as if it would be popular with certain children. I remember how when I was about nine I waited for my mother to get through a Henry Moore exhibit. I almost strangled myself in the hole of one of his mother and child pieces, I was so bored.) Jakobson's dry humor is a relief in the midst of all the piety. Still, the question of whether or not children should be exposed to material that they may not have the capacity to understand and that might confuse or frighten them does need to be addressed. Children deserve the same serious consideration here as in relation to any comparable medium, be it the movies, television, or comic books. There's the strategy museums have employed for years with Mapplethorpe's work: a placard informing viewers that some of the material is sexually explicit. Although this idea of warning people may be useful in controversial situations—for adults as well as children—ultimately, ratings for art are a sad solution. It's not just that if ratings are applied to art they are even more likely to be used absurdly and hypocritically than they are with movies. It's that to think about art in these terms is not to know what art is.

At the beginning of this year, when all the corks popped to celebrate photography's 150th anniversary, it looked as though the spotlight would be on the medium because of the role it had played in the past. Instead, what is happening with photography in the present has grabbed all the attention. And it makes sense that it was photography that launched the latest attempt to define proper versus improper art. Almost a hundred years ago, Bernard Shaw wrote about the effect of photography on people's sense of propriety:

"Photography is so truthful—its subjects are so obviously realities, and not idle fancies—that dignity is imposed on it as effectually as it is on a church congregation. Unfortunately, so is that false decency, rightly detested by artists, which teaches people to be ashamed of their bodies. . . ." Sometimes what photography reveals is a reality that people find intolerable. We saw that lack of tolerance in the reaction against Mapplethorpe's pictures. To take part in any effort to bury his supposedly offensive images is to be an accomplice in bigotry, to aid in the wiping out of his subjects by once again rendering them invisible. That, finally, is what is so disappointing about the Corcoran's not standing up for Mapplethorpe's work.

The Corcoran also betrayed its social contract with artists and viewers—not that it was the first museum to make such a mistake. Many museums operate from a position of fear, always worrying that images may be too graphic or extreme and upset the audience. Often, though, it is the people in charge of these museums who have the closed minds; and the audience, as Mapplethorpe's crowds prove, is fully capable of dealing with the controversial material.

Mapplethorpe understood that what he wanted to see—homosexuality brought out of the closet and into the light, sex brought out from the dark or up from under the counter, strong women, black men who are vigorous, beautiful, and classical instead of the usual bottom-of-the-pile image—others did, too. But, obviously, not everyone. One of the loudest voices to be raised against Mapplethorpe's work is Hilton Kramer's. Kramer is one of the few writers on art who made a statement in support of the Corcoran. His July *New York Times* article on the Mapplethorpe-Corcoran episode, "Is Art Above the Laws of Decency?," could be read as a disgorging of bitterness against contemporary art and its values, and was full of anger at the professional art world—a community that by and large has stopped listening to him. Of all people, it was Minor White whom Kramer cited as an example of a photographer who approached male nudity the right way—that is, inoffensively.

Kramer wrote, "There are male nudes in the Minor White retrospective now on view at the Museum of Modern Art that no one, as far as I know, has made any fuss about." And he left it at that. He didn't tell the reader that White's nudes had never been out in public before, because of the very issues now surrounding Mapplethorpe. Kramer, touting White as a symbol of acceptability, either didn't see the connections between the two photographers or didn't want to get distracted by them. For instance, there's that cancellation of White's exhibition at the California Palace of the Legion of Honor. Although the theme of that show was war, not sex, its disturbing images and text had quite a bit in common with Mapplethorpe's S & M pictures. White's allegedly unpatriotic "Amputations" sequence was criticized for its focus on the physical and emotional suffering of soldiers. Mapplethorpe's subjects are civilians, and their clothes are costumes rather than uniforms, but they, too, are creatures who live in battle, and it's a battle that both Mapplethorpe and White experienced at first hand: the struggle not to be condemned by society because of whom and how you love.

In the obvious ways, some of Mapplethorpe's photographs are harder to look at than White's. Mapplethorpe intended his work to challenge us. When he first got rolling, he didn't want to make the same old art. He wanted to get to us. He wanted to tap our most personal, least understood feelings. It is not possible to have an impersonal reaction to his sexual imagery—the part of us that it hits is the part that is most raw—so it's not surprising that his pictures have elicited both love and hate. They have always had enormous personal meaning for me, extra-pictorial as well as pictorial. I first saw them when I was in my mid-twenties. It was at a time in my life when I was afraid of what would happen—and worried about how my parents would feel—if I said I had a girlfriend, not a boyfriend. It was a relief to come upon an artist who addressed homosexuality in an unqueasy, honest, and often beautiful way. It was an inspiration to see self-portraits that were so candid, and at the same time so cool. It meant so much that he didn't project himself as "a loser." Later, Mapplethorpe and I became friends. His imagery wasn't all that was honest about him. He was a straightforward man. It was his willingness— actually, his need—to reveal himself that made it possible for him to treat his subject so directly. I've written about him once before, for the book that was produced on the occasion of his retrospective at the Whitney. I remember struggling with the section of my essay that addressed his S & M pictures. They are so tough to look at that they brought on a horrible thought: What if these criminal-looking images were exploited by those who see homosexuality as a crime? What if the fact that Mapplethorpe had AIDS was to color the reception of his work? It didn't happen then, but a year later, in Washington, we saw the exploitation and ignorance in action.

That Mapplethorpe was going to succeed was in the cards. He worked hard, all the time—and he understood what was missing from most of the other imagery that people were being offered. Like Minor White, Mapplethorpe was a figure of his time, but times had changed. He was able to photograph the transition of homosexuality from a dirty secret that people felt they must hide to a vision of lives that could be led out in the open, without fear of recrimination. To some, his pictures seemed to be the mirror they had been waiting for all their lives. And his attitude toward his material was also welcome. No apologies, no disguises, no theories: He just laid it all out. Minor White didn't have this chance; that's what is so painful about his work. In the end, it is much harder to look at his photographs than to look at Mapplethorpe's most frightening images. Photographs like Minor White's suggest how much is lost when the public becomes an entity to be afraid of rather than a body of people to whom one tries to tell the truth.

The New Yorker, November 13, 1989

Sam Wagstaff's Silver

Sam Wagstaff looked and acted as though he was born with a silver spoon in his mouth. It always seemed to me that he was the handsomest man in the world. And it always seemed as though he could have been anything and done anything he wanted. He could have, and he did. He was known first as a dynamic curator of modern and contemporary art—working at the Wadsworth Atheneum and the Detroit Institute of Arts—and then as a collector. He was really a collector all his life, but he went at it full-time in his last twenty years. This is where his genius came out.

Still, people were surprised when he started to focus on American silver in 1984. We're talking about someone who ate out, opened a can, or ordered take-out, so the very idea of silver pieces cluttering the shelves seemed out of character, too fussy and retro for a man who traveled so light. That's why collecting photography, the modern medium of light, had matched his image so well. But here, too, when he first started buying pictures and talking about photography as more magnetic for our time than painting and sculpture, he didn't find unanimous agreement in either art or collecting circles. In fact, in the early 1970s, there were very few people having serious love affairs with what a person with a camera could achieve. Yet by 1984, when Wagstaff sold his collection of nineteenth- and twentieth-century photography to the Getty Museum, he had more than proved his argument, so much so that you could hear something virtually blasphemous in the chauvinistic New York art world—an admission of envy that the most important private collection of photographs was on its way to California.

With American Victorian silver Wagstaff's prescience becomes evident again. And again, when he first entered the field, only he and a few others wanted the stuff. Most connoisseurs disdained its eccentric designs, its democratic use of mixed metals, its embracing of sources as diverse as Alaska, ancient Greece, and the East; they preferred something more European, less

Robert Mapplethorpe, *Sam Wagstaff*, 1979

wild. Wagstaff and those few others comprised a tiny world where everyone knew everyone else and agreed that everyone outside that world was dead wrong. That was part of the fun for Wagstaff—the intimate underground aspect of collecting, the renegade angle that challenged the ruling orders of taste. Wagstaff's air of entitlement came in especially handy.

Arrogance served—such a smooth way to get beyond the rules of the game. He didn't even have to attack orthodoxies he didn't respect; he simply appeared above it all. You could say he was a bohemian in patrician's clothing—a combination that guaranteed surprises.

Such as the time silver spoons were coming out of his pocket. A few of his friends were at the restaurant Da Silvano, seated and waiting for him. When he showed, he had that swallowed-a-canary look he could get. Even before sitting down, so it wasn't the slightest bit subtle, he pushed away the existing flatware from each of our settings and produced a set of spoons he had just bought, saying they were for strawberries and ice cream. At dessert, he wouldn't hear of any of us begging off. (He couldn't identify with dieters, which always pro-

vided me with an excuse to eat uncomplex carbohydrates.) He wanted us to taste the spoons, to feel the solidness of the scoop compared to the melting ice cream that filled it. We did as we were told (each for our own reasons). The spoons were left to sit on the plates, returning to his pocket, after a cursory wipe with his napkin, only when the waiter was clearing the way for coffee.

Wagstaff made his silver earn its keep; it was used, which was his way of drawing us into the excitement. I remember waiting and waiting for one Christmas dinner at his apartment, not because the food wasn't ready but because the silver vessel he had chosen for the stuffing had to be polished until it came up to par. This was in 1985, before he had amassed the approximately six hundred pieces that would eventually make up his collection, built largely in just over two years and cut off by his death in 1987. He would keep some of the objects lined up on the white floor of the living room in front of the windows, adding to the glamour of the view down to Fifth Avenue as it goes into Washington Square. Despite the chicness, some problem with air trapping had developed between the floorboards and the white linoleum. Walking around was like treading on Bubble Wrap, and the sound of popping would punctuate conversation. So at his place even the acoustics contributed to the Wagstaff electricity, the expectation that he would unwrap and reveal something amazing. I was never disappointed. In a way, it was permanent Christmas up there; but outside in the middle of nowhere he could give you this feeling, too.

Many years ago a bunch of us were on the beach having a picnic. Sam decided to take a walk and disappeared into the distance. Sometime later we spotted him way up on the beach, heading back toward us. As he got closer, we spied these bizarre jumbled things dangling from both his hands. When he reached our temporary camp, he bent down, handing out his treasures, and said, "I've made you sandals and brought you something else to eat." Our Poseidon had collected bark, seaweed, beach plums, and other plants and found materials; he claimed some of it could be eaten, and the rest he had tied together into shoelike contraptions with bits of net and string.

This food he offered and these sandals he had made rendered it utterly clear that Sam Wagstaff couldn't stop collecting and that his compulsions were free from extrinsic notions of status. This isn't to say he was a socialist. He would go very high in the bidding. And this isn't to say that he didn't discriminate among people—but he argued with people's discriminations against certain materials.

The point is that he particularly liked to choose the orphans of art, the stuff that hadn't quite been let into the pearly gates of fine art. Wagstaff never cared if others agreed with his choices—that was their right or, more accurately, their problem. Consensus wasn't his aim. He had a favorite free-spirit story, which goes along these lines: The art dealer Betty Parsons once asked some people what the difference was between cats and dogs, and after hearing their answers, gave her own— cats aren't afraid for their jobs. Nor was Wagstaff. His job was to get us to look.

In a fundamental way, he put out-of-fashion American Victorian silver through the same regenerative process that he did the bark and string of our sandals that day on the beach. Silver had seemed to me a leftover, useless to the needs of modern life, all that polishing a pain in the neck. But because of Wagstaff's eyes I looked again. Many people did, and the history and pleasure of American silver made in the second half of the nineteenth century is once again a subject.

Sometimes I think his decision to collect these works, particularly silver of the 1870s and 1880s, was like sending us a message in a bottle. As our decade spins in its fin de siècle mood, the analogies between then and now multiply, and the old objects become radically contemporary in the context of today's ornamentalism, stylism, decorativism, and, of course, our social Victorianism. Wagstaff did it again; he threw the light onto objects that were waiting for him as though in the wings. He is, in a roundabout way, responsible for yet another light turned on them—Robert Mapplethorpe's photographing some of them for this issue of *H&G*. Silver is photography's elemental relative, and Wagstaff always wanted his friend Mapplethorpe to show the beauty in these things, usually considered ugly and scorned, as only a Mapplethorpe can do.

On January 20, 1989, the Sam Wagstaff Collection of American Silver goes up for sale at Christie's. Picture him sitting in the audience, shining as much as the pieces.

House & Garden, January 1989

Belief

At the Museum of Modern Art, they have the same troubles with their office machines that the rest of us do. And the same types of instructive notes about how not to have a breakdown when they break. Item number four on a sign taped up at one of the copying stations in the corridors of the curatorial offices reads, "Please try not to take it personally when the machine has its problems . . . it's just a machine. In other words, please don't bang, bruise, beat, bump, or otherwise abuse it. It won't help." I happened to be at that machine because the one that visitors to the study center of the Department of Photography usually get to use was—yes, out of order. I was reproducing some pages

from a book by the photographer Chauncey Hare that appeared in 1984 and got none of the attention it deserved. The book is titled *This Was Corporate America,* and its subject is the opposite of people bruising and beating up on machines out of frustration: It is about people being beaten down and psychologically bruised by the corporate machine.

Although Hare's work has been honored—with a MoMA show and Guggenheim grants—he is not famous. He doesn't have the reputation of an Avedon, a Penn, a Leibovitz, or a Weber—probably because his work is not about limelight figures. The photographs in *This Was Corporate America* are of ordinary people, people who go to work on the subway. He shows person after person in a cold, anonymous-looking, dead-feeling office—in other words, unspotlit people, who sit under fluorescent lights. So his work slips out of the media's attention—too humdrum. A sense of alienation like his is what one used to expect from an artist, but today it seems almost old-fashioned, and not at all postmodern; and in his career, there was no split-second leap from art school to art gallery and wealth. There was a jump, however, to save his life. "In 1977 at the age of 43, after 21 years' employment, I left my engineering job with the Standard Oil Company of California in Richmond, California, where I still live," he writes in *This Was Corporate America.* "At Standard I swallowed until I choked and the programs literally caused me to vomit."

Before Hare became a photographer, and about the time he went to work for Standard Oil, in the fifties, some revered figures in the history of photography, such as Walker Evans and Ansel Adams, were also going in and out of executive offices, photographing them for magazine articles about the growth of American industry. A lesser-known figure, Dan Weiner, was on this beat, too. The work he did then is the subject of a small show now at MoMA. And

Dan Weiner, *Kaffeeklatsch, Park Forest, Illinois,* 1953

the difference between Weiner's portraits of people in the fifties and Hare's eighties pictures could break your heart.

What's missing in Hare's work is the look of belief in the faces of his subjects. In Dan Weiner's photographs you find belief to spare, and you also have a chance to consider picture taking at its most ungimmicky. And that's odd, because the gimmick is so often Weiner's subject: the search for the gimmick, the selling of it, the buying of it—in short, "American enterprise," as it was called in the fifties. We can never know how Weiner would portray us now, with our desk computers and our faxes, because he was killed in a plane crash in 1959, at the age of thirty-nine. In his day, he was something of a success. His photography was showing up in *The New York Times* and in some of the biggest magazines—*Fortune* and *Collier's*—and in some smaller publications, too. But, as the years went by, his work practically disappeared from circulation. Except for an occasional show (there was one at the International Center of Photography in 1980), he has been inadequately honored, especially in books on photojournalism. (*The Eyes of Time: Photojournalism in America,* by Marianne Fulton, which appeared this March, virtually ignores him.) But history is like a bed: It's made, unmade, made again, and so on. In conjunction with Weiner's exhibition at MoMA, a book by Bill Ewing is about to appear. It has the same title as the show, *America Worked: The 1950s Photographs of Dan Weiner,* though it has additional photographs, critical essays, and material from the period.

The photographs at MoMA were made after the war; the bombing had stopped, but this is an exhibition of battle pictures. Now the target is the public, and the weapon is the psychological warfare employed by advertising. Weiner's photographs look more like images from TV and the movies than like photographs of real people doing real things. The subjects exude such naïveté that they seem more believable if you think of them as characters

Dan Weiner, *Kenneth Spencer, Head of Spencer Chemical Company, Kansas,* 1952 in ads or as actors playing fifties parts. There's a home-products vice president demonstrating how to sell clothes brushes. (He suggests listening to "the music of the bristles," according to a quotation on the wall at the exhibition.) The president and top executives of Campbell's taste soup and make the event seem as momentous as the discovery of the Dead Sea Scrolls.

A good number of the males in these photographs resemble Feds as they have been imagined by Hollywood—in boxy suits and fedoras. When they're together at a strategy meeting, or checking inventory at a company they've just taken over, or surveying an idyllic piece of land for a possible real estate development, they huddle like football players. The women (except for the showgirls) look neat and uptight. The children look worried. One little boy is really suffering as his exhausted-from-shopping parents try to decide on a dinette set in a Brooklyn store. (I hope they got it; they could resell it for a fortune today.)

Weiner's most brilliant portraits are the equivalent of pictures you'd see now

in a company's annual report, except that the people are less obviously posed. Everyone's on the go. As one of the show's two curators, Susan Kismaric (the other is Bill Ewing), points out, people seemed much less self-conscious then in front of the camera, more open and more natural. Weiner's method of taking pictures encouraged this naturalness that now looks so unnatural. He'd get to an assignment a bit early and hang around until he fitted in with the new furniture or the new car or the plane, and then start working. His "decisive moment" was different from Cartier-Bresson's: It wasn't the instant that stands out because what's happening is so exceptional; it was the stretch of time when supposedly nothing much is going on. And that's why everything is there—all the dynamics between people that most other photographers missed because they were holding out for the remarkable. It's clear why Garry Winogrand, who sought that same artlessness in his snapshots, admired Weiner's work.

A large proportion of the photographs in the MoMA exhibition come from

Weiner's assignments for *Fortune,* and it's different seeing the images where they originally appeared. The pages of *Fortune* used to be as scrumptious as paintings; the illustrations, the photography, and the ads often came from the best artists around. Even the printing was opulent. (The writing was a complex mixture of gung-hoisms and criticisms, of racism, sexism, and enlightenment, of acuity and horse blinders.) *Fortune* was not only about the material world; it was monthly proof of that world's achievements. In its pages, Weiner's photographs sometimes shine, but often they're no more special than the next guy's. Surrounded by similar views of America selling itself on itself, they are really pretty generic, lacking the spin that emerges thirty years later, when they're clustered on the walls of the Modern. Weiner's is not the only work that has sharpened with the years. Walker Evans's pictures also often look run-of-the-mill when you come upon them in their original frame of reference. Photography is slippery that way. Isolated and framed, a photograph takes on a different life from the one it had on a contact sheet or in a newspaper or magazine.

Weiner had his complaints about the way publications used the photographer, as if he were "a plumber"; as he put it, "when they have a hole to fill, they rush him out." But he wasn't always dissatisfied, and he was counting on time to look after his work. He said as much in a short text titled "The Camera to Me": "Photography combines those elements of spontaneity and immediacy that say, this is happening, this is real, and creates an image through a curious alchemy that will live and grow and become more meaningful in a historical perspective."

Actually, it was a lucky thing for Weiner that his *Fortune* photographs didn't stand out. On their own, they make you wonder how he could have got away with some of his asperities. *Fortune* may have had its irreverent and critical side, but it was neither *Mad* magazine nor *Das Kapital.* At the MoMA exhibition, you hear people laughing out loud at some of Weiner's images, and you see

Dan Weiner, *James Moran, Chicago,* January 1952

them staring in amazement at others. On the museum's white walls, the pictures reveal that almost everyone in them is under a spell—the spell known as the American Dream. One dream is to be the boss, and it is illustrated by a secretary-with-boss shot that is almost a cartoon of bossiness. The boss has the girth of affluence and holds in his hand a piece of paper that seems to be mobilizing both of them for action. The quotation from *Fortune* above the picture says, "Advice to Organization Wives: Be a phone pal of your husband's secretary." The same man, the industrialist Henry Kaiser, appears in Ewing's book, along with four executives, in what may be the first group to "reach out and touch someone": Each man is holding a phone to his ear. Why, you wonder, do they all have to be in the same room? There are other novel situations. A rather handsome man holds a meeting in his Bel Air home, in a room that seems to be a combination of tree house, boardroom, and appliance store. The men sit around a table that is cluttered with papers and has a tree growing out of its middle; a television set seems to be growing out of another tree. (This same man had a bomb shelter that you arrived at via the swimming pool; the dip was meant to wash off the radiation.) But Weiner didn't photograph just the serious stuff; he was there for the fun times, too—the planned office parties. Except for the presence of typewriters, these affairs look like funeral gatherings.

Others of the photographs are an invitation to reminisce. John Wendelken, who works at the museum as a guard, remarked to me, "These pictures take me back to the days when they used to build quality refrigerators. Not anymore. Now they fall apart." The picture that inspired that good-old-days remark is of men and women in a store, admiring the latest convenience: a fridge that contains a freezer. The year is 1954, the store is Macy's, and the photograph was made for *Fortune*. Wendelken's lament about fridges comes from the same place as my nostalgia for top-quality printing. We all fall into one nostalgic trap or another. The Weiner exhibition is so effective because it forces us to catch ourselves in the act.

There are no good old days. Weiner's pictures brilliantly debunk the myth that "things were better then," through what they reveal about people who are supposed to be in Paradise—or, at least, on their way. There are a few photographs that outdo Diane Arbus on this score. One was taken in an environment that she, too, frequented—Scarsdale. It's a tableau of Dad, Mom, and the kids in front of their home, looking as though they were waiting for the executioner. In another picture, there's a family in their living room, but no one's lounging; they're having "a conversation." In order to have it, they have to raise their hands, as we see in the picture, before being given permission to speak by Dad. It's scarier than if the family were in their bomb shelter on a drill. Then, there's a young man waiting for an interview in front of a sign that shouts ARE *YOU* READY FOR YOUR INTERVIEW? and lists how he should look, what he should know, and how he should behave. His tie wasn't the only thing that had to be straight.

Above all, "America Worked" is about conformity and the making and spending of money. Weiner's photographs are puppet-show pictures, with the dollar controlling the strings. The costumes are, of course, versions of "the gray flannel suit." What else would "the organization man" wear? The man who wrote *The Organization Man,* and who understood the mirages lurking in the dream better than anyone else, William H. Whyte, is the presiding spirit of "America Worked."

Some of the pictures depicting marketing strategy made me see red, such as an image of two little girls with two miniature shopping carts in a supermarket. The image is accompanied by a quote from *Fortune:* "People think that these tiny carts are very cute; the operator thinks they are very profitable. The small children go zipping up and down the aisles imitating their mothers in impulse buying, only more so." But it's too simple to see this show as an illustration of the evils of making a buck. Yes, there are photographs that bring out the snake-oil aspect of advertising, and photographs that display people at their most self-important. And there's proof of how tight the door to the new Paradise was. With all the bossiness on view, there's only one woman boss, Catherine Loretta O'Brien, the president of Stanley's Home Products. Otherwise, women play their stereotyped roles as wives, mothers, secretaries, members of kaffeeklatsches, floor-show entertainment. The young Martin Luther King, Jr., and Coretta Scott King and their baby are among the few black faces in the exhibition. They do more than stand out; they remind us of a different dream. The social realities emerge very clearly in "America Worked." But we don't need to go to the Modern to learn about them; life gives us plenty of such opportunities. What the pictures at MoMA do teach us is how a certain kind of photojournalism works. What did Weiner do? He made visible the hardest subject of all to visualize: belief. And he did it convincingly, partly because the people themselves were convinced and partly because of his narrative approach. He was a master at including the activity around the edges of his subjects. (You don't just see "Smiling Jim Moran, the Courtesy Man" smile as he sells a car to the people at home watching TV. You see what's happening "off camera"—a TV camera, the wires, the lights—so you also see the shaping of belief.) Some of the people in Weiner's portraits may have been angels and others terrible jerks—who knows? But most of them really seem to have believed that the work they were doing and the things they were buying were going to make their country great and their lives "happy." And Weiner clearly realized that this pride in work and faith in purchased goods was essential to understanding the culture of the fifties.

Weiner was a member of the socially conscious Photo League—yet another organization that Senator McCarthy misdiagnosed as subversive. And although the MoMA exhibition is almost solely about bullish America, it's important to know that he didn't take photographs only of flush times; as the book demonstrates, he photographed poor America, and old people. And he worked in Russia, Eastern Europe, and South Africa, as well. While the pictures he made

Dan Weiner, *Fashion Show on Show Train, New Haven Railroad,* July 1949 in other countries reveal him as a photographer determined to express the dignity of people, these are not his most charged images. American industrialization is the subject at which he excelled. The closer he got to the people who believed in its powers, the better his work became. This is the area of his photography that is a surprise. It's so filled with the suspense of people high on the new that you're left wondering where they landed. These photographs treat the workaday and domestic life of the fifties as though it were as much a subject for revelation as the court was in Velázquez's time, or the battlefield in Delacroix's. This is still true of daily life today, although today we mostly find in it not belief, but pessimism. Now when we go to the copying machine we're not shocked when it's broken.

The New Yorker, May 22, 1989

Selling Dreams

IT'S WAR, screamed a headline more than half a foot high on the front page of the *New York Daily News* last month. An even catchier headline, in *Newsday*, warned, "ATOM BOMB" OF CUSTODY. There was no reason for panic, though; no one was heading for his shelter, or for the Canadian border. These dire headlines were not proclaiming a threat to the nation. No, they dealt with a personal, family crisis. This was a war that was drafting not citizens but lawyers and publicists, for a frontline battle on a very unmilitary front line—in the press. And the press got so apocalyptic because this family crisis involved two American stars as big as they come: Woody Allen and Mia Farrow.

It's hard—maybe impossible—to imagine what it feels like to be the subject of headlines like these, creating excitement and mass debate in offices, at newsstands, on buses, in restaurants all over the land. It's much easier to relate to the feelings of a far larger group of people—the fans. Hasn't each of us carried on, at least once, an unreciprocated love affair with a star? Maybe it was a high school football hero, maybe it was John Kennedy, maybe now it's Michelle Pfeiffer, Luke Perry, or Jackie Joyner-Kersee. The chosen ones may remain important to us or we may eventually laugh at our infatuations, but I don't know anyone who hasn't felt the emotions that come with being a fan.

In America, over the years, we've changed the way we treat our big-time stars, whether they're in the movie business or in areas that bear more directly on real life. We've gone from regarding the very famous—or, at least, certain aspects of their lives—as if they were untouchable to the opposite: to a form of cannibalism. Nowadays, every aspect of a public figure's business is, if we want it, available to us—as if it were *our* business. Bill and Hillary Clinton's marriage, Jodie Foster's sex life, William Styron's depression, some celebrity's drug habit, history of abuse, or story of personal "madness" (the latest thing in celebrity bios)—these topics fill the dailies, the weeklies, and the monthlies.

The classic among American stars is Elizabeth Taylor, a woman whose marriages, history of backaches, habit of lateness, fluctuations in weight, affection for diamonds, and addictions have fed the media for decades. To witness Taylor on the celebrity stand is to see an audience absolutely mesmerized by the presence of a star they seem to know intimately. Last year, she gave a press conference at the Plaza to help launch her new fragrance, White Diamonds. The reporters who attended seemed to have as much interest in the actual scent as I did: *What* scent? It was Taylor's personal life that they pressed her about, and the questions got very frank, right down to whether or not she practiced safe sex. And, as often happens with Taylor, throughout her appearance the cameras were going. Shortly before her exit, she commented on the nonstop flashes of light in her eyes. "I can't see," she said. But that didn't stop the cameras.

What a different life Taylor might have had as a star if, instead of growing up at MGM, she had been one of the girls in Japan's Takarazuka Revue. If she had been, the great majority of the people taking pictures of her through the years would have been fans, not the press, and had she told her fans that their flashbulbs were hurting her eyes, those violet pools would have had instant relief, because the crowd's paramount concern would have been her comfort. And she would never have been subjected to a barrage of personal questions, for she would be treated as someone whose privacy was precious, and not as public property to be dissected. If she had announced plans to get married, there would have been weeping, rather than a rush to get scoops about her sex life. And the fans would have been sobbing because, in essence, their star would have been dying before their eyes. Takarazuka actresses are not allowed to have any public connection with anything that even suggests a sexual relationship, so a Takarazuka actress must retire when she announces her marriage.

Had marriage meant the end of Taylor's career, that career would have stopped in 1950, when she was eighteen.

We have no stars like Takarazuka's in America. We have no equivalent to this theater in America. To Americans, and to most other non-Japanese, the whole thing seems very odd indeed: An all-woman theatrical extravaganza, whose audience is almost 100 percent female, but whose biggest stars present themselves onstage as men and are treated as such—offstage, as well. It's not enough to say that Takarazuka is the flip side of Japan's most famous theatrical form, Kabuki. On the surface, there are correspondences: Whereas Takarazuka has women playing all the parts, male as well as female, contemporary Kabuki uses men in all the parts; and both genres specialize in visual spectacle. But Kabuki, despite its popularity, has something highbrow about it. Not so Takarazuka: Although its followers practically constitute a cult, it's as accessible as a Vegas stage show.

If you ask your Japanese friends about Takarazuka, you risk being laughed at. They may tell you that their mother or their maid likes it but that they themselves have no interest in it at all—that they've never seen it, and have no desire to. Which may explain why, although I'd come upon mention of Takarazuka in print, it took years for me to actually see it. As it happens, I had had a passing encounter with the phenomenon ten years ago, in Tokyo. Looking out of a window in the Imperial Hotel, across from the Tokyo Takarazuka Theater, I saw an enormous crowd on the street below, obviously waiting for something, the way people lining Fifth Avenue wait for a parade. I can't remember whether or not I noticed that the throng was female, but I do remember being aware of how orderly and disciplined it seemed. At the hotel information desk, I asked who the people were and what they were expecting to see, and was told, with a dismissive laugh, "Oh, those are the Takarazuka fans. All women and girls."

.   .   .

I completely forgot about my aerial view of the Takarazuka lovers until I went with a friend—I'll call him B.—to see the company perform at Radio City Music Hall in 1989, when it was on tour. (A small group from the company will be performing in New York this November, at the Joyce Theater, in an atypical all-dance show, of both Eastern and Western pieces, choreographed by Kayoko Nakura and Linda Haberman.) The Radio City event contained many standard elements of Takarazuka: There was singing, dancing, and acting, in a surreal mixture of East and West; the women played both female roles and male roles, and were dressed accordingly; there were thirties-style Hollywood numbers, with plenty of Busby Berkeleyesque lighted-up-stairway-to-the-sky shtick and razzle-dazzle costume changes. The incomparable sound of Takarazuka was there, too—the strangely haunting, even grating, quality of the women projecting their miked voices "girlie" high or else low "like a guy." And Radio City itself, with its Deco architecture and its history of theatrical spectacle, was a suitable place in America for Takarazuka to perform. But although the audience consisted primarily of Japanese, I didn't notice that they were getting any special kicks. There was no real sense of excitement in the air—or on the stage, for that matter.

Our perception began to change a few months later, when, on the first morning of a visit to Tokyo, B. and I spied the Takarazuka Theater all brightly lit and busy. On the outside of the building were giant posters advertising the stars of the current show, *The Rose of Versailles,* the company's all-time hit. (It has been revived again and again since its premiere, in 1974.) The billboard-size photographs stopped us in our tracks. The top male and female characters had been thoroughly airbrushed and were done up to the max in eighteenth-century outfits, including wigs that could turn ordinary men into rock-and-roll stars and jackets fit for Liberace. Their eyes popped out of turquoise eyeshadow emphasized by bold strokes of purple, and their mouths were superseductive via generous helpings of crimson lipstick. These figures projected an aura unlike anything we had ever encountered. Dietrich, DeMille epics, kitsch are points of reference too limited to suggest the shock value of Takarazuka's iconography.

Inside the theater, a dress rehearsal was taking place. Thanks to the luck of running into a high-level technician who spoke a bit of English, we were allowed in to watch several scenes being rehearsed—over and over and over, for almost eight hours. I'm sure the rehearsal was less confusing than the whole performance would have been. Consider this plot summary, taken directly from the English translation included in a program for the show, under the heading "A Takarazuka Grand Romance; *The Rose of Versailles*":

The story takes place in the last half of the 18th in France. General Jarget's wife was expecting their sixth child. The General loved his five daughters but was praying with all his heart for a son. When his wife gave birth to another daughter, the General gave her a boy's name, Oscar. He decided to bring her up as a boy.

Oscar grew up strong and brave. She became the commander of Queen Marie-Antoinette's Royal Bodyguard. Oscar cut a gallant figure in the Court and was respected for her superb swordsmanship. The Ladies of the Royal Court idolized Oscar and the Queen herself held her in high esteem.

Oscar's subordinate, Andre was a grandson of Oscar's nurse and was brought up along with Oscar as if they were real brother and sister to each other and became a bosom friend of her. But now he was secretly in love with Oscar as a woman. He knew his love to her was a hopeless love. . . .

Oscar learned of Andre's love for her and realized that she had found true love. Beside the river Seine Oscar made every attempt to prevent a violent incident. But the King's troops opened fire on the citizens and started a bloody battle. Oscar, in spite of Jerodel's objections, threw his support to the citizens and fought against the King's soldiers. During the course of a long battle Andre was shot and then Oscar was gravely wounded.

A white flag appeared over the castle wall. With the victorious cheers of his fellow citizens ringing in his ears, Oscar quietly breathed his last.

A grand romance, to be sure—and a grand freedom with pronouns. However, there wasn't much that was grand about the rehearsal itself. Like any dress rehearsal, it was full of interruptions, people checking details on the stage, the orchestra stopping and starting, stagehands dragging scenery behind (or in front of) the performers, a lot of cigarette smoking and exchanging of notes by those in charge. What stood out was the behavior of the actresses. They gave the impression of being the sweetest schoolgirls on earth, not a grumbler among them, and certainly no sign of a prima donna. This would have been striking in any case, but, given the roles that some of them were playing—men with enough strength to lead armies, to change history—the gap between image and life impressed us and sucked us in.

A few nights later, from the back entrance of the Imperial, we saw what happens when the mob that waits outside the theater gets its reward. The actress who played Oscar in *The Rose of Versailles* had just come through the stage door. There was a tiny flash from a camera here, another one over there, more and more hints of light bouncing out of the assembled fans as this assured woman strode past, leaving them behind, their order and quiet unbroken. None of the bursts of light came anywhere near her face, and everything else in the immediate environment was business as usual. To the fans, a star was walking among them, but to other Tokyoites passing by, there was no reason to pause. No longer in the sparkling jacket, ruffled shirt, and shiny pants that we'd seen her wearing at the rehearsal, and without her reddish wig, she had a plainer appearance but a no less engaging one. Her face was obviously made up, her short boyish hair was on the dusty side of blond, and her street clothes—a cream trouser suit and a crisp, tucked-in white shirt—had an androgynous look. She was nothing like any of the Japanese women we'd been seeing every day. As we would come to realize, though, her public look resembled that of every top "male" Takarazuka star.

Accompanying the actress was another telltale sign of Takarazuka stardom: an assistant—someone who contrasts with her the way a paper towel does with Christmas wrapping. *Dumpy* might be the word for the assistant, who was carrying her star's typical paraphernalia—a few bouquets and some shopping bags. Crossing the street, they walked by a few scattered groups of fans, each of which held still as the star came past, close enough to be touched. But nobody tried to touch her. Instead, people stared, as if gazing at a masterpiece in a museum. Or they bowed. A few fans chased after the two women, at a respectful distance. Me, too. (Not B., who was enjoying the blackmailable sight of me in the grip of Oscarmania: He knew I hadn't been a groupie since my schoolgirl days in Scotland, twenty-five years ago, when I retired as president of the Illya Kuryakin fan club.) When our star and her assistant reached the back entrance of the Imperial, their followers stopped as if its glass double doors had been barbed wire. *Whoosh*—the doors parted, and in went the two women, while the fans remained outside. The dividing line was clear. But "off-limits" is not a notion we New Yorkers care for, and, besides, I was staying at the Imperial, so I crossed the border, in pursuit. Inside the hotel, the excitement that had surrounded the star instantly evaporated. She stopped at the newsstand, glanced at the candy and the magazines, and then kept on walking, her assistant beside her, until they made their unceremonious exits from the front entrance of the Imperial. It was after this epiphany that B. and I decided to find out what Takarazuka was all about.

Back in Tokyo this past summer, we made straight for the Takarazuka Theater and acquired standing-room tickets—the only ones left—for a performance already in progress. I can't remember ever being so stunned by another sequence on a stage as I was by the finale of Takarazuka's version of *Spartacus,* which we saw from our perch in the third balcony. Spartacus and "his" cohorts are surrounded by Roman soldiers led by an evil general. The heroine—Spartacus's great love, in blue chiffon—snatches a sword and kills the general, and is slain in turn. The bodies are borne away, and Spartacus is left alone onstage to sing a dirge of protest, anguish, and heroism. (The music, which made Andrew Lloyd Webber's button pushing seem subtle, was accompanied by another sound: a subdued weeping throughout the huge house, which couldn't be muffled by the white handkerchiefs that had been pulled out and put to use by the audience.) The dirge ended, the lights went down, and the lights came up—on two lead performers in sequined jackets and razor-sharp trousers, backed by forty girls in white tights and little red bunny dresses, huge plumes in their hair, all dancing and singing, more or less adequately, to "Arrivederci Roma."

Here, onstage and off, was what had been missing that day in Radio City Music Hall. How could one quibble about technique or talent or narrative logic in the face of the kind of pleasure we saw all around us? This was a full-scale, all-out performance for an audience of fans who are crazy about the company, who plan their lives around getting tickets for it, who have favorite stars they'll wait hours on the street to see. And not just wait. Plan the wait, choreograph the wait, treat the wait as a ritual that leads to paradise: the sight of *them.*

When *Spartacus* was over, hundreds of fans clustered outside the theater, and the stars gave them more thrills by emerging at intervals, smiling just enough, bowing, accepting a note or two, occasionally signing an autograph, and then disappearing either into waiting cars or into the Imperial. And for the final performance of *Spartacus,* the next evening, there were still more fans outside the theater. Here was a fan send-off that spared no love. There were so many bouquets lined up on the sidewalk in front of the fans that it seemed like a state occasion. And many of the fans were divided into groups by special uniforms—outfits that they'd had made to identify them as belonging to a specific fan club. A whole section of the crowd was dressed in light blue denim, another in red and white stripes, another in pink or brown checks, another in green, and so on. (The outfits, in general, had the look and the appeal of Girl Scout uniforms.) On this gala evening, the actresses left the theater by the main entrance, not by the stage door. Each time one of them came out, the fans roared with pleasure and remained at attention until she had passed out of sight. None of the women in the front rows took photographs, though, because, they told us earnestly, they were the "guards." When the star who had played Spartacus appeared, there was a moment of silence before the collective explosion of happiness. As B. remarked, "Spartacus did not die in vain."

While we were waiting with the fans, we spoke to some of them, with the help of our friend Kazue Kobata, who interpreted. Of the many people we talked to, only one group seemed uninhibited by the fact that I identified myself as a reporter from New York and had a tape recorder in my hand. This group was made up of fans wearing no special uniforms and standing in an unprestigious spot far from the main entrance. An older woman in the group showed a boldness that seemed to encourage the others.

"Why do you like Takarazuka theater?" I asked her.

"It's good because there's music, singing, dancing, and drama, too. Given the price, that's a good deal. I go to other kinds of theater as well, but Takarazuka offers the best value."

"How often do you come to see Takarazuka?"

"Almost every day. I spend so much money on Takarazuka I can't believe it! I get a pension; I used to be a child-care worker, so that's how I can afford it. Often, my husband comes with me. It's cost us over ten thousand dollars."

"Why do you think so many people love Takarazuka's top 'male' stars?"

"Because they're much more manlike than real men."

A pair of twins in their mid-twenties had been listening to our conversation, and one of them put in, "And they're more delicate than real men. The charm is that we all know they're women, and yet they are like men."

The older woman added, "And they sing better than men."

When we spoke to other fans, almost everybody agreed that the actresses who played male parts had something extra, which they thought real men lacked—something "ideal." But this "ideal" something seems to reflect the image the stars project rather than anything they actually say. When I asked one uniformed woman how her fan club's favorite star behaved at its get-togethers, she said, "Our star doesn't make any speeches. She doesn't give any lectures. We ask questions, and she answers." I didn't ask if the star had her own agent and publicist; I knew the answer. But then Hollywood stars don't have front-row guards.

A couple of days later, B. and I received what we'd been hoping for—a fax from Haruhiko Saka, the president of the Takarazuka Revue, inviting us to visit the company at its headquarters, in Takarazuka City. The invitation was the fruit of a phone conversation our friend Kazue had had with Mr. Saka, which went on so long that we were afraid we'd requested the inconceivable. After she hung up, though, she told us, "It will be okay," and she added, "When I mentioned your interest in going behind the scenes, he didn't say yes and he didn't say no. He only said that some things might not be possible, because they are selling dreams in Takarazuka."

The president's fax, which was in English, was gracious—just as gracious as he himself proved to be from the moment we met him—and it had its own dreamlike surprise toward the end:

Mr. Tommy Tune is now staying in Takarazuka working with us in preparation for his work of stage direction and choreography with Takarazuka for a world-premiere production scheduled in April 1993 to open at new Takarazuka Grand Theater.

Mr. Tune is leaving Takarazuka on July 5th for U.S. If you can arrive in Takarazuka by the noon of July 4th (Sat), it will be possible to arrange your meeting with Mr. Tune.

We had heard that at the time the theater was founded, in 1914, Takarazuka City was a peaceful spa. By 1992, it had become part of a belt of prosperous urban communities in the Osaka-Kobe-Kyoto area of Japan, served by a commuter-railroad system that would make believers of a million drivers from Long Island, New Jersey, and Westchester. But peaceful it is not. With an amusement park called Familyland, a ballpark, a racetrack, a Kentucky Fried Chicken franchise, a Thoroughbred Grill, serving "Soup Any Style" or, if you prefer, "Seafood Any Style," Takarazuka City would make a suitable location for an episode of *Wayne's World*. Wayne and Garth would probably love the sweatshirts that B. and I kept seeing on people in town, which were printed with phrases like "Recession Wear" and "Muncie, Indiana We're Full of Nice Surprises." Equally full of nice surprises was the state-of-the-art (or nearly) Takarazuka Hotel, with its neo-Italian fountains, neo-French eating spots, luxe splashes of red carpet and marble, and distinctly Japanese service. Breakfast was an abundance, ranging from traditional Japanese to traditional Western to chocolate éclairs—possibly a local tradition. Yet simple requests could cause havoc. In the hotel's "European" café, when I tried to get some milk for my iced coffee instead of heavy cream, my waitress didn't understand, and she turned to the maître d' for help. He solved the problem Takarazuka-style: He acted out my desires. Squatting down, he performed a gesture on his chest that most of us associate with farmers milking their cows.

The café was obviously too casual for our first meeting with Mr. Saka; that took place in the Renaissance Room, the hotel's formal tea lounge. During our talk, as waitresses knelt beside our chairs to serve us Campari and sodas, Mr. Saka gave us a brief account of Takarazuka, speaking fine English, for which he kept apologizing, and answering our questions without a trace of impatience, though he must have answered the same questions countless times.

The account started with one of Mr. Saka's favorite subjects when he discusses Takarazuka—the company's highly successful production of *Gone with the Wind,* first performed in 1977, repeated often since, and seen by about two million people. "Katharine Brown was very enthusiastic about our production," he reported with pride, referring to the agent for Margaret Mitchell's estate. Then he laid out the basic elements of the theater company. There are four troupes of performers—Snow, Moon, Star, and Flower—each of which averages two big productions a year. Each production plays about forty-five days in Takarazuka City and then goes to Tokyo, and each troupe also puts on small-scale shows and traveling shows, both national and international. Altogether, the company has about 350 performers.

It turned out that Mr. Saka's career as Takarazuka's leading executive had a history similar to that of other men we eventually met within the organization. He had worked for many years in the administrative division of the Hankyu Corporation, Takarazuka's parent company, before receiving this assignment sixteen years ago. The connection between Takarazuka and Hankyu may seem a stretch but it is tight. The Takarazuka form of entertainment was the brainchild of Ichizo Kobayashi, who founded Hankyu, one of Japan's most powerful railway networks. For him, Takarazuka was both a dream and a goal—a reason, early in the century, for vacationers to travel to the town he was busy establishing as a resort. Although Kobayashi died in 1957, he remains a kind of godfather to both the city and the theater. In fact, the official brochure of the revue opens with a message from Mr. Kobayashi's grandson. If its last sentence is politically incorrect, and even archaic—"I hope that you will enjoy this dazzling entertainment performed by charming girls of the Orient"—elsewhere the brochure's text suggests just how contemporary Kobayashi's invention is. His approach has a distinctly 1990s flavor in the way it connects to the latest stylistic trend in rock and roll, the movies, and the visual arts—the collaging and the montaging that have become known as sampling. The brochure describes how Kobayashi added elements of Western musicals, dance revues, and novels to his new entertainment concoction, and it declares that Takarazuka is "an instant history . . . [and] a playback of how the Japanese see and interpret the West."

Kobayashi's idea worked from the start: The theater quickly took off as a favorite family entertainment among the middle class and not quite middle class. In addition to all the other treats on the stage, here was a chance to observe "charming," well-bred girls—and in performance! To this day, many of the actresses come from economically comfortable families, and it appears that parents approve of their daughters' choice of Takarazuka as a suitable extension of their upbringing, and as a useful preparation for their future. In Takarazuka City, as opposed to Tokyo, one still sees a few families in the audience, but, in general, today's spectrum of fans is much narrower: girls in their teens, unmarried women—many of them office workers—in their twenties and thirties, and older housewives whose children are grown and whose husbands are off, as we were told, working like dogs or playing golf. Mr. Saka, who had told us apologetically that he had two sons, and not the daughters we might expect of a man in his position, also confessed that his sons had never seen a Takarazuka performance. "Some people never taste special dishes," he said philosophically.

He was just as philosophical about those who have acquired a taste for, not to say an addiction to, this special "dish"—the fans. We told him we had seen them waiting for hours outside the theater in Tokyo. "The excess of that kind of thing can spoil the stars," he said. "The most popular members of the company are those who play the male roles. They especially appeal to our audience of ladies, and that is some kind of psychological matter I cannot evaluate. We have our very old novel *The Tale of Genji,* which symbolizes the ideal male from the viewpoint of a female writer. I think it may be the same kind of phenomenon. However, I am not a scholar of that."

Mr. Saka told us that it takes about ten years to become a top "male" star. "Stars usually stay at the top for three or four years and then retire," he said. "If they stay too long, they know that they will lose something. They want to leave at the height of their careers. We call it 'graduating.' " He said that his organization draws a strict line between its official fan club, the Takarazuka Friendship Group, and the many clubs for which the organization claims no responsibility and to which it grants no official approval. If these individual clubs were acknowledged by the system, he said, the actresses would be stimulated to seek more and more attention, and that kind of ego boosting would not be appropriate. After all, he went on, the motto of Takarazuka is "Modesty, Fairness, and Grace." (This motto was translated in a variety of ways for us over the next few days, depending on who was quoting it.)

We asked Mr. Saka what determines whether a girl is to play male or female roles. "Height," he said, and he added, "Depending on the girl's physical type—on the type of body she has—she is advised whether she's right for a male or a female role."

"Can a person switch? Can someone have a role change?" I asked.

"Sometimes," said Mr. Saka, manifesting what we found to be surprising flexibility in a system that on the surface appears so rigid.

Our first night in Takarazuka City was a Saturday night, and it was a VIP-studded splash. It began with Mr. Saka escorting B. and me to a conference room in the hotel, where Tommy Tune and two of his colleagues, Jeff Calhoun and Wally Harper, were sequestered, like national treasures. Mr. Saka's presentation of them to us and of us to them was so full of restrained pride, so exquisitely choreographed, that the least we could do was greet each other like long-lost relatives. That done, and Mr. Saka having discreetly left us to some high-strength margaritas, we responded to each other the way I imagine explorers once did when they ran into their countrymen in remote corners of the world: We had fun comparing notes about the exoticism of it all, and we caught up on news from home. We also learned a little about the production Tune was planning for Takarazuka. (The combination sounded like a marriage made in heaven.) Just as Tune was wrapping up his over-the-top description of his future Takarazuka collaboration, Mr. Saka reappeared and, playfully cautioning "Top secret" about the sketchy preview we'd just been given, led us to another private room, for a pull-out-all-the-stops dinner to honor Tune on his last night in town.

Everybody who was anybody within the infrastructure of Takarazuka seemed to be there, but it felt less like a show-business dinner than like a catered cabinet meeting, because, apart from a translator, one ceremoniously silent wife, and me, it was an all-male affair. Perhaps the actresses, being the stars they are, were at an even more glamorous shindig somewhere else—but I don't think so. This was a power fête, and while the actresses have the power to mesmerize their audience, it is clear that they don't call any shots within the organization. This is not Hollywood, where box-office stars choose whom they work with, and decide if their fee is large enough. Takarazuka actresses receive a modest salary, and seem to have no say whatsoever about the productions they appear in.

Apparently, Tommy Tune was viewed as such a big celebrity that when he first saw Takarazuka, in 1985, a special welcome was arranged for him onstage, in which the actresses took their grand-finale positions on the famous lighted-up staircase and in full regalia. Mr. Saka's dinner party for Tune was not as climactic as that, but it wasn't without its mix of East-West rituals. Business cards were flung at us across the table, and there were gifts for every guest, followed by appreciative speeches and toasts all around, many expressions of affection for and from Tune, suggested plans for future meetings, and then a lot of hustle-bustle around his and his colleagues' departure for Osaka. At this dramatic point, B. and I were led to a late-night work session with Mr. Saka and some of his top colleagues (including his second in command, Takusuke Tanaka, director of production), at which our schedule for the next few days was plotted out as meticulously as though we were drawing up the Treaty of Ghent.

The administrative headquarters of Takarazuka are fairly new. There's an open floor plan, with almost all the staff members, who number about fifty-five, working at their computers and desks or watching television monitors that allow a view of dress rehearsals and performances. In Japan, as in America, smoking has become a habit that has to be negotiated around, but the arrangement at Takarazuka offers, to nonsmokers, more conceptual benefits than health benefits. Plunk in the middle of the open space is a sitting area—neither walled off nor screened off—where people can go if they want to light up. And it was in this spot, from which smoke wafted over the rest of the floor, that we did most of our talking with the Takarazuka staff through the next several days. There were moments when the image of peace-pipe powwows crossed my mind.

It is only a few minutes' walk from the administration building to Takarazuka's amusement-park complex, but in mood they are worlds apart; you stroll from a place that is devoted to the daily realities of work—budgets, organizing, long-range planning—to Familyland, which at first glance looks like an enormous miniature-golf course. The theater is inside the amusement park, and within its mall-like lobby there is for sale such an orgy of knickknacks, stuffed animals, flowers, cassettes, and East-meets-West snack food that one could be happily occupied there even without attending a performance. No wonder people make a day of it at the theater, shopping and noshing before the show, during the long intermission, and once more after the final curtain.

It was the Moon troupe that was performing when we were in town. The show began with a musical, *Puck,* and continued after intermission with a multinumber production called *Memories of You.* It is fairly standard for a Takarazuka entertainment to be divided into one part "classic" and one part Folies-Bergère song and dance fest of radically different numbers—cucarachas, Balanchine-influenced waltzes, disco, Latino, Broadway, and so on. But we shouldn't take all this too literally, because Takarazuka doesn't. It uses these forms as diving boards from which to jump into spectacles that are kaleidoscopic in both look and content. A Takarazuka show requires from us, with our Western sense of linear narrative, the same suspension of disbelief that the entire audience has to have in the matter of gender.

How to describe *Puck*? Perhaps as something you might dream on a midsummer night in a place so hot that your sleep is full of the fragmentation and surrealism that can surface when the unconscious takes over. Imagine Shakespeare's play remembered and then forgotten as it's transformed into a theatrical bonanza with no precedent other than previous Takarazuka extravaganzas. (Over the years, Takarazuka has "modernized" many classical Japanese plays and has also adapted such Western favorites as *Romeo and Juliet, Oklahoma!, Hamlet, Wuthering Heights, War and Peace, The Sound of Music, Le Rouge et le Noir, For Whom the Bell Tolls*—a smorgasbord as unpredictable as the productions themselves.) *Puck* is a show that by turns evoked drawing-room comedy, *Miami Vice, West Side Story,* Toys "R" Us stores, Elvis, menswear advertisements, an average wedding with a less than competent rock band, go-go clubs, fairy tales, gangster movies, the musicals *Grease* and *Gigi,* and a town meeting about a controversial real estate project. All these things may reflect the show's narrative and visual components, but they don't explain why the faces around us were expressing ecstasy. That had to do with the actresses—especially those who played the lead male roles. Without the magic they provided, the show would have been like MTV in 3-D, but, as things were, instead of seeming canned, the performance was electric with expectation, and most of all when Mayo Suzukaze was onstage.

When I told Takarazuka fans in Tokyo that I would be seeing the Moon troupe in Takarazuka City, they spoke of Suzukaze the way people in New York might speak of the Statue of Liberty—as a world-famous sight that has to be visited. They were right. She carried off the nutty transitions that were required of her as Puck with a grace, a seriousness, and a degree of immersion in her job that completely justified her top billing. Whether she was required to be a roller-skating child in overalls, a dolled-up bumpkin bellboy, or an ethereal sprite in the woods, she established her presence as the glue that held this ultimately nonsensical collage together.

And when, in the second half of the show, she appeared as a glittering singer-dancer-stud in *Memories of You,* Suzukaze showered upon the crowd all the romance and glamour it had come for. Suzukaze wasn't the only actress who made the girls and women in the audience hold their hands up to their mouths in amazement, but it was clear from the way she inspired the audience that she has an extraordinary understanding of what makes her fans tick. Appropriating certain gestures and ways of walking that are associated with men, and always in men's garb, she embraced the line between boy and girl and between man and woman in a manner that fully suspended one's sense of gender. She never wholly became one sex or the other, nor did she ever turn into a caricature, and it is this that makes her a sex symbol—however indeterminate the sex—to so many of her fans. It also prevents her act from becoming camp. And, because it's not camp, the audience doesn't laugh at gender-crossing the way crowds often do at drag shows, in recognition of truths being revealed. Those watching Takarazuka are relating not to imitation but to otherness— "to something that doesn't exist in real life," as they say.

The acceptance of rules and discipline and self-censorship is ordinarily more normal for everyone in Japan than it is for Americans, and, of course, being a member of Takarazuka is for many Japanese girls a dream come true, but I couldn't help assuming that at times an actress would feel as if she'd been put in a straitjacket, rather than the festive tuxedo that made her want to join in the first place. The strict code of behavior that Takarazuka imposes on its members is one reason we were curious about the training that Takarazuka students receive before they go into the company. We wanted to find out about their social and psychological indoctrination, not just about how they learn proper Takarazuka technique.

At our first meeting with Mr. Saka, he explained that Takarazuka trainees, who can be anything from fifteen to eighteen when they join, spend two years in a school that is very different from, say, Juilliard. "The Takarazuka Music School operates not only as an educational institution for young girls but also as a kind of finishing school," he said. We learned that they study dance, singing, music, and drama. When I asked if the curriculum included literature, Mr. Saka shook his head. And when I asked about mathematics, he smiled. "Most Japanese girls are not good at mathematics," he said. I decided to suppress the nature-versus-nurture speech on the tip of my tongue and instead asked to see the school.

It's about a ten-minute walk from the theater to the school, which sits back from a pleasant suburban street. As one enters the building, one notices, hanging above the center door in a plain frame, a print of a simple fan, opened wide and bearing calligraphically Takarazuka's often-quoted motto. Here at the school, it was translated for us as "Modesty, Purity, and Grace," while in a brochure it was "Purity, Honesty, and Beauty." Like the rest of the school's interiors, the office where we were taken for an orientation session was a study in simplicity, and was impeccably neat—as were the three-piece dark suits of the two men who talked with us. By their calm, correct manner, Yoshiro Maeda, who is the school's deputy principal, and Shoji Tamaki, whose title is supervisor, conjured up those aging gentlemen who appear in so many of Ozu's great films of the forties and fifties. They were, it turned out, two more veterans of the Hankyu Corporation, and they seemed as bemused as we were by the fact that they were helping to run a girls' finishing school. Maeda, he told me, had been involved in "matériel procurement" for Hankyu for forty years. Perhaps to compensate for a schoolgirlish impulse to giggle at this information, I quickly asked, "Are the students very good?"

"About a thousand girls apply each year, and only forty are selected, so they have to be good," Maeda said. "And we believe that even after they go on the stage it is necessary that they behave properly, so we discipline them very well here."

It had begun to seem as if we were discussing broncos that needed breaking in, and not schoolgirls, but I went ahead and asked how the disciplining is done. I was expecting almost any answer other than the one I got: "When the girls enter the school, we bring in members of Japan's self-defense forces. These men provide basic training. They teach the girls how to walk, how to keep a straight posture without moving, how to bow. All these things are managed by the gentlemen from the self-defense forces. Also, the senior students will always watch how the juniors greet people, and how they enter the classroom." When we were shown around the school, it was hard to imagine that the presence of Japan's equivalent of the military was necessary to get these girls walking and bowing correctly. They were so respectful of the teachers and of each other that they seemed to have been born with good manners.

But the job of turning the students into competent singers and dancers clearly isn't as easy as perfecting their etiquette. Like the performers in the company, the students showed very different levels of technical skill. In ballet class, turnout was considerably less in evidence than thigh girth. And in voice class, one courageous singer in training to be a "male" gave new meaning to what people say about a teenage boy: "His voice is changing." Nevertheless, her fellow students listened as if she were Maria Callas singing "Ave Maria." (The generosity of all this extends to an understanding that every student will go into the company—a policy that is in sharp contrast to most professional schools. The School of American Ballet, for example, feeds an average of four dancers a year into the New York City Ballet.) In the tap-dance class, many of the girls weren't exactly tapping in time to the music, by Milli Vanilli, that was being played, but no doubt when they leave the charge of these former railway executives, they'll keep time as perfectly as the Hankyu trains do. Proficiency aside, what all the girls displayed was a desire to please, and that's what really counts in Takarazuka theater.

The fees for the school aren't high by American private school standards (Takarazuka's two-year training course is 25,000 yen a month, or about $200), and although there is an extra fee for being a boarder, it is negligible. The administration was very precise about the cost of the girls' education, but the answers got fuzzier when it came to other costs, such as the emotional toll of the nunlike commitment to Takarazuka that is required from the students. There doesn't seem to be much concern about the girls' psychological state, nor is there any of the kind of social programming that has become almost de rigueur in many school systems elsewhere in the world. No one talks about anorexia or drugs or condoms, as the personnel of a suburban school in America might do. And there are no guidance counselors or therapists available. When we asked if the students had any special person they could go to for advice when they had worries or personal problems, we were told, "There are two older women, clerks, whom the girls can talk to. And, in addition, there are female teachers who can attend to these matters." When we asked what "these matters" might typically be, the example we were given was a sore leg.

And no wonder legs get sore or stiff, considering a remarkable demonstration we witnessed of student training, discipline, and self-control. It took place not at the school itself but at a rehearsal we attended for a dance performance that the Star troupe was giving on the following day in Takarazuka's smaller theater. The students, there to observe, were sitting in the house: to our left, the juniors; to our right, the seniors. Within each group were girls with long hair and girls with the short cut that one sees on every Takarazuka performer of male roles, but dye had not yet touched these shiny black heads. Although the girls all had on the same uniforms—gray pinafores and white shirts—the seniors wore white shoes with a hint of heel, while the juniors wore black flats. For the juniors, wearing less sophisticated shoes was an easy character test compared with another: They all had large black plastic schoolbags on their laps, and their hands were folded on top of the bags in exactly the same way, whereas the senior students, though their hands were folded, too, not only were allowed schoolbags of different colors but could stow them on the floor!

From their total stillness and the rigid positioning of their hands, we could tell that none of the students from either class was supposed to move. During the hour and a quarter that we watched the rehearsal, we noticed only a few transgressions: One student stretched a couple of fingers; another sneaked in a short scratching session on the underside of her left wrist; and one girl went all the way, by putting a finger in her mouth for a few seconds, until she realized her indiscretion. Everybody sat straight up, as if each had a board behind her back; nobody whispered or passed a note. Given this sensational exhibition of stiffness, we were relieved to notice a fair amount of catnapping. (Apologies to any student who feels betrayed, but there's nothing like being reminded that everybody's human.)

Ironically, the person in charge of the rehearsal was the choreographer Akiko Kanda, whose dances were being practiced. She was clearly more interested in the dancers' expressing themselves than in their constant apologies for having missed certain steps. Every time Kanda's credentials had been cited by Mr. Saka or his colleagues, the first on the list of her accomplishments was the fact that she once worked with Martha Graham. She was a member of Graham's company from 1956 to 1962, and as soon as we saw her—thin, supple, authoritative—it was clear that Graham formed a part of her identity. She incarnates everything that Graham stood for in dramatic looks, in body language, in opinions, and in spirit. And, in a place that brings in self-defense forces to teach girls how to bow, who could better encourage the expression of self, and freedom of movement, than a dancer who performed Iphigenia in the years when Graham's company was at its height?

Self-expression and freedom are valuable concepts in dance, but what about an open show of them in actual life? That takes some courage in this environment. It wasn't just the actresses who were kept on a tight rein. Most of the fans seemed nervous about what might happen if their names ended up in print. And members of the staff we spoke to were obviously concerned that the right impression of the company's behavior be conveyed to the world. (One of the directors, who had married a Takarazuka actress, hastened to assure us that their alliance was made *after* she left the company, not *before*.) People's desire to remain anonymous was sometimes hard to understand, since most of what they said appeared to us quite harmless. One fan, for instance, requested anonymity after remarking, "I am single, but if I had a boyfriend I'd bring him to the show, because I'm sure he'd like it." Other requests to be kept off the record were more understandable, like that of a woman who said, "Japanese men are boring, so of course women love Takarazuka. The husbands work so hard that they have no time for their wives, and Takarazuka is a place for wives to go that doesn't threaten their husbands. At Takarazuka, women can express the emotion they can't show their coldhearted husbands. Takarazuka never disappoints them." In the context of such pervasive anxiety about giving the wrong idea or upsetting people, it was always memorable when someone broke the pattern. (I, too, didn't want to offend, and found myself accepting courtesies I would normally refuse as a journalist, such as Mr. Saka's offer that we stay at the Takarazuka Hotel as the company's guests.)

For a while, we suspected that all this diplomacy was getting between us and the real story. But eventually it became clear that there wasn't a big gap between what was told to us officially and what we discovered for ourselves. Just a human gap. A few people were willing to discuss taboo subjects, and most weren't, but isn't that always the case? A wider gap had to do with where Takarazuka fits into Japan. It's as if Takarazuka were its own world within the country, with a way of life that has ties to Japanese tradition but also stands apart from it. In Takarazuka City, however, the network of connections seems infinite; it's difficult to come across someone who hasn't had something to do with the theater.

For instance, it turned out that one of our interpreters, Chieko Sakuta, has a sister, Chiho Asadori, who is a former "male" star of the Flower troupe. (I was told by a fan in Tokyo that Asadori had been especially splendid as Rhett Butler in *Gone with the Wind*.) These days, she teaches at the Takarazuka Music School, and—like some other former stars we met—she occasionally performs in a dinner show at one of the better local hotels. Although it has been years since Asadori retired, she still has that giveaway short haircut and that low, sonorous voice.

Asadori was a star in the late sixties, and her view of Takarazuka reflects the changes that have taken place since then. "When I was in the theater, Japanese women, in general, were supposed to be good wives," she said. "They were not working as career women. So I think that for many years we were the pioneers of working women. Nowadays, there are many working women, but not then. Many of us were not very mature, even though we practiced very hard; we enjoyed it all very much. When I look at my students now, I feel they are more serious than we were, and they want to become more professional. Today, many of the students consider their work in the Takarazuka a career more than a hobby."

When I asked her how the women in her time met the men they eventually married, her answer made us all laugh, and especially her sister: "When the Hankyu Corporation's baseball team, the Hankyu Braves, became the champions one year, there was a big party, and we were invited because of our affiliation with the company. Many of the girls in the theater got married to the players."

Asadori was not one of the baseball wives; in fact, she remained a star for an unusually long time—seven years—and then departed for an arranged marriage, and motherhood. But even now she is clearly proud that she was once a star, and she is grateful to the Takarazuka system of education for giving her a sense of purpose in life. Asadori is not comfortable discussing anything that might embarrass the organization. When I pressed her about difficulties that she or the other girls might have had with the social curbs that are part of Takarazuka life, she said simply, "We have to prevent scandals."

"But in life there's often some kind of scandal, isn't there?" I said. "Even if it's something small that seems big?"

Her measured reply: "The people in the theater hate scandals."

"With men?"

"Mm-hmm."

Later, I tried again, with "Before, you said that they didn't like scandals in the theater. What kind of scandals was it that they didn't like?"

I got a little further this time: "In my day, there were very few such scandals. We were very well disciplined."

"But those few—what do you remember about them?"

Asadori: "Even if you were going with a boyfriend, it should be hidden. I used to go out with friends, and we would go to a place, a very nice restaurant, where we didn't think we'd be seen by the fans. And one day we were eating and a waiter came over to me and said, 'May I have your autograph?' "

I didn't quite grasp the scandalous nature of this anecdote, so I tried yet again: "Are you saying that girls could not go out with friends who were boys?"

This time, Asadori's answer revealed both the flexibility in Takarazuka's system and its black-and-white way of thinking: "If we were going with a boyfriend and planning to get married to him, it was okay, but if you didn't have any intention of getting married, you were considered to be a playgirl. The theater doesn't want the actresses to be playgirls. It was okay to have a boyfriend that one planned to marry, but one would be in a very difficult position if this was disclosed to everyone before you had a chance to make a public announcement that marriage was going to take place."

"So the biggest scandal you remember is that an actress was known to have a boyfriend?" I asked, almost ready to wrap up this delicate part of our conversation. And then, when I imagined wondering for the rest of my life why I hadn't had the courage to ask what I really wanted to know, I asked it: "Can you remember an incident when a girl had a problem because she was pregnant?"

Asadori didn't seem shocked by my bluntness, but she didn't confirm my view of what can happen in life, either. She replied, "No. In my day, there was no such scandal. If you are in the theater, you have to be pure. If you want to live with a man, you should leave the theater and continue your career as a singer or dancer."

This woman of firm standards hardly seemed like someone whose head could be turned by opportunities for perks such as we'd heard were available to top stars from their fans. But it seemed worth asking her about them anyway, and, as I expected, she listed flowers or a cake as the kind of present she might have been given. Since we'd been told of situations in which stars were treated to pianos, and even houses, by their wealthiest and most devoted fans—called patrons by those in the know—B. tested the waters by throwing in jewelry as an example of another possible present that might come from a hypothetical patron.

"Oh, no!" she said, and then added, "Maybe a dress from a friend, but I would not call her a patron."

As she described them, the privileges that came with being a top "male" Takarazuka star were modest both in their proportions and in their monetary value. In fact, modesty seemed to anchor Asadori; it was impossible to imagine this solid citizen ever being carried away by the headiness of adoration. She made me understand how Takarazuka stardom could be a significant self-strengthening experience, something that could help a young woman develop a kind of inner authority that could stay with her for the rest of her life.

While many of the actresses like Asadori end up teaching or entertaining at dinner shows after they retire, some go on to have professional careers in television or on the stage. One former "male" star, Miyako Asuka, has a current career that doesn't fit into any of these categories: She is a jazz singer, and when we met her she was preparing to sing "Amazing Grace" at an upcoming avant-garde art event. Like the other former stars we met, Miyako Asuka has kept her stage name from her days in Takarazuka. But she has dropped the other obvious signs of her former life, starting with the hair; these days, hers is almost shoulder length. She was very open about the problems she had had as a "male" star.

Male and female stereotypes, she said, are so artificial that they can be put on and taken off like masks. She didn't go to Takarazuka because her dream was to become a top star; she went because she wanted to train her voice. She succeeded, but she also got some lessons in sexism that aren't without their humor. She told us, "In Takarazuka, I did not think, Oh, I'm a big star, but, rather, I kept trying to sing better, and deal with the complexities of playing a male and being a female. I didn't think that it was wonderful to have to pretend I was a male all the time. It was sometimes hard for me on my holidays to switch myself over. Some of the actresses who played the male parts enjoyed staying in their roles, even on their days off. They really acted the way they thought men act. For example, normally, if you're a Japanese woman you wash your own clothes, and clean your room, and cook, but if you're a Japanese man you just let somebody else do it. In Takarazuka, some of the big 'male' stars would ask the others to do their cleaning and cooking."

When Asuka retired, she celebrated by doing all the so-called female things she hadn't been allowed to do as a Takarazuka star, or had done on the sly, when no one in authority was looking. "After playing the part of men for so long, when I left I thought, How wonderful—now I can realize the fact that I'm really a female. When you're in a male role in the company, you have to wear pants on the stage at all times, and whenever I'd go to places that had nothing to do with Takarazuka I'd wear dresses. Once I had left the company, I wore a skirt every day. It had been my dream to have long hair, so I grew it. I looked in mirrors all the time to make sure I was being properly feminine, and I studied how to do it better with the use of these mirrors. I taught myself how to walk in a feminine way."

I asked her to demonstrate this walk, and B. and I got Asuka's equivalent of that sublime character from *Monty Python's Flying Circus,* the Minister of Silly Walks. Asuka told us that she had tried out her most feminine walk on a visit to New York, and it had worked, because—and she said this almost triumphantly—a large group of construction workers had cackled and whistled. At this point, I remarked that, of course, it was just that kind of whistling that made many American women furious, because it symbolized the way women are treated as objects. Before responding, Asuka looked at us, one at a time, with fierce concentration, and then she said, "I didn't like it, either, really. I found it frightening."

Perhaps Asuka's directness and candor stemmed from her evident desire to be helpful to us, but, whatever the cause, the effect brought out things that none of us had expected to be sharing when we sat down to what was a rather formal afternoon tea. When Asuka would pose questions like "Why would women want to dress the same way as men?" we'd answer with one of the obvious points of reference—Marlene Dietrich, say. And then Asuka would react with such enchanting attention to our information that we kept wanting to give her more. The next thing we knew, we were spilling the goods on Dietrich's famous bisexuality. And *Garbo's.* This really called a halt to any standing on ceremony. When we assured Asuka that these facts were relatively common knowledge in the West, you would have thought we'd told her that B. had once been a top Takarazuka female star. She stared at us as though it were impossible for things like that to be widely known and accepted. Yet she also seemed delighted by a world that would allow such a departure from the way a movie star was meant to act. By the end of the afternoon, we had discussed men, women, and sex almost as candidly as if we were supplying data for a Kinsey report. And each time another frank fact would emerge, Asuka would reward us with her sense of liberation at being part of a discussion in which people—men and women together—could talk to each other so openly.

But however enlightening Asadori and Asuka had been, neither of them was the person to help paint the big picture of just what Takarazuka is. For that, a major clue came from the man who had written and directed *Puck* and, some time before that, *The Great Gatsby*—Shuichiro Koike.

In the context of the other Takarazuka insiders we'd met, Koike was unexpected. His demeanor was hip, his responses were spontaneous, and he understood very well that we saw Takarazuka from a perspective different from that of the company's executives. The clever collaging that we'd been struck by in *Puck* became much less of a mystery once we'd met Koike. Clearly, he had the advantage of many perspectives—Eastern and Western, contemporary and traditional. Knowing a good deal about European and American culture, and being fluent in English, Koike assumed that we would approach Takarazuka as something out of the ordinary, even kinky. So he approached head-on our struggle to understand it, saying, "It's our tradition, maybe in combination with our religion, that in many of the arts an innocent girl performs the part of a man, or an innocent boy performs the woman. One sex acting both sexes is not unnatural to us at all. Sometimes foreigners, even Japanese who don't know anything about Takarazuka, tell me that I'm very lucky because I'm surrounded by all these girls. They think I live like Hugh Hefner." To us, having observed something of the life of the actresses by now, this notion of their carrying on with Koike was hallucinatory. The reality had more to do with something else that Koike said: "Really, the company is popular because of its innocence. Some people say it's just amateur, that the singing, dancing, or acting isn't professional. But the audience loves that. If the performers were real professionals, then people wouldn't come to see Takarazuka. They love how the performers try so hard."

Koike was well aware that Takarazuka might appeal in different ways to different people for very different reasons. For instance, he said that if Takarazuka were being shown in a nightclub in Paris it would probably take on a whole different meaning, and could perhaps be seen as a drag act. He also agreed to a suggestion that the performers might be viewed by some as akin to rock-and-roll stars like David Bowie, Annie Lennox, and Mick Jagger, all of whom have experimented with the line that usually divides our image of male and female. Both from Koike himself and from his work, I had the feeling that it was these considerations, as well as Takarazuka's traditional charm, that had attracted him to the genre, and that gave to his work its special sophistication in the context of so much innocence.

In the West, we tend to hear mostly about stars in terms of their high-profile romances, their fights, their cleavages, their disasters, their recoveries, and, most of all, their secrets. There are those who interpret our culture's addiction to news stories about famous people as a product of modern life's vulgarity. It seems to me, though, that this hunger is an expression of something else: a desire for fantasy and for confirmation that one is not alone—say in one's marital troubles—and for proof that even stars suffer. Which is not to say that at times the relationship between stars and fans can't lead to hurt in the West, or even in Takarazuka. In Tokyo, B. and I heard a story that contradicted some of what we had heard from Chiho Asadori; it was about an emotional collision that shed light on the other side of the dreams and ideals specific to Takarazuka. The story was reported by a fan who asked for anonymity before she began:

> *I first encountered Takarazuka when I was sixteen or seventeen years old. My mother took me to see a show. When she was younger, she'd wanted to be in the company, but at that time joining the entertainment world was very difficult for a daughter of an ordinary family. Although she didn't have a chance to join the theater, she and our maid often discussed it. My mother didn't talk about Takarazuka with my father.*
> *The minute I saw Takarazuka onstage, I knew it was a great thing. Many*

of the other fans I knew had boyfriends—I personally don't think the women were as crazy about them as they were about Takarazuka. Anyway, for me seeing Takarazuka made the dormant volcano erupt. My attraction was sexual. You see, the reason I asked for anonymity is that I work in a straight world. I have to be careful about my homosexuality.

When I entered university to study sociology, I was still crazy about Takarazuka. And after I graduated I went to the United States. In America, I became a feminist activist. When I returned to Japan, I found that among the Japanese feminists the norm was that you shouldn't like Takarazuka. They criticized me for liking it, because they thought that what it did was just perpetuate the notion that women are sex objects. Plus, they said it had a fixation on the whole idea of sex roles. So I kept my distance from Takarazuka after coming back to Japan. Then, one day, I saw Takarazuka on television, and I went crazy about the star in the main role, who is now retired. I started following this star, going to her shows locally and in other towns. I chased her, in fact. Once, I took a cab for fifty thousand yen to where she was, by the Japanese seaside.

On that very first day I saw her on television, I had decided to join her fan club, and I enrolled. But I became dissatisfied with the club, because I never had any real contact with the star, so I said I have to quit. Then the chairman of the club introduced me to someone who said, "Why don't you join the Exclusive Club?" and told me that it required a ten-thousand-yen membership a month and a thirty-thousand-yen entry fee. I joined, and longed for the four-times-a-year dinner opportunity with the star—the dinner, of course, cost each member an extra amount each time.

The Exclusive Club had twenty members, while the general fan club membership for this particular star at this time was about six hundred. Already, I was paying about a hundred and fifty thousand yen, and then they asked me if I would like to pay for the lunch box that the star would eat from, or if I wanted to pay for such-and-such day's bouquet. The money was endless—three hundred thousand, three hundred and fifty thousand, half a million. A hundred and fifty thousand yen was about six hundred dollars, and it was equivalent to the monthly salary that a new university graduate might be paid.

The chairman was very close to the star. She controlled the situation with the fans. Sometimes she'd approach me and say, Can you pay an extra three hundred thousand yen this month? I refused. But she did this with others, too, and eventually we came to wonder what was happening. Then somebody checked the club's bank account and found that there was only two hundred yen in it. The chairman asked another member to lend her a million yen to buy tickets. The woman, a rich housewife, took the money from her husband's bank account without telling him, but the chairman just kept the money for herself and never repaid the loan. When we learned about this, we fired her, and decided to have collective control of the club. Eventually, we paid back the money. I think the star may have known what the chairman was doing, but she played dumb when I talked to her about it.

We asked if this event had ended her affection for the star.

No. Although it's kind of a secret, I started giving a lot of money to the star. And gradually we became close. Finally, I became very disappointed in her. Around the time that she started thinking of retiring, she moved from Takarazuka to Tokyo. And I wanted to give her a gift for her new house, so I asked what she would especially like to have, and she answered, "Give me money!" I'd wanted to choose something meaningful to her, and she wanted money. I was so disgusted I said, "Go away. Bye!"

What I have told you is not a special case. But nobody talks about things like this. And I wasn't even really a patron. Patrons can pay a star's rent. When certain stars are still young, when they're at the bottom of stardom, they find wannabe patrons.

This fan didn't claim to be speaking for others, nor did she make any generalizations about the morals of the stars or the sex lives of the fans. But she very deliberately changed the phrase about selling dreams to "They're selling sexual energy in Takarazuka." When she had finished her saga, I asked her if she had stopped falling in love with Takarazuka "male" stars.

She smiled and produced a Takarazuka program. Pointing to a photograph in it, she said, "This star's terrific. Mayo Suzukaze."

To observe Mayo Suzukaze in *Puck* and *Memories of You* from backstage—as we were permitted to do one afternoon in Takarazuka City—was to witness someone utterly focused on her work. That afternoon, she pushed herself like a racehorse that seems to sense the presence of people out there counting on it. Suzukaze brings off the killer costume changes that are required of her at a pace so fast and so constant that her limbs never stop moving: overalls off . . . jacket and pants and hat on . . . face checked . . . more makeup . . . hat off again, then back on . . . one last confirmation that the wig's on straight . . . and seconds later she's back onstage, knocking herself out for the audience. Although there had been concern that our watching Takarazuka from behind the scenes would destroy the fantastic aspect of the revue for us, looking at the whole thing from the inside had the opposite effect. It was here—where we couldn't avoid registering all the artificiality—that the beauty of Takarazuka revealed itself.

When it became apparent how much energy went into this spectacle, how much traffic of people and costumes and props was involved, how absorbed everybody backstage was in making sure that all details were in order, from the knotting of a necktie to a frill's splaying the right way, when we saw the girls flying past us to make their costume changes in time—the mechanics of it all became more wondrous than a lighted-up stairway can ever be. This was the magic that can happen when everybody pulls together.

It's true that some of the performers hang around and schmooze. Watching the girls joke with the distinguished Mr. Tanaka, our backstage chaperon, and then help one another by straightening a bow tie or adjusting a bunny outfit was further reinforcement of the fact that these performers are a special breed. One doesn't find this kind of ubiquitous sweetness backstage on Broadway. And their politeness and openness weren't only for us. The many helpers who work behind the scenes, from the stagehands to the wardrobe mistresses and the laundresses, were treated by the performers with gratitude and respect and also with the kind of familiarity that can include some affectionate kidding around. Although the special forces may have taught the girls how to bow and sit with machine-like precision, the girls are certainly not machines.

After the audience finished applauding the last glitzy lineup in *Memories of You* and the curtain was down, the actresses went, as they always do, to relax by soaking themselves in large communal baths backstage. It had been arranged that I would subsequently meet Suzukaze inside the stage door. This may sound like a simple plan, but until I actually saw her there, in an unexpectedly kooky outfit, I wasn't at all convinced that we'd get that far. For a rendezvous with Suzukaze had turned out to be much more of an on-and-off business than any of the other meetings Mr. Saka and Mr. Tanaka had arranged for us. Her schedule, her plans, her to-and-fros from the theater all had become incredibly complicated, and surrounded in mystery—as if someone weren't certain that she *should* be interviewed. But her arrival put an immediate end to the murkiness that had developed around her: She herself was just too vivid. Her outfit that day could be described as New Wave Brechtian; it consisted of a baggy kidlike version of a pants suit with clashing plaids, topped off by a black straw hat designed by Milan's fashion wit, Franco Moschino. When she, Mr. Tanaka, and B. and I left the theater, her ensemble was not lost on the crowd of fans who had collected outside the building to watch for her. They reacted enthusiastically, a few of them snapping their

Instamatics and many of them rushing to fall in behind her as she walked to the administration building, where it had been settled that we would convene. The three of us fell back and watched her handle her fans with ease.

That my official interview with Suzukaze was a summit occasion was indicated by its taking place in a private room, not in the smoking section. Mr. Saka was there, and so were B., Mr. Tanaka, and an interpreter. One can imagine how free Suzukaze and I felt to have a frank discussion. Yet, remarkably, even with an audience around us, Suzukaze managed to create an intimate situation in which small talk quickly vanished. Her eagerness to provide thoughtful answers to my questions dominated the mood in the room. Yet she addressed me with an embarrassing degree of respect—I was startled to find her treating me as if she were not my equal. To me, she was a star of Takarazuka; if anybody should be in awe, it was I. To make clear how I felt, I said, "I admire the way you are on the stage. And I admire the way you treat your fans."

Suzukaze talks as evocatively as she performs. When I asked what she experienced when she first saw a Takarazuka show, at age fourteen, she answered, "I felt lightning in my heart."

"Why?" I asked.

"I was impressed with the theater because it consisted only of girls. To see only girls acting on such a huge stage was so impressive! At that time, the big star was very tall and she had a beautiful voice and beautiful style. And I was also very much moved by the magnificent costumes and all the stage sets."

"Do you think that the fans are especially excited by the actresses who play the male roles because equality for women in Japan is still so far away, and the fans are happy to see women playing such strong roles?" I was testing a theory I'd been developing since I first encountered Takarazuka.

She did not confirm it. Instead, she said, "No, I don't think that's why the fans become so inspired. I believe they love the gorgeousness of the theater. And also there may be the factor that when women are young we tend to have an adoration for women, not men. They can express this adoration for the stars in Takarazuka."

"What does it feel like to be so deeply loved by the fans? Is it difficult for you in any way?" I asked.

"Difficult? Oh, no! When I was very young, I adored Takarazuka, and so I understand the feelings of the fans. Now that the situation is reversed, I want to be as careful with them as I can. I want many fans to love me. This is the good part of Takarazuka theater. Without this, Takarazuka theater can't be Takarazuka theater." Clearly, the fans who had chosen her as a star to worship had chosen wisely.

Just as we began to talk about New York, we ran out of time, because Suzukaze had a class to teach. I leaped at the opportunity this gave me to interview her privately: "I hate to end this conversation, so I want to ask you if it would be possible for us to meet again afterward. We don't have to spoil your image with the fans. If it's just us gals, as we say in America, we won't have the problem of your being seen with men. If you'd like, we could go to one of the places in the Takarazuka Hotel for a drink or a bite to eat."

"Yes," she replied.

After Suzukaze's class, she and I went outside, to find her fans still waiting. To no one in particular, but for the benefit of them all, she said, very distinctly, "Since I am going to have two performances tomorrow, I will be leaving home by nine o'clock." This was her way of showing consideration for a fan's need to know when the next pleasure would be available. After waving and bowing to the fans, she stepped into a car that was waiting for her. So did I and Michiko Matsumoto, who had taken over that day as interpreter, and, with a silent fan at the wheel, we took the couple of minutes' ride to the hotel. The fan dropped us off, still not saying a word, and once we were inside the hotel Suzukaze chose Le Premier, a Frenchish restaurant, for our meal.

I think we both felt freer without witnesses to our exchange other than our interpreter. Suzukaze was as much the interviewer as I was, asking about my life, extracting my opinions, keeping things between us balanced. To put it simply, this was not a self-involved actress.

I knew she cared for the fans, I said, but, beyond sympathizing with them, was there anything else that made her such a devoted star?

"Yes. They help me a lot. For me they are like my family. Everybody else thinks that since I am a star I am always eating delicious food, but I'm not. When I go home, I'm so tired I just go to bed. The fans are the ones who are worried about my health, and about what I eat."

I asked her to tell me about the extra responsibilities that go with her life as a Takarazuka star. She listed dinner shows and recordings, as I expected, and then said, "Sometimes I am asked to present a bouquet to a famous person, or to a politician. I don't particularly hate it. This is a little selfish to say, but it can take up a whole day, and I don't care for that too much."

Suzukaze asked me to talk about life in New York, and she eagerly offered her own impressions. "The first thing that surprised me when I arrived at Kennedy Airport was the rough driving of the taxicabs," she said. "I think the Japanese are the only people who say 'I'm sorry.' I had the same kind of shock when I saw people in Manhattan that I had when I first saw Takarazuka. I was amazed to see individuals with blue eyes. I had never believed that people with blue eyes, or people with such black skin, really existed in the world. It was strange to see them actually living in New York. That was something that I knew only from magazines or TV, or in the movies."

By the time we ordered dessert, we were chatting about the fact that going to bars and going dancing were taboo for Takarazuka stars in places where they were known, but Suzukaze also had a story about what can happen when you're a stranger in town and look different from everyone else: "In New York, I was mistaken for a teenager," she recalled. "I wasn't allowed into a discothèque."

"Which club?" I asked, laughing.

"The church."

"The Limelight, on Sixth Avenue?"

"Yes, that's it."

Instead of explaining the complexities and exclusivities of door policies in New York clubs, I took another direction. "What's good about the Limelight is that all kinds of people go there," I told Suzukaze. "I don't know if you have the words *gay* and *straight,* but the Limelight's a club where everybody is welcome, so it's very popular."

The very next question that Suzukaze asked me was about AIDS. "Is it a big problem in New York?" she wanted to know. After I gave her the bad news, we talked for a long time about AIDS, and she had a lot to say. Part of it went, "When the first AIDS patient was discovered in Japan, it was treated just like a scandal. And even today people who are suffering with AIDS are hidden away from the society. Sometimes I am very frustrated, because we have such a big misunderstanding in Japan about AIDS. I realize that in America there are many charity shows organized by famous people to help find a cure. I hope such a movement will come to Japan. But this has nothing to do with Takarazuka. Some people might say that I should just be a big star in the theater, and not have any worries about the outside world. Yet I was brought up in a very ordinary family, and in a very natural environment. I lived in a place that had beautiful nature, and I was moved by many things in that world. So I would like to stay an ordinary person who has contact with the world. Even though what I say may mean very little to the larger world, inside of me there is someone who would like to do something. But what I have told you is not known to my fans!"

Talking to me about AIDS was very daring in Suzukaze's world, far more so than it was, say, for an American movie star in the early eighties, when there was still a possible stigma by association. We may or may not have gone beyond that, but Japan definitely hasn't, and the actress's candor was especially moving because it seemed so uncalculated. One of Suzukaze's fans described her as being like glass: clear, sharp. Glass seems ordinary rather than fancy, yet glass, like Suzukaze, is a fragile product. Even so, during my long conversation with Suzukaze, she never gave the slightest sign of feeling burdened by the necessity of upholding everybody's idea of her, or by her vulnerability if she should fail. On the contrary, she said to me, "I believe that my life now is the happiest I can lead."

When it was time for Suzukaze to leave, she made a quick phone call, and almost instantly her driver of a few hours before pulled up in front of the hotel.

I saw her one more time. The next day, I happened to be backstage right after *Memories of You* finished; Suzukaze heard that I was there, and came downstairs from her dressing room to say good-bye. She had left upstairs all the signs of her status as a star. There was a towel around her head, she had on a robe and fluffy slippers, and her face was scrubbed clean of makeup. We kissed each other on the cheek, Continental-style, and as we did I imagined what this everyday way of communicating would mean to one of her fans: everything.

At this point in her life, Suzukaze has a sense of purpose that separates her from the other stars I met in the Moon troupe. They, too, were highly individual, though. The top "female" star, Kayo Asano, who played Hermia, Puck's love, had the air of acceptance that people often have when they understand but don't resent the fact that their role in the shadows helps create spotlights for others. She told me that one of her favorite movie stars was Audrey Hepburn, and, in fact, she has the sort of ballerina-like allure that made Hepburn such a class act for Hollywood. I don't know whether this is coincidence, or whether it has to do with Asano's playing female roles, but she seemed to be much more traditionally "Japanese" than her "male" counterparts. When she laughed, for instance, she would always put a hand to her mouth.

By contrast, Yuki Amami, the Moon troupe's second "male" lead, who is young for such a distinction, appears to be someone who wouldn't have any trouble if she woke up tomorrow to find herself in New York. She's up on everything in pop, loves MTV and blue jeans, and is a fan of Bruce Springsteen, Matt Dillon, and, particularly, Robert De Niro. After all the protocol and all the old-world beliefs I'd encountered, Amami's noncovert assertiveness seemed exceptionally spunky. I first became aware of her in *Puck,* playing the part of the rock star Bobby, which she did with a savviness that picked up on Elvis and the kind of toughs who were made into entertainment icons by *West Side Story.* After spending some time with Amami, B. and I told her we'd heard rumors that she might well become a top star one day. "They didn't tell me," she said, not in the least implying that they should have, but with a hint of humor at the idea that she would be so little in the know about her own career. At this point, Amami does not appear to consider her role as a "male" star a calling, the way Suzukaze does; nor does she seem to have Suzukaze's soul-to-soul connection with her fans. Amami's future is open. Give her a bit of time, and she could take the Paris/Milan/New York fashion catwalks by storm—she has the height and the confidence. Still, she seemed surprised when we told her we could imagine her on a runway, or on a stage or a screen outside Japan. I didn't sense that she'd ever considered such a possibility. Instead, here was another young woman who had fallen into the Takarazuka world because she liked to sing and dance, and had an idea other than early marriage. As Chiho Asadori had suggested, there is a difference between the recent generations of Takarazuka actresses and past generations. The administration may believe, as Mr. Saka put it, that "when the girls are going to be married, our mission is completed," but the girls we talked to did not seem to concur. Amami may or may not go on with her career, and may or may not get married sooner or later, but the notion that she might graduate from top stardom into an *arranged* marriage—as Asadori had done—is inconceivable.

As for Suzukaze's future, every possible answer seems to evaporate as it arises. All I can see is Suzukaze on that stage wowing the fans, or perhaps letting them know, on leaving the premises, when she'll be back. When someone is so deeply committed to her work, when she and it come together as one, why pull them apart before life does? Suzukaze's fans know that time will end their pleasure, whether it's the clock declaring that a show is over, or the calendar eventually making it necessary for Suzukaze to stop performing. Perhaps the short span of stardom is what makes the fans treat each second as if it were precious. They grab every chance they get to immerse themselves in this world of heroic men and women, of sparkle and color, of singing and dancing—and of a dreamy erotics that transcends the usual division between the sexes. For the fans, too, Takarazuka is likely to be an experience that ends when their own marriages occur—at least, until they return to it, decades later.

So, for both the audience and the players, Takarazuka is an adventure, a suspension of "normal" life. There are people who dismiss it as an *escape* from life, a way of avoiding the difficulties of "real, grown-up" relationships. And certainly Takarazuka seems like another world. That's true whether it is the "finishing," disciplining, marriage-preparing institution that the men in charge believe it to be, or whether it's the heaven on earth that makes the fans love it so. But Takarazuka is also a distillation of the complicated relationship that exists wherever there are stars and fans. What makes it unusual is that it keeps this dynamic human. We didn't meet one star or ex-star who pretended to be anything other than an ordinary woman. We didn't observe one instance of rudeness, either to the fans or from the fans. Everybody treats everybody else with respect; it's as if they all realized that they're giving one another something they wouldn't otherwise have in their lives.

Of course, no one claims that any of these stars or former stars are supreme talents. Nobody in the Takarazuka office talks about "geniuses," just as none of the actresses seems to think they're above the laws of human behavior because they're stars. In fact, the word *star* is bandied about so often that it ceases to imply "one in a million." Practically any girl in Japan who wants to have a go at being a star can put herself to the test, though it's true that the gift of a couple of inches gives a girl a better chance to be a bigger star—a "male" star. Takarazuka isn't a perfect world—it's full of inconsistencies and paradoxes. But it's also full of qualities that we don't normally associate with stars: modesty, fairness, and grace.

On our plane coming back to New York, B. needed to stretch his legs, and when he returned to his seat he said, "Guess what! The assistant purser is a Takarazuka fan." I found the assistant purser, Maki Ohbayashi, in the service area, taking a break with her colleagues.

"I hear you enjoy Takarazuka," I said to her. "When you were growing up, did you see it often?"

"Yes. My mother and my grandmother took me. We liked it very much." As she started to tell me why, one of her male colleagues, who spoke better English, offered to help translate. But whatever it was that she was saying in Japanese seemed to confuse him. "It's very complicated," he told me, and he started to get tangled up in pronouns. Obviously, the idea of female "male" stars had stumped him. So I kept my questions simple.

"And you're still a fan, I gather. Is there anybody you especially like?" I asked.

"Yes."

"Who?"

"Now? Mayo Suzukaze."

Trust Suzukaze to crop up just before we got home and witnessed the crash landing of some of our own stars. It was only a short time later that the *New York Daily News* was announcing "A Midsummer Night's sex tragedy for Woody." Where is Puck when we need him/her to help us dream up a happy ending for that star-crossed story?

The New Yorker, September 28, 1992

Lee Friedlander: Nudes

After such an immersion in women's bodies, it's natural to ask about the photographer who took these pictures, to want to turn the tables for a minute on the beholder. What about Lee Friedlander? He's a big guy, unbuttoned-up, easy to be with, familiar-feeling. When his hair hasn't seen a barber for a spate, the time off brings out the cowlicks, putting an accent on the boyishness that's already there, preserved in him. It's that lightness that makes Friedlander ever so slightly different from most other men who are nothing special when it comes to physical appearance. It's a subtle quality you can sometimes notice in people who have a different relationship to their work than a nine-to-five clock-in. But it wouldn't make him stand out in a room, or on the street. What might, however, lead you to know it's him is the fanny pack he's wearing, containing the photographic gear that's such a part of him, when he's out and about. If the police were looking for him the fanny pack would be his "outstanding characteristic."

I hadn't seen Friedlander for a few years when I spotted him one day, shooting on the street. I was late, stuck in a taxi, in midday, midtown traffic; he was up the block a bit, and my view of him was from the back. But he's done so many self-portraits in which his photographic apparatus is part of his silhouette that the sight of this similar figure just had to be him. When it turned out so, New York felt like the small town that it is, but that's not all—I watched Friedlander photographing the buildings, the shop windows, the people on the street. Although he was alone, it seemed like he wasn't. It was as if Eugène Atget were there, too, and Lewis Hine, Brassaï, Walker Evans—other legendary photographers who had paced the life of cities, and small towns, before him. Although I'd looked at their work often, I'd never pictured them actually out on the streets,

Lee Friedlander, *Nude,* 1979

doing it. Seeing Friedlander among the crowds on the sidewalk—melting right in, if it weren't for his hands up to his camera—made what they had done before seem less mythic, simple, and therefore even more amazing considering what they got. It must have been a double eyeful to have come across Friedlander and his friend Garry Winogrand shooting on the street together, as they did sometimes when Winogrand hit town. The image of Winogrand snapping away jumps to life when Friedlander describes him, remembering, "He would come to New York, and it would be like being with somebody who was horny or something. He just had to photograph everyone. Nobody could pass him that he wouldn't take a picture of." With that kind of attraction to people, no wonder Winogrand left millions of unprinted negatives as part of his legacy.

Winogrand isn't just a name one mentions to conveniently place Friedlander in his generation of American photographers. No, the tie between the two was stronger than that of people who happened to be working at the same time. They were lifelong friends, who met when they were both starting out, who ate casseroles at each other's houses, who talked on the phone at least every three weeks, who went after the same work, who produced very different kinds of pictures, two obsessive photographers who were obviously vital points of connection for each other. When Friedlander talks about Winogrand, you can feel the wonder he has for what Winogrand did—and his loss. He'll tell you that Winogrand became a real photographic intellectual as well as a great photographer, and his language reveals such respect it takes on a beauty. "He was such a force that was out there working," he states, and goes further. "He was like a reflecting block." When we were talking about Winogrand's writings, Friedlander's hands embraced the air while he marveled, "Those pieces are the size of the moon."

It is striking that Friedlander sees Winogrand as an intellectual, but not himself. So many of Friedlander's projects—his pictures of American monuments, his series of cherry blossoms, for example—exercise the mind as well as the eye. But then this is a man who loves the jazz that he grew up with—and that was one of his earliest subjects—so his focus on the improvisational scatting that comes out of his instrument is in keeping. He'll say, "What you need to know is in the pictures." Still, even the tiny riffs that he'll throw your way will tell you more about himself and his medium than most. Often he begins slide lectures with a self-portrait and the comment "Don't ask me any complicated questions, because the photographer, as you can see in this picture, has straw in his head." Winning the MacArthur "Genius" award didn't make him pull this slide to protect his image. And indeed from the looks of all of Friedlander's self-portraits the photographer's happy to reveal himself as imperfect as the rest of us. The "straw shot" is not only unglamorous, it's funny. It's a reflection of Friedlander's shadow on the ground, and so whatever was there on the earth has also been incorporated into his form. His shape's all off; the rocks look like protruding organs, he's got lumps and bulges in all the wrong places. Friedlander's someone who can't be accused of pretension.

His choice of camera echoes his insistence on the modesty of what he does. It's a Leica. "With a camera like that," as Friedlander explains, "you don't believe that you're in the masterpiece business. It's enough to be able to peck at the world. If I was using a piece of equipment that was big, and I had to carry that thing around all day, I'd probably think twice about what I did with it. But when you're using such a small piece, it doesn't matter. The more junk you put in, doesn't cost you any more. It's a wonderful little medium." And his use of flash is in keeping with his connection to the present. He's a photographer of our time. He'll take the picture of the highway, and of the TV; he's not a nostalgic image maker. And so he wants his materials to be able to reveal the feeling of contemporary life. As he says, "Flash renders everything. And everybody knows when you've taken the picture. It's not a secret. It's not a quiet moment." Right there is the reason Friedlander's nudes may at first appear to be so aggressive. We're used to images of naked women being passive, not ones that jump out at you. Here in Friedlander's photographs some-times the bodies twist, and the camera shouts. But they also rest together. Flash doesn't just make it patently clear that a picture is in process, it's the perfect tool for a photographer such as Friedlander, who wants to bring out elements that are usually so avoided you'd think you were the only one who had them. (Pubic hair is just the most obvious example.)

Perhaps that's why Bob Guccione, Sr., the publisher of *Penthouse,* was once quoted in the *New York Daily News* as saying that the idea of publishing Fried-lander's photographs "was like scraping the bottom of the barrel." That's the kind of insult a man like Friedlander lives for. Funnily enough, Guccione was talking about photographs Friedlander had made of the "Material Girl" in 1979–1980 when she'd worked as an artist's model. About Friedlander's pho-tographs of Madonna, four of which are in this book, Guccione apparently complained, "She wasn't well-groomed, there was lots of hair on her arms and hair sticking out of her armpits." Hair! Can you imagine that? What a scandal! Madonna has hair! What a relief, actually, of reality, after all the fake images that bombard us day and night. "I always have a distrust of subjects that look perfect," says this photographer. Ditto, I.

Friedlander, himself, offers the same kind of here-on-earth acceptance that his pictures have. He says things that most people are afraid to admit, lest they look like Okies. When he talks about his early admiration for the heroes of pho-tography he confesses, "And I didn't even know how to pronounce Atget." How many of us looked at that name and thought, At get? He seems to be comfort-able enough with himself to state, "I'm not much for refinement. In Europe, it seems to me it's full of refinement." And witty enough to want to "photograph French people eating. I'd like to be there in the middle of the table with a flash. Wouldn't it be interesting to take pictures of people eating, especially people that make such a fuss about it?" Clearly he's an iconoclast. And all that's what gives these nudes their earthiness, their punch, their flesh and blood bodilyness.

They're not just different from the coy nudes one sees in titillation magazines. They're not like the usual nudes one finds in an art context either. Obviously they're much more concrete than painted figures. Even if the emphasis on realism is high in a painting there's still the fact that paint has a very different quality than skin. Photography can't be the real thing either, but it can bring it to you less mediated. Still, with most fine art photography that involves the nude, it tends to be much more artificial than Friedlander's, much more concerned about declaring itself art, with a capital *A*. Have you ever noticed how many photographers do nudes that look like peppers? Friedlander's not ambitious that way. His goal with these images was inherently photographic—to make nudes that felt as real as possible, of course using all of the vocabulary of his medium, highlighting, cropping, angling, et cetera, and ultimately the alchemy that happens in printing. (For the production of the book, Friedlander had the services of a true artist of the printing process, Richard Benson.) To make something seem real is harder than it sounds for, of course, here one's dealing with a human subject. And we humans have become pros at posing for the camera. With professional models one can have an even more static situation than with people one knows, or just finds, but that's not what happened here. Apparently some of the sessions got so relaxed that on a couple of occasions his models fell asleep.

There's about a baker's dozen years of work in this book. Like most of Friedlander's projects the nudes was a slow one that built up as it did, not according to a schedule. Friedlander found his models through an informal network of friends, painters and other photographers, and he took most of the pictures in this country, in various cities where he'd go for work, but a few were done in France. The models were paid for their time, and Friedlander usually went to their homes, solo. (He's never had an assistant.) He says that most of the time he followed the models' leads in terms of posing, and apparently his instructions were usually on the level of "Turn to the left" or "Can you do that again?" All of the women are between their mid-twenties and early thirties; this age range seems to have been the only constant Friedlander was looking for. "I figured everybody has something that's interesting" is his comment. And he proves his point. He doesn't make a mountain out of a bruise, or a beauty spot, but he lets these kinds of features be part of the general assertion of each woman's individuality. In his hands, nudes have as much topographical information to look at as landscapes, and as much psychological potential as the viewer is willing to admit. And the surroundings that envelop the women fill in the images with additional fragments from life—a soft sofa, a radiator, a lace curtain, a creased bedspread, a shag carpet, patterns, weaves, cushions, a hardwood floor—these kinds of bits and pieces of information come with where the women lie, sit, or stand.

The idea of photographing nudes began when Friedlander got the Mellon chair at Rice University for a semester. His two kids were in high school in suburban New York (where Friedlander and his wife, Maria, have lived since 1959), and so Friedlander went to Houston alone. There he had much more time on his hands than usual. His friend George Krause was employing models for the photographs he was working on, and Friedlander asked to go along. But it obviously wasn't just convenient circumstances that inspired Friedlander's interest in photographing female nudes. He stuck with the subject for over twelve years. When asked if the nudes were tougher to do than, say, his pictures of American monuments, he affirmed, "The nudes are harder. With a monument, if you found the damn thing, you could always go back, unless somebody stole it, or removed it. Not so here." It so happens that all the women turned out to be white. I asked him about this, and his explanation was, as usual, matter-of-fact. "That's who cropped up."

Time has such a different meaning in these pictures than in others he has taken. With the monuments you feel their endurance over time, emphatically so because of the way Friedlander encourages other telling details within the frame of the image. With the nudes you can almost feel the seconds passing. You can just about see these bodies breathing. You witness them open, closed, turning away, contorting, arching, stretching, moving any which way, as well as not. Although Friedlander's such a master at anchoring his photographs with a sense of place, just look at all the details and textures he captures and juggles—the bedcovers, the windows, the bedside tables, the droop of a couch, the light at a certain spot in a room—these photographs are more about getting up close to see what things really look like, rather than being claims of intimacy. You'll notice many of them are cropped so there's no face, and that when the head is included the subject is rarely looking at the viewer. See, Friedlander's not pretending to know these women, nor is he promising that we can, even with the right-in-your-face perspective that he gets. That's what makes me trust his pictures. They're about his curiosity.

They're different from what we're used to, even if they look familiar, in fact *because* they look familiar. At times they seem disorienting, but isn't that what happens in real life when you're so close to another person's body that your perspective goes "off balance"? What you see can get surreal, cubist, hyperreal, as it does here. No matter how much Friedlander admires Edward Weston's beautiful, sensual nudes, or Bill Brandt's sculptural, graphic ones, his work is not derivative of either photographer. Their work has had such an impact, conscious and otherwise, on anyone who pays attention to the subject that it's often somehow present when one looks at photographs of nudes. And in these images one can find moments where one's reminded of either Weston or Brandt, but these are like flashes of memory, more than copycat shots. Friedlander despises the idea of redoing what's already been done. This is not a postmodernist we're talking about. "I'm not Walker Evans in Saratoga," he declares, continuing with, "Don't you think that the real difference between photographers is that they each lived in their times? If times didn't change, there'd be nothing to photograph. It would all still look like Atget's pictures."

There's no mistaking these photographs as being a product of any other time than the one in which they were taken. In fact, they're so specific that they already mark time, as well as indicate something about their maker. Friedlander says he wanted to photograph "women in their prime," before their bodies "start to slide." He clearly has a broader view of prime than is usually the stereotype, but he also has an old-fashioned sense of aging when it comes to a woman. And something else is noticeable: He doesn't seem to have run into women who have gym and weight lifting as part of their daily routine. Who would have thought there were this many women left in America in the eighties who didn't work out? These women may not have articulated biceps, triceps, or quadriceps, but that gives them the softness that women who pump iron don't always have.

Does it make a difference that the photographer who took these pictures is a man? Would we react to them differently if they were made by a woman? Or if they were of men nude, instead of women nude? You don't have to ask these questions. An old-style approach might be to talk about the pictures purely from the point of aesthetics. But one might as well be as candid as the photographs are. In 1991 if you look at a series of images that are as blatantly focused on women's bodies as these are, it's a different experience than it might have been, say, thirty years ago. We've made advances in consciousness, if not always in action, about women's lot, and that has affected the way we see images of women that could be said to be using them as objects. Shaking up accepted mores of how women have been treated and represented has meant more self-consciousness for both sexes. Perhaps the most honest way to begin to get to what the pictures are about is to involve oneself.

As a woman, when I see women zoomed in on as assertively as Friedlander does here, I'm not neutral about it. In general, the subject itself is too loaded, too burdened with "piggyness," to not set off instant alarms in me. How long do they ring with Friedlander's photographs? Well, it's complicated. There's no getting around the fact that he's been dressed in a room while his subject has been naked, and *he* is the one who's capturing *her,* so the antennae do go up. Sure, I guess I could pull back and remember that nudes are one of the oldest subjects of art, or I could balance the fact that these are women with the fact that they might have been men, and then what would I say? But why do any of that, why tone down what's there, or what really happens at the sight of these photographs? One's later thoughts are an important part of the process of looking, too—they are how we understand images in large ways—but that first gut response is to be grabbed. I relaxed as I went through the photographs, and started to examine the different elements that caught my attention. I trusted them as honest and open acts of looking. Each person will react differently, depending on who they are, what's happened to them, what else they've seen, what they feel when they see women in these poses. They're personal images that way.

And their personal aspect starts with their creator, the man who decided to do this, and then spent years on the subject—Lee Friedlander. Now, he could have said, "No, that topic's too hot to handle," or he could have been unaware of how it implicates him. I doubt he wasn't at least conscious of the weight of the issues. It's our gain that he followed his instinct to say yes to the subject. "Yes, I'll follow my attraction to this enormous subject." Friedlander uses his curiosity as a guide to what he photographs; afterward he finds what he brought back with him in the picture. But make no mistake, he's not casual in terms of his work. You have to be very focused to stick with a theme for the years that he takes with his projects. This is a photographer who has spent years photographing trees. Trees, another subject that, like nudes, in someone else's work might look monotonously the same. His trees aren't boring. But no matter how curious Friedlander was about trees, nudes are a whole different, if you want, formal, emotional, psychological, political set of problems. Friedlander's first step on this score is to not get too caught up in the problems and instead pursue his interest. Over and over he says the one thing he cared about when he did the photographs was that they feel "real." He succeeded, not only in the kinds of pictures he got, but because the pictures themselves give one a sense of the photographer's curiosity about women's bodies that feels very real. He isn't hiding his fascination. He's revealing it.

The results are fairly strange. To me, a few are beautiful, but they're not all so. Some are tense, others have an awkwardness that's oddly like Egon Schiele's figures. Still others have humor, as the body can. There are erotic images, and analytic ones, and pictures that generate no electricity whatsoever. But each photograph is a clear presentation of how Friedlander met his subject. And that's what makes art bigger than many things—when it can bring to the surface something that feels convincing about an individual's response to the world, it has done something profound. Then we the viewers can say, "I'm not alone," or "I'm different from that"; agreement doesn't matter. Revelation's much more important than consensus.

Friedlander's photographs don't just light up the women who are in them, they light him up, and they call forth memory and history and what comes with all that—questions. The style of Friedlander's photographs is so strong, they are obviously the result of lots of decisions. Some photographs are so neutral that you don't feel the presence of their maker; a finger pressed the button, but it could have been any finger. This is not the case with Friedlander's pictures. You can sense the photographer getting up close, angling, moving about. When the voice of the photographer is this clear, something special is happening. A vision is being presented, not just visuals. You get interested in the person behind the vision.

Why only women? Friedlander's answer was that he's not curious about men. Why did he do these pictures when he was in his fifties? Friedlander's response was that there are certain seasons in a photographer's life when a subject becomes possible. But during our talks he gave me other clues about this work which also seemed to fit with its emotional tenor. He kept on saying that he has a bad memory. And I, psychological creature that I am, kept wondering whether this desire to photograph women at what he sees as the prime of their lives had to do with his sense of his own aging.

Then, at the very end of our discussion, he gave me something I think I'll never forget—an early memory, and with it an image as mistily clear as his photographs are crystal clear. "I had a great-uncle who was a farmer," he said. "I'm a first-generation American. My mother was from Finland. My father was German, German Jewish. My mother died when I was quite young. But before that we'd go to her uncle's. He and his family had a sauna in the backyard. Every Saturday he'd get up in the morning and light the fire on the rocks. And every Saturday night all of the family from the area would come, and all the men would go take a sauna, and then all the women would go. We only went three times a year, because it was such a long car ride, but it was amazing. My cousins and I were always the youngest. There were about four tiers of benches. We, who weren't used to it, who were littler, were down at the bottom, trying to get air on the floor. There was the whole male side of the family there—the oldest were at the hottest place, which was at the top. When you see your whole family naked in the steam, it is a great scene."

"That whole event would have been a great photograph," I thought out loud. He agreed, "It would. But it's like a photograph in my mind. It's indelible." So he doesn't have such a bad memory, I mused. "And the women?" I asked, "Did you see them?" "No," he replied, "they came second when the stones weren't as hot, but it was really warm." And then I couldn't stand not asking, "So if you didn't see the women, are they part of that photograph that is in your mind?" "No, see the women went after the men." Isn't that what art's all about? Seeing what had been waiting in the imagination?

Lee Friedlander: Nudes, 1991

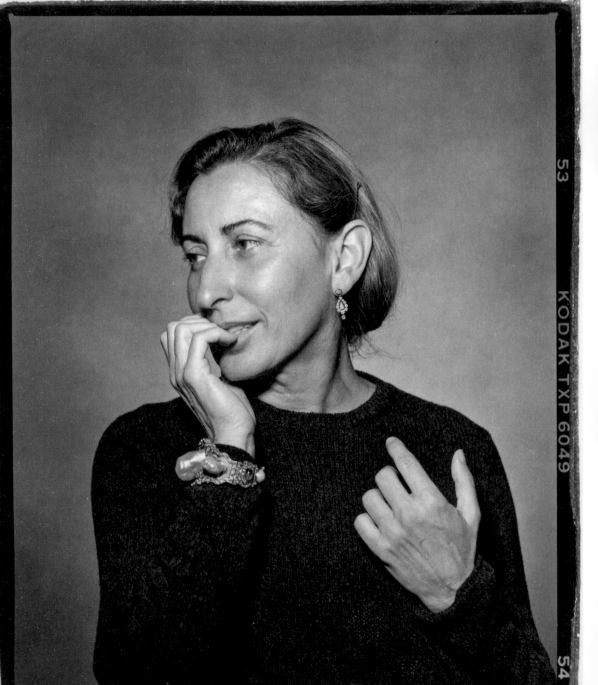

Some Clothes of One's Own

For most of her forty-four years, the designer Miuccia Prada shuddered at the notion of working in fashion. Like lots of people, she thought of fashion as basically silly, and as a stupid, superficial way to spend much of one's time. She wanted a life with real meaning. Her family, which owned a Milan leather-goods company, had money, and she was smart and well educated. In keeping with a tradition of socially aware upper-class Italians, she joined the Communist Party in the seventies, while she was attending university in Milan, where she received a doctorate in political science. By her mid-twenties, she had risen in the ranks of the feminist section of the Party, and was spending many of her days demonstrating, leafleting, or confronting local government officials, and her nights debating or giving speeches at meetings. It's funny to think of her now as someone issuing manifestos and holding forth in public, because she's shy, and everything about her resists formulas, including her looks. She's been described as a woman one might find in a painting by Modigliani. Her face veers between beautifully plain and plainly beautiful. She has brown eyes and shoulder-length auburn hair. It wouldn't be true to say that she's slim, or that she's not; she's what old-fashioned doctors used to call "the right weight."

Even back when Prada's opinions of fashion were dismissive, she didn't dress like the rest of her crowd. She wore antique dresses, not jeans, and even a few pricier outfits; her favorites were by Yves Saint Laurent. She realized that

Guido Harari, *Miuccia Prada*, 1999

this way of presenting herself might undercut the idea that she was serious about her politics, but the draw that such clothes had for her was greater than any concern about what others might think. "Although I was ashamed of the desire I had for these clothes, I refused to reject this part of myself," she says.

Perhaps an extra reason that Prada had shuddered at the thought of working in fashion was that such a career had been in the cards for her all along. The family business wasn't just any leather-goods company—it was Fratelli Prada, one of the great Milan stores, whose goods had helped establish Italy's reputation for craftsmanship and fine quality since the beginning of the century. In 1958, Miuccia's mother had stepped in as boss at Prada after the death of Mario Prada, the patriarch who created the business, and by the late seventies the question of Miuccia's tie to her heritage could no longer remain up in the air. She'd been helping out more and more, liked it, and found herself absorbed in the question of Prada's future. But the decision to work permanently for the firm was difficult, not just because of her take on fashion as a world of smoke and mirrors but also because of the political climate in the seventies. "Being so involved in the women's movement then, and in everything that it was trying to accomplish, I thought that making bags or shoes or dresses was the worst way I could spend my time," she says. "I was embarrassed, since most fashion had been such a nightmare for women. And I never actually *decided* to become a designer. Eventually, I found that I was one. I wanted to be something more. But I am what I am. Not everyone can be Albert Schweitzer or Karl Marx."

The fact is that Miuccia Prada has ended up doing more with accessories and with fashion than one might think possible. When she took over, in 1978, the company was in the doldrums, just plugging along. In a way, she has continued what her grandfather Mario Prada began when he established Fratelli Prada, in 1913. But she has done it from a completely different perspective, and with completely different results. Like Miuccia, her grandfather approached his work as though he were an explorer. He made long, arduous journeys all over the world to discover the finest materials for his opulent luggage and other luxury items, including some fancy ladies' handbags that were the epitome of elegance. Italian leather wasn't good enough for him: He used leather made in Vienna, because it was the best then. In those days, you had to be rich to afford Prada, and in the twenties and thirties Italian aristocrats and European royalty were crazy for the company's products. Classic Prada suitcases of that period were so heavy that you needed servants to carry them. The cases were fabricated from walrus skin, and they included toilet articles made of tortoiseshell, ivory, and gold. Inside, there were as many compartments as in a gentleman's dressing room, some of them packed with grooming tools that don't exist anymore. But with the Second World War that way of life disappeared. The family kept the business going by selling goods that were still of high quality but were much more mundane.

It's anybody's guess what Mario Prada might say if he were alive to see the backpack that his granddaughter created—the item that initially put life and prestige back into the business. This bag is so light that when it's empty it feels like nothing. It's black, and very practical-looking, and it doesn't always have a lining. And it's made of a material that has no snob appeal at all: nylon. The backpacks, run up on machines used for making parachutes for the Italian army, initially appeared in the early eighties, and at first it seemed that nobody wanted them. What was hot then was anything that blatantly suggested status and money. Prada's only positive reinforcement came from the fashion vanguard. Mostly she received the kind of advice you often get when you've done something ahead of its time: People tried to persuade her to add elements that would transform her creation to fit the moment's formulas for success. They said she should put initials on the backpacks, the way

Gucci does on its bags. She refused. She'd hated those initials the whole time she was growing up. After a couple of years, her instinct and conviction paid off. The backpacks and other handheld bags started to attract more and more customers, and then she did add a metal PRADA tag, taken from historic Prada steamer trunks. Women became so attached to the bags, carrying them day and night, everywhere and on every occasion, that they were almost like cult objects. They still are; it's just that now there are more members of the Prada-bag tribe. Constant use was exactly what Prada had in mind: We have so many things to lug around, she believes, that we need something light to carry them in; we go out straight from work, so we have to have something that functions no matter where we are; we can't be worrying that a spill or a splash will lead to ruin; we need something washable, flexible, tough, and soft.

The bags also caught the eye of the man who became Miuccia's husband and partner, Patrizio Bertelli. She got to know him at a trade fair, where she discovered that he was selling bags that looked a lot like the ones she'd designed. She hunted him down, pointed out the faults in his versions, and engineered things so that the competition would end up working with her. Soon the team of Prada and Bertelli was running a company that was producing clothes as well as shoes and bags. "From the moment we met, we started disputing," she told me, laughing, "and we haven't stopped yet."

Recently, I spent a few days with Miuccia and her husband in Milan, and on the last of them I was partly responsible for a spat between them, because she and I had been talking so long, she'd kept him waiting. When we walked into the Prada offices, it was obvious we were in the doghouse. She was about an hour late, and the looks on the faces of the young women running the reception area flashed storm warnings. From the top of the stairwell, Bertelli's voice rained down at us, and, while I couldn't understand the words, their tone was enough to make me want to scram.

He didn't give a hoot that his wife had been talking to a reporter. This is not a fellow who spends time trying to seduce the press. "Miuccia! Miuccia! You have work to do!" he scolded. And, turning to me, the other culprit, he said, "I'm going to kill you later!" "*At* or *with* dinner?" I asked, referring to plans we had for that evening. Except for quick smiles, neither Miuccia nor Patrizio allowed my presence to distract them, and therein lies a significant difference between these two and most of the fashion pack. There's none of that faking of harmony, of confidence, or of success, which is constant in the fashion business. With Prada and Bertelli, you don't have to pick your way through the hype. They don't waste energy pretending things for the sake of their public image.

It's a whole other kind of pretending that keeps the house of Prada moving—the dreaming and fantasizing that go on in Miuccia Prada's head. The first time I saw one of her runway shows, a few years ago, a friend whispered, "What an incredible interior life that woman must have." These words—surprising for a fashion show—struck home, because they seemed to pinpoint what was so riveting about what we'd seen. The clothes seemed to have something extra to them—or, rather, *in* them. They suggested that someone, not something, had caused them to be. A while later, I started to wear some simple Prada stuff myself: sweaters, shoes, an anorak, one of her black nylon backpacks. Immediately, they seemed familiar and intimate.

At first glance, some of Prada's work looks plain and undesigned. How it feels on the body is something else altogether; its power remains the wearer's secret. Her ability to give clothes this strong inner quality has to do with her own experience. Her imagination is a huge part of who she is, of how she does her work, and of how she gets through life. She confessed to me, "I always live a double life. There is my real life, and then there is the one I would like to live. I am never in my real life only. I am always also in my dreams, or hopes, or thinking about somebody. It's always like this for me." Where her mind travels is often, but not always, reflected in her clothes and accessories. But what can always be discerned in her creations is Miuccia Prada's worldview—her view of fashion, her view of women, and even her feelings about the ways the sexes relate to each other. (She recently launched a small line of clothes and accessories for men. Most of them aren't that different from her sporty women's clothes.) Also discernible in anything by Prada is her understanding of materials, of what they can give us—or take from us. Many of her creations mix different materials, different textures, different weights, different values, different traditions, different processes, different associations.

Since the beginning, with her 1988–1989 collection for autumn-winter, her ready-to-wear shows have frequently had a schoolgirl theme. The models have been styled to look like the kind of girls that are considered trouble: the ones who are a bit too bohemian as far as their teachers and parents are concerned, who sleep with a guitar-playing dropout, or who smoke, or spend too much time on art class and not enough on math. The clothes themselves don't necessarily have misfit connotations, and they're not even particularly geared to young women, but, the way Prada imagines them worn, they're like uniforms for the slightly disenfranchised. I asked her if she'd been one of those rebellious kids she likes to create on the runway. She said, "I tried to be bad, but I couldn't be as bad as I would have liked—not as bad as the girls I really admired, and not as bad as the ones who are in my dreams."

From the outside, Miuccia Prada appears to be what society expects of a woman of her standing. In many ways, she seems the epitome of the good daughter, the good wife, the good mother, the good Italian. She and her husband and their children—they have two small sons—live in the building she grew up in, and her brother and her sister (who went to work at the firm after Miuccia took over), her ex-sister-in-law, her mother, and her aunt all have apartments in the same building. Most Americans would find such an arrangement stifling, but Miuccia's designs prove that roosting at home can be a way of taking flight. She describes her working life as "exactly like school," and it's as though out of all this institutionalism she had wrung its opposite: freedom. Her designs have freedom of movement, freedom from definition, freedom from constriction.

Bohemians, avant-gardists, beatniks have been constant motifs in her designs, but she has also had fun with clothes that signal money and bombshell allure. Prada's outfits allow a woman to feel glamorous yet convey the sense that she's playing with glamour—she's not owned by it. Prada has done lunch outfits, hostess dresses, ski-bunny ensembles, and twin sets of all types, but in a way that suggests they're part of a movie, not real life. Their colors, including a citrus green that she's particularly fond of, are often as candylike as early Technicolor. Box pleats, bows, snoods, puffs, fashions of the fifties and early sixties, and a memory of the designs of Balenciaga, Courrèges, and Givenchy are just some of the elements that come into play in these clothes. Her collection for autumn-winter 1991–1992 recalled Hollywood heroines— especially the kind who went on heists. Some of the outfits seemed made for cat burglars, for roles in the *Pink Panther* movies, or perhaps for Grace Kelly in *To Catch a Thief.* The young Audrey Hepburn would have looked fantastic in every single outfit.

You can tell what kind of evening Miuccia Prada has had by the shutters in the courtyard of her house in Milan. If she's been smoking and drinking, chances are that the clothes she had on the night before will be hanging outside. And then she'll do everything that's supposed to be healthy, but you don't hear her promising that she's going to give up cigarettes or alcohol. She says that this outdoor fumigating is the best way to get rid of the smell of her sins, but I think it's also a ritual that reflects her personality. As she points out, she's a "Catho-Communist"; that is, she has experienced the moralizing of both Catholicism and communism. She uses notions of goodness and badness as if they were the oil and vinegar without which her fashion wouldn't mix into what she wants. And she isn't afraid of living with contradictions and conflicting desires. Rather, she seems to need to express their presence. "Everybody makes a choice when he or she gets dressed," she says. "It's not true when people say, 'I don't care what I have on.' Your way of dressing is something you can go to the psychoanalyst to find out about, because there are so many personal things involved. Women, especially, have complexes when it comes to dressing, because of all the attitudes toward women—about who we are supposed to be, what's supposed to be sexy, and so on. Look at Mrs. Clinton, whom I admire. You can tell exactly what's going on. You can see that she's clever and badly dressed. Maybe she doesn't care, maybe she doesn't understand fashion, maybe she has bad advisers."

Prada's own solution to the trauma of shopping—or a trip to the closet—was to return to a phase of her life when her clothes were without all that sexist baggage. She paid a visit to the Ferrari sisters, on Via Bigli, who are Milan's most exclusive tailors of children's clothes, and had dresses and coats made to order, scaled up to her size and with "corrections," such as a bigger or smaller collar than the one that was there. She commissioned the Ferraris to create her wedding dress, too, and even though she mostly wears her own designs now, on occasion she still places an order there, and also at shops such as Cirri, in Florence, which she says makes the best sailor dresses around. You can trace her love of children's clothes in some of the details that she likes to include, such as smocking, and in the way she uses undergarments modeled on children's underwear. Her newer line, Miu Miu—which is her nickname—evokes everyone's childhood memories. But grown women, not children, are the point of Prada's work.

"Today, a designer of women's clothes has to express something that is deep enough so that it represents what a lot of women feel," she says. "Maybe that's why, in general, it's the women designers who are so successful at this." By sneaking her own experiences and her dreams into what the company manufactures—coats, pants of all kinds, sweaters, bustiers, jackets, suits, skirts, dresses, pinafores, shoes, bags—she has done something revolutionary. But her work hasn't always been recognized as such, because it isn't obviously radical.

First of all, Prada isn't cheap. Like her grandfather, Miuccia Prada goes for the best of whatever material she's using. And the products are utterly beautiful, sometimes in a new way, sometimes not. What makes her work revolutionary is the way it makes so much other fashion look outdated. Even though Prada has designed women's clothes based on men's fashion, her newer designs have rendered stale the whole idea of women wearing men's clothes. Prada herself says she has bought and worn plenty of men's clothes in her day; for a long time, that approach seemed the only alternative to clothes that made women feel bad. But the symbolism is starting to get empty. The singer k.d. lang said to me recently, "You know I have this image of being someone who wears men's clothes. But I didn't wear clothes that are associated with men because I wanted to come off like a man. It's just that there were no other kinds of clothes that had to do with confidence and authority instead of vulnerability and stereotypical sexiness. I wish there had been a third choice." Then she reported her latest discovery: "I was in a department store shopping with a friend. I went through the men's department. I went through the women's department. Then my friend brought me this beautiful jacket. I tried it on, and it fit. I said, 'Where's this from?'

She replied, 'The women's department.' I said, 'You're kidding me.' I was shocked. The label was Prada."

This is how Miuccia Prada would explain what lang experienced: "In the end, there is something that goes through one person to another." But how many designers can communicate as quickly as that through their clothes? How many others are in touch with what people really want? Prada's magic is that she makes the consumer feel understood. Her clothes are driven by her own feelings and by her sharp sense of where we are in the world. "I have the sensation that happiness is forbidden," she says. "If you have it, you need to hide it. How can anyone be happy with so much terribleness around, with so many reminders of all the problems that exist? But sometimes, thank God, someone feels happy anyway, perhaps for some personal reason. The way to express this joy or sense of beauty has to be subtle. You have to keep it personal—you have to wear this richness in a manner that is private." Many of her clothes give joy in that private way, and the element of privacy may explain why Prada, which has taken off as a business, is still a kind of secret. It isn't logo fashion. During collection season, top fashion editors and stylists typically make a point of wearing the clothes of big-name designers, but at the Prada stores in Milan, which have the biggest inventory, you also see them shopping for themselves.

For all her receptivity to others, Miuccia Prada is very sure of what she does—most of the time. She still gets worked up about her 1989 autumn-winter collection, her third; it stank, she says. Her next collection faltered, too, and it took a while for her to find herself as a designer again. In those collections, she used conventional, Seventh Avenue solutions. The clothes were overdesigned, and it seemed that commercial considerations and self-consciousness, not the usual articulation of her unconscious, were leading her. Some of the models looked wrapped like presents, without any of Prada's characteristic humor. Her third collection included two of the least Pradaesque things she has ever done: power-suit shoulder pads and cardigans with buttons in the shape of letters that spelled out the name Prada. That show made her miserable, but it was a lesson, too. "The whole time I was working, I hated everything," she says. "It was not me. It was a nightmare. If it's my mistake, it's okay. In fact, I like mistakes, because mistakes are what life's about—they tell you something's alive. Yet this was something that made me crazy. For ten days, I was mad. I hated all the people around me, and I told them it was the last time others would push me to do what I didn't want."

It has been only five years since Prada began doing runway collections, but next week the company will receive the International Award from the Council of Fashion Designers of America. Prada and Bertelli should get a prize for trusting themselves as well as the intelligence of the consumer. As they've gathered more experience, they've become increasingly convinced that their company's success is based on its personal approach. Miuccia Prada is the critical link, for it is her sense of touch, her desires, her feelings, her memories, her problems, her dreams that are passed on. This creates enormous pressure, and enormous problems as the company gets bigger (there are now forty-five Prada stores worldwide, twenty of them owned by Prada, and two Miu Miu stores), but Miuccia admits that she enjoys coming in to fix things, thus reasserting her indispensability. This is a long way from dreading a career in something as trivial as fashion. Miuccia claims that her husband would be happier if it were possible to do the work without her, but that's the only thing she told me that I don't believe. Bertelli, who oversees everything, is very aware of the importance of his wife's role. He is a charming combination of opposites himself, and it's clear that they rely on each other.

The dynamic between Miuccia and Bertelli is part of the Prada recipe:

It keeps the passion for the work high, it guarantees constant debate, and it clarifies the roles of both players. The two are capable of polemics that could exhaust even Miuccia's old Communist comrades. Bertelli didn't kill me that night in Milan, but their debate over dinner about the merits of different types of rare Venetian glass almost did, because I laughed so much. Out came a bottle that Miuccia had commissioned from the Pauly factory in Venice, which has produced handblown glass for hundreds of years. Then another, and another, and another, until the table was covered with bottles. The issue was which was the right color. Just when I had given up on the possibility of there ever being agreement between the two, Miuccia got up and presented the one example that satisfied them both. It was an antique piece of her grandfather's, a broken violet-colored lantern. They concurred that it was perfect.

Such hypersensitivity to details is a bond between them. So is their love of art, especially art that was truly avant-garde when it was made. Prada shops are designed in ways that are reminiscent of the art galleries of the sixties. They have that same emphasis on a clean space, on an environment that heightens perceptions. But the indirect neon lighting isn't gallerylike at all; it's a way of reconstructing that catchword of the fifties—*glamour.* While *glamour* may be as suspect a term today as *elegance,* Prada has reinvented it in new forms. Some of her clothes allow one to have a private experience of feeling glamorous, and others provide the glamour of iconoclasm. One inspiration for this is the work of Italian filmmakers of the early sixties. (Her advertising campaign for this spring was shot at the Castello di Donnafugata, in Sicily, where Visconti filmed *The Leopard.*) She credits Antonioni, for example, with influencing her first two collections. And when one looks at the clothes she presented there, it's clear why: The dresses, sportswear, and slips, mostly in black and white, echo what the stylish, lonely people in his films wore. There's a line in

L'Avventura that sums up the approach Prada took when she began. A father asks his daughter if young people going sailing still wear caps embroidered with the name of the yacht, and she replies, "It's not done anymore." And the scene in *La Notte* where the guests throw caution to the wind and jump into a swimming pool in full evening gear epitomizes Prada's boredom with the whole old idea of elegance. She knows that it's a dead issue.

Her most recent collection, which has just arrived in stores, is her most intimate statement yet, and has many of the same elements as her first collection. There is a lot of black, and sheerness, and lace-up shoes worn with ankle socks. One dress, made of black organza and trimmed with black knit—the whole thing slightly crumpled—was shown so that the black underwear beneath looked like a mirage. But there was nothing here that reminded me of anybody's movie. I couldn't help thinking she'd dreamed this collection rather than drawn it. Many of the clothes seemed to float down the runway, grounded only by the sureness of the models' feet in their lace-ups and socks or stockings. These clothes often display Prada's love of showing opposites together. There are knits, silks, cottons, linens, gauzes, leathers, viscoses, velvets, suedes, nets, and the industrial material that represented Prada's first breakthrough: nylon. The beauty of it all was unmistakable, but it didn't conform to any formula for beauty, so some in the audience looked puzzled. But the clothes had an answer for problems that are rarely faced in fashion: "It's okay if you've made mistakes, if you're scared, if you're aggressive, if you're fat, if you're beautiful, if you're ugly, if you feel crazy, defensive, happy," the collection seemed to say. "Come into my arms." I watched it, entranced. Especially the dresses. It was the first time in twenty years that I'd been able to picture myself wearing one.

The New Yorker, February 7, 1994

Good Intentions

Sebastião Salgado is the photojournalist of the moment. His reputation has been on the ascent, and although the heyday of photojournalism is past, his career proves that there is still a hunger for the kind of social-documentary picture stories that flourished in magazines in the thirties, forties, and fifties. In a relatively short time, he has had a number of books published, his images have been used prominently in major news stories, and there have been heavily publicized exhibitions of his work. He has, in fact, had two shows this year, only six weeks apart, at New York's International Center of Photography. In the spring, the uptown branch of ICP housed Salgado's traveling retrospective "An Uncertain Grace," which originated at the San Francisco Museum of Modern Art; and this summer at ICP's midtown branch one could see "Kuwait Epilogue," an exhibition of his shoot of oil-well firefighters in Kuwait, done right after the Gulf War, and, in another room, his photographs of gold miners in Brazil, many of which had just been on view in the retrospective uptown.

It's rare for a photographer to be as widely trumpeted as Salgado. And it's rare—even rarer today than it was in the past—for a working photojournalist's pictures to be shown in a museum. That limiting, fragmenting system that divides people who use the medium into categories—fine-art photographers or commercial photographers or news photographers—may have had many exceptions and challenges over the years, but it's still firmly in place. No matter that, for instance, a photographer's imagery is highly inventive, and stands on its own: If it was originally produced on assignment, he or she is still pigeonholed as "less" than an artist, and has a harder time being taken seriously than someone whose pictures are first seen in an art gallery. Salgado's photographs, though, have been welcomed in a variety of milieus. They are generally the result of self-assigned projects, and they look as carefully composed as still lifes. Indeed, this "art" quality has contributed greatly to the work's success as photojournalism plus much more.

"Kuwait Epilogue" underscored how bright a spotlight there is on this photographer, while confirming that there's something exaggerated about all the attention he's getting. The Kuwait pictures are mostly stagy shots of men at work, trying to cap the gushing wells, or at exhausted rest. But they constitute an expression of Salgado's ongoing interest in manual workers—for the last few years, he's been involved in a project called "The End of Manual Labor"—more than they constitute a narrative of what happened to Kuwait's landscape in the Gulf War. There's no deep observation of the place and its new scars. The oil that's such a looming presence in the photographs and that appears to cover everyone and everything identifies the series as a product of the war, but the images add no special meaning to the sense of ecological devastation transmitted over the wires while the war was going on—something they seem to be striving to do. Salgado's portraits of the firefighters are remarkably similar to his portraits of gold miners; the firefighters just happen to be covered with oil, not mud.

What stood out most about this exhibition was its promotional tone. Two press displays were installed in Plexiglas boxes, one showing spreads from the issue of *The New York Times Magazine* in which the Kuwait images first appeared, and the other containing an appreciative article on Salgado, from the same issue. You don't come across press clippings as an installational element at many exhibitions. It could be argued that there's interest in seeing Salgado's Kuwait images in their original photo-essay format, but why display the article on the photographer? It's a piece of feature journalism about his life and his work that, though it covers his time in the Gulf, is the type of background article that usually stays in the background, separate from an actual presentation of the work. Just imagine what it would be like if curators regularly displayed magazine articles on artists as part of their exhibitions—a show, say, of Jasper Johns's paintings and, with it, his press clippings. Nor was this the only place in the ICP exhibition that hinted at a collapse of the usual separation between curatorial practice and publicity. Salgado's biography, installed on a placard, ended with something more like an after-dinner speech than like an educational device: For the years 1988 through 1990—years in which Salgado did a great deal of work—all it cited was a list of awards.

It makes sense that the International Center of Photography is enthusiastic about Salgado's pictures, which are clearly trying to echo the endeavors of the group now referred to as "concerned photographers"—the group whose humanistic mission was the inspiration for ICP's founder and director, Cornell Capa, who is the brother of Robert Capa, a hero in the field. (Cornell Capa, in fact, is credited with coining the term *concerned photography,* and Robert Capa was a founder of Magnum, the prestigious agency of which Salgado is a member.) Yet ICP isn't exceptional in its fanlike attitude toward Salgado's work. From the tone of other recent Salgado projects, including the texts that are part of his books and shows, it's clear that neither he nor his admirers believe his photographs to be anything short of acts of enlightenment, and great pictures to boot, the premise being that they bestow honor on the people in them. Included in this claim is the suggestion that the images are powerful enough to change perceptions. The cult of appreciation that has developed around Salgado sets him up as a photojournalist whose pictures have a transforming power over, say, ethnocentrism, racism, and classism. From Salgado's choice of projects, from his titles, and from the photographs themselves, it appears that he aspires to be a spokesphotographer for forgotten people and also for soon-to-be-lost ways of life—a worthy ambition, but one, unfortunately, that resists the oversimplified yet heavy-handed means by which he attempts to achieve it.

Salgado's subjects are often so weighty, and are so weightily presented, that it is inevitable that his work has come to be credited with weightiness. It's no coincidence that his images of starvation, and of other situations in which human beings undergo intense physical stress—such as slogging in and out of a barren mine—are the ones that have brought him the most notice; subjects like these embody matters of conscience and, by their very nature, pull at the emotions. But other photojournalists have photographed such subjects. It's Salgado's manner—his visual rhetoric—that has given his work so much clout. His compositions, crops, lighting, angles, and toning stand in sharp contrast to the usual lack of insistent style in photojournalism. He goes in for aura. What's more, many of his photographs suggest both religious art and the kitsch products resulting from the commercialization of religion. Salgado is given to including crosslike forms in his pictures, for example, and all too frequently he presents people in a way that implies a connection to saints, martyrs, and various other figures familiar from Judeo-Christian iconography. It is work that is sloppy with symbolism. And his religiosity seems to be catching. At times, a curator's or a commentator's partisanship can become so extreme that it feels as if the artist's work is being worshipped instead of examined. You can see this happening in the exhibition "An Uncertain Grace," and it's there in the book of the same title, which was published last year, by Aperture, when the show opened.

"An Uncertain Grace" is a package deal, with basically the same format, plus or minus a few images, at each museum where it appears. (It is now at the Chrysler Museum in Norfolk, Virginia, and will eventually be seen at San Diego's Museum of Photographic Arts; at Washington, D.C.'s Corcoran Gallery; at Harvard's Carpenter Center; and at the North Dakota Museum of Art, in Grand Forks.) The photographer's proponents may make claims for the power of his pictures, but the presentation of this show doesn't reveal much faith in the viewer's ability to grasp what Salgado is doing without help and hype. The captions that accompany the photographs have an inflated, pseudoeducational tone, and the introductory wall label, written by Sandra Phillips, of the San Francisco Museum of Modern Art, who conceived of and organized the show, begins this way: "Sebastião Salgado, a Brazilian by birth, is probably the most important contemporary Latin American photographer and one of the most important artists in the Western Hemisphere." No faint praise here. There's something off-key about the lionizing of the "artist" that informs "An Uncertain Grace" (both the show and the book) when one considers Salgado's subjects—particularly the people in the Sahel region of Africa, whom he has photographed, it appears, in order to convey the effect that famine has had on them. The photographs of these people have been fostering discussions of courage, but not the courage of those who really deserve recognition for it. It is Salgado everyone seems to end up admiring—for getting so close to such suffering. (You also hear people discussing the Sahel photographs as if what mattered were whether or not they themselves had the courage to look.)

At ICP, "An Uncertain Grace" was installed so that before you got to the photographs of starvation and death in the Sahel, you came upon a statement from the American branch of the French aid organization Médecins Sans Frontières telling you that the group was "proud to be associated with ICP for this exhibition," and that Salgado's "humanitarian concerns parallel our own." No doubt, the doctors have great respect for Salgado and for his work, and there is plenty of evidence that he is serious in his efforts to help fight starvation. (For his most recent Sahel pictures, he was working with the cooperation of Médecins Sans Frontières, and when the photographs were published as a book in France and Spain he donated the profits to it.) But his seriousness cannot eliminate the evident disparities—between claims for the work and what is actually there in the images; between intentions and results.

Certainly, what Salgado is trying to accomplish is difficult to achieve. He wants his portraits from the Sahel to reveal the inhuman scale of the tragedy there, while also capturing the dignity of the people he is photographing. Furthermore, the images are supposed to work as educational vehicles, as calls to action. But this is the kind of endeavor that requires an El Greco or a Goya, and though Salgado is treated as if he were such a visionary, regrettably he isn't one. In the history of photography, there are many who have tried to use photojournalism to change the world as well as to capture it, and a few have had some effect. Others have simply been naïve—even deluded—about what they were doing. Still others are complicated mixtures of high aspirations and presumption. It seems to me that Salgado is one of these.

Salgado's imagery is often linked to the work of a photojournalist whose pictures include moments of brilliant humanitarian communication: W. Eugene Smith. Indeed, Smith's work has been a strong influence on Salgado, and the two men have much in common, most particularly their passion for making the world "see" injustice. Smith's photographs of war-ravaged Saipan and Okinawa, of the leper colony where Albert Schweitzer worked, and of the mercury-poisoned Japanese fishing town of Minamata are among the projects of his that remain a touchstone for many who practice concerned photography. Smith took photographs you can never forget once you've seen them, and he also took pictures that were heavy-handed and hackneyed. But Eugene Smith is his own story, and its usefulness to viewers of Salgado's work lies in something that Smith once said: "I frequently have sought out those who are in the least position to speak for themselves. By accident of birth, by accident of place—whoever, whatever, wherever—I am of their family. I can comment for them, if I believe in their cause, with a voice they do not possess." Such presumption is at the core of what is self-aggrandizing about Salgado's photography. To quote Smith again, in a moment of clarity about his work (and he had moments that went in the other direction), he described his camera and film as "the fragile weapons of my good intentions."

Salgado is working in a time very different from Smith's. As has frequently been remarked, the advent of television—with the resulting loss of mass-circulation magazines committed to supporting and publishing photo essays—has meant that photojournalists have few outlets today; there is no way they can compete with television in terms of immediacy or the public's attention. And in responding to the remaining magazine opportunities, they do not have the same sense of authority they had a few decades ago. Even though they never had real control over the presentation of their images, at least back then there was a healthy editorial demand for what they did. That has changed, and so has the way photographs are viewed. For instance, we, today's audience, know that pictures can "lie," and, like the photographers themselves, we assume that magazines can use pictures to slant things. Meaningful photojournalism today requires an appetite for challenge, a belief in the power of the medium, and an internal alarm system against stereotyping. For the first two of these, Salgado deserves credit, but his work suggests that his consciousness of the deeper issues of representation in this kind of photography—such as how one's approach can skew things or how the subjects themselves might feel about being "honored"—is only partly developed.

Still, it's tricky to unravel what is meretricious about his work, because it's all so uncompromisingly *serious*. His dedication to making people visible whom powerful institutions—governments, say, or the media—have typically ignored is strong, and he is aware of how the image of "the victim" can perpetuate victimization; he features pride instead of its absence. But often there is something else in his compositions: beauty. In fact, *beauty* is a word one hears a lot when Salgado's photography is discussed, and you can see why people respond to the formal beauty of his pictures. You can also understand and appreciate why he has chosen to challenge the usual clichés about poverty by underlining the beauty in its midst—he means to negate the revulsion that can take over when disease and hunger are on display. But beauty as a formula—and this is what it has become for Salgado—is as much of a cliché as what he's trying to avoid, and as artificial as any other blanket approach. A photographer can't lose with heart-wrenching subject matter like the situation in the Sahel: a fleshless child hoisted up in the air to be weighed; two sick-looking children sucking on breasts that look more like wrinkled pieces of leather than like oases of nourishment; a man bending over a child who has a skeleton's body and an old man's face. Getting our attention with such material is easy; what a photographer does with that material is what counts. Salgado is far too busy with the compositional aspects of his pictures—with finding the "grace" and "beauty" in the twisted forms of his anguished subjects. And this beautification of tragedy results in pictures that ultimately reinforce our passivity toward the experience they reveal. To aestheticize tragedy is the fastest way to anesthetize the feelings of those who are witnessing it. Beauty is a call to admiration, not to action.

Salgado's approach has inspired much laudatory writing, such as that by Fred Ritchin, who wrote the main text of *An Uncertain Grace,* and who is the guest curator of the exhibition. Ritchin's expertise in photojournalism, as well as his long professional relationship with Salgado, which began in 1979, made him a natural choice for these tasks. His knowledge of the work is evident, as is his respect for it, but this very closeness to it seems to have forestalled an overview. To Ritchin, Salgado's use of biblical themes is impressive, not pretentious, and so is the formalized beauty of the Africans. In fact, he makes a point of the contradictions between the look of the pictures and what's happening to their subjects:

> *Fathers march for days with dying children draped across their arms. . . . Children are weighed, suspended as if in the agony of the cross. . . . There is an exalted beauty to the people—an emaciated boy using a cane stands nude before a withered tree on a carpet of sand, a woman with diseased eyes radiates a visionary sadness. A bruising conflict is created between the formal radiance of the imagery and their agonizing content as a proud, attractive people suffers so.*

No question, Salgado's depiction of the woman with diseased eyes gives her an oracular presence. But the fact that her affliction has been turned into something spiritual-seeming is exactly what's disturbing about the photograph. Yes, he's trying to counter the fear and horror that her disease can cause others to feel: He's attempting to attract people to her plight—to involve us in it. And, yes, it's a "beautiful" photograph. But Salgado's strategy here fits into a long and convenient tradition of coupling human suffering and God's will. Finally, the photograph suggests that the woman's blindness is holy—in other words, that it needn't be seen as something to cure.

There is a widely felt yearning today for photography and art that *matter,* and Salgado's work has benefited from it. But what do his pictures really succeed in doing? In a photograph of people in a refugee shelter in the Sahel, two young figures loom in the foreground, one sitting and the other slightly propped up. Salgado's perspective creates the impression that the viewer is close enough to touch the boy who is propped up: His elongated body and bald head stretch along the bottom half of the picture. His bone-thin legs are spread apart, and his shorts bunch around the tops of his thighs, which have a much smaller circumference than the shorts seem made for. Yet despite the sculptural image that he has become in Salgado's photograph, this boy is made of flesh, not wood. The shock of what he looks like is strong, but Salgado's objectification of the boy's body makes the image a setup—and, like most setups, it evokes reactions that are mechanical. Typical of the comments I overheard during several days of visiting the show at ICP was one made by a young woman standing in front of this image: "I can't look at this picture. It makes me cry." Yet she looked at it, and she didn't cry. It isn't fair to make Salgado responsible for how we do or do not respond to the content of his pictures, but there are certain gimmicks and attitudes in them that seem designed to trigger specific reactions and reflexes that are insulting to the people being portrayed.

Ritchin explains Salgado's approach this way:

> *It is a romantic view that he espouses, one that is loyal to the dignity of the person depicted while circumventing some of the complexities of his or her existence. But when one juxtaposes the images with their various contexts, the lyricism can become particularly searing—the fact, for example, that in the Third World 40,000 children die daily of diseases we in the industrialized world have learned to cure long ago, like measles and diarrhea.*

The statistics about the children are an effective way for Ritchin to segue out of the issue of Salgado's romanticism, but they don't resolve the big problem with his work—the unrelenting application of the lyric and the didactic to his subjects. His is not photography in which the facts are allowed to sing for themselves, which is how Lincoln Kirstein once described Walker Evans's work. Evans's approach to photojournalism was the polar opposite of Salgado's.

As Kirstein so trenchantly put it:

The most characteristic single feature of Evans's work is its purity, or even its puritanism. It is "straight" photography not only in technique but in the rigorous directness of its way of looking. . . . It is also the naked, difficult, solitary attitude of a member revolting from his own class, who knows best what in it must be uncovered, cauterized, and why. The view is clinical. Evans is a visual doctor, diagnostician rather than specialist. But he is also the family physician, quiet and dispassionate, before whom even very old or very sick people are no longer ashamed to reveal themselves.

There has been no need for Evans to dramatize his material with photographic tricks, because the material is already, in itself, intensely dramatic. Even the inanimate things, bureau drawers, pots, tires, bricks, signs, seem waiting in their own patient dignity, posing for their picture. The pictures of men and portraits of houses have only that "expression" which the experience of their society and times has imposed on them. The faces, even those tired, vicious, or content, are past reflecting accidental emotions. They are isolated and essentialized. The power of Evans's work lies in the fact that he so details the effect of circumstances on familiar specimens that the single face, the single house, the single street, strike with the strength of overwhelming numbers, the terrible cumulative force of thousands of faces, houses, and streets.

In general, Salgado's subjects are too much in the service of illustrating his various themes and notions to be allowed either to stand forth as individuals or to represent millions. He's a symbolist more than a portraitist—the people in his pictures remain strangers. It is true that what certain men, women, and children in the Sahel are suffering has overwhelmed them to such a point that they appear to be embodiments of hunger, thirst, and disease. Still, there are choices a photographer makes every time a picture is taken, and Salgado's strategies here consistently add up to aestheticization, not reportage.

．　．　．

While the Sahel photographs stand out because of their distorted humanism, they constitute only one chapter of Salgado's work. "An Uncertain Grace" is divided into four main sections. There's a section titled "Diverse Images," a nonthematically grouped collection of photographs taken between 1974 and 1987 in Asia, Africa, and Europe. There's a group from the worldwide project "The End of Manual Labor," begun in 1986. And then, under the heading "Other Americas," there's a gathering of images taken in Latin America between 1977 and 1984. In these portraits from Ecuador, Mexico, Bolivia, Peru, Brazil, and Guatemala, Salgado is just as hooked on displaying his artistry in matters of composition as he is in his African pictures. But here it is the picturesque that dominates, rather than beauty. (Actually, the African work, too, offers a number of images in which one can see Salgado pursuing picturesqueness. A couple of the photographs from the Sahel aren't all that different from the chic desert shots in Bertolucci's ponderous film *The Sheltering Sky*.) Some of Salgado's Latin American photographs recall images made by others—Bravo, Penn, Sander, Arbus—and his attraction to the cross motif really gets a workout in this section. But at least here the religious content is appropriate, not dragged in, the way it is in the African work. It's still empty, though, because it's still formulaic. Taken as a whole, the "Other Americas" images—men in ponchos, a village wedding, a fiddler, bright-eyed kids—have that special Salgado weightiness; they're making points, but not very original or interesting ones. And in the group called "Diverse Images" there are shots very similar to the work of earlier influential photographers such as Cartier-Bresson and Robert Capa. A 1976 photograph of a soldier running in the Spanish Sahara is so close in feeling, if not in detail, to Capa's famous Spanish Civil War picture *Loyalist Soldier, Spain, 1936* that it almost qualifies as a remake. It's possible, even probable, that Salgado intended his picture as an homage, but he is not a postmodernist appropriation artist, so it's hard to believe that all his derivative works are intended as quotes—certainly, that's not how they've been presented.

"The End of Manual Labor" is perhaps Salgado's largest-scale *Gesamtkunst-werk* to date. It already includes photographs taken in Cuba, Bangladesh, India, the Soviet Union, North America, South America, and France, and apparently Salgado plans to shoot in forty or fifty locations eventually. From Ritchin's text it appears that "The End of Manual Labor" is conceived literally as an homage to laborers—he tells us that the project is "a paean to the end of an era before robots, electronics, and computers take over production." No wonder that in their earnestness some of these images would look at home in corporate annual reports, or the *Fortune* magazine of the thirties. Occasionally, the content of a photograph—such as pigs waiting in a slaughterhouse—leads one to believe that the project may turn out to be deeper than it seems. But that hope may stem from the overall confusion in Salgado's work between what is actually present and what he intends.

Salgado himself seems to sense that there's more to his topic than celebrating the worker. Consider his alternative title: "The Archaeology of Industrialization." Nevertheless, unlike many works of art that deal with industrialization, Salgado's photographs are basically uncritical of its effects on human beings and on the environment. This is characteristic of his approach—it's his way of being "sentimental, nostalgic, heroic, lyrical," as Ritchin puts it. Such a romanticizing of this multilayered subject is almost breathtaking in its narrowness—particularly in the light of Salgado's supposed attunement to the lives of the powerless. His stiff photograph of a coal miner in India and his arty depiction of a silhouetted worker in an iron plant in the Soviet Union seem startlingly inadequate when looked at in the context of photographs that have been taken of subjects like these ever since industrialization went into gear. Compare Salgado's "Archaeology of Industrialization" with Lewis Hine's early-twentieth-century indictment of industrialization's inhumane use of lives. Hine was a photojournalist who did affect injustices: His photographs of children in factories and mills were so lucid and convincing that they can be credited with hastening the creation of America's child-labor laws. Salgado's work here, as in the Sahel, is too aestheticized, too caught up in itself, to fully acknowledge what's happening to others.

Within the workers series there is, however, one group of photographs that stun the viewer—the pictures of miners in Serra Pelada, in Brazil. Like the Sahel images, these have immediate power. They can evoke awe and horror, for they are of an immense human spectacle: thousands of men working a gargantuan gold mine. Visions of such waves of labor and physical exertion, of a mass of men so jammed together that their backs and sacks and legs look like a repeating pattern, are the stuff of nightmares and of wonder. But even these powerful pictures reveal Salgado's reliance on cliché. There's one shot, for instance, that looks like a gloss on Michelangelo's Sistine *Creation of Adam* and *E.T.*'s appropriation of it. When I first went to the "Uncertain Grace" exhibition, I had just seen the film *Spartacus,* and several of Salgado's other images recalled the more kitschy slave-crowd scenes in that movie. And his use of his favorite sign of the martyr and the miraculous—the cross—mirrors the climactic shots of Kubrick's movie, except that with Salgado there is no Tony Curtis and no Kirk Douglas.

When Salgado's admirers want to make the point that he understands what it is like to be outside the spheres of power, they bring up the fact that he lived in Brazil before moving to Paris. But since when did being a Brazilian qualify someone as the voice of Africa or of India—another assumption that creeps through the Salgado myth? A second aspect of Salgado's earlier life that buoys his reputation as a man deeply in touch with his themes is that he started out as an economist. Fred Ritchin explains in his text how Salgado made the transition from economics to photography: "It was while on a work assignment [for the International Coffee Organization] in Africa that he decided, on the basis of initial attempts with a camera he borrowed from his wife, that rather than work at the remove of a social scientist he preferred spending more time with the people he was drawn to, photographing them. He found that he could depict them more vividly in photographs than in economic reports." Vivid Salgado's photographs are, but the people in them, and the situations that he is supposedly penetrating, rarely are.

Actually, Salgado's most vivid image is one that is atypical of his work as it has progressed, and it's not about a subject that seems close to his heart. It's his "lucky break" picture: an on-the-scene shot of the attempted assassination of President Reagan. Salgado was tracking Reagan on an assignment from Fred Ritchin, who was then picture editor of *The New York Times Magazine,* and the famous photograph that he took in the instant after the bullets were fired is in almost every way the opposite of the imagery that has led to his current acclaim. It looks like something from a whodunnit movie: The image explodes with energy and action. The punch of the Reagan image comes from our realization that here is a figure of megapower made vulnerable before our eyes. The photographs that have made Salgado's reputation also have punch, but it comes from the pathos of the lives of his subjects.

And therein lies his power over the viewer. This is photography that runs on a kind of emotional blackmail fueled by a dramatics of art direction. Salgado undoubtedly gets away with so much because of viewers' sympathy and guilt. What is more terrible than someone starving? What is more tragic than a dead child so thin that his or her body looks like a stick wrapped in a piece of cloth? Unless we have no heart, when we see such things something happens to us. The feeling can last for a moment, it can last forever; it can make us want to help, and it can make us actually help. Salgado's work has produced all these reactions, but I believe that this speaks more for the power of his subjects than for the quality of his work. Two photographs in the "Kuwait Epilogue" exhibition were almost identical—of a bird covered with oil, drowning in it, as it were, since the bird could no longer fly. We had seen such images during the war; in fact, one just like it, taken by someone else, became a symbol of the madness that the Gulf War was. It is in keeping with Salgado's approach to his work that he picked up on such a "button pusher" of an image. But the button pushing may not end there. Salgado used the phrase *paradise lost* in a caption he wrote to go along with one of the bird pictures—and both his image and his reference to paradise reminded me of the more kitschy aspects of Eugene Smith's work. Smith used the phrase *paradise garden* in a title for a photograph, one that ranks among his most famous—and schmaltziest—images: Two small children walk hand in hand, in a forest, their backs to the viewer. This is greeting-card stuff; it became the emblem of Edward Steichen's "Family of Man" exhibition, and has been reproduced countless times in advertisements and as a greeting card. Some of Salgado's photographs have appeared in postcard form; as yet, they haven't been reproduced as greeting cards. But who knows? The manufactured poetry that is so dominant an aspect of his aesthetic could turn the people in the Sahel into emblems on greeting cards for all of us who want to express our humanity. These photographs are less than their subjects deserve. We can be sure that if truly appropriate images should ever surface they will not be so "beautiful" that they could work as packaged caring. Salgado's sentimentalism, for all its earnestness, isn't any kind of breakthrough. Unfortunately, his champions aggravate the bullying quality of his work by presenting it as if it were the Second Coming.

The New Yorker, September 9, 1991

Exposure

Last July, the up-and-coming menswear designer John Bartlett presented his new collection in a packed, sweltering loft in Chelsea. The two main themes were preppy with a twist and studied bohemianism. The slacks were ankle-high and the socks were sheer. One man wore a jacket, stiletto heels, and no pants; there was glitter makeup and lipstick; there were a few women, too, butched up and proud of it. Many of the male models looked as if they'd just stepped out of a Hockney painting or an Isherwood novel. Healthy-looking young men and the frank commercialization of homosexuality were part of the pitch. But the most striking model in the show was a tall, thin man in his late sixties, who, despite his ravaged features, was still handsome. The moment he stepped out on the runway, dressed in a gray windbreaker and navy pants, you could feel the audience sit up and take notice. You see sucked-in cheeks at fashion shows, but not the kind that people get when their teeth fall out and their faces cave in. His attitude was as dramatic as his appearance. "I may be old," his expression seemed to say, "but I'm cooler than all of you put together." Few in the audience that day knew his identity—*The New York Times,* in its review of the show, singled him out, without naming him, as "a white-haired man with wrinkles"—but those who did know had special reason to take notice. Three decades earlier, in another life, he had been the revolutionary fashion photographer Bob Richardson.

My introduction to Richardson's work occurred just a few years ago, when I came across a haunting picture in *Appearances,* a book about fashion photography, published in 1991, by the art historian Martin Harrison. The photograph, which originally appeared in French *Vogue* in 1967, didn't look anything like a typical fashion picture. It seemed so casually true to life that at

Bob Richardson, *Untitled,* 1967

first I took it to be just a color snapshot—a simple, melancholy memento of a day at the beach. On closer inspection, one could see that this was not the work of an amateur. A young woman and a man lie together on the sand—a couple very much uncoupled. The man is stretched out on his stomach, facing away and looking out to sea; the woman, in a cropped black tank top and shorts, reclines against his back, using his behind as a pillow, but you get the feeling that their touching is a matter of habit rather than of affection. The emotional distance between them, not what they are wearing, is the subject of the picture. A tear is crawling down the woman's left cheek.

If this photograph had been taken today, it would probably have a tough time getting by the editors at the fashion magazines, because it's not about pushing the goods, and it's "down." The woman—Donna Mitchell, who was one of Richardson's favorite models—is young and beautiful, but she has strong features, which convey character and introspection, not the malleable, blank beauty that fashion likes to promote. The picture is a completely convincing image, without a speck of sentimentality, and almost defiantly anticommercial. Below the model's bare midriff, near her crotch, a small cross dangles from a set of rosary beads clipped to a belt loop. The beads and the cross seem less like accessories than like tokens of an inner life. The image is desolate and sensual, and suffused with a mixture of superstition and faith. It made me want to touch wood.

In the sixties and the early seventies, Richardson was one of the edgiest talents in what was then a small international circle of fashion photographers. He worked in Paris, London, Milan, and New York, and in all kinds of exotic locations. Even though he had a reputation for being wild and exceptionally difficult, he earned the loyalty and respect of powerful art directors and editors. At the height of his fame, when he was jetting from one job to another, Richardson was the epitome of the photographer as cultural hero: He was successful *and* rebellious. But something more than ambition and rebellion were fueling his erratic behavior and repeated blowups. By the late seventies, many people in the fashion business considered him to be a monster—he'd been rude, he'd been overbearing, and he'd taken his problems out on others too many times. And then, after nearly two decades of doing work for the fashion magazines, he seemed to evaporate. In fact, he had gone to California, dropped out, and cut himself off from his family and everyone else he knew. He had hit bottom, and was homeless, living on the beach in Santa Monica.

Despite the books, the exhibitions, the curators, and a growing body of memoirs and reminiscences, the history of fashion photography is full of gaps and uncertainty. The sixties are particularly hazy. In the helter-skelter of the time, there were lots of casualties, and fashion was often disorderly and chaotic. Magazines were notoriously cavalier about preserving their archives, and in Richardson's case both the pictures he took and the clear outlines of his story are hard to come by.

In conversations with Richardson over several months, I occasionally got the feeling that he was saying and doing things for effect. Sometimes he appeared to be Bob Richardson *playing* Bob Richardson. He could be volatile and unfair; more often, he was frank, modest, insightful, and sensitive. For a while, he seemed to be torn between a desire to tell his real story and a combination of fear and anger and illness. Since I've come to know him, he's been on and off the wagon a number of times. After he agreed to let me write about him, there was the risk that he might sabotage the process at any minute, but he never did. He'd hang up the phone when he felt like it. Then he'd get in touch again, and be in a good mood and optimistic, and we'd go on until the next mess. The explosions seemed to coincide with the peaks of his frustration at not getting the work he wants—photographing for magazines and directing videos—and his frustration with his generally rootless existence. He can't afford an apartment of his own. He lives on Social Security, and what tiny income he has in addition derives from teaching photography and selling prints of a few of his pictures.

The word was that Richardson had become a drug addict and an alcoholic.

But he himself suggested to me that his problems had deeper roots. In his early forties, he told me, he had been found to have schizophrenia. At various times, he said, he had been treated with medication, hospitalized, and given electroshock therapy (which he believes has caused him to have lapses of memory). These days, he doesn't seem to be receiving any treatment, and he told me that, apart from marijuana, he long ago swore off drugs, legal and illegal. When he reported his schizophrenia, I thought that he had given me the key to his story. But nothing about Richardson is easy or clear.

The first time I interviewed Richardson, we met at a Chinese restaurant in the West Village. His innate sense of style and an aura of intensity held in reserve reminded me of the late trumpet player Chet Baker. His clothes are plain but hip. He was waiting for me when I arrived at the restaurant, and he was dressed in a duffel coat, a sweater, and jeans. He had ordered a glass of red wine, and after I sat down he pulled out a news clipping; it was Patric Walker's horoscope column from that day's *New York Post.* He read the predictions for our astrological signs. As I soon learned, he has a penchant for the melodramatic.

He leaned forward to tell me, "I was born in the Year of the Dragon. I'm a Capricorn. That means I've probably managed to stay alive out of spite. Nobody's ever asked me my side of the story. When you have all this scandal and tragedy stalking you all the time, nobody ever hears your side. And I'm normally too proud to tell. But I'll tell you. I know I'm not going to last much longer. I have a bad heart, I smoked myself to death and did a lot of other things that destroyed my face, but inside of me is a beautiful nineteen-year-old boy."

When Richardson was a nineteen-year-old boy, in 1947, he was studying at the Parsons School of Design, in New York, in preparation for a career as an artist. It took almost fifteen years before he settled on photography as the best way to express himself. Robert George Richardson was born in Brooklyn in

1928 to Irish Catholic parents. In the early 1930s, his family moved to Rockville Centre, Long Island, and that is where he grew up. After high school, he went to Parsons and the Pratt Institute; dropped out of both; married the girl he had been going out with in high school, Barbara Mead; and had various jobs connected with the fashion industry. In 1951, he was drafted into the army, and served in Korea. When he got out of the army, he and his wife had a daughter, Margaret, but the marriage soon fell apart. Richardson says that by his mid-twenties he had undergone a series of crack-ups, and that his ignorance of the cause persisted for the next two decades. He continued to work in fashion, and the jobs included designing textile patterns and creating department-store window displays—"like Andy Warhol," he says. In the mid-fifties, he hit the road for California.

In Los Angeles, Richardson discovered photography. A wealthy friend gave him a camera, and he took a picture of his friend's table after a long lunch, with an empty wine bottle, an ashtray with a cigarette butt, and other remains of the meal. Richardson says that it was a moment of recognition: He had found his vocation. "It all came out with the camera," he recalls. He wasn't content with still lifes, however. In the late fifties, he returned to New York for a time, and then made his first extended trip to Paris. By the time he came back to New York, he had decided to become a great fashion photographer and, as he puts it, "photograph my kind of woman." He had also settled down with a young actress named Norma Kessler, and she eventually became his second wife. (In 1965, they had a son, Terry, who is now a photographer in New York.) In 1963, after serving a short apprenticeship as an assistant to Dick Hyman, a successful commercial photographer, he got his first fashion assignment, for *Harper's Bazaar.* He says that he was drawn to the magazine by his admiration for the famous art director Marvin Israel, and he recalls their meetings as seminal moments in his education as a magazine photographer. Apparently, Israel's critique of his first pictures was crucial, and he began to find his identity as a photographer.

. . .

Right away, Richardson did attention-getting, formula-smashing work for *Harper's Bazaar.* He had landed his first assignments at a propitious moment. The magazine's innovative art director, Alexey Brodovitch (Richardson had studied with him in a master class), had left in 1958, and Israel, who had come to *Harper's Bazaar* in 1961, and whose support and admiration had been of deep importance to Diane Arbus, Richard Avedon, and many others, was fired shortly after Richardson arrived on the scene. Even though Richardson often cites Israel as his mentor, in fact it was two women—the new art directors, Ruth Ansel and Bea Feitler—who commissioned Richardson's first portfolio and made the case for him, persuading Nancy White, the editor of *Harper's Bazaar,* to publish his work for the next three years.

Ansel remarked to me that Nancy White "went to church to say her novenas every time she saw a sexy picture." Richardson must have caused her to recite a lot of prayers. "Fashion always seemed so artificial, and I never liked that," he says. "I wanted to put reality in my photographs. Sex, drugs, and rock and roll—that's what was happening. And I was going to help make it happen. Boy, they did not want that in America. Some of those editors were still wearing white gloves to couture." Nancy White may have been from the old school, but her two art directors took their predecessors' farsighted ideas and ran with them. Moreover, Ansel and Feitler *got* Richardson's work: It spoke to their lives, not necessarily in obvious ways, but in profound ways. The women's movement and the counterculture were bubbling beneath the surface, undefined, yet Ansel and Feitler sensed that Richardson was managing to point to changes that would eventually sweep through the culture.

The two art directors entrusted Richardson to a young editor named Deborah Turbeville, who would go on to become a significant fashion photographer herself. Because she had a taste for the moody and the uncanny, she was the perfect editor for Richardson. She had been put in charge of a section of the magazine called "The Fashion Independent," where a freewheeling, experimental approach was encouraged. Diane Arbus did some remarkable work for that section, but the first photographer Turbeville worked with on it was Richardson.

"Bea and Ruth told me, 'Remember, we want very important photographs,'" Turbeville recalled recently. "They asked what I'd like to do, and I'd thought maybe it would be fun to do a child. So they replied, 'Fine, but this is *Harper's Bazaar.* The photographer has to be someone who *really* addresses his subject and takes it seriously.' Then they told me there was someone they were incredibly excited about. His name was Bob Richardson."

Turbeville remembers Richardson as "a skinny, gangly guy with curly hair and gaps between his teeth," and says, "I was very impressed with him. He was articulate, he had a sense of drama, he was very forceful, and he could be *very* charming. He went to see the six-year-old girl we had chosen for the shoot, and afterward he called me up and said, 'She's very sexy, and she has amazing charisma. I think that we should do her in a little woolen coat in the winter by herself in the park.' When we did the shoot, he *directed* this child. He would tell her, 'I think we should play Monkey See, Monkey Do.' He'd say, 'Curl up your feet, like this,' and her little bare feet would twist the way he showed her. Beautiful photographs came out of it. *Everybody* loved them."

Not long afterward, Richardson and Turbeville collaborated on another shoot featuring children, for a spread called "The Littlest Americans in Spain." Some of the shots were done in what Turbeville describes as "a decadent villa in Madrid, on the most decadent bed I've ever seen, with about ten crucifixes and photographs of the Duke and Duchess of Windsor all over the walls."

The pictures that resulted are brilliant—naughty, witty, and knowing. Like Lewis Carroll's photographs of children, they bring out a quality of seriousness that is usually attributed only to adults. Richardson shows that it belongs to his young subjects as well, but the shots also provoke the full range of responses to children depicted in ways that can be interpreted as sexual. There is a beautiful and disturbing nude of the four-year-old Caroline Smitter. In another picture, she is coiffed and dolled up like Brigitte Bardot, and in another, her sister, Victoria, and her brother, Matthew, are dressed up and posed to look like children whose rich parents have left them to find their own impertinent amusements. There is a shot that shows Victoria leading what the caption calls "a flock of priests"—a sly reversal of the way things are usually seen. Children in Richardson's photographs have *presence.* They are depicted not as decorative objects but as subjects of immense import. In other stories, Richardson's solemn images of children rank with the nineteenth-century masterpieces of Julia Margaret Cameron. Richardson says that all his pictures are self-portraits, but he singles out his photographs of kids as the truest mirror images.

Richardson's first period at *Harper's Bazaar* came to an end in 1966, when Ansel and Feitler stopped giving him assignments. (He took pictures for the magazine again in the late sixties and in the early seventies.) Even though his drug habit was well known—he'd talk about his speed doctor, for example— Ansel says that drugs were not an issue in the split. "A lot of people were doing drugs," she says. "Some people discussed it, and some didn't." The problem was that Richardson and the editors had got sick of each other. Depending on whom you talk to, Richardson in his heyday—the sixties and seventies—was a genius or a manipulative pain in the ass. Richardson himself views the editors he worked with as ranging from brilliant to stupid. In any case, after he had spent three years at *Harper's Bazaar* everyone had had enough. He wrote a vindictive letter to Nancy White and went over to the competition, at Condé Nast.

Richardson started to spend the bulk of his time working in Europe. He wanted to kick the drugs, and several times in 1966 and 1967 he went to a sanatorium outside Paris and took a "sleeping cure"—a regimen of tranquilizers and bed rest. He says that this treatment was the only thing that ever got him clean—for a while, at least—until he finally "bummed out," in the eighties, and tried to recover alone.

His greatest feature dates from this period. It was shot in Greece in 1967, for a sixteen-page spread in French *Vogue*. It hardly seems to be a fashion spread at all; it's more like scenes from an extraordinarily passionate life. The protagonist of Richardson's story is Donna Mitchell. She is seen dancing with abandon in the Baboulas tavern, in Rhodes. She contemplates candles in a church, plays with a naked toddler (Richardson's son, Terry) in a bathtub, does her makeup, and walks through the streets as if in mourning. On a rocky shore, she lies supine as a godlike nude swimmer emerges from the water at her feet (and then makes love to her, we're supposed to think). One of the shots in this Greek spread is the picture of Mitchell crying on the beach that was reproduced in *Appearances*. Mitchell wears designs by Christian Dior and Daniel Hechter, among others, but as we look at the pictures we're aware of fashion only indirectly. The overwhelming impression is one of emotional richness and physical actuality. Richardson managed to convey a sense of place, of real lives, of sex and joy and loneliness and broken trust. Richardson's wife, Norma, helped him; there were no editors or assistants along on the trip.

Joan Juliet Buck, who is now the editor of French *Vogue,* remembers seeing Richardson's Greek pictures when they were published, in the spring of 1967. She was eighteen at the time. "I was completely knocked out," she told me. "It was just before the Summer of Love. Our mothers wore those sleeveless dresses that seemed to be made out of cement. And even the new clothes by Courrèges and Ungaro were very structured. Richardson's pictures had the opposite feeling. They said, 'This is what I can be: I can be sad, I can be involved, I can relate, I can be sexual.' In those pictures, there was light—a world where sex and style didn't cancel each other out. They were destiny photographs."

Indeed, those photographs conveyed some essential qualities of the sixties: the drugginess, the sexual freedom, the growing gulf between men and women. Without clichés or fake grooviness, Richardson put these elements into fashion photography. Like Buck, the fashion photographer Steven Meisel remembers encountering Richardson's work when he was very young. "I was in the sixth or

seventh grade, around 1968," Meisel says, "and the minute I looked at his pictures, although I wasn't aware of what I was seeing, I knew there was *something* that stood out. Now I realize that, in addition to everything else, the photographs have an intoxicated feeling. The youth thing and the drug thing—it's all there. The greasy black eyelids that the models used then—they're a big thing again now—gave you the feeling that the girls were so zonked out that they could barely keep their eyes open. There were *guys* with black eye makeup in his pictures, too. The women he photographed were unusual beauties, and they often looked as if they were lost, desolate, or frightened. Once, when I was in ninth grade, I saw Donna Mitchell on the street. It was drizzling, her hair was frizzy, and she had on a black cape. She looked like a Bob Richardson picture waiting to happen."

Though Richardson says he doesn't remember a lot of what he created, he has a clear recollection of his general aims. He was succeeding at bringing "my kind of woman" into the fashion magazines. "People say I am someone who brought reality into fashion photography," he explains. "Schizophrenics are critically aware of reality. In fact, a schizophrenic's awareness is so intense that he tries to escape from it—sometimes into fantasies—in order to survive. I'm sure that's why I became an artist in the first place. I brought me into my pictures. Nobody else could do that, because nobody else *was* me."

His style had its cost. Over the years, there were nightmarish shoots, marked by tantrums, feuds, and other lavish displays of temperament. Some of the craziness and drama was funny. Editors were locked in dressing rooms, dropped off in the middle of nowhere, or subjected to sudden, expensive whims. (Once, Richardson decided to photograph the models and the clothes underwater, because they looked so much better in the soft blue light.) He may have terrorized some editors, but others loved working with him.

To a certain degree, Richardson faced what every commercial photographer faces. A lot of his work ended up unpublished. "I lived on the cutting-room floor," he says. "It was my home away from home." Mainstream magazines have always been afraid of too much sex, too much edge, too much body, too much pain, too much sickness—too much of anything, in fact, that seems as if it might scare readers away. It was no accident that many of Richardson's most provocative pictures appeared in European magazines. And even though a lot of his work was killed, some of his fellow photographers recognized the significance of his mission. Richard Avedon recalls, "There was a moment in the history of fashion photography when the turbulent woman, reckless in her lassitude, became heroic. She let herself be used by life, and looked it, and that was the essence of her beauty. That moment was brief. When it ended, some of us adapted. Richardson refused."

He was continuing to find work, but that wasn't much comfort. "The success of my photographs didn't mean much to me, because I knew I was not going to be able to keep doing the things I was doing," Richardson told me. "I knew I couldn't

Bob Richardson, *Untitled,* 1967

sustain it. Every once in a while, my life would fall apart and I'd go bananas. I wound up, again and again, in a straitjacket. After a doctor finally told me that I had schizophrenia, I was put on medication. Then another doctor gave me an experimental drug, and then yanked me off it and tried another one on me. That's the way it is for people with this disease. I'll never take another drug for it."

But there was a time when Richardson was willing to try anything. By the mid-sixties, getting high had become a way of life. He took speed and heroin and cocaine and everything in between.

"The first time I got stoned, it totally changed my life," Richardson recalls. "And it changed my photography, that's for sure. A model I'd been working with got me high on marijuana. Later on, she took me to see Max Jacobson—the famous Dr. Feelgood. Everybody went to him. He showed me how to skin-pop and mainline speed. Other doctors prescribed legal drugs for me, and I got hooked on those, too—on Valiums, on sleeping pills. That's the way it goes. If you're frightened, you take something to take away the fear, and if you're too nervous you take something to calm down, and if you can't sleep you take something for that. I was shooting up all day long, and then at night we'd go out to dinner, but I could never eat, because the drugs take your appetite away. After that, we'd go to clubs, and then finally come home, and then I'd start to edit the whole day's film. How long can a human being do that, day after day, night after night? It wasn't only me—the times were like that. People were passing out at my sittings, and often it had nothing to do with me, but once you get a bad reputation, everything is blamed on you."

As Richardson remarks, plenty of people were experimenting with drugs, and that is probably why it was so hard for people to see that he was in deep trouble, and wasn't just living the lifestyle of the moment.

Still, no matter how far out of control things got, Richardson always nurtured his talent for bonding with his models. It was an approach that made his shoots more dramatic than most. In 1969, Joan Juliet Buck was working for Julie Britt, a fashion editor at *Glamour,* who did a lot of shoots with Richardson. Buck assisted Britt on an issue about college girls. She accompanied Richardson to a field on Staten Island, and there, she says, the photographer labored mightily to portray the student models "as creatures of deep poetic weight." She remembers Richardson asking one of the young women he was photographing "to pick up the earth and hold it up to God." The approach was guaranteed to impress a young person of those times. Buck says that he was very Dylanesque—that he talked a lot about integrity, ideals, ethics, and the importance of not selling out. He still does.

Not long after the Staten Island shoot, Anjelica Huston, who was eighteen at the time, and whose mother had died a few months before in a car crash, came to New York to stay with Buck. The two girls had grown up together, and were as close as sisters. When *Harper's Bazaar* asked her to set up a photography session with Huston, Buck suggested Richardson for the job. The forty-one-year-old photographer and his young model began a four-year romance and an important artistic collaboration. Soon after Richardson met Huston, he and his second wife, Norma, divorced.

His involvement with Huston wasn't his first extramarital affair. An editor told me that she remembers Bob and Norma as the Scott and Zelda of their time. And Richardson is open and matter-of-fact about all this. "Sex became a raging thing inside me," he said. "It absolutely overwhelmed me. It was part of my working structure. Often a session would wind up with sex." When I asked him if his experience was typical, he replied, "There was nobody cooler than me." He had no difficulty explaining how actual sex and mental sex played a part in his photography. "My secret for taking many of those good photographs was turning people on, and getting them so freaked out before I took the picture that I got it almost immediately," he said. It may have been an economical way to use film, but it was not the key to domestic bliss.

According to many witnesses, Richardson and Huston had a tempestuous, consuming relationship, but the affair also produced some of Richardson's greatest portraits and fashion photographs. A number of these pictures convey that intoxicated feeling that Meisel describes. On a visit to England, Richardson made an unforgettable image of Huston standing between two horses: She has the same feral beauty as the animals. Richardson also concocted an eye-popping color photograph of Huston in a big hat, and one with Huston, a second woman, and Serge Lutens—the art director, who was a makeup artist at the time—in a photographic studio. The woman, who is sitting fussing at Huston, is meant to portray an editor, while Huston plays the part of the model. The trio is surrounded by camera lights and photography equipment, which make for a kind of behind-the-scenes view, a peek at the inner world of fashion. Richardson's approach, however, is different from the kind of backstage shot that is ubiquitous now. His is like a critique of fashion, and it's almost surreal.

Richardson's relationship with Huston ended in 1973, and when one looks at the photographs that followed it's hard not to think that the breakup marked a turning point. (According to Richardson, he lost contact with his first wife and his daughter around this time; he says that he hasn't heard from them since and has no idea where they are living.) He continued to work for six more years—for American *Vogue, Mademoiselle, Glamour, Harper's Bazaar,* and other magazines. By and large, his photography became dutifully professional. Once in a while, there's that old Richardson verve, but for the most part the spirit, the originality, and the passion are gone. And, soon, so was he. He says that his sickness—compounded by years of drug abuse and the stress of his career—had finally made the old life impossible.

"I kept going for years, but I had lost interest—it vanished," Richardson said. "It was like waking up one morning and finding yourself all alone and wondering what you're going to do. In the end, I just gave up. I'd been taking lousy photographs, and I didn't want to work anymore. I think I wanted to find out if I wanted to live or if I wanted to die." In the late seventies, acquaintances used to see him hanging around Gramercy Park, near where he lived. He was clearly unstable. One day, in 1982, he seemed to simply disappear.

"I left for California," Richardson told me. "Somehow, I knew I was going to end up living on the street." For a while, he moved around Southern California. Not long after he arrived, his son, Terry, who was eighteen, visited him in a run-down motel in San Diego. Terry was living in Hollywood at the time, and a few months later he took his father in, but they argued, and Terry asked his father to go. "He told me to get lost," Richardson recalls. "There are times when nobody can help you but yourself. I left my Louis Vuitton suitcase, filled with all my nice warm clothes, at his house, and that was it. I see now that I had to follow this road into hell and go all the way through it."

When he talked about his experience of being homeless in Southern California, it was the only time he said we had hit on a subject that was difficult for him to discuss. There were harrowing interludes of humiliation and discomfort, and he endured being filthy and hungry and scared. He said he found that it was safer to sleep during the day, in order to stay alert at night. He was arrested for stealing a blanket from a car, and spent time in jail. He drank: He said, with wistful sincerity, that his dearest friend during this period was a bottle with the names Ernest and Julio Gallo on it. But there were also strange encounters with his former life. Wandering around Santa Monica at night, he would peer into well-lit galleries and see pictures by photographers he'd known. Being homeless didn't change his standards. "I'd often wonder how they could do the same thing over and over again," Richardson said. "No wonder I'm crazy, I'd think. At least I'm not stupid like some of the photographers my age who are just repeating themselves." He once found himself standing in front of a theater in Hollywood, and discovered that Anjelica Huston was starring there in a play, about the painter Tamara de Lempicka. He spent the next few days in the neighborhood, hanging out and sleeping in Huston's vicinity.

Terry Richardson says that his father was homeless for about two years altogether. At one point, the son arranged for his father to move into an apartment, but he soon abandoned it for the streets again. Richardson seemed to be living by his wits, and occasionally hooking up with strangers. He once called Terry from jail; he said that he had been living with "a millionaire guy" who had got fed up with him and had summoned the police to get rid of him. Another time, he called from a pay phone on Hollywood Boulevard and said he'd been attacked. Terry went to pick him up. "He was all bruised up," Terry told me. "He looked and smelled like he'd been living on the street—like a homeless person, which is what he had become."

"What ultimately saved me," Richardson says, "was that I started going to the library in Santa Monica every day and reading everything I could about schizophrenia. Finally, I had a way of understanding what had been going on inside me all these years." He took another big step when he walked into an unemployment office and asked for work. Eventually, he ended up in San Francisco, doing odd jobs, driving delivery trucks, and living in an SRO hotel in Chinatown.

Richardson might never have come back to New York to try and start again if it hadn't been for Martin Harrison's obsessive determination to find him. Harrison, an English art historian, was researching the history of fashion photography in the sixties, and Richard Avedon kept bringing up Richardson's name and praising his work, but when Harrison tried to find the photographer and his photographs, he discovered that both seemed to have disappeared. Then, in 1989, Harrison tracked down Richardson's son and also Richardson's second wife, Norma, who had changed her name to Annie Lomax. They knew that Richardson was living in the SRO hotel, but Richardson wouldn't respond to messages that Harrison left there, or reply to letters he wrote. Harrison got on a plane and went to California to try his luck in person.

"The hotel was a spooky place," Harrison recalled. "I knocked on Bob's door, and he opened it and said something like 'I don't want to be rude, but I don't want to be in your show, and I don't want to be in your book. I'm not interested in my old pictures.' I wanted to burst out crying. But then he lit up a cigarette. I'm a smoker, too, and when someone lights up a cigarette it's an invitation to share about seven minutes of killing yourself. I joined him, and that sort of did the trick. He invited me into his room. There was a bed, a sink, a tiny wardrobe, and there were newspaper photographs all over the walls. He had tacked up a Kertész poster and a picture by Bruce Weber torn out of a magazine. After a while, I pulled out some photocopies of his work, and he'd say things like 'God, I was awful.' But mixed in with the self-deprecation was a definite sense of professional self-esteem."

That visit resulted in a few of Richardson's pictures being published in *Appearances,* Harrison's enormous book. The book gave him recognition of a kind he hadn't had in years. Meanwhile, Terry Richardson, who had started to take pictures himself, moved to San Francisco, and he and his father began to spend time together, with the older man teaching the younger. In 1992, Terry moved to New York. A few months later, his father followed him back to the city he had deserted ten years earlier. Soon, Richardson was going around town saying that he and his son were a photography team: the Richardsons.

When the news that Bob Richardson was back began to circulate, some old friends and colleagues were amazed and others were horrified. There were also those who were glad to see him alive and healthy, and were ready to do what they could for him. Richard Avedon and Steven Meisel helped him get teaching jobs at the International Center of Photography and at the School of Visual Arts. He and his son together completed several assignments, including projects for *Town & Country* and one for *Interview,* the magazine I edit. (Recently, the two have gone their separate ways professionally.) On his own, Richardson has directed a rock-music video for a New Jersey band called Negative Male

Child, and a contemporary video adaptation of *Sweet Bird of Youth,* starring Donna Mitchell, for *Mirabella,* which published stills from the video as a fashion feature. Both videos contain something of Richardson's old photographic vision and themes—drama, sex, fights, tension, and fashion—but they also seem to revisit old territory; the clothes may be new, but the results really aren't.

Richardson is still living an economically marginal existence. He stays in fleabag hotels and borrowed apartments. He isn't nostalgic about the penthouses, the state-of-the-art studios, or the twenty-four-hour limousines of his old life. The one thing that he does seem nostalgic about is the days when he could get all the sex he wanted. He likes to talk about his need for young lovers, and he says that he is bisexual, that he has always been interested in both women and men but didn't advertise it.

Richardson views the modest revival of interest in his past work with pleasure but also with detachment. For a long time, he didn't own a single one of his photographs—he lost everything when he became homeless—but two friends liberated some of his old negatives from the storage closets of various Condé Nast magazines in Europe. Steven Meisel may have the largest "official" collection of Richardsons in the world, and he has only about eight prints. Two new prints of Richardson photographs are now on display at the Staley-Wise Gallery, as part of a show of color fashion photography since the sixties. Still, the only way to see more than a few of Richardson's pictures is to find vintage copies or bound volumes of the various fashion magazines he did work for. Someday, I hope, there will be a retrospective of his photographs, but the task of finding and assembling them will be herculean.

Richardson's recent activities don't really add up to a second career in photography. When he worked with Terry, it was Terry who actually took the shots. Although Richardson has spoken to me at length about pictures he says he took when he lived in San Francisco and after he returned to New York, he has been unwilling to show me any new photographs. I repeatedly expressed my interest in seeing them, but there were always reasons that he couldn't let me look at them: He had no money to make the prints, or he was dissatisfied with the results. Richardson's critical abilities are very sharp when it comes to his own work. He once told me, "I used to be afraid of doing mediocre photographs, and in the end I did just that." He certainly has no illusions that he created one fantastic picture after another, even in his prime, yet his self-criticism may be too sharp.

He complains a lot about not getting the work he wants, about not getting to do more videos and photography projects. But Richardson's story is more complicated than that of someone trying to have a second chance for success. It may be that his fear is stronger than the passion he says he has for photography. In fact, he may not be ready to get behind the camera again. He may be terrified that he will be terribly disappointed when it comes down to just him and a camera, two old friends who know each other well. He may be afraid that the world will be disappointed by his new work. I recently asked him, point-blank, "What would you do if some magazine editor suddenly said, 'Okay, Bob, here's an assignment for you—just you. What do you say?'"

Richardson looked me straight in the eye for a few seconds. Then he replied, "I would answer, 'I've been rehearsing for ten years. Is that long enough? I know all the mistakes I made, and I'm really sorry. I've been to confession and I've received Holy Communion. When are you going to absolve me? If I can forgive you for being vulgar, for not being as bright as me, can't you forgive me?'"

I think the real question may be, Can he forgive himself? Just before this issue went to press, Richardson seemed to be on the verge of sending the magazine a new self-portrait. Instead, he sent the recent portrait, by another photographer, that appears in this article. The portrait arrived with a note from Richardson explaining why he substituted someone else's work for his own. "When I looked at my self-portrait," he wrote, "I couldn't bear the look in my eyes."

The New Yorker, April 10, 1995

A Picture of One's Own

The last time I saw John Ropetzoh was at the Johannesburg Railway Station, in July 1961. As far as I know, there is no photograph that has survived of this man, and I am spelling his last name out phonetically because it was really a tribal name. The most honest way to describe John's official status would be "servant," which was why he was standing off by himself that day at the station, and not in the company of the relatives and other friends who had come to see our family off, as we began the journey of our immigration to the new lives that were ahead of us.

Even though John in private had become the other father of our family, a new life wasn't an option for him. The law forbade it, just like it forbade the kind of close feelings that really went on in our household with John. By government rules he had to stay behind, just as he had to stand behind the group that day at the station. In fact, it was even an issue that John, a black man, was there at all as a member of the group that was sending us off.

The train hooted and there was only a minute or two left before the wheels started turning. Nobody said out loud that we were leaving for good. It was John Ro-pet-zoh's face that made me understand the forever part. My mother never liked pretending, so of course her eyes had landed where the portrait of the truth was: John. As her nine-year-old daughter, my eyes tended to follow where her eyes went, so I was watching John, too. If anybody had had a camera, the portrait of John in those last few minutes would have looked like this: a largish man in his sixties, dressed in his Sunday best, weeping, the tears glistening up his African black skin.

The last whistle went, the chug-chugging started, and didn't stop for two days. At Cape Town, we boarded a ship to England. It was a crossing that lasted two weeks, and John and what would happen to him was a topic we spoke of often.

I remember mourning the fact that I didn't have a picture of him. After that, we only heard from him once. It was almost miraculous that we got the one letter we did. He'd put the stamps inside the envelope instead of on the outside, and somehow the mailman had delivered it to us anyway. It said that he was leaving Johannesburg and going to work in the mines because he had lost us, his family.

Soon, my sense of connection to South Africa disconnected. Unlike John, who could never exercise the option of rage, I went all the way with it as far as South Africa was concerned by the time I was a teenager. My anger that a government would do what that one did, with its inhumane policies of apartheid, made it that I cut myself off from being a South African.

Twenty-five years later, Nelson Mandela got out of prison on Robben Island, and it wasn't long before South Africa had begun to transform itself into a democracy under Mandela. The country that had so betrayed human rights had turned into a place of mass collective hope. For many ex–South Africans it became possible to connect with the country in our hearts at least—there was a chance they wouldn't be broken again. And also for many non–South Africans it became possible for the first time in decades to think about visiting the place without feeling like one was condoning evil.

When Bruce Weber went there to photograph and we were talking about it, I remembered something that I had not really thought about since our train ride: that I don't have a single personal picture from when we lived there. But for years after our family had left South Africa, I'd had an image in my mind that sat there like a dream. In it, I was the child of a Bantu tribe. For more than thirty years, I believed that this flash that I'd get of being with a group of Bantu men, women, and children was something that I'd imagined. As I'd gone on, I'd treated it as a fantasy, even as a product of guilt; I'd come to understand it as a way I'd disassociated myself from the bad nationalist white guys and rewritten things so I could be with those whose lives had haunted me in all sorts of ways. This notion that I'd made up the story didn't arrive all by itself. When I was younger and first spoke about this feeling I'd had of being far from home, and with a man in tribal dress, I'd been told that it had never happened. I am sure that this denial was the result of an effort to make me unafraid. What had really happened could terrify a kid, not because of who it happened with, but that it had happened in the first place. In fact, the truth is that I had crawled away from our front yard, where I was meant to be under supervision but wasn't. And I had been found a ways down from our house by a Bantu man who returned me to my family—but only after some hours, because he'd been afraid of being accused of stealing me.

When I finally discovered the truth behind this image that had for so long seemed like a product of fantasy, it was like finding a missing piece of my life. I started to wish that there was a photograph of the man who had rescued me. I'm sure a picture would help bring back a day that I have been searching for all these years. To me, it would be a priceless gift. And when Weber showed me the boxes of pictures that he had from his trip, it was as if someone had given me the same kind of present.

Although Weber's photographs of South Africa can't show me that particular man, or that particular day, his work is all about the gift that photography can be for people. Whether it's for an ad, for a magazine assignment, or for a project for himself, when Weber's photographing, no matter who the people are, he always says that he wants his subjects and the audience to be able to remember the day in which they were taken.

When I look at Weber's pictures of South Africa, I often think about my rescuer, and about John Ro-pet-zoh, and the last time we saw him. Weber's pictures have a personal feeling, and many of them seem to open out into stories. Now that I'm older, I know what it was that made John so inspiring to all of us to whom he meant so much. In essence, it was his dignity, his grace,

Bruce Weber, *Cape Town, South Africa,* 1995

and his victorious transcendence of anger. You see these same qualities, and the same victory in many of the portraits that Weber ended up taking when he was in South Africa. You see a particular kind of deep beauty in the faces of its people. Whether it's his shots of the great Mandela, or his series about some kids who are struggling to keep their boxing club alive—it's a beauty that made all the hate seem all the more hateful.

Branded Youth and Other Stories, 1997

Kid Haring

When you're young
You find inspiration
In anyone who's ever gone
And opened up a closing door
She said, "We were never feeling bored."
Cause we were never being boring
We had too much time to find
For ourselves
And we were never being boring
We dressed up in faults
And faults make amends
And we were never holding back,
Worried that
Time would come to an end.
—From "Being Boring," by Chris Lowe and Neil Tennant

For decades now, New York has been stereotyped as the place for those seeking a place. But Keith Haring, the boy from Kutztown, Pennsylvania, who would become an art icon of the eighties, needed less and more. As an artist, he connected emotionally naturally; his images became internationally recognizable in a heartbeat. Yet as a gay kid brought up, like most, with an essential component of himself under wraps, he needed a home, a place where his uncensored self could really emerge.

New York gave him that because of the moment when he arrived. Haring hit the city in the late seventies. He needed to join the dance.

Tseng Kwong Chi, *Keith Haring, New York Subway,* 1983

And they were dancing.

Keith Haring's struggle for recognition as a "serious" artist was not won in his lifetime. But he is the kind of lively figure who calls the importance of "seriousness" into question. The real communities that nourished Haring had little to do with dealers, curators, collectors, or critics. Despite the flashes of support from art powers, the safety, comfort, and sense of connection that freed him and spurred him on came from the work itself, kids, other artists, and the life he found in the heart of gay New York.

Some of his most characteristic imagery involved figures twirling around and playing together, happy but never aimless. To understand why such uncomplicated and effortless-looking art is actually meaningful, one needs to look at it all in conjunction with Haring's story, gay lives, and a specific moment in time. It is easier now, with some years elapsed, to sort out. Haring's legacy is the joy of a spirit, once restrained, taking flight and making leaps. Dancing safely, *finally.*

And in Haring's later work we can feel the safety give way to danger and loss.

Born in 1958, Keith Haring had a churchy, pie-baking, your-parents-and-country-are-always-right upbringing. "We were staunch disciplinarians," his father, Allen Haring, says. But Keith was no Beaver Cleaver Little Leaguer. He didn't take to all-American boyhood.

Mr. Haring worried about his son's lack of stick-to-itiveness. Drawing and doodling were this boy's life, but from early on he had little interest in the purely representational. He didn't see things straight, as it were—he went for cartoons, that lightly subversive pop form. He would grow up to look like one himself—a caricature of normalcy, a Cub Scout askew.

Haring's youthful ambition was to work for Walt Disney. But he also believed in his destiny as a "fine," as opposed to "commercial," artist. He saved jottings in notebooks maintained in pristine condition, and in the eighth grade signed his name twice in the school record. (He noted that the more glamorous version was his "art signature.") By Haring's sixteenth birthday, his parents, Allen and Joan—deep-rooted in several generations of the Pennsylvania Dutch—thought Keith had gone haywire. No more the kid who looked like a baby Buddy Holly. First he was a Jesus freak. Then came drugs. Not the example his parents had planned for his three kid sisters. Not the White Picket Path.

Instead of attending his high school baccalaureate in June 1976, Haring hotfooted it to the Jersey Shore. Then he headed off for art college in Pittsburgh, quit, and drove cross-country with his girlfriend. In San Francisco, where you could smell sex in the breeze, he looked at a guy. The guy looked back. It probably wasn't the first time such glances had been exchanged. But San Francisco '76 seems to mark the end of Haring and girlfriends.

Upon his return to Pittsburgh there were odd jobs, classes to zone out in—and a boost when the Pittsburgh Arts and Crafts Center gave a show of his work. None of that was enough.

Allen Haring was worried. But if God insisted that his only son be delivered into a Life of Starvation and Failure—in the form of Manhattan's School of Visual Arts, on East Twenty-third Street—he would do the driving! Though the trip from Kutztown took just a few hours, the Harings had routinely avoided the metropolis, and Keith's father was not certain about where it was legal to park. Keith was dropped off on a curb outside the YMCA (where Allen, who had dutifully paid the tuition to SVA, determined his son should stay). His dad can't get over it now: "*Where was I?*—dumping him in the middle of New York City, putting him on the sidewalk with his boxes of belongings. I couldn't even go in with him. I didn't want to leave the car."

Keith arrived in 1978 with a few basics: a certainty about making himself an artist, uncertainty about everything else—and a lively shot of talent. I always think of him as the "Smalltown Boy" in that Bronski Beat song. Before more than a few years had passed, he had established a reputation as an up-and-comer in a scene where the newest urgent ambition was "to mix things up." A budding synergy of visual art forms, music, film, and performance combined with a need to incorporate the textures and politics of real life was shaking out old postures and dried-up intellectualized expectations; Haring had neither. But by the early eighties he had all kinds of friends in the art hoods and on the dance floor; one was the ambitious, not so blond Madonna, who shared what a friend called his "jungle fever." According to club owner and DJ Johnny Dynell, who worked with Madonna when she was a coat-check girl at Danceteria in the early eighties, she and Keith always clicked. "Haring would get boys from Madonna."

Without shedding his geek look, Keith Haring eventually became a media star befriended by Yoko, Princess Caroline, Timothy Leary, and William Burroughs, not to mention rock stars, designers, and a publicist's dream list of the hip and glamorous. Haring definitely seemed seduced. But he remained Keith.

He did it all in a short time, because a short time was all he had. In 1990, at the age of thirty-one, he died of AIDS, leaving more art than most octogenarians. In his vast, multifaceted body of work, you can see one still rarely represented chapter of our very modern times. Julia Gruen, who worked with Haring for six years and who now runs the Keith Haring Foundation, remarks, "This is what differentiates Keith from the other artists; he incorporated so much of what was going on day to day in his life, and in all of our lives." Charged with the energy and rhythms of American pop, he worked with confidence, unwavering purpose, and dazzling speed. Those who saw him create were amazed at how quickly he tossed off images; to belabor was to risk the pure exuberance and spontaneous feeling he so often transmitted. He was not one of those guys who sweated over a handful of canvases per year. No—he kept it moving, making thousands of things, from buttons to enormous murals. This speed and productivity did not enhance his reputation among high-minded types, but other artists were as quickly won over as the "regular people," who couldn't turn away.

Kids always say that Haring's work makes them happy. And yes, the good-naturedness is part of what sucks people in, even when a second glance reveals something heartbreaking. Because of the stick-figure simplicity, Haring's art can seem Gumbyesque, almost dumb. But there's undeniable humanity in his unindividuated little people; at their best, in fact, they seem infused with the essential spirit of life. But Haring, the rare artist with the becoming modesty to harness his talent to unpretentious, childlike forms, can also be breathtakingly intricate. Yet, embarking on even the complicated work, he never began with a sketch; he had it all in his head. He expressed himself in every medium, but the point is how he drew. Whether it was with chalk, markers, or paintbrushes, Haring had an almost miraculous ability to energize a line and give it personality and meaning. Although he knew color's punch, the black-and-white work most clearly reveals his gift, demonstrating his ingenuity at making much of what superficially seems so little. This is one of the things that make Haring's art worthwhile. And, ironically, it is part of what has stopped the Establishment from seeing how it shines. They associate value with what looks worked on or complicated. Haring's art is so at ease it doesn't look like stuff for the history books. The ultimate subversion.

Of course, by the time Haring appeared, Andy Warhol was already the pop of Pop. And Pittsburgh isn't all these two very American artists had in common. Both were prolific, dared to create all over the place, and had the audacity to be informal and casual-seeming about art, which misled critics already determined to find them frivolous. Both were gay and—perhaps, at some level, because of that—had an extra drive to be anointed as popular and famous. Haring didn't have Warhol's range, or complexity, or genius at getting under the skin of the culture. But one could say that Haring became a sort of mini Warhol and, in one way, went beyond his idol. Because of the tenor of the times, Haring's queer sexuality was much more out-front than Warhol's enigmatic image, behavior, and sensibility. But Warhol's need to *belong,* to be a star among stars, was shared by Haring. He was an American kid who equated—at least at the beginning—success with public recognition and media validation.

Haring's open homosexuality cost him with critics who just couldn't go there and who didn't see sex as art, politics, a language all its own for a generation absorbed in exploring it. This summer, when the first major American Haring retrospective opens at the Whitney Museum, we'll see whether time has changed these attitudes. We'll also see whether the museum has the vision, and the guts, to honor its best intentions by truly representing Haring's journey and including a full range of the graphic, unabashed celebrations of gay sex that are so crucial a part of him. American museums, unlike their European counterparts, have always shied away from Haring's boldly licentious material, perhaps shrewdly. After all, the Whitney has not been able to find a corporate sponsor for the show, which would seem to have the makings of a popular blockbuster.

The last time I saw Haring was in August 1989. I ran into him in a restaurant in the West Village. He was just the type to understand the sultry magic of New York on a charged-up summer night; he wasn't the kind who checked into the Hamptons once he had a checkbook. But, dressed for the bleak midwinter, he looked like hell, eyes receded, his brainy-boy forehead marked by Kaposi's sarcoma lesions. I can't remember what we said; I remember only the heaviness that had replaced his fizz.

We'd been acquaintances for about ten years. I had been editor of *Artforum* when he was coming up, and over the years the magazine had published both pro and con assessments of his work. In 1988 I'd bumped into him at an ACT UP demonstration on Wall Street. As part of the group's AIDS awareness strategy, Haring lay in the street, blocking traffic and finally getting arrested. I had already been told that he was HIV-positive, though not sick. But by the summer of 1989, sick he clearly was. Days after I ran into him, I read an interview with Haring (by David Sheff) that had just appeared in *Rolling Stone*. In it, the young man looked back on his life, as so many others were doing in those days of borrowed time.

After the article, Haring's prices shot up and he accelerated his already furious work pace until he became too sick to go to the studio. Near the end, he received a letter from Disney, asking for a meeting. He couldn't believe it, but he couldn't actually read it. He was just too sick.

He died on February 16, 1990, leaving an estate of $25 million. His last weeks were spent, without life support, saying good-byes to family and friends in his New York apartment. Not long before, his bedroom had been transformed—by designer and friend Sam Havadtoy—into a suite reminiscent of those at the Ritz, his favorite Paris hotel. Such luxury was the antithesis of God-fearing Dutch frugality, but aesthetics actually represented the most superficial of the distances he had traveled. Haring's personal life had become so different from what he had known as a child that, as far as his parents were concerned, he might as well have moved to the moon.

He had to have felt it, too; it hardly seems possible that he, any more than his parents, could have avoided the tension of change. So much had been jettisoned out of necessity. Or choice. Practically the only constant through the hectic, dizzying years was children. He could not live without kids around him. The Haring estate's creative director, David Stark, says, "Everywhere he went, he wanted to do some kind of outreach program with kids." His feelings went beyond sentimentality; he needed to connect with them, to join their games and play. If he'd go to a friend's house for a holiday dinner, he'd ask to be seated at the children's table, and nine times out of ten, he'd end up down on the floor doing pass-along drawings. This was a game his father had taught him.

Once he arrived at the School of Visual Arts, the games exploded. Haring's friendship with fellow student Kenny Scharf was sealed after he helped Scharf drag about fifty broken televisions, to be used for a sculpture, through the New York streets. According to Scharf, "Keith was the most fun, funny, happy person. He was the best go-go dancer." Then he added, "Even then we knew that it wasn't just regular times . . . it was something special."

Part of what was extraordinary is the fact that everything was happening at once—on both the conceptual and theoretical fronts. In the subway and on the street, vital talent was bubbling up. At SVA—no ivory tower—Jean-Michel Basquiat, who was not the application-form type, sneaked in to use the walls as canvas. Haring, who would later go Basquiat one better, was tuned in to all this—and turned on: Gay New York was alive as never before. The old shame was being exorcised. It was a tribal moment.

Haring, along with so many, improvised each step in his continuing sexual evolution, sometimes hiding, sometimes pushing others to accept him as he really was. At SVA, he made a video entitled *I'm Looking for My Tupperware Book,* which juxtaposed footage of his mother puttering around her kitchen ("Where *is* my Tupperware book?") with scenes of the family dog twirling on its hind legs, and three guys, probably including himself, having it off together in a bathroom. Keith never actually described himself as "gay" to his parents, but clearly wanted them to deal with his sexuality. His attempts to enlighten them were awkward, sometimes cruel. His father recalls his son's once coming home with what might as well have been a bomb. "It was a tape of him taking a bath," Allen Haring remembers. "I guess he thought it was art or something. He even brought the VCR. He was proud of this, but he was not proud of the way we reacted. That's for sure. We told him to turn it off." The dialogue was always half unspoken. Later, Keith would introduce his first boyfriend as his "bodyguard."

Keith and friends did a lot of things people would consider outrageous—some pharmaceutical (he favored "happy drugs"—pot, acid, and later ecstasy), and a great many sexual. "Are you kidding?" Scharf says. "Back then it was like a big orgy. Everyone was having sex in front of everybody all the time, in many different ways. That was the way it was." There were other antics. One day Scharf offered to "customize" Haring's glasses. Scharf's optical improvisation pleased Haring so much that he had his pal paint and repaint the frames. Haring documented the evolution with photographs and eventually brought guest artists into the act.

Like kids, Haring loved clubs—all kinds. He frequented the Club Baths for sex, and he especially liked fringe hangouts. (He didn't have the right look to get beyond velvet ropes.) In 1979, at Club 57, a place that attracted a group of media-mixing artists, Haring became the "curator." Scharf remembers, "At Club 57, Andy Warhol and the Factory were always in the backs of our minds. . . . All we wanted was for Andy to walk in. He didn't."

But Haring's involvement got him noticed by Steve Maas, who invited him to create a gallery environment for his place, the Mudd Club. This was truly "arriving" for Haring; Maas ran an original joint. Johnny Dynell, owner of today's Jackie 60, worked there as a DJ and recalls, "Steve would say, 'The club is too crowded. So, no fat people tonight—unless they're famous, like Meat Loaf.' . . . Or Steve might say, 'No leather tonight, unless it's Robert Mapplethorpe.' Now, of course, you know ninety-nine percent of the people in the club were wearing black leather!"

Leather wasn't the only thing that was dark and popular at the coolest of the downtown clubs. Once again, black culture was "it," although Latin and Hispanic voices and themes eddied into the swirling urban synthesis. It was an era of passions, obsessions, visceral thrills. Directness was a virtue; everything was about feeling, powerful feeling: If you didn't feel strongly about what (or whom) you were doing, you might as well have caught the Kutztown bus.

The source of the heat was the street. Haring felt it so much that he dropped out of SVA in 1980. Everything seemed to lead to the city, not the classroom. Graffiti—and new kinds of images made out of letters—yelled out on trains, subway walls, and sidewalks, announcing the beginning of a metropolis that was part village, part *Blade Runner.* These were the days that witnessed the beginnings of break dancing, hip-hop, and rap; new sounds, new visuals, new styles. Everything was a mix, a layering, an amalgamation. Grandmaster Flash, a popular DJ, didn't just spin records. Using his tongue and elbow, he'd scratch the

Tseng Kwong Chi, *Keith Haring, Pop Shop Tokyo,* 1988

vinyl, creating new sounds, and, sampling from records of previous eras, he'd add his own rap. The result was the sound of a different city, deep inside the old.

Haring connected, really *feeling* the beat for the first time in his life. For him, this was it—the city that he had dreamed of finding and that he was helping to create. At first he didn't understand where the work of a white boy in thick glasses fit in. But he found his way. His 1980 breakthrough, a series of white chalk drawings on the empty black spaces in subway stations, distinguished him from the graffiti artists but also—in the kind of synthesis that the era loved—linked him to the medium and messages of black visibility. Haring refused to allow his race to condemn him to a lifetime of stark galleries. He hip-hopped around boundaries, creating an urban iconography of babies, barking dogs, space raiders, pregnant women, dancing legions, and men with TV heads. He used image as language, as the graffiti writers around him were using language as image.

By 1980, Haring, Scharf, and another friend, Samantha McEwen, were sharing an apartment on Sixth Avenue between Thirty-ninth and Fortieth Streets. Eventually, they were asked to depart because of an out-of-control party where a man who had just been stabbed in Bryant Park came stumbling in, dripping blood. The German guests had believed it was performance art. After that, Haring always lived downtown.

Altogether, 1980 was a big year for Haring, who, to make ends meet, was freelancing as a wildflower picker on the New Jersey Turnpike and delivering rent-a-plants. He was in a bunch of shows, and briefly became a gallery hand for Tony Shafrazi, who would eventually become his dealer. Then, in June, came "The Times Square Show." Organized by a group called Collaborative Projects, it was multileveled, multicultural—and dynamic. Haring was proud to be included. So was Fred Brathwaite—better known as Fab 5 Freddy, graffiti artist and rapper.

"Lee Quiñones and I walked into the gallery where our paintings were hanging, and there's this white guy with funny glasses on looking at the work.

He tells us that they're by Fab and Lee, that these guys are really important. We're like, *What's with him?* Then somebody yelled, 'Fred and Lee! Is everything cool?' Keith was mortified. He said, 'Oh man, I feel like such a fool.'"

Their bond held when, a while later, Haring came out to his new friend. "It was a revelation," Brathwaite recalls. "I remember thinking, This guy and I are really good friends, we're buddies, and he's telling me he's gay, and that's cool. . . . I had to respect Keith, as did all the others in graffiti who eventually found out he was gay. Nobody dissed him. It was a sign that we were on a new playing field."

Walking one night with Brathwaite, Haring discovered the place that would be for him what Tahiti was for Gauguin: the Paradise Garage. Haring's Nirvana, where cars had once actually been parked, was just off Varick Street. Here he watched the city kids who turned dancing into declaration—the soft-skinned Spanish boys, the Snap Queens, the drag royalty from the Houses of Labeija, Xtravaganza, and Ninja whose voguing would inspire Madonna. He also met the lovers he would stay with the longest (Juan Dubose, who is now dead, and Juan Rivera). At the Garage he witnessed gay life at its most pagan and communal. A night of dancing at the Garage became a ceremony of "coming in" to a community, to a lifestyle, to a circle of friends, to sex. The titles of the songs that Larry Levan played in the heyday of Haring's fixation with the place—"Heartbeat," "Walking on Sunshine," "Can't Get Enough," "Life Is Something Special"—would have also been appropriate for his art. They were anthems—mantras really—of affection and brotherhood, expressing the sorts of sentiments that usually make sophisticated New Yorkers recoil. But don't forget what Kenny Scharf said, "It wasn't just regular times."

"The Garage was the best club that ever existed," recalls Johnny Dynell. "It was about happiness, music, and dancing. They didn't serve alcohol, but there was plenty of acid around and later, ecstasy. The big thing wasn't the cocaine of Studio 54 and all the bullshit that came with that. The Garage was a lifestyle. People went to it as much for the communal experience that it offered as for the entertainment. Keith would totally lose himself. You can't fake that. . . . For a white boy . . . it wasn't the easiest thing. He had his obsessions. After you see somebody with different boys, and they're all black or Spanish, it becomes obvious that this is what he likes. He was always popular, but once he got known, he was a real boy magnet. He became the official artist of the Garage. He designed T-shirts, did parties, and created invitations that we always saved."

The inclusive energy of the Garage fed Haring's creativity. By 1982 he had exhibited in dozens of group shows and was being repped by Tony Shafrazi. Toward the end of 1981, the poet Rene Ricard wrote an article in *Artforum* that dealt with a number of artists, including Basquiat, but Ricard titled it "The Radiant Child," in honor of Haring's recurring image of a baby with lines of energy emanating from its body.

Haring's first show at the Shafrazi Gallery involved some collaboration with LA II, a gifted graffiti painter whom Haring admired. At the exhibition, there was abundance: wall upon wall of drawings and paintings, filled with zigzaggy currents of energy, sharp visions and gentler ones. One memorable work showed Mickey Mouse doing something with his penis; there was also a black-light installation and all sorts of objects bursting with imagery. The point was to make the place as full and vital as the world.

Tony Shafrazi had kept his eye on Haring since the young artist had worked for him. Recently I asked the gallery owner what had impressed him about the young, prefame Haring. "He was incredibly fast and attentive to everything," Shafrazi recalled. "He had the peculiar habit of looking at something and doing a double take. To me, it signified extra curiosity. At the end of the day he would leave all his things—his brushes, his sneakers, his tools—all neat and clean and lined up in a row. Then he was gone. You had to run to catch him."

While I was thinking about this article, I happened to go to the Byzantine exhibition at the Metropolitan Museum of Art, and despite all the obvious connections that Haring's work has with twentieth-century art, from Jackson Pollock's "all over" strategy to Pierre Alechinsky's more banal patterned abstractions, to Sol LeWitt's Minimalist wall drawings and Jenny Holzer's pithy social criticisms, it was in the Byzantine era that I found the most interesting Haring parallels. After all the censorship that had gone on earlier with the puritanical church, these Byzantine artists expressed their feelings, beliefs, and new freedoms. They put their stamp on everything, as did Haring. His work also came after a long period of puritanism in art, and his images of the body, sex, and homosexuality were part of the taboo busting that was as intrinsic to this period as the Reagan right-wingers.

By 1983 he had also finally met his hero—Andy Warhol. Becoming friends with Warhol propelled Haring into an even higher orbit of pals in high places. Alba Clemente, the wife of artist Francesco Clemente and one of Haring's close friends, recalls a night when they hooked up with Sean Lennon and wanted to move on to a club. Lennon was quite young and getting him in anywhere was an issue. Haring instructed Clemente to tell the doorman who he was, and she, not one to name-drop, became flustered and got her Seans mixed up, blurting out that they were with Sean Connery.

Even with all his clubbing and socializing—or perhaps because of it— Haring kept expanding his résumé. By the time he was done he had created fabric for Vivienne Westwood and worked on the Fiorucci store in Milan. He had designed Swatch watches and collaborated with Richard Avedon on a project involving Brooke Shields. (Haring's contribution was awful.) He had produced a backdrop for the Palladium and painted Grace Jones's body for a big night at the Paradise Garage. He had made album covers and antiapartheid posters, had created a powerful drawing for the Berlin Wall. And on it went, from Japan to Pisa. In addition to all this, there were thousands of drawings, hundreds of paintings, a huge array of sculptures, and much, much more.

But there had also been the news and the reality of AIDS, and with it a kind of change so radical it will take decades to understand. You can't really measure what happened, but something did. In the clubs they played "I'll Be Your Soldier" and Madonna's "Keep People Together." Everywhere there was this soft whisper of sadness. The losses built, as did the fear. And Haring worked, socialized, and tried even harder, as if he knew. Once he did know that he, too, was infected with the virus, which was about 1988, he became compulsive about using his time for all it was worth. He worked like a maniac and got even more celebrity-happy. More than ever, he needed to know that he had become a somebody. But that didn't mean that he denied what was going on. He put a lot into AIDS activism and, of course, he brought everything that was going on into his work. The art from this period in his life tells it all. He painted knives going through hearts, sperm that seemed to shoot with an epic force, people being pulled apart, bodies piling up. Eventually, in 1989, he made a diptych that includes a skeleton touching an image that looks like an emaciated baby or a key. He also did a large pattern painting, leaving a corner unfinished, as if to point to the work he would never get to do. By this time, the Garage had closed. The people who pushed night past noon soon moved on to the Saint and later, the Sound Factory, where DJ Junior Vasquez pioneered a darker house style.

Haring started to go back to Kutztown much more often than he had before. His mother remembers that, when he arrived, he always talked about how good it smelled. As news of his illness spread and some of his celebrity friends dropped him, he passed most of his time with his old buddies, such as Adolfo Arena (his last assistant), Kenny Scharf, Julia Gruen, Francesco and Alba Clemente, Lysa Cooper, and a few others. Gil Vazquez, a man Haring had fallen for, was often by his side. Haring and Vazquez were never lovers, because Vazquez is straight, but by all accounts their friendship gave Haring a kind of companionship he'd been longing for.

As the years go on, questions like "Who was Keith Haring?" and "Why does he matter?" get both simpler and harder to answer. Time has allowed the work to assert itself; it is a document of a time. Haring's eternal boyishness has joined somehow in our minds with the memories of all those who came to the city and died before they ever really had the chance to grow up. Because of this, the Whitney show will have special meaning in New York. The Whitney staff understands this, and Elisabeth Sussman, who is the curator of the Haring show, says that everyone intends "to do it right." A lot of planning and care have gone into this exhibition. Everybody involved seems dedicated to the idea of showcasing as many facets of his talent as possible. But good intentions often aren't enough. It's hard to physically re-create the mood of the times without hokeyness or condescension; in addition, we still live in a country where if a show has too many penises and too much homosexuality, there's an outcry. So, I imagine Haring's most sexually explicit art will need to be circumvented, or there will be warnings.

Fear of sex in art is often rationalized as concern for children. Nina Clemente, who is now sixteen years old and who adored and was adored by her parents' friend Keith, got it right when she said to me, "I have a cartoon of two little boys having a conversation. The one says to the other, 'I found a condom on the patio.' The friend replies, 'What's a patio?' People who say that kids can't absorb information about sexuality or are frightened by it are preventing their children from learning about the world. The problem is the adults, not the children."

For Nina's seventh birthday, Haring made her a book called *Nina's Book of Little Things!* It has a purity that is reminiscent of the glorious feeling that Matisse could give his books. One of Haring's instructions in his opening note to Nina is "Don't be afraid to draw in the book." Nina told me that Keith is her biggest inspiration for being brave. Her father hates the idea that people will think Keith Haring has finally made it now that his work is being celebrated at the Whitney Museum. He says, "Keith doesn't need art-world legitimacy. He found a much more interesting legitimacy. He invented an audience for himself. There's nothing better than that."

I keep thinking about Haring's relationship with his parents and about theirs with him. The fact is that in the end he did what they had wanted *and* what he had dreamed of. They had always hoped he would become a commercial artist, and he was. He also had an impact, which is what he came to most desire. As Sussman points out, "He made the line so flexible an animal, and he made it work on so many levels that spoke of the time." Haring's parents wanted him to be an inspiration to others, and he is—just not the way they had planned it. I keep imagining their faces when they come to New York for the exhibition. Their pride in their son was obvious when I visited them for this article, as was their sorrow. The Harings have moved to the outskirts of Kutztown, to a beautiful spot on a hill. For the first fifteen minutes after I arrived, we talked about the tree swallows, the wonderful weather, and the prop that Allen Haring was making for his granddaughter's school play. Joan Haring served homemade vegetable soup and homemade coffee cake, and gave me extra slices to take home. Their decency is as unmistakable as their son's art, of which they have a few modest pieces.

The Harings have gone through enormous changes since Keith's death, including a questioning of many things they believed in before. When Keith was growing up, his father was patriotism incarnate. The night he saw Lee Harvey Oswald on TV being taken in for the assassination of John F. Kennedy, Mr. Haring shouted, "My God! That's Ozzie!" Ozzie, as he called him, had been in the same squadron in the marines as Allen Haring. Keith's father remembers teasing his tent mate one night because he was studying a Russian dictionary. Now he laughs at the naïveté of his Red-baiting, but much else about the past, especially in regard to his son, brings out his pain and regret, not his humor. You can see how all of it tears up his wife.

. . .

I asked them if they experienced injustice once word spread that Keith was suffering from AIDS.

Allen Haring: "There were some incidents."

Joan Haring: "Keith was to be a godfather, and the head of the church said he didn't think he should be allowed to even come into the church. That was the beginning of our being turned off."

Allen Haring: "It was just the opposite of what the church is supposed to be about."

And it's a tale of what goes on in the name of righteousness. Keith Haring did everything he could to fight that kind of obscenity, and to celebrate the moment when people liberated themselves from hate with flying leaps and deep embraces. After I left the Harings, I wanted to send them a passage from an interview with Michel Foucault that was first published in *Ethos* in the autumn of 1983. In it, Foucault says:

> *You see, that's why I really work like a dog and I worked like a dog all my life. I am not interested in the academic status of what I am doing because my problem is my own transformation. That's the reason also why, when people say, "Well, you thought this a few years ago and now you say something else," my answer is [laughter], "Well, do you think I have worked like that all those years to say the same thing and not to be changed?" This transformation of one's self by one's own knowledge is, I think, something rather close to the aesthetic experience. Why should a painter work if he is not transformed by his own painting?*

Haring transformed himself, and he also transformed others. Silence equals death.

Vanity Fair, July 1997

That Feeling in the Stomach

"It was around 1980. I was twenty, and Robert was thirty-three," Edward Mapplethorpe explained when I asked him when he discovered that his older brother, the late Robert Mapplethorpe, was gay. "He had basically cut himself off from the family, but I'd tried to stay in touch with him, and he'd gotten me on the guest list for a Patti Smith concert," he continued. "We had been back-stage, and I didn't want to be the little brother getting in the way, so I said, 'You do your thing, and I'll go out and watch the show from the audience,' which I did. At one point I looked over at the speakers and there was Robert perched on top of one of them with a guy's arm around him. My reaction was surprise. The thought of it was easier than seeing it. This was the first time I had actually seen my brother in an intimate situation with a man. To tell you the truth, as a kid I was told Robert was married to Patti Smith. They'd had such an incredible rela-tionship, and that's what he'd told our parents. In fact, I have a bunch of post-cards that Patti sent to my mother in the early seventies that say, 'Dear Mom.'"

By the time Edward spotted his brother with another man, Robert, who was born on November 4, 1946, had been living his life as a gay man for a number of years. But it's not unusual that a person's family would be in the dark about the fact that he or she is gay. Double lives, or misrepresenting the details of one's life, particularly in the area of girlfriends or boyfriends, is an old tale for homosexuals. Fudging things has been a survival strategy for gay people for eons. Silence has been one, too—which leads to why Mapplethorpe is an important figure. He may have committed that earlier sweet, sad lie when he pretended to his relatives that he'd tied the knot with his then lover Smith, and she may have been a partner in keeping the folks happy, but he sure didn't lie in his photography, which went for the truth like it was the only thing that mattered. In fact, Mapplethorpe's modus operandi was candor. His strongest work went against the silence that has so often surrounded the subject of homosexuality in a way that is unforgettable once you've seen the pictures.

There's no pretending some of them aren't shocking. Because they break taboos and don't try to be politically correct, they can be shocking on so many levels—race, sex, pain, beauty, politics, history, love. But surely the issue isn't their shock value, but whether they give us the kinds of things for which we turn to art. I believe they do. Of course Mapplethorpe isn't the only artist to have broken the usual silence about homosexuality. There have been many in his generation or ones past, such as Oscar Wilde or Francis Bacon. Like these two artists, Mapplethorpe's story and work have a shape of their own, and the imagery pulses with the feeling of the times in which it was created. When they were first taken, Mapplethorpe's photographs signaled the changes that were going on with gay liberation in the seventies and eighties. Today they encapsulate that period. They articulate the hope, the craziness, the sense of emerging freedom, the battles of self-esteem, the fight to be proud of one's love, the defiance, the bonding, and so much more that gay people were experiencing. Although Mapplethorpe couldn't have anticipated this, as it turns out his photographs have also become an eloquent record of loss.

There has been a lot of attention on Mapplethorpe in the last twenty years. But despite it, not much has nailed why his work is really something. I think it has to do with how he dealt with stigmas against homosexuality, confronted taboos, and presented his content with such a sense of perfection and aesthetic sophistication. It's difficult to have the full view of Mapplethorpe as a taboo breaker because most often it is not his taboo-breaking work that is seen. It has served to give the rest of his work a buzz, but it's often treated as "too hot to handle." His portraits, nudes, and flowers may have become a staple in photography shows, books, articles, and collections, but many of the sex pictures have remained like land mines that the photography world is afraid to touch. What a shame. This is to miss the full scope of what he did, and why his work matters. Explicit pictures of homosexual sex don't make up a huge proportion of his work, but they are its underbelly. This is the subject through which he found his photographic voice, and it's here that one can see the incredible balancing act between form and content that makes a Mapplethorpe really fly. That doesn't mean he didn't do other kinds of photographs that are memorable. He did. Plenty of his photographs have power, but the all-male sex pictures are where one sees him finding his place in history.

In any serious discussion anyone ever had with Mapplethorpe about the development of his vision, he'd always indicate that this imagery was pivotal to his art and his personal education. As he once explained, "I learned about my own sexuality through taking photographs of sexuality. It was all interrelated. It was as though I wasn't documenting anything but myself in a way." Of his sex pictures, the most difficult images for most people are the ones that depict sadomasochistic rituals. It is understandable why people have a hard time with these photographs. Witnessing a man choosing to have his genitals bolted down, tied up, and strangled until they bleed—which is what one sees in certain Mapplethorpe images—is to encounter pain on many levels. But since when did art only cover "nice" things? Since when was art supposed to pretend that certain things aren't a part of reality? Within his body of work Mapplethorpe shows a broad span of what occurs in sex between men—including pleasure. Mapplethorpe's images cover ground that definitely isn't represented in *Everything You Ever Wanted to Know About Sex,* But Were Afraid to Ask*.

A compilation of his sex photographs, such as this book, is something Mapplethorpe wanted to organize for years. Although he continued to involve sex as an important element of his work, he shot all his "hard-core" images in the space of a few years. If one only heard about Mapplethorpe's most graphic images, instead of looking at them, one might think they resemble pornography. But there is a world of difference between a Mapplethorpe image and pornography. For a start, his subjects weren't for hire. The relationships depicted are real. As Mapplethorpe once bluntly said, "The people involved in those sexual pictures are really involved in what they were doing. It's their thing. If there was somebody that happened to be drinking piss in the photograph, he was, in fact, into drinking piss. He wasn't doing it for the pictures." The word *shocking* has been used often to describe his explicit pictures. I think what shocks isn't just the material but how it is so artfully presented. The content, lighting, composition, sense of order, and aesthetics all combine to give the photographs an unforgettable impact. If one listens to the comments of viewers as they absorb these images, one will often hear someone say with surprise, "I can't believe how beautiful they are." In fact, beauty was Mapplethorpe's bullet. He loved it, and he used it to wipe out old notions of the pitifulness of homosexuality. It shouldn't be forgotten that the men in Mapplethorpe's pictures, who came from all walks of life, wanted to be photographed. In a way these images always reminded me of Mathew Brady's Civil War pictures, taken right before the soldiers went out to battle.

It's very rare that one comes across a Mapplethorpe in which one's first emotion is that the view is pathetic. The series that he informally titled "Baby Larry" is an exception. In these pictures one views a grown man completely done up like a baby—bib, bow, bonnet, and all. Mapplethorpe catches the moment in one shot, when his subject has the kind of tantrum only babies usually get to enjoy. The infantilized man dumps a bowl of yuk on his head, and it drops down his face like a scene from the Marx Brothers. These "Baby Larry" shots are both heartbreaking and hilarious, and they feature something very rarely seen in a Mapplethorpe—mess. His work is usually impeccable. This gives the sex pictures all the more tension—because of how the sense of perfection contrasts with the fact that the images themselves bring up all sorts of "messy" issues.

Mapplethorpe admitted that he knew he had to do something shocking in order to make a name for himself, but his decision to involve sex in his work went beyond calculation. He didn't refer to himself as brave, but he was. His is not the work of a coward. It took guts to do this kind of work in the art and photography worlds that existed then. Neither world had ever shown real support for visual work that was openly about homosexuality. It's different now than it was then. Skip twenty years or so and one sees Mapplethorpe's courage again in the self-portraits he did right before his death. Mapplethorpe wasn't an intellectual. He had street smarts, though, and was smart enough to know that what he felt, others might feel, too. What he said on this score is often quoted in one version or another:

> The first time I went to [adult magazine] stores on 42nd Street and saw those [physique] pictures in cellophane, I was still straight and didn't even know that those male magazines existed. I was sixteen and not even old enough to buy them. I'd look in the window . . . and I'd get a feeling in my stomach. I was in art school then and thought, God—if you could get that feeling across in a piece of art . . .

What's remarkable is that Mapplethorpe achieved this. His sharpest work goes right to the stomach and gets a visceral response. Many different feelings have been expressed by those who have seen these pictures. There are those who identify with the photographs, and those who say the images make them sick, with varying responses in between. But it's impossible to talk about the public reaction to this imagery without talking about his private reasons for doing it. As Mapplethorpe himself said, his photography was a means to learn—about himself, sex, homosexuality, and life. It was also a means to make something beautiful that was often considered ugly.

During the early seventies, even before he shot the images in this book,

Robert Mapplethorpe, *Helmut, N.Y.C.,* 1978

he was taking hundreds of Polaroids, many of which were self-portraits. Mapplethorpe is often naked in them, or wearing some provocative item. Qualifying these images in the context of his later work, one might say these earlier Polaroids—like the objects he made by cutting out pages from pornographic magazines—were the prologue of the drama to come. They are exercises in self-discovery and photographic seeing. These shots feel very personal. This is also true of his Polaroids of men kissing one another, and engaging in sexual contact, or his images of friends like Marianne Faithfull, Candy Darling, and Lucy Ferry. Among the gang is Sam Wagstaff, who played a monumental part in Mapplethorpe's life as a lover, teacher, friend, benefactor, and someone who believed fiercely in his pictures.

By the time Mapplethorpe hooked up with him, Wagstaff was legendary as a curator who understood new art, and as an independent thinker. He had stopped working and was enjoying the life of a free man, with money to spend as a collector. Even though Wagstaff already had decades of developing his eye before he met Mapplethorpe, it was the young photographer who turned Wagstaff on to photography in a serious way that made him a champion of the medium. There are many parallels between Wagstaff as a photography collector and Mapplethorpe as a photographer. Wagstaff's collection, now housed at the Getty Museum in California, brought down the walls of the photographic canon. Wagstaff disregarded the history of photography as it had been written and went at it from a different angle. Ultimately, he showed that many more things belong in the pearly gates of what is considered art than what we are usually taught. Mapplethorpe and Wagstaff educated themselves about photography together. One sees that education at work in Mapplethorpe's pictures. There's a consciousness of photographic history—of, say, the achievements of Fox Talbot, Nadar, Cecil Beaton, George Platt Lynes, and Diane Arbus— which is the foundation upon which he built his imagery. Take the way he used lighting. Mapplethorpe learned about glamorous lighting from the work of George Hurrell, one of the Hollywood greats, and translated it brilliantly into his own work. Nowhere is this clearer than in his graphically explicit sex pictures. Rather than hide details that usually aren't shown because they are considered scandalous or dirty, Mapplethorpe lights them for all the world to see, as if they were Garbo's face.

An intimate, personal approach was essential to Mapplethorpe's way of working. This was not a photographer who used big crews and many assistants when he went at it. There's no way he could have captured the images he did had he done that. He didn't consume reams of film the way so many commercial photographers do. Dimitri Levas, who designed this book and worked with Mapplethorpe throughout the eighties, remembers, "It's as though he would see an image before he took it. When it came to shooting the picture, he knew exactly what he was going to focus on. In a regular portrait session he'd begin by chatting with someone for a bit of time, all the while checking out how they talked and moved. Then when he'd get them in front of the camera, he'd know exactly what he wanted to capture. I'll bet that's how he worked on the sex pictures, too. He'd look at a scene and see what the essence of it was and try to figure out how to make it into a perfect form." Levas recalls something else that's vital to understanding Mapplethorpe: "He was so consciously aware of himself as an artist. One could see it in the way he lived his life, the way he presented himself, the way he presented his work." Indeed, when Mapplethorpe went for some of his most taboo-breaking shots, the furniture—which is used like an altar— isn't just any old chair, but one by Gustav Stickley. When he took his picture of a man role-playing as a "policeman," he had him "sit guard" on a Charles Eames chair. Where else can one find an S & M scene featuring a flawless Biedermeier bed? Much has been written about the way Mapplethorpe's

Catholic upbringing informed his aesthetic. It, of course, also informed his rebellion against sexual taboos.

Sometimes a situation couldn't be shaped into something that had the aesthetic rigor that Mapplethorpe insisted upon. When things didn't pan out, Mapplethorpe didn't push it. He took it as fate. As Levas points out, "He'd always say it wasn't meant to be. The word *magic* was an important part of his vocabulary. 'Magic,' for instance, was the way he described pictures that turned out great by some unforeseen technical accident, such as a lighting misfire or the bump of a camera. And he'd always talk about the magic of the moment."

To Mapplethorpe, there were elements of fate and magic involved in the fact that he was an artist who found himself in the middle of a world that was uprising. Toward the end of his life, in a BBC interview he said, "It was a certain moment, and I was in a perfect situation [to represent it], in that most of the people in those photographs were friends of mine, and they trusted me. I felt almost an obligation to record those things somehow. I thought, Well here I am. I have a certain vision and it's an obligation for me to make pictorial images that nobody has ever seen before and do it in a way that's aesthetic."

Sometimes Mapplethorpe's sex pictures are so obviously provocative that they're plain old funny, such as his famous self-portrait with a whip going up his backside. Sometimes they're surrealistically bizarre, like his shots of a man who has his mouth plugged with clothespins. These images are reminiscent of the performance work done later by the British artist Leigh Bowery. Other Mapplethorpe pictures have the elements of absurdity that occur in life at the strangest times. As Levas says, "There are photographs that remind me of *The Bell Jar* where Sylvia Plath writes that seeing male genitals for the first time reminded her of a turkey neck and gizzards." Then there are Mapplethorpe's darkest photographs—his toughest scenes of crime and punishment, and self-hate. The sight of a swastika in the midst of a picture that is about power, domination, and obedience, as happens in a few of Mapplethorpe's pictures, can be understandably horrifying to many human beings. There's too much history involving the swastika to be casual about it. Why do the very people the Nazis would have wanted eliminated appropriate Nazi symbolism in their reenactments of power and submission? Many people have tried to untangle this awful paradox, but to me none has hit it in a way that feels more to the point than philosopher Michel Foucault, who used his own experiences as a homosexual to try to unravel these kinds of questions. In "Sade: Sergeant of Sex," he said:

> *The Nazis were charwomen in the bad sense of the term. They worked with brooms and dusters, wanting to purge society of everything they considered unsanitary, dusty, filthy; syphilitics, homosexuals, Jews, those of impure blood, Blacks, the insane. It's the foul petit bourgeois dream of racial hygiene that underlies the Nazi dream. . . . The problem raised is why we imagine today to have access to certain erotic phantasms through Nazism. Why these boots, caps, and eagles that are found to be so infatuating, particularly in the United States? . . . Is the only vocabulary that we possess for transcribing the grand pleasure of the body in explosion this sad fable of a recent political apocalypse? Are we unable to think of the intensity of the present except as the end of the world in a concentration camp? You see how poor our treasure of images is!*

Foucault also wrote about seventies style in which so many gay men appropriated signs and symbols of "obvious" masculinity—such as sideburns, beards, and as much leather as possible. The fashion parade of the era, and the role-playing that went with it, is well represented in Mapplethorpe's photographs. Their inventory of types include policeman, cowboy, Nazi weirdo, biker, and lone ranger.

I didn't see either of the exhibitions that occurred in 1977 and 1978 when Mapplethorpe was right in the middle of doing many of the sex pictures. These shows are now legendary. They took place at "alternative spaces" in New York and San Francisco, because Mapplethorpe was already having exhibitions in galleries in these cities and it was thought these particular pictures were too controversial. Instead of cutting them out entirely, alternative shows were organized so this work could be seen along with the rest of his production. (The invitations on the covers of this book go back to that time in 1977 when Mapplethorpe's work was exposed in New York with two concurrent exhibitions.) The next year he had two simultaneous exhibitions in San Francisco. Photography dealer Jeffrey Fraenkel vividly remembers what happened when a selection of the sex pictures hit the West Coast and were presented at 80 Langton Street:

> *The opening was packed. The word was out. No one could have predicted sex pictures like these. They were photographed so carefully, lit so beautifully and sensitively, and presented in such an artful manner. There is no shortage of sex pictures in photography, but with these pictures, unlike, say, Victorian photography, there was no aspect of shame, no feeling that they should only be viewed privately or secretly. With Robert's work you never got the feeling that anybody was being coerced. You definitely got the feeling that people were busting out after decades of holding back. They were placing this out for everyone to see. I think a lot of people connected with that sense of defiance.*

AIDS is now in the back of many people's minds when looking at these pictures. How could it not be—even though no one knew anything about AIDS when all this was going on and the photographs were being done. Many of the subjects in these pictures have died due to the disease, as did Mapplethorpe himself. It was right after he died, in 1989, that the Corcoran Gallery in Washington canceled the exhibition of his work, "The Perfect Moment," because of institutional fears about the public's reaction to his work about sex. In fact, when the same show went up elsewhere in Washington, it was proven that the audience, which went in droves, appreciated the opportunity to see what he had done. At the time, I wrote a piece in *The New Yorker* about two photographers: one who censored himself, Minor White, and one who didn't, Robert Mapplethorpe. The article included the following passage:

> *He didn't consider his condition God's punishment. He understood it for what it was—a virus, not a sign that he had sinned. He had no shame about having AIDS. . . . [But] the outcome of the Corcoran's cancellation of Mapplethorpe's show has been a debate in which his photographs have been treated by some as though they were a virus that curators have to be careful about exposing the public to.*

Ten years have gone by. AIDS is still a disease that needs to be eradicated, but enormous progress has been made in treating it. There's been progress, too, in terms of the public's understanding of the disease. Isn't it time that there was progress about understanding the public, as well? We are always hearing about how the public can't handle this or that. Isn't it time that people stopped appointing themselves the guard dogs of culture and started to let the audience determine what they want to see? I know Mapplethorpe had great faith in the audience's ability to look at all of his work. That's why he always wanted to publish a book of sex pictures. Here it is. I don't think he could have known the layers and levels that this work would eventually take on. But here's how he summed up what he did, "I captured something at a certain time that couldn't be captured anymore." How true.

Pictures: Robert Mapplethorpe, 1999

Artist, Interrupted

"I grew up in a little town and it was dull, and I was so bored that I looked for something exciting," recalled the painter Alice Neel, then eighty-four years old, as she charmed late-night viewers on *The Tonight Show* one evening in June 1984. True to form, within minutes the artist was telling Johnny Carson that she should paint him nude.

Neel died a few months later, before Carson's nerve could be put to the test. There was the usual flurry that comes with the passing of an important cultural figure, but soon Neel's work went back into the shadows where it had been for much of her life. One could say that her work has been a kind of twentieth-century secret, known to her supporters and art-world insiders but not the general public. During decades when abstraction reigned, she had been committed to realism, and most of all to figurative art, which meant she was considered "less important." But even though her belief in portraiture cost her in many ways, what she accomplished did not go entirely unnoticed: Whether consciously or not, painters such as Eric Fischl and Lucian Freud invoke her work in their art, and to a new generation of portraitists such as Anh Duong and Lisa Yuskavage, she is an avowed inspiration.

Alice Neel, born in 1900, daughter of Alice Concross Hartley (a descendant of one of the signers of the Declaration of Independence) and George Wash-

Alice Neel, *Alice Neel Self-Portrait,* 1980

Neel '80

ington Neel, has been called a modern American van Gogh, in the sense that she never got her due in her own lifetime. Well, her work is about to have a moment of redemption: Ann Temkin of the Philadelphia Museum of Art has organized what is essentially the painter's first full-scale retrospective; titled "The Art of Alice Neel," this thoughtful show will travel extensively after debuting at the end of June at the Whitney Museum of American Art in New York (an institution Neel picketed twice, once in 1968 and once in 1971, over shows that she and others considered either racist or exclusionary). Neel has also been portrayed on the big screen this year, and while she might have been flattered to know that Susan Sarandon was chosen to play her in the Stanley Tucci film *Joe Gould's Secret,* what would have really pleased her is the fact that the movie showed her unforgettable portrait of Gould, a homeless philosopher who claimed to be writing a comprehensive oral history of the world—in his head, as it turned out—and who cut a notable figure in the Greenwich Village of the 1930s and 1940s. The sensational part of Neel's picture is that she painted him naked with not one, not two, but three very baroque-looking penises. But it's the look in Gould's eyes that truly shocks: In them one sees the up-and-down manic-depressive moods that were his painful reality.

Though Neel's work can revel in a painterly loveliness, she doesn't pander to her audience or to her subjects, and it's not unusual for her paintings, like the Gould portrait, to be tough. As she confessed to a critic in 1984, "Cézanne said, 'I love to paint people who have grown old naturally in the country.' My statement is, 'I love to paint people mutilated and beaten up by the rat race in New York.'"

On another occasion she said that life was more brutal than she was. She knew from whence she spoke.

Although she spent her first twenty years living a sheltered existence outside of Philadelphia, where her father was a railroad clerk and her mother took care of home and family, the rest of her life was the opposite of conventional. When I asked Nancy Neel, one of her daughters-in-law, with whom she had a close relationship (and who helps run the Alice Neel archives today), what initially drove Alice to leave the security of home so far behind, I was told, "She saw her mother be tied to the house and be bitter about it. She didn't want her life to be that way. She wanted to take charge of it. That didn't mean she didn't run into pitfalls."

In fact, Neel's troubles were more like abysses. By the time she was thirty, her first daughter, Santillana, had died from diphtheria, and a second daughter, Isabetta, had been taken from her by her Cuban husband, Carlos Enríquez, who placed the child in the care of his wealthy family in Havana. A nervous breakdown followed the double loss, as did at least two suicide attempts; Neel spent over a year at an assortment of psychiatric wards and a sanatorium, where she was encouraged to continue making art, which had been important to her since childhood. Enríquez had by then more or less abandoned Neel, and she would only see Isabetta a handful of times, painting her on at least three occasions. I don't know if Alice was given the advice to pursue her art by people who had seen the paintings she had done when her first baby was dying, but all one has to do is look at works from that period, such as *Futility of Effort* (1930)—which depicts the accidental hanging of an infant from a crib while the mother is absorbed in household chores—to understand how painting was Neel's way of connecting to her own life.

Somehow Neel put herself back together enough to reenter the world. In 1932 she began living with Kenneth Doolittle, a sailor she'd met through friends; they set up quarters on Cornelia Street, in Greenwich Village. As Nancy remembers, "Alice loved interesting people, poetic people, intellectual people, out-of-the-ordinary people, ones who were down on their luck." She used to say that if someone didn't have character she couldn't paint that person; the Village, then, was perfect for her. She called herself "a collector of souls," and she lived the life she painted, for good and ill.

In 1932 she found herself embroiled in the kind of censorship battle that has become all too familiar in today's art world: The Catholic Church objected to her painting *Degenerate Madonna,* which showed a sickly, alien-looking mother and child, and was partly done as a way of expressing her feelings of abandonment when her daughter died; the work had to be withdrawn from the first Washington Square Outdoor Art Exhibit. (When Robert Mapplethorpe photographed Neel in 1984, just weeks before her death, their similar experiences with the art police, fifty years apart, gave the image particular resonance.) Still, Neel's bold canvases got her noticed, and it wasn't long before she was brought into various government-funded art programs of the thirties and forties, which were responsible not only for the survival of numerous painters, muralists, sculptors, and photographers during the Depression but also for some extraordinary work. For Neel, as for others, the thirty or so dollars that the government sent each week was a lifesaver.

Some of her strongest pieces from the thirties are very personal watercolors and other works on paper; small images, they depict scenes from her domestic life, such as a drawing of Doolittle sitting around the house projecting a cocky sense of entitlement. No one can say for sure what else Neel accomplished during this period, because man trouble visited her again: In 1934, Doolittle slashed and destroyed more than three hundred of her works in a fit of jealousy over Neel's attachment to the aristocratic John Rothschild, a dabbler in the travel industry, who was a sometime lover and lifelong friend; he appears in a number of her paintings, including some incredible bathroom scenes of such extraordinary clarity and verve that six decades later they still feel utterly fresh. Neel's next love affair produced a group of beautiful, seductive images—her most romantic. She'd met José Santiago Negron, a twenty-five-year-old Puerto Rican guitar player, at a nightclub, and by 1938 the two of them were living in Spanish Harlem, where Neel would remain for more than twenty years. This union produced a son, Richard. Another son, Hartley, followed in 1941, reportedly fathered by Sam Brody, the Russian filmmaker and photographer. (Both Richard and Hartley grew up in Alice's single-parent household and kept her last name; today one is a doctor, the other a lawyer.)

During the mid-1930s to the early 1940s, Neel also created some of her most powerful political and social imagery. As Nancy says, "She always looked at life from the point of view of forgotten people." In her painting *T.B. Harlem*, which was done in 1940 and depicts a gaunt, bedridden young man, bandaged at the chest and hollow-eyed, she renders as haunting a picture of sickness as any I have seen, and yet the portrait leaves her subject with his grace and dignity.

Even though Neel had a strong social conscience, she had an ego and worldly needs, too, and so the occasional gallery show and positive critical response helped keep her going. But the outside affirmations stopped by the late 1940s, when abstraction, particularly Abstract Expressionism, became the ruling art form. These genres may have been about freedom for many of those who practiced them, but their hold over the American art world became nothing short of tyrannical. As a female figurative artist, Neel was generally considered a pest, doing lowbrow, inconsequential work. Her infrequent commissions dried up altogether, as did her shows, her reviews, her paltry-at-best sales. If she had a crowd during those days it was the Beats, with whom she was friendly, though not intimate, and whose disaffection was something she understood. (In the mid-1960s, she would produce a posterlike counterculture portrait of Allen Ginsberg—not one of her best.) She appears in painter Alfred Leslie and photographer Robert Frank's 1959 film, *Pull My Daisy*—basically a record of a bunch of Beat boys hanging around in a loft. Neel plays "the bishop's mother," looking less like an elder hepcat than a member of the Salvation Army.

Neel credited the psychiatrist she began seeing in 1958 with helping her turn her career around. As Nancy remembers, the therapist said something like "Why don't you go to some of those openings and ask some of those important people to sit for you?" The idea clicked—with shrinks like that, who needs agents or dealers? The body of work that followed, and that pre-occupied Neel for much of the rest of her life, is a vigorous record of artists, critics, writers, historians, and other art-world figures of the time. This move on Neel's part—to start to represent the powerful instead of the powerless—has been interpreted as a careerist step. But that's overly simplistic. In fact, Neel seems to have been born to paint this world, a world in which she had one foot in and one foot out.

As Nancy says, "It's not as if she had compromised by doing portraits of CEOs and presidents of the board, or [members of] the Harvard Club." Looked at together, these art-world pictures are a fascinating collective portrait. Her paintings of poet and curator Frank O'Hara, artist Robert Smithson, curator Henry Geldzahler, writer and editor Cindy Nemser, and critic David Bourdon, with his lover and fellow critic Gregory Battcock, are classics. From a contemporary vantage point, there's something touching in the sense of self-importance that can come across in these images of people who once wielded great authority but are in many cases now forgotten. And yet it's the awkward-looking painting of a shirtless and scarred Andy Warhol, done in 1970, after he was shot in the chest and abdomen by Valerie Solanas, that is the master-piece of this period. It also serves as a testament to both Neel and Warhol: to her for being able to get so deep into his emotional and physical being, and to him for allowing himself to be represented in a manner that must have gone against all his feelings of shyness and vanity. (It's worth noting that Warhol also allowed his scars to be photographed by Richard Avedon, and that the result proved more glamorizing than piercing.)

By the time Neel died, she had not only painted a kind of archaeology of the American art world in the sixties and seventies but had also produced a sizable number of nudes and paintings of pregnant women. In addition, she had done portraits of people such as Che Guevara and Kate Millett who were intrinsic to the era. (Neel painted Millett as a commission for *Time* in 1970, back in the days when the magazine used serious painters regularly for its covers.) Her portraits of such icons, done from photographs, can be a tad too illustrative to have the real Neel punch; at other times her work from this period can feel overly folksy, or cramped. (It shouldn't be forgotten that Neel worked in modest circumstances, in a room in her apartment; her views weren't conducive to the sense of infinite space that one feels, say, in the work of Jackson Pollock, who had those wide-open Long Island horizons to gaze at.) But when Neel is at her best—boom! Take her 1970 double portrait of the Manhattan transvestite Jackie Curtis and her boyfriend at the time, Ritta Redd, both of whom were part of Warhol's circle. What makes the painting unforgettable is that Neel doesn't sensationalize the fact that these are men breaking taboos in multiple ways. She depicts the ordinariness that was such a part of what Curtis and Redd were after. In the painting itself, Curtis comes across as all woman, while Redd, who has been called a part-time transvestite, looks like much more of a "guy." This portrait of their relationship never goes for the cheap shot. It's pure Neel—honest, direct, and human.

She once said, "If I have any talent in relation to people apart from planning the whole canvas, it is my identification with them. I get so identified when I paint them, when they go home I feel frightful, I have no self—I've gone into this other person. And by doing that, there's a kind of something I get that other artists don't get. It is my way of overcoming the alienation. It's my ticket to reality."

This identification shows, and it's what makes the work really something.

Vanity Fair, July 2000

Outskirts

When the designer Gianni Versace was murdered three years ago, all sorts of writers, after the shock, weighed in on whether he had been a great talent. But no one focused on his sense of humor. It was major. And it could be wicked. He especially got a bang out of things when they had to do with some kind of fashion foible. I never saw him laugh as much as when I first told him the tale of my gray corduroy skirt. It was an ash gray, asexual number that was unexceptional in every way, but it turned out to have an enormous influence on the rest of my life.

When I picked it out in 1977, I had no idea it would be the last skirt I would ever wear, or that it would end up like a character in a crime novel—at the bottom of a river. It was actually the first skirt I'd bought in ages. Sarah Lawrence College, where I had gone just after the height of the student revolts, hadn't been a dress-code kind of place, to say the least. So, a few years later, when I was sitting in the public affairs office of an important New York cultural institution, being told to report for work on the following Monday and not to wear pants (which were against the dress code for non–security staff female employees), I should have run as fast as I could in the opposite direction.

But instead I went to Bloomingdale's and spent all the money I had on a pair of black loafers, a salt-and-pepper tweed jacket, and the gray corduroy skirt. When I put the skirt on for my first day of work, it just felt like a skirt—no big deal. But by the end of my tenure it had come to feel like prison bars. All in all, my entire sentence lasted only about three weeks. It wasn't the actual work that posed an obstacle; the job itself was elementary. The problem was elsewhere. I, who like a chameleon had until then adapted to any environment into which I had been placed, found myself in a situation in which I didn't fit. It was bad enough that I didn't have or want a boyfriend—I had a girlfriend by then and wasn't about to pretend that I didn't. But what could be worse than not knowing who Salvatore Ferragamo was?

The fact that I had never heard of this shoe designer was so shocking to my office mate that it seemed to be the equivalent of telling her I hadn't heard of God.

Of all the books that have been written and all the films that have been made about office hell, Cindy Sherman's black-humor movie, *Office Killer,* comes closest to capturing, in a fabulously exaggerated way, what it was that had me counting the days until I was free. In Sherman's film, the very campy central character gets her revenge on the office tyrants by doing them in, and then propping up their bodies in her basement, where she dispenses cookies and milk and advice on etiquette. The plot to my tale has a different twist. Instead, I did myself in—I got myself fired.

What a feeling it was, coming home on the bus after my last day at work. I swore to myself that no matter how much I needed a job, I would never take on one that felt wrong again. When I got to my apartment on Riverside Drive and removed my skirt, I had an idea. I would formalize the pledge I had made to myself with a ceremony symbolizing my emancipation. From the banks along the West Side Highway, I threw the skirt into the Hudson River. Weighted by a cement block I had found on the street, it went down like a rubbed-out body.

A short while later I had the good fortune of being offered a fellowship under John Szarkowski, the legendary photography curator at the Museum of Modern Art. No matter how excited I was by the prospect, though, first I had to use my litmus test. "Will I have to wear a skirt?" I asked him. Szarkowski answered, "Why would a person need to wear a skirt to look at photographs?" I jumped at the chance to work with him and am still glad I did. I am also still skirtless. But I could have made a tidy sum if I had taken the dare that Gianni Versace challenged me with a few years ago. There was a big fashion event coming up. Versace sent a mischievous fax offering me $1,000 if I would dress up in an exact copy of that gray corduroy skirt, designed by him. Guess how I responded.

The New York Times Magazine, August 20, 2000

The Whole Clemente

"It was a brush made of one mouse hair," the painter Francesco Clemente kept insisting. "No, no, no," said the poet Rene Ricard. "There were two, two, two—there had to be two mouse hairs!" Clemente countered: "They told me it was one mouse hair, and made a specific point of showing it to me." Which made Ricard even more dogmatic: "One hair will not hold paint—it has to be two hairs to act as a conduit." The painter and the poet kept at it for a few more rounds, and I kept laughing at them. Who wouldn't?

We were at Clemente's home in Greenwich Village, a town house formerly owned by Bob Dylan. It was a scorching summer day, and the air-conditioning wasn't on, so the doors to the garden were thrown open, and the place felt surprisingly cool. A quality of certain Clemente artworks is that he knows how to take the viewer someplace else with a left-of-center palette—slightly skewed Mediterranean blues, pumped-up Pompeii reds—and how to leave large expanses of canvas or paper unfussed with; the same restraint, the same easy use of space and color, is at work in the house. You won't find wall colors like these in Martha Stewart's Kmart collection; the artist mixes them out of the pigments he uses in the studio. Yet nothing is overdone. Nothing feels "expensive" or "precious"—except time, which Clemente and Ricard were quickly running out of.

For some days Ricard had been installed at the house, working on an emergency writing job, a chronology of Clemente's life for the catalogue accompanying the artist's much-anticipated exhibition opening this month at New York's Guggenheim Museum. A chronology had already been produced by the Guggenheim, but Clemente felt it was too "bureaucratic." Considering what

David Seidner, *Francesco Clemente*, 1999

else was happening in his life at the time, considering how many people were calling or banging on his door due to all sorts of deadlines, or the fact that he was leaving that night for a weeks-long stay in Europe, some people might find it hilarious that he made himself completely available to Ricard while the poet put in marathon day-and-night writing sessions, working on a task most museums consider so unimportant, and even boring, that they often leave it to interns. This kind of concern with detail is classic Clemente. (In the end, by the way, he and Ricard never agreed about the mouse-hair brushes, which are used by young Indian boys schooled in the craft of miniature painting; some of these artisans had worked with Clemente in Jaipur in 1981, when he produced "Francesco Clemente Pinxit," an important series of miniatures.)

Hands-on can't begin to describe how involved the artist is with all things relating to his work. He is a master at blocking out external noise, at ignoring everything except that which he considers a priority. Phones ring and messages aren't returned. Faxes never receive replies. He'll eventually get around to dealing with what he feels is most important in the pile, he'll always make good on a promise, but the rest of it can wait forever. Sometimes Clemente's inward focus can lead to gaffes that people think are rude—turning up late at a wedding, missing appointments morning, afternoon, and evening. He's usually forgiven because he's horrified by his own faux pas and shows it—and because he's "Francesco." As his friend painter Alex Katz puts it, "Some people hit all the notes socially. Francesco doesn't. He leaves notes out, that's all."

Early one morning many years ago, I spied Clemente on his bicycle on Bleecker Street in the Village. He'd just taken his two daughters to catch the school bus and was off to his studio to put in a day's work. He looked very proper in a suit and tie, which he often wears when painting, but at the same time he was riding in the wrong direction, against traffic. When I asked him about it later, he said, "It's safer to go against the traffic than with it." That's an apt metaphor for what he's done in his art.

A glib description of Clemente's work might be "Matisse with content." When he was starting out in Rome in the seventies, no "serious" male painter would have been expected to deal with complex sexuality—nudity maybe, but not the intimacies and neuroses of the body. Yet Clemente took up that challenge and has never put it down. The kind of personal, obsessive, self-aware stuff that he was producing then was usually associated with the work of what some people have dismissed as "bedroom" artists—that is, "women" artists or "gay" artists. The machismo that was reigning in Italian art didn't encourage a man busy drawing images of himself with his finger in his nose, or up his ass, as Clemente was doing. Not only did he dare to enter an area of art that was considered—Picasso notwithstanding—more fluff than substance but he made something illuminating and original out of it. He also put the flesh and blood back into painting—showed that it could be as visceral and contemporary when it comes to sex as, say, a taboo-breaking photograph by Mapplethorpe.

By now, Clemente's work is so associated with sexuality that it's often the first thing people talk about when his name comes up. "I can't think of another artist working today whose work is more erotically charged than his," Helen Harrington Marden, the wife of painter Brice Marden and a painter herself, told me. "Those big lingams and yonis are hard to mistake," she went on, using the Sanskrit words for penis and vagina, and laughing. When I left a message on model and actress Lauren Hutton's machine, explaining that I was writing about Clemente and wanted to talk to her, since I knew they have been friends for years, within twelve hours I received a fax from her from Kuala Lumpur that included the following statement: "To see a man paint directly about sex after all these sly-puss references we've had for the last millennium! Well, I positively trill. It practically turns me into Diana Vreeland." As with Picasso—whose erotic art was thought of as secondary until only recently—Clemente's erotics are simply part of a very large whole, which also involves an enormous amount of self-portraiture.

But the key to Clemente is his prodigiousness. Because he does it all—abstraction, figuration, still lifes, landscapes, portraits, allegories, visual meditations—he's a nightmare for people who like to fit art into slots. By the same token, his art can't be defined in terms of medium either, as Clemente is at home with the whole enchilada—charcoal, ceramics, pen and ink, oils, fresco, watercolors, printmaking, pastels, sculpture, mosaic, paper, canvas. Due to the fact that all of the work is intensely tactile and visually pleasurable, people don't think of Clemente as a conceptual artist. But he is that, too. His fellow artists often comment on his dexterity. Katz told me, "My opening sentence to Francesco when I met him in the early eighties was 'I think you're the best thing to come out of Italy since de Chirico.' He's a major stylist. There hasn't been one out of Italy with that much energy for a long time."

Apart from some early experiments with photography, however, Clemente has left the more technological media to others. I remember a few years ago, when it felt as though almost every major artist who had ascended in the eighties was directing a movie—Robert Longo, David Salle, Cindy Sherman, Julian Schnabel—Clemente would say in a self-mocking (yet not entirely so) way he has, "I'm just an artist." He did, however, end up in a movie. Much to his amusement, his friend Gus Van Sant, the film director, asked Clemente to play a small part in *Good Will Hunting*. Van Sant, who years before he'd ever met Clemente clipped a photo of the intense-looking artist out of *Interview* magazine, told me, "He's so amazing-looking that I thought he'd be interesting as the hypnotist."

Spells actually do come into play with Clemente's art, in a very real way. Raymond Foye, a writer and editor who has worked with him on many projects, including their line of mystical Hanuman Books, which they copublished, said, "Whenever I go to his studio, when the elevator opens I feel like I'm descending into the subcontinent. It just has a different feel. He cannot work in a pristine, antiseptic environment. He's very good at evoking moods. Out of that mood comes the work. It's a spell that's taking place when he's painting, it's enchantment." These kinds of things—spirit, spells, et cetera—can sound very hokey. There's an enormous difference when it's the real thing, and with Clemente it is, just as it's genuinely India that makes its presence felt in much of his art. Thousands of Western artists have trekked to India and been involved with its philosophies and practices, but few have given all of it new life in their work as he has.

"For the last twenty years we've called Mr. Clemente the little monk (behind his back of course), because of his trances, his moods (that can last a year), his deep mental retreats." This was also on the fax that Lauren Hutton sent me from Kuala Lumpur. She continued: "But now that I think of it, his art is often religious; it is not being made for buying and selling, but in order to know ourselves." Hutton is spot-on. Clemente's religiousness is not limited to the Judeo-Christian tradition, or even by his deep reverence for and knowledge of Indian culture, but really communicates a broader idea of spirit. Certainly his work enters the art market, and has done very well in it; but, for Clemente, the process of making it and looking at it is what counts. One day when we were at his studio, he got a call about something he'd promised to do and went flying out of the place. He knew I didn't have a key to lock it up, so he said he'd be back in a few hours. He wasn't. I was lucky that the cleaning lady soon arrived, which meant I would not have to bear the guilt had his life's work been stolen. When I saw him a couple of days later, he explained that he'd thought I'd just close the door behind me and not bother with a key. I said, "But, Francesco, all that work and all your paintings were in there." He looked at me and laughed. To Clemente what is most valuable cannot be stolen, because it has to do with the process of making art, with what is inside of him.

The full scope of what he has done as an artist is only beginning to become clear. He may sometimes come across as a gentleman of leisure—those paint-stainless clothes he wears, and that laid-back, "I don't really do anything" demeanor—but he's created a monster volume of work. Even though there's been no shortage of shows and books on Clemente, the last extensive exhibition in America was organized by the Philadelphia Museum of Art in 1990. The Guggenheim's show will be the first here to really address the story of his work in a large way. Considering how long Clemente's art has been in the limelight—he broke through to a significant worldwide audience in 1980—it's amazing how much mystery still surrounds it. Clemente himself has been partly responsible for the smoke. He is so protective of the atmosphere which he needs to do his work that he doesn't kowtow the way some other artists do. He doesn't spend a lot of time explaining himself. He doesn't even spend time helping himself—he's never had a regular studio assistant, which is unusual, given how much work he's produced. Raymond Foye laughs. "He once said to me that I was like one of those slaves in the pyramids who had to be sealed up with the pharaoh after the burial because I knew too much." Clemente likes to quote de Chirico: "What shall I love if not the enigma?" And he lives up to this statement. When the Guggenheim exhibition goes up and we finally have access to the full range of his work, it will be like the opening of a dam.

An only child, Clemente was born on March 23, 1952, and grew up in the same building as his father and grandfather—the Palazzo Calabritto in Naples. The palazzo is famous for its staircase, designed by the great eighteenth-century southern Italian architect Luigi Vanvitelli. Though Clemente never brings it up, his father, Lorenzo Clemente, is a marquess. He was also a judge; I'm told he was a favorite among Neapolitans in trouble because he was lenient and often let people off. Alex Katz says you can sense Clemente's blue blood in his work. He told me, "In this respect, the guy I find Francesco most like is [the fifteenth-century artist] Fra Angelico—his paintings are sort of primitive and yet they're so refined and elegant. You see those white walls with those frescoes on them and you say, This fellow must have been some fancy dude. Francesco's work is like that."

Bianca Quarto, Francesco's mother, was clearly nuts about her son, and qualified as his first big fan. When I told an Italian critic who has been around the Italian art scene for a long time that I was writing about Clemente and curious about his family, he said, "Now *that* was a pushy mother." Her adoration got him tailor-made suits from Naples when he moved to America, but it also brought mortification to Francesco on at least one occasion, which he now laughs about: "In the fifties there was this fantasy going around about child poets. There was a famous one in France, about whom there was a whole mystique, and my mother was obsessed with it all. Since age four or five, before I could write, she would take down the poems that I would make up. She collected all of it and then had the poems published in Naples without my knowing it. She went to a really fancy publisher, and the whole thing was a huge trauma for me. I was twelve, and Naples is such a small city. The last thing I wanted or needed was a book of poetry displayed in the window of the local bookstore on the way to school. I was angry at my mother for about ten solid years." He laughs. "I decided never to write again, and to become

Following spread: Francesco Clemente, *Alba,* 1997

a painter. Initially I became a painter so I would have my privacy. Before my mother died in 1995, I wrote one hundred small poems for her, had them printed, and gave them to her."

There's even more drama than meets the eye in this anecdote about Clemente and poetry. He may have stopped writing it, but he's done something else with it. In fact, his art is intertwined with poetry. His work is regularly described as poetic, and the adjective only begins to suggest the deep connections. Ours isn't exactly a time when poems are on the tips of people's tongues, but Clemente has done much to keep this art form visible. Writers often remark on the obvious links Clemente has to William Blake and Ezra Pound, just two of the many historic figures whose work has been a springboard for the artist. As important is Clemente's long love affair with contemporary American poetry. This passion has produced collaborations with poets such as Allen Ginsberg, Robert Creeley, and John Wieners. It has also led to a powerful group of portraits covering the field from John Ashbery to Rene Ricard.

But this bond with American poets isn't something that could have been predicted when Clemente threw down the pen for the brush. That change didn't come out of left field, if you consider that by the age of twelve Clemente had traveled all over Europe with his folks during holidays, visiting museums, palaces, and churches in Spain, France, Germany, England, Scandinavia, and, of course, Italy. As time went by, Clemente, like many precocious kids, developed a voracious appetite to see, hear, learn, and experience all he could; especially important to his growing sense of himself as an artist was the work of Bob Dylan (the owner of his future house), Allen Ginsberg (with whom he would later collaborate on a number of projects), and the psychoanalyst Jacques Lacan. College was the University of Rome, where he nominally studied architecture but spent most of his time either working on his art—largely drawings at that point—or hanging out at the Campo dei Fiori, where, day or night, one could find artists debating ideas (while not producing much actual work). Clemente's college years, the late sixties and early seventies, coincided with worldwide student unrest, the rise of conceptual art, and, more specific to Italy, *arte povera* (basically the art of found materials). Rome, a city where philosophy has always mattered, was home to some major figures in those arenas.

That group included Alighiero Boetti, who became a key mentor of Clemente's. Boetti, now deceased, was an utterly original artist whose work, often involving maps embroidered in Afghanistan, expresses a love of craft and a respect for craftsmen; it is especially admired by visual artists because of its processes and integrity. For Clemente the friendship with the older artist had profound meaning: "I was already a painter for myself, but a turning point for me was to stop being a painter for myself and become one for another artist. It was as if my process was to say, Okay, I really admire Boetti's work. What am *I* going to make that he can look at without my being embarrassed?" That breakthrough would occur in a few steps. First there was an outpouring of drawings which were done in Rome, and which established the basic subject matter of his work; some of it involved images of self-protection, like shields, and some was an elaboration of body imagery that had emerged when the artist took LSD while traveling in South America. Following this spurt of productivity, Clemente made his first trip to India.

Back in Rome in 1974, Clemente was with friends one day at the Piazza della Rotonda when he heard a big, heavy, low-pitched laugh. He looked for its source and found Alba Primiceri. He'd seen her around before, hanging out with a mutual friend, and couldn't help but take notice. Comparing Alba's dark glamour to that of Anna Magnani, which many people do, doesn't get to the half of it. Andy Warhol did better in his diaries, writing, "She could be the best movie star." Like Francesco, she had gone north to Rome, moving there from Amalfi, where she'd given her lawyer father palpitations by deciding to pursue a life in the theater. By the time Francesco met her, Alba, then twenty-one, was a well-known actress in Italy. She had recently caused a scandal in her hometown because of some magazine photos of her performances that had been published. She laughs now when she remembers trying to persuade her mother that she wasn't nude in the pictures, but had on a leotard. Anyway, she already had quite a following the night Clemente fell in love with her distinctive laugh. He introduced himself and sat down. "He ordered a chamomile tea, which I thought was very weird for a twenty-two-year-old," Alba recalls.

That was the extent of their first encounter. Clemente left for Afghanistan the next day with Boetti. It would be another year before Clemente and Alba would once again cross paths. Though he didn't really know her at all, feelings of jealousy stirred in him—according to Alba—when he saw her with another artist, Gino De Dominicis. Clemente asked Alba to go for a car ride, and that was it. She told me, "We never left each other after that." Clemente adds, "She came to my house, and fifteen minutes later she was pregnant." They finally got married in 1980 so that Alba could see her family again. By then Chiara, their older daughter, was three; they have three other children, Nina and the twins, Pietro and Andrea. Although Alba continues to perform on rare and much-anticipated occasions, she largely stopped acting after she met Francesco.

By the spring of 1975, Boetti had been impressed enough by some of Clemente's installations—one of which involved enlarged Polaroids of little mounds of tea, shot so that they looked like war photographs—that he took his dealer, Gian Enzo Sperone, around to see the young artist. As a result, in quick succession, Clemente got himself a gallery, some shows, a bit of cash, and a trip back to India, this time with a pregnant Alba. They found their way to Madras. Right away the city inspired Clemente to create bold graphic pieces in collaboration with local movie-billboard painters; one, for instance, is of a map of the world painted on a hand so huge that it comes out of the sea and touches the sky. These Pop works could be considered his first truly substantial pieces. Thanks to certain connections, the Clementes were staying at the Theosophical Society, an institution of enormous historical resonance for the interdisciplinary pursuit of religion, science, and philosophy, situated on the Bay of Bengal. In the course of many visits through the years, the society's library gave Clemente the opportunity to delve deeply into matters relating to the spirit, including mystical traditions such as the cabala and gnosticism, as well as Oriental religions, notably Buddhism and Hinduism.

It was during Christmastime in 1977, just after Chiara was born, that the Clementes, now on their second trip together to Madras (which, for them, had become something of a refuge from the violence and political convulsions of late-1970s Italy), first heard a lecture by the guru Krishnamurti, then eighty-two years old. In his lifetime Krishnamurti—who disdained organized religion and instead preached individual notions of spirituality—attracted a long list of listeners, including many artists and writers; W. H. Auden, Christopher Isherwood, and a young Jackson Pollock all went to see him in the twenties. On the same trip—perhaps inspired by Krishnamurti—Clemente finally broke free in his art. He had already been working with images of the body that were entirely his own, and that are recognizable both because of their particular mix of naïveté and sophistication and because of their attention to orifices. Soon he was creating a group of paintings involving the image of a harlequin which got insiders talking. The pieces are impressive for the way they combine tight rendering and freehand, almost automatic drawing.

. . .

The work showed up in *Flash Art,* a European art magazine. This is when Clemente experienced his first brush with art labels. He was included in a new movement that went by the name Transavanguardia, supposedly a new and paradoxically retrogressive avant-garde. It was a largely meaningless package, but there's nothing like a new ism in art to get the media going, and a few months later Clemente's art was included in the 1980 Venice Biennale. His life would never be the same. For the Biennale, Clemente had created a triptych in fresco entitled *Coi Sentimenti Insegna alle Emozioni,* which loosely translates as *He Teaches Emotions with Feelings.* The work, which boldly uses yellow and red, was a standout. Two of the panels are self-portraits, and the third is a delicate-looking tree with a heart at its root. The piece was installed as part of a section on young artists that included other newcomers such as Julian Schnabel, David Salle, Sandro Chia, Enzo Cucchi, and Mimmo Paladino. After more than a decade of being looked down upon as a medium, painting was back with a bang. Moreover, much of it was figurative painting that invoked history in some way—something that had been "out" for years. Now, rather than America's being the center of the art world, as it had been since World War II, Europe appeared to be just as, if not more, crucial. "Venice," Clemente says, "was an overnight kind of deal. You went to bed and there was one art scene, and you woke up the next morning and there was another."

But to many artists, dealers, and critics from previous generations, all this painting and invocation of history seemed like a conservative throwback. Now that Clemente's identity was that of a painter, and not a conceptual artist, Boetti stopped speaking to him. (They made up fourteen years later, shortly before Boetti died.) Fights were breaking out all over the Biennale. Clemente remembers, "Konrad Fischer, the German dealer, was dead drunk, screaming and shouting, 'I go out. You go home! I go out. You go home!'" But there were plenty of other dealers who wanted to hook up with Clemente, such as the Swiss gallery owner Bruno Bischofberger. "Lots of people were warning me that Bruno Bischofberger ruined Andy Warhol," Clemente recalls. "My answer to that was, 'If he ruined Andy Warhol, I want him to ruin me, too.'" (Alex Katz is very funny on the subject of Clemente's ambition: "I'll ask Francesco over to the studio, and if he sees something that he thinks is a real good painting, he'll say, 'This makes me sick.'")

It was after the Biennale that the Clementes moved to America. While India remains essential to Clemente's life and work, and the family spends part of every summer at Alba's house in Amalfi, New York has been home base for the last twenty years or so—"the only city," Clemente says, "that was able to match the wealth and diversity of visual and personal experience that I felt in India."

Soon after the move, Francesco and Alba drew in a tight circle of friends that included Keith Haring, Jean-Michel Basquiat, Julian Schnabel, Robert Mapplethorpe, the Mardens, and Henry Geldzahler, who was then commissioner of cultural affairs for the city of New York. Socially, Alba made as big an impression as Francesco. Rene Ricard well remembers his first encounter with the two of them: "I met them at One University Place, which was the place to go in New York at the time. Well, you don't expect when you meet a painter that you are going to meet a wife, too. It's not automatic, right? There was a dressmaker in Naples who had all the patterns for the Paris couture clothes, and Alba had gone to her when she was choosing her wardrobe for America. That night she was wearing a perfect copy of a charcoal gray Chanel suit, a matching ivory silk blouse with a little mandarin collar, black pumps, and huge pink plastic flower earrings that didn't go with the outfit at all. Her hair was pulled back in a knot with one little wisp hanging out. At one point I went to push the stray hair back and she said, 'Oh, no! I am not so perfect.' Francesco was sporting that little three-day-growth beard that would later take over and set the fashion. It was as though he had arrived fully formed from the head of Zeus. The couple was an event. They knocked the socks off this town." The first major piece Clemente created and showed in Manhattan was a coup, a canny one in terms of endearing himself to the downtown New York art world. The painter approached this work as if he were a film director, enlisting Diego Cortez, one of the most interesting entrepreneurs of the time, to choose a cast of New Yorkers, protagonists of the early-eighties downtown scene, whose portraits Clemente then painted in twenty frescoes on movable panels.

There are great descriptions of Clemente's early years in New York in Warhol's diaries. One entry reports on a lunch at Da Silvano: "Clemente, the Italian artist, was there, and gee, I like him a lot—he's picked up the American attitude. He understands American humor, which is so strange, because you don't understand how a person from another country can pick it up. He doesn't say much, he just sits and eats and watches." Clemente's silence was due partly to the fact that he wasn't entirely comfortable speaking English, but it also added to his magnetism. Chiara Clemente told me this about her father: "The stereotypical Neapolitan is very rough and kids around. The other side of that is the Neapolitan who is smooth, has things under control, but is very nonchalant. My dad's very good at the latter. I always saw him as having the ability to bring people in. He was always sucking them in by doing nothing. He'll just be sitting there, cross-legged, very quiet, and people would just come and sit by him or talk to him."

One of Clemente's most important patrons in the early eighties was Sir Nicholas Serota, who is now director of England's Tate Gallery but who then ran the Whitechapel Art Gallery in London. I asked Serota what it was about Clemente's work that had caught his attention, and he answered, "More than anything I was struck by his unusual, penetrating sensibility into people's psychology. It struck me as a really new and fresh vision that grew out of an awareness of Italian art, and early-twentieth-century European art, which was being translated into something quite different from what we'd seen before." Two of Clemente's strongest pieces from this period were created in Madras toward the end of 1983. One of them, *1152,* is a haunting sculptural work that includes sixty-four figures made of papier-mâché; each figure is two and a half feet tall and has nine holes, characteristic of the way Clemente often draws attention to the human anatomy. The work feels at once old and new, tribal and personal. Then there's *Indigo Room,* a series of exquisite works of indigo-dyed paper with charcoal drawings bound together with cotton and overlaid with silver, which together literally make up a room. (It will be shown in its entirety in the Guggenheim exhibition.)

Around the time that Clemente made *Indigo Room,* he finally met Krishnamurti. Over a lunch that has since become legendary, the guru apparently spent a lot of time asking the artist questions about being a painter. He particularly wanted to know where Clemente's images come from. This is always one of the big questions for an artist. Clemente's best answer might be the description he once gave me when I asked why he likes the poetry of John Wieners so much. Clemente responded, "When you read Wieners's poems, there is no boundary between what he is seeing in the world and how he is feeling in the deepest recesses of his psyche. There is a total flow between the inside and outside, as well as between what is pop and what is holy. His poems make one feel awkward without wanting to shock. He says things that are hard to say. It is plainly embarrassing sometimes to listen to what he has to say." Clemente's work also has this sense of flow, and sometimes embarrassment. As the years have progressed and his work has made fewer and fewer obvious references to history, it has grown even stronger in this respect. His study of meditation, yoga, and chant—none of which he makes an issue of, but all of which he has practiced seriously on and off for years—has assisted him in creating this kind of art, since these disciplines are very much about examining the texture of consciousness and observing the mind.

Consciousness is exactly what has allowed Clemente to deal with big subjects in his art without turning ponderous or pretentious. Nowhere is this clearer than in "The Funerary Paintings," which Clemente did around 1987. This was the work that came after the glory years for eighties artists, when they had gone from being hailed as "the new rock stars" to being attacked as yesterday's hype. When things began to turn in 1987, it seemed as though one was always reading about the impending crash of the art market, a favorite media topic. But what was really affecting many individuals in the art community, in measurable and unmeasurable ways, was AIDS. Fighting the disease is what I heard artists talking about then, not the rise and fall of their bank accounts. By the early nineties, the art world—like the world in general—had lost many individuals to AIDS, a large number of whom were close friends of the Clementes: Mapplethorpe, who was the godfather of their twins; Haring, who practically lived in their house; art critic and actress Dorothy "Cookie" Mueller and her husband, Vittorio Scarpati, at whose wedding Clemente had been the best man. Thomas Ammann, Clemente's foremost collector, died in Zurich. Then there were the sudden deaths of Warhol and Basquiat, both of whom Clemente had collaborated with. Some of these deaths had not yet occurred when Clemente made "The Funerary Paintings," but the siege mentality was certainly in place. These works—some are abstract; some deal with religious symbols, some with death imagery—have the scale of an enormous battle; in them, emptiness gives one a palpable feeling of loss. The artist had visited the Valley of the Kings in Egypt, and he brought this experience with him to these paintings, which have a sense of history and the feel of a tragedy that can't simply be digested and gotten over. "There is nobody in the paintings—the room is empty," Clemente told me. "It's the most out-there work I've done." It's also among his best.

When I was talking to Lisa Dennison, the curator of the upcoming show at the Guggenheim, she explained that it would be arranged by themes rather than in a linear way because, as she put it, "chronology gets one nowhere with his work." She's correct. Clemente is always returning to certain themes, and one of his biggest, lushest, and wildest themes is women, a subject that has received a particular focus in his work in the last decade. He says, "Through the years I have always joked—or not so joked—that I am a great woman artist. Twenty years later, finally, all of my favorite artists are women." He has produced thousands of images that depict female anatomy or female genitalia. Recently he created a group of paintings that have an undeniable potency: They're all square, they're all red and green, and in them women, with double sets of eyelashes, contort and dance across the canvas. Clemente seems to have taken every conceivable approach to depicting women in his art, including transforming himself into a woman, and another recent series of oils plays with the traditional theme of reclining women. These paintings are anything but passive, but then, his subjects include Jerry Hall, Helen Marden, Fran Lebowitz, Gita Mehta, Toni Morrison, and Alba, who shows up in Clemente's art almost as often as he himself does.

Helen Marden can be extremely amusing about life with a painter. The Mardens and the Clementes have been pals for a long time, and Helen cuts straight to the chase: "Alba totally grounds Francesco. They had a fight once, and he said he couldn't live without her for three seconds. Alba and I, we'll bitch about Francesco and Brice for hours. We go to Bar Pitti to have lunch and complain about both of them through the whole meal. Francesco wasn't a surprise to Alba. She knows southern Italian men. Enough said about that. When we're finished with lunch, we always say, 'Well, they're really wonderful.' But we've spent the preceding hour and a half totally complaining about how they talk about themselves all the time. For instance, I say, 'How are you going to get through the Guggenheim show? You're going to have to hear every damn thing over and over again.' Then we both laugh."

As the Guggenheim show approaches, Clemente admits to feeling the anxiety artists often experience when a large portion of their work is brought together. It isn't the first time. Helen Marden told me, "Once I went over to Francesco's studio to look at a new group of paintings right before they were picked up for a show. We were standing in the kitchen, and there was a chocolate cake on the counter. Well, as you know, he's usually very elegant and controlled, but he just jammed all this chocolate cake into his mouth. I knew how nervous he was then. He laughed because I'd seen him do it; in fact, we both started laughing. It was so un-Francesco, and yet so Francesco."

The artist had better steer clear of cake shops this fall, because the Clemente news doesn't stop with the Guggenheim show. Forthcoming are two additional publications, one on his portraits, from PowerHouse Books, the other a portrait in pictures of Clemente, his work, and his life, shot by Luca Babini and released by Aperture. Beyond normal jitters, Clemente's apprehension about all this stems from a smart intuition about the perils of too much limelight. He is honest about how important it is for him to keep his freedom. He explains, "I am on the run from wherever I am. I miss one appointment out of two. It is part of my career and craft to have an exit always ready, and to have a triple identity and a quadruple life." Whenever I try to get to the heart of what this freedom is about for Clemente, I remember something that he told me when we started talking for this piece. He said, "You have to remember that I am from a country where artists were once the equivalent of the prostitute or the drug dealer. During Caravaggio's life they were the criminals, the lowest of workers. The poets of Venice were slaves. In Roman society no free man would dream to be an artist. In India the poet is supposed to be the son of a warrior and a prostitute to emphasize that he is an outcast and partakes in lawless activities. It is sort of a comedy that art has become so respectable."

Sir Nicholas Serota made his own allusion to Caravaggio when we were talking. He said, "Francesco manages to deal with concerns, even neuroses, that one finds in Italian Renaissance painting, particularly in Mannerist painting of a certain kind, and give them a very present-day relevance. People were as anguished in the sixteenth and seventeenth centuries as they are today, maybe about slightly different issues, but certainly in terms of their place in the world, how they relate to other people. One thinks of Francesco relating back to Caravaggio, back to Pontormo, as an artist who deals with anguish."

Once when I was speaking with Clemente, something made me stop asking the usual questions and ask instead what he thought the deepest reason was that he had become an artist. He looked at me, a bit horrified that we were going into areas that can be treacherous. But then he answered, "Because I am heartbroken." This made me think of something that John Wieners, his favorite poet, wrote:

Poetry is the only way we
Can keep in touch though not enough.

To Clemente art is the way to keep in touch.

Vanity Fair, October 1999

Triumph of the Still

In the introduction to *US at War,* a 1945 book produced by the magazine *U.S. Camera,* editor Tom Maloney plugs photography like there's no tomorrow. He writes, "These pictures are probably a greater heritage than most of us will ever realize. We've had a better coverage by artists in this war than ever before. These photographs make the best painting dull. Even Ernie Pyle, unquestioned peer in portraying G.I. Joe to good old stay-at-home Joe Doakes, can't tell it better than these pictures can. This is it."

US at War is a true artifact of the period. It's as patriotic as can be; it's also peppered with racism and ethnic slurs. Looking at it today, as we go deeper into what threatens to be a war more hellish than anybody's worst nightmare (or Hollywood's worst movie), I take some comfort from the book's faith in imagery, innocent as it is. The object fairly vibrates with a sense of romance about photography, and about risking one's life to get the picture. These images are a living embodiment of the philosophy of Robert Capa, one of war photography's greatest heroes: "If your pictures aren't good enough, you're not close enough." These guys, and in the forties they very much *were* guys, definitely got close enough.

Capa is also said to have come up with another piece of basic advice for photographers: "If you call yourself an artist, you won't get any assignments. Call yourself a photojournalist and then do whatever you like." In the last few decades, photojournalists have been the ones left out in the cold, but that predicament may have been reversed by recent events. How can we understand the current war when we know so little about the people and places where so much of it is being fought? Television, which repeats more than it illuminates, cannot tell us everything we need to know—we need a communications arsenal. It's the Internet's big moment, and as for photography, the public is hungering for images that make real what is all the more frightening for seeming so abstract. One witnessed this hunger immediately following the events of September 11; it continues to grow. How ironic that the Taliban regime, which prohibits graven images, which executes those who create them—and which first caught the full attention of most Westerners last year when it destroyed those unbelievably beautiful and majestic Buddhas in Bamiyan—would be one of the forces leading to a renaissance of photojournalism after almost three decades of its being off in the wings.

The photographs in *US at War* were all shot by servicemen. A few, such as W. Eugene Smith, went on to become important figures in the history of photojournalism, but most didn't. In fact, what's striking about the book is how so many of its powerful images—the kind you wake up at night thinking about—were shot by nonprofessionals and nonartists. (In the preface we learn that the pictures were chosen by "Commander Edward Steichen, U.S.N.R.," who had been *Vanity Fair's* principal photographer in the 1920s and 1930s; two years after the war, he would become the curator of photography at the Museum of Modern Art in New York.) *US at War* subverts the whole notion of a star system in photography; it shows that the events themselves were so vibrant and unforgettable that almost anyone who picked up a camera ended up capturing something worth looking at. As Maloney wrote in his introduction, "Eighty-five years ago, an indefatigable little Irishman named Mathew Brady gave up the best photographic business in America to record the actions of the Union Army. He did such a masterly job it became a monumental work. The name Brady is one of the great names of the Civil War today. . . . In this war there are thousands of Bradys."

Maloney was right. And what he observed also held true this past September when the Pentagon and the World Trade Center towers were hit and nearly three thousand lives were lost, so many literally disappearing into thin air. One result was a flood of pictures for our tears to drown in. Some were taken by the medium's biggest names; plenty of others just as powerful were shot by ordinary citizens. Wherever one looked—in the newspapers, in the weeklies, in the many special editions, which sold by the million—there were photographs to make one gasp, to break one's heart, to inspire and move one. Within days people were predicting the rebirth of photojournalism.

One may argue, correctly, that photojournalism never went away, and that there have always been photographers deeply committed to reportage. But the fact is that the genre as a whole has been in crisis for decades. It has been a long time since it has merited Steichen's 1951 description of it, in his foreword to the catalogue for a popular MoMA exhibition called "Memorable *Life* Photographs": "Photographic journalism is generally accepted as an authoritative source of visual information about our times. It now regularly reaches audiences all over the world on a scale unheard of a decade or two ago. It is becoming a new force in the molding of public opinion, and explaining man to man."

The takeover by television and the consequential demise of mass-circulation magazines such as *Life* and *Look,* both of which were defined by their commitment to publishing photo essays, is just one reason that photojournalism lost its influence. There is also the fact that today's awareness of issues such as stereotyping, racism, voyeurism, and exploitation of one's subjects makes it difficult to go along with the sometimes innocent assumptions that were part and parcel of the field years ago. Photographers once believed they could change the world with their pictures, the way Lewis Hine had at the turn of the last century when he helped reform labor laws by exposing the cruelties and injustice children were subjected to in factories and sweatshops. Or the way the Farm Security Administration did in the thirties when it sponsored the work of brilliant photo-documentarians such as Walker Evans, Dorothea Lange, Ben Shahn, and Russell Lee, whose Dust Bowl photographs captured the poverty, pain, and dignity of Depression-era America.

But over many decades, much photojournalistic work has become hackneyed and formulaic. The "Family of Man" exhibition, which drew record crowds at

MoMA in 1955 and which then toured the world—forever, it seemed—offers a good example of how socially concerned photojournalism can turn into the equivalent of a Hallmark card, reassuring rather than enlightening. For decades it has felt as though, outside of a handful of exceptionally committed photographers, the genre lost its steam. As the curator John Szarkowski wrote in 1978 in his introduction to his influential and controversial show "Mirrors and Windows" (which was about the medium's transformation from one that looked outward to one looking increasingly inward), "The failure of photojournalism stemmed perhaps from the sin of hubris. Like President Johnson, photographers thought they could deal with anything. . . . As the influence of the professional diminished, the content of American photography became increasingly personal, and often progressively private." While the climate in recent years has never been better for art photography, fashion photography, and celebrity photography, socially concerned photojournalism has been marginalized. America by the end of the twentieth century had become like a country living in a bubble. It wanted to know very little about the injustices going on inside its borders and even less about those in the rest of the world.

When that bubble burst on September 11, the camera, after years of being taken for granted, got to show us again what a great invention it is. The events were so overwhelming and so alien to anyone's experience that there was no time for grandstanding or pretense. People shot pictures out of instinct and need. What resulted is an incredible mass of imagery, so much of it produced by amateurs that the medium's singular democracy really showed.

This virtual mountain of pictures has the eerie quality of evoking not just crucial images in the history of photojournalism but the entirety of Western art. There are pictures of the rescue scene that look like paintings by Brueghel or Hieronymus Bosch. In others the chaos recalls the way Cubism turned Renaissance perspective on its head. There are those photos of the World Trade Center's husk that make one think of the Roman Colosseum, and sometimes when one imagines all of those souls suspended in the smoke above the site, it is hard not to think of Tiepolo's angels ascending. You can see the history of the Western still life in the iconography we saw printed in the magazines, newspapers, and tabloids; there are photographs of an ash-covered tea set in an apartment, for instance, that remind one of the work of the Italian artist Giorgio Morandi, who painted and repainted many still lifes of jars and bottles. Then there are shots that bring back horrors captured by past works of photojournalism. How many pictures did we look at that have discomforting similarities to the famous shot by Huynh Cong Ut of the naked Vietnamese child running from a napalm attack? Images of workers leaping from the burning towers engender horror and disbelief, much like Sam Shere's pictures of terrified passengers escaping the *Hindenburg*. Echoes of the work of Diane Arbus, Garry Winogrand, Magritte— it's all there, all shot basically in one seventy-two-hour period "by thousands of Mathew Bradys." (Clichés got a workout, too: One of the most popular images from Ground Zero, of three firemen hoisting the American flag, was a conscious reworking of the famous Iwo Jima shot by Joe Rosenthal.)

This phenomenal outpouring of imagery did not go unnoticed. Already, books are being published, and shows have come and gone. Almost immediately, the Digital Journalist, a popular Internet photography site, hailed "the Return of Photojournalism," and came up with an astonishing factoid: The days immediately following the tragedy marked the first time that more people logged on to news sites than pornography. The Digital Journalist also offered comments by a number of well-known photojournalists who had shot the devastation in Lower Manhattan. One of them was James Nachtwey, who almost died on the job dodging debris. He said, "I have never seen more amazing pictures from so many photographers as this story. New York must be full of incredibly talented photographers who probably very rarely have a chance to show what they can do."

· · ·

Larry Towell, *A Minister Amid the Wreckage of the World Trade Center,* September 11, 2001

An unusual number of photojournalists were in town that day, in part because Magnum, perhaps the most historically important cooperative agency for photojournalists, had had a board meeting the night before. Still, when the agency opened for business on the morning of September 11, no one was prepared. David Strettell, Magnum's director of cultural projects, remembers: "We didn't know how many of our photographers were able to get to the site. It was very difficult to get through on any of the lines—cell phones were busy—so we decided to do something which we don't usually do at Magnum, which is send out our interns and some of the darkroom printers, anyone who had a camera." By the end of the first day, it became clear that many of Magnum's most famous photographers had indeed been shooting since the buildings were hit. But the interns and people who usually print their more famous colleagues' work also had their photographs put up on the agency's website and made available to magazines and newspapers.

Adam Wiseman, a Magnum printer, ended up having four two-page spreads published in *Le Monde 2,* and his photographs are also reproduced in the book that Magnum has just released chronicling the attacks and their aftermath. But Wiseman didn't plan to come out of this a published photographer. He recalls, "I wasn't thinking about shooting for publication or for Magnum, or for anything, in fact. It was purely instinctive as a photographer, and as a New Yorker, to want to document what was happening. Absolutely everyone who had access to a camera was shooting. I saw this one man in SoHo, on West Broadway, who was obviously a fashion photographer shooting away with a large-format Polaroid, which is very burdensome. And then there were people with disposable cameras. In my pictures you see half the people in the crowd have cameras on them."

Susan Meiselas is a Magnum photographer who has worked all over the world, including Iran, Iraq, Turkey, Tajikistan, northern Afghanistan, Kazakhstan, and Nicaragua. She was once wounded by a land mine in El Salvador while working for *Time.* Her photographs from September 11 of people running for their lives with the volcanic smoke behind them are some of the most emotional images to have emerged thus far from the tragedy. Disquieting in a different way is her shot of a banal sculpture of a businessman with his briefcase open, now covered with and surrounded by tons of paper and debris. But after photographing in New York night and day through the first weekend, she grew understandably uncomfortable with the spectacle the tragedy had become. I asked her about the stampede to photograph the World Trade Center, and she tackled the subject as someone who has struggled for years with what it means to record human suffering: "It's sort of unspeakable to be watching with whatever lens one is using, whether it's one's eyes, or with a camera. . . . The tourism of it all was not something I saw in the kinds of war settings where I've usually been, be it Central America or the Middle East. The question is, how was *our* lens different? What is it that we do that's different? How much is photography about just being in the right place at the right time, and standing still and watching?"

Like many of the photographers I spoke with who have worked in the Middle East and Central Asia, and who have endured the media's and the public's previous lack of interest in what they have witnessed in those corners of the world, Meiselas sees some sort of cause-and-effect relationship between America's blindered isolationism and the current crisis. She said, "People didn't want to see those images [from overseas] and deal with those realities, and that's another cost of this. How do we prepare ourselves now for what the world is really like?"

Good question. Let's face it: Most of us have been embarrassingly ignorant of the places and people we are now receiving crash courses on. Since its invention, photography has been one of the great tools of enlightenment, though the medium has at times been oversimplified as a conductor of truth. But it does offer a way of getting to know the world, which is how photojournalist Steve McCurry sees it. McCurry, who is one of the most passionate photojournalists shooting today, has worked all over the world, including Kashmir, Sri Lanka,

Cambodia, and Yemen. He covered the Gulf War and the violence in Lebanon, and has worked in Pakistan and Afghanistan some sixteen times. Many of the images that we are now seeing of the Afghan people were taken by McCurry—such as his most famous shot, a 1984 portrait of a young Afghan woman with black hair and pale green eyes. (When I was in Paris this October that image was ubiquitous at newsstands, in bookstores, and on kiosks. *Portraits,* a book by McCurry that features the picture on its cover, has become very "in" with the fashion set; when I asked Karl Lagerfeld what it is about the picture that seems to be grabbing people, he replied, "The hopeless beauty of it.")

McCurry had arrived back in New York, his home, on the night of September 10, after a grueling trip that had taken him through China, India, Nepal, Hong Kong, and London. In New York, he lives in the same Village building where André Kertész once had an apartment. Like many of the photographers I spoke with, McCurry has a clear view from his home of where the World Trade Center once stood. (Kertész's pictures of the buildings, shot from there, now have even more power than they did when they were taken.) McCurry was opening his piles of mail when the Twin Towers were struck, and he remembers, "I ran up to the roof, and what I saw was so horrific and unmentionable. Words can't describe the kind of horror that I was feeling, but it didn't even come close to the kind of emotion I felt when I actually saw them start to crumble. It was just about the worst moment of my life. You kind of felt like the world was coming unglued. I wasn't thinking about anything other than to record this thing. I didn't call the agency. . . . I wasn't thinking about assignments or magazines. I was just thinking this is something which is so monumental I just had to be there to record it. That's basically what I do. I'm a photographer. It's how I think and operate, covering situations that are pivotal."

Nowadays McCurry, who decided he wanted to be a photographer when he first saw the work of Henri Cartier-Bresson and W. Eugene Smith, works mostly for *National Geographic.* He is enormously respected in the field, but as he says, "It's not as though my phone is ringing off the hook." I have a feeling all of that is about to change. His image of a fireman, seen through a shattered window, climbing up a pile of destruction is among the most chilling pictures we have seen from September 11.

Like many others in downtown New York, I saw it all with my own eyes—my office window, twenty blocks north, is like a camera lens pointing toward the World Trade Center site. When the first tower was hit, it seemed inconceivable that such a thing could happen—and impossible that the other tower could be hit. It was. There was no way I could imagine the buildings would come down. They did. I saw the glass and metal fill the sky, and the people jumping. When news spread that the Pentagon had been struck, too, like many other people I kept wondering if our culture had itself provided the narrative to whoever was responsible. After all, this was a plot familiar from so many Hollywood movies, which now looked tame compared with what I was witnessing through my window. But it was only later, when I began to see the still photographs, that the human scale of what had occurred started to come into focus. For me, it was the intimate shots of people looking up in utter terror, or running for their lives with makeshift masks to keep them from choking to death, that really hit home. When I look now at the photographs of people high up on ledges trying to save themselves, or down on the ground with a shroud of ash all over them, I think of something that Gilles Peress, a staff photographer for *The New Yorker*, told me: "It was a moment of pulverization, essentially of everything, of the buildings, the people, the meaning of the continuum of history."

I think of September 11 as the day photography got back one of its most important jobs, the day it regained its potential. Now let's watch it go to work as we try to stop the world from blowing up.

Vanity Fair, December 2001

Koons, High and Low

It was a recent winter evening in New York, and the artist Jeff Koons was overseeing the completion of one of his new paintings, *Cheeky*. With its grilled cheese sandwich and flying bikini, the work is an eccentric marriage of Surrealism and Pop art. Koons's eyes never left what his assistants were doing on *Cheeky* for very long as they fine-tuned certain parts of the work, sharpening details. Every once in a while, his face a complete deadpan, he ever so politely corrected them—it was as if they were medical residents assisting him at an operation. But considering that they were trying to intensify the deliciously melted look of the grilled cheese sandwich, the solemnity of the enterprise would have definitely made some people shake their heads at the crazy art world. Another thing that might have startled people was where all this was going on. We weren't in the artist's studio, but at his New York gallery, the dealer Ileana Sonnabend's new place in Chelsea. The picture had already been up on the wall for almost a week!

If one has to ask, How can he still be working on a piece that has left the studio and is considered finished enough to be on view?, then one doesn't know Koons. He calls it "tweaking," and over the years he has tweaked his work in nearly every important museum in the world. His notorious perfectionism is a key to what has made his life as an artist so theatrical, and his art so powerful. It has also meant that some of his work has taken years to complete, and it has led some people to call him impossible. In fact, Koons's belief in the importance of not letting his audience down, of showing nothing but flawless art, has on a number of occasions virtually bankrupted him.

But on the winter night when the finishing touches were being administered to *Cheeky*, the mood was very up. After a biblical-seeming period encompassing

Grillo Demo, *Party Hat, Jeff Koons's Studio*, 1997

seven years of artistic struggle, coupled with a personal saga of familial, legal, and financial hell, Koons, forty-six, one of the most successful and controversial artists of the 1980s, is once again on a major career roll. He has finally begun to exhibit some pieces of "Celebration," the technically daunting sculpture and painting project that he began in 1993 and that so often looked like a Sisyphean task. Furthermore, in the last two years he's begun, finished, and exhibited a number of new bodies of work, and after a long and unhappy split, he is back at the Sonnabend Gallery, where he began his career. Meanwhile, his prices at auction have been impressive—his 1988 porcelain sculpture *Pink Panther* sold for $1.8 million at Christie's last year, a record for the artist. At the end of March he'll unveil yet another body of work at a much-anticipated show at the dealer Larry Gagosian's Los Angeles gallery. All in all, not bad for a guy whose career obituary was being written just a couple of years ago.

But not everything has turned around in Koons's life. He is entangled in various lawsuits over his finances, including one with some of his ex-lawyers, and he is still fighting to enforce his custody rights to his eight-year-old son, Ludwig, which were awarded him by American courts in 1994. That decision went the way of the wild, however, because Ludwig's mother and Koons's ex-wife, Ilona Staller, had already taken the baby to Italy, where she lives. The story of what's gone on between Koons and Staller makes the fights between Muhammad Ali and Joe Frazier or the marriages of Elizabeth Taylor and Richard Burton pale in comparison. This is drama with a capital *D.* It is also deliriously nutty. The ex–Mrs. Koons has her own claim to fame: One of the most popular international pornography stars of all time, Staller, forty-nine, who also goes by the name of La Cicciolina, stunned the world in 1987 when she won a seat in the Italian parliament, which she held for five years as a member of the Radical Party. (Her friendly campaigns, which included a nude ride through Rome on top of a horse, make our own recent election look substantive.) She and Koons met in 1989, and their head-spinning union produced not only Ludwig but some of the most talked-about and controversial artworks of the twentieth century. The relationship itself was so out there that many people thought it was a publicity stunt. If only life, or Koons, were that simple.

Ed Paschke, the Chicago-based painter who mentored Koons during his college years, tells a story about Koons that suggests how singular his devotion to art was even during his student days: "On one occasion Jeff was assisting me in my studio as I was preparing for a show that was going to Paris. There were a bunch of real large paintings that he was stretching for me. I didn't have canvas pliers, so he was doing it by hand. I noticed that he was developing blisters on the tips of his fingers, so I said, 'Jeff, you know, maybe we should stop that and do something else because you're going to hurt yourself.' He answered, 'No, I'm determined to finish this and do it right.' He continued and the blisters broke and the tips of his fingers were bleeding. So there's a Jeff Koons stigmata on the edge of one of these canvases."

The story captures Koons perfectly—a man who will literally bleed for art (though he himself doesn't actually paint or sculpt or draw anymore; like many contemporary artists, he's more an *auteur* in the cinematic sense of directing a complex collaborative enterprise). There are very few artists who will push themselves and their work to the edge the way he does, and even though his personality can come across as flat in the way of a mechanized figure, Koons is actually quite theatrical; along the way—with a little bit of help from a few artistic forebears such as Salvador Dalí and Andy Warhol—Koons invented a persona for himself as a kind of art salesman, mischievous yet also achingly sincere. By now he's become that persona so completely that one can't tell where it begins and the original Jeff ends. The total package, Jeff Koons, is like a great American character one might find in a book by Walker Percy or James Thurber or Sinclair Lewis, but updated. When I was talking to the designer Helmut Lang about Koons, Lang said, "It's as though he's the son of Pee-wee Herman and Lucille Ball." That's close.

Koons has always reminded me of Darrin Stephens, the very courteous husband in the sixties TV show *Bewitched.* They have the same clean-cut appearance and an "I want to be liked" aura. Koons isn't literally in advertising, as Darrin was, but in a weird way he's in a related business—selling the beauty of vacuum cleaners, for instance, in the sculptural works that first won him notoriety in the early eighties. But where Darrin had to count on the women in his family when a touch of magic was required to make things better, Koons, whose own wife proved less accommodating, is an expert at casting his own spells.

Part of the magic of Koons's art is the way he melds high and low and keeps the work feeling so alive. He may spend years developing his projects, but by the end you'd never know it, because for all his intensity over the finish of his art, Koons is a master of the light touch. And yet, there's always more with him than meets the eye. The artist's work is packed with an art historical consciousness, and critics and historians have linked it to Surrealism, Hyperrealism, Pop, Minimalism—you name it, it's all in there—but the results are never didactic or academic. They're as accessible as products in a supermarket. Take his "Celebration" painting *Play-Doh:* It looks as if the whole history of Abstract Expressionism came crashing into Pop art. Think of Willem de Kooning and James Rosenquist producing an heir and you've got it, but you've also got a work that communicates to everybody—a painting, after all, of Play-Doh. Or how about a massive sculpture of a kitten peeking out of a sock? If the imagery sounds obvious, that's part of the point with Koons. He doesn't have the ambivalence, or the cynicism, that comes with postmodern thinking. What he does have is a need to make things that can connect to other people. Like Warhol and Roy Lichtenstein, whom he credits as major inspirations, he has completely integrated the American idea of democracy into his art. To Koons, everything and everyone is worthy of art. His work is the successful result of the more idealistic movements of twentieth-century art—he actually *has* made art for everyone. Once, in his brasher days, he said, "I've made what the Beatles would have made if they had made sculpture. Nobody ever said that the Beatles' music was not on a high level, but it appealed to a mass audience. That's what I want to do." The truth is, I've never seen an artist who wanted to reach the general public more than Koons does. This has made him the most popular artist of his generation. It has also made him the most misunderstood.

Jeff Koons was born in 1955 in York, Pennsylvania, an industrial town with a population of some sixty thousand. During one of the many talks that we had for this article he told me, "My life experience has been through my art." The reverse is also true: Through Koons's art one can witness the story of his life. In his telling, his childhood sounds like the living incarnation of a TV version of a stereotypical all-American, whiter-than-white family of the 1950s and early 1960s. His father, Henry Koons, owned a furniture store and also did some interior decorating for the local swells; his mom, Gloria, was always waiting with cookies and milk when Jeff and his sister, Karen, came home from school. When Jeff was five they moved to Dover, a suburb right outside York, where they had found a bigger, better home, a Georgian colonial. By then Koons had already started to act the part of the little artist. There's a portrait of him in which he is proudly sitting with a box of Ethelbert crayons. Apart from the fact that Koons is just a tot, the picture looks remarkably like those photos of budding industrialists from the period that one would find in *Fortune* magazine. Koons has the same scrubbed look, the same haircut, the same cock of his head as he looks directly at the camera that those on-their-way-up-the-ladder businessmen had. But instead of a cigar he's holding a crayon, and instead of a suit he's wearing a flowered shirt that seems very Pop today. The artist used the photograph in an artwork twenty years later, titling it *The New Jeff Koons*—that's how telling it is. In the picture, he already had a version of what would become his signature look—part Frankie Avalon, part Elvis Presley, part pleased-to-meet-ya Rotarian.

In Koons's recollections of his early life, there are no tantrums, no pot scandals, no deep traumas. There were family outings to amusement parks—not to museums—and visits to his grandmother who lived nearby. He still speaks fondly of the saltine crackers with jam that she'd dole out to him and his sister—not quite your Proustian madeleine, but it is the kind of imagery that Koons loves to put in his art these days. In tenth grade, he fell for Shelly Myers, a straight-A student who encouraged Jeff's artistic ambitions, and who still bakes him an occasional pumpkin pie. It can all sound too good to be true, not at all like the torment artists often describe when they talk about growing up. Koons has said, "My life was innocent and beautiful," and, whether or not the reality was that uncomplicated, one can feel in much of his art a drive to capture those feelings.

This was not a situation where, when the kid said he wanted to be an artist, the parents broke out the smelling salts. On the contrary, they'd been encouraging him with lessons since he was five—and, as if conscious of the historical importance that his art would eventually have, they'd also saved almost everything he'd done. Weekends, Jeff's proud dad would take him along to work, where Jeff pitched in at the store, or helped out on house calls to the wealthier clients, or at least acted as though he was doing these things until he was old enough to really contribute. This introduction to the world of appearances left a deep impression. As Jeff remembers it, "The furniture store really seemed like theater. It was like a stage set, because it was always changing. I realized that through different aesthetic choices my emotions would be affected. If I would go into one room and there would be red carpeting and a dark couch, it would create one kind of atmosphere, and then if I'd go back the next week and there'd be a gold-and-turquoise setup, the feelings would be completely different. I enjoyed that." The store would also become Jeff's first art gallery. When he was about eight he painted copies of old masters and signed them "Jeffrey Koons." He made this Duchampian move without knowing anything about art history, and his dad recognized a good thing. He put the paintings in the windows of the store. Soon they were selling for as much as a few hundred dollars each.

There was never any question about whether Jeff would go to art school, and after graduating from high school in 1972 he chose the Maryland Institute College of Art in Baltimore. It was during his first year there that he finagled an appointment with one of his art heroes, Salvador Dalí. There weren't many art books in the Koons household when Jeff was growing up, but Dalí was among the handful of artists whose work made it onto the coffee table. One might even say that he was Jeff's first role model. In any case, Koons had read in the local papers that the older artist, then sixty-eight, was in New York, staying, as he always did, at the St. Regis. Koons rang him up. Dalí—possibly the most narcissistic artist to have ever existed, although he's had a lot of competition—must have been happy to hear from a young fan, no doubt one who flattered him, because the painter invited Jeff to come up and meet him. The following Saturday, Koons took the train to New York, and, at least for the budding artist, the meeting at the hotel was a hit. The mustachioed Dalí was dolled up in his drama-queen cape, with a young trophy blonde on his arm; Jeff was decked out in his Sunday best—it's a threesome I would love to have witnessed. They got along so well that they moved on to the Upper East Side's M. Knoedler & Co. gallery, where a show of Dalí's had just opened. It was only when Jeff started to take too long with the photos he was snapping of Dalí (which he still keeps in his studio) that the big-shot artist decided enough was enough. "He was saying, 'Hurry up, kid. I can't hold this pose all day,' " Koons remembers. But Jeff went back to Baltimore that night with big dreams.

At college, Jeff definitely got himself noticed. Paschke, his teacher-hero, remembers, "He had a disarming way about him that has allowed him to network in a very effective way, but aside from all those personal skills, he had abilities as an artist." Koons's paintings and drawings from that time, figurative works that incorporated religious iconography, tied into not only art history but what he saw around him, including the local bars and strip joints that Paschke would take him to. "There was a certain edge about the work," the older artist recalls. "I think it attempted to tap into the relationship between spirituality and the carnal aspect of the human spirit."

After college, which included an exchange year at the Art Institute of Chicago—where he met Paschke—Koons moved to New York City. This was 1977. Within two weeks he got a job at the Museum of Modern Art. Lots of artists work in museums, particularly when they start out—it's almost an initiation rite, and the list of artists who have worked at MoMA reads like a who's who. But the few years that Koons spent manning the Modern's membership desk in its front lobby have become legendary. Koons relished his interactions with the public and the opportunities to get visitors excited by art. He was a kind of half performance artist, half salesman, and he invented all sorts of getups to attract customers. He dyed his hair red and would often cultivate a pencil mustache, after Dalí. His inventory of outfits included paper bibs, loud polka-dot shirts, a double tie that he'd match with a sequined jacket. One of his favorite accessories was an inflatable flower—the kind that you buy at a toy store or variety shop. He'd wrap it around his neck, and it attracted people like a magnet. This inflatable was actually related to the art project that Jeff was working on in his two-room apartment on East Fourth Street. In the playfully subversive spirit of Marcel Duchamp, who had turned everyday objects such as urinals into art pieces (which he called readymades), Koons was experimenting with all sorts of store-bought colored inflatable flowers and inflatable bunnies, combining them with plastic, Plexiglas, and mirrors to create what are now considered his earliest serious artworks.

These lowly inflatables would eventually lead to some of Koons's most brilliant, iconic work—and they also helped him stand out at his job at the Modern. But while his sales techniques may have been popular with the public, they weren't a hit with everyone. William Rubin, then the chief curator, who had enormous power at the institution, was one person who could have lived without the Bob Hope–like entertainment factor that Koons was bringing to the serious matter of art appreciation. Koons says that on a number of occasions, when visiting dignitaries were expected at the museum, the museum's director, Richard Oldenburg, had the task of telling Koons to beat it. "He was always very nice about it," Koons remembers. "He'd say something like 'Jeff, we really appreciate what you're doing, but we wonder if you'd mind not coming into work just for tomorrow.'" While Oldenburg doesn't remember having to ask Koons to leave, he does recall him fondly, and remembers that, despite whispers of Koons's flamboyance, he sold five times as many memberships as any other salesperson.

Plenty of others who watched what went on at that desk could tell that Koons had a big future, and he had no shortage of job offers, especially in sales. One of these offers helped give Koons the courage finally to leave the museum in 1980, when he was twenty-five. He got himself licensed to sell mutual funds and stocks, began working at First Investors Corporation, and was thus able to finance his first breakthrough pieces, which involved household appliances and lights. These works—displaying a fantastic variety of vacuum cleaners and shampoo polishers, always presented in clear Plexiglas containers and illuminated by industrial fluorescent lights—ultimately occupied Koons's attention for the next six or seven years. These pieces work by giving the viewer a series of shocks—the shock, say, that vacuum cleaners have been recontextualized as art, and the shock that they look so beautiful. (These aren't just any appliances, but the visual caviar of vacuum cleaners and shampoo polishers—Hoover Deluxes, Hoover Celebrities, and Shelton Wet-Dries, among other brands, all gorgeous examples of design and craftsmanship.) To many observers, these impeccably packaged sculptures, glowingly lit to suggest an aura of holiness, are like shrines to the gods of American consumerism, and a comment on our love of the new. Some take that to mean Koons is being ironic about our culture, even cynical. Actually, though, when one talks to Koons about this work, it gets much more interesting and personal—Freud would have a field day with the artist's interpretations of the sexual identities of these objects. "The sexuality sometimes goes back and forth," he told me recently. "I can look at an upright Hoover Convertible and think of it as being masculine because of the handle. A moment later, I can look at the same vacuum cleaner and read it as feminine because of the womblike quality of the bag. This type of duality is also stated in the Shelton vacuum cleaner, which has written on its side WET/DRY."

By 1980, some positive critical response to the vacuum-cleaner pieces, including a mention in *Artforum,* the magazine that I edited in the eighties, had helped secure him a window installation at the New Museum of Contemporary Art, as well as given him a presence in a variety of group shows. But he was having a harder time getting a dealer to make a commitment to him. When Koons told Mary Boone—who was showing many of the decade's new art stars, such as David Salle and Julian Schnabel—that he wasn't going to stick around and wait for her to give him his first exhibition, she said, "Good." Another powerful dealer offered to try out one of his vacuum pieces in her home; the next day she told him to come and cart it away. Making the piece had taken every cent he had. Evicted from his apartment and broke from spending all his earnings on his art (fancy European vacuum cleaners cost quite a bit more than, say, oil paints and canvas), Koons feared his career was over.

But after a summer respite with Mom and Dad, who had moved to Sarasota, Florida (Koons took on a brief job there as a political canvasser), he returned to New York, now twenty-seven, determined that this time he was going to make it. Thanks in part to the contacts he'd made at the Modern, he found a new career on Wall Street as a commodities broker, first at Clayton Brokerage Company and then at Smith Barney. (He recently told me that he liked selling cotton commodities the most. When I asked why, he said it was because he is an artist and cotton is soft.) There is no doubt these experiences helped Koons hone his skills as a salesman. He needed to earn well, too, because he had fixated on a new, even more expensive idea for his art.

The series of works he eventually created is titled "Equilibrium." It has all the multiple layers—psychological, social, physical, sexual, and art historical—that inform Koons's greatest works. There are bronzes—of a life jacket, for example—in the series that refer to the art of Jasper Johns, especially to his famous bronze beer cans. There are photo-based pieces that play on the influence of advertising and sports iconography, especially the publicity campaigns of Nike. But the most famous works in the series, basketballs suspended in perfect equipoise in aquariums, are what really stand out as original. The artist had become so obsessed with figuring out how to pull this idea off—it proved to be quite a technically complicated feat to suspend a basketball in a tank of distilled water—that he was spending a lot of time at work on Wall Street on the phone with scientists he thought could advise him. He finally tracked down Dr. Richard P. Feynman, a Nobel Prize winner in physics, who pushed him toward a solution, helping out with the science of density gradients. (The trick is that you have to make the basketball too light to sink and too heavy to rise. The solution, to vastly oversimplify, involved filling the ball itself with water and then layering the bottom two-thirds of the tank with salt water and the top third with pure water. For all that, the suspension lasts only about six months; collectors need to have the pieces serially reinstalled, for which Koons provides a video and manual.) As metaphors for life these works have infinite power, from the way they evoke the goal of staying in balance to the way they embody a desire for immortality. And the choice of a basketball in a tank to convey this message is pure Koons. It's interesting to look at Damien Hirst's famous formaldehyde tanks in the context of this work, and almost impossible to miss how Koons influenced his younger British colleague.

Following spread: Grillo Demo, *A View of Works in Progress, Jeff Koons's Studio,* 1997

．　．　．

Some critics were appalled when Charles Saatchi, one of the most important collectors of American art at the time, paid seventy-five thousand dollars for a Koons work—a stainless-steel bourbon train—from a subsequent show, held in 1986, at International with Monument, an artist-run gallery that was the "it" place that year. It was only a matter of time before Koons would end up in one of the big-league galleries, and this finally happened when he joined in a group show with three other young artists—Peter Halley, Ashley Bickerton, and Meyer Vaisman—at Sonnabend in the fall of 1986. The exhibition became the only subject in the art world for a minute. (It was somewhat misleadingly referred to as the Neo-Geo show, because of Halley's geometric abstractions.) All four artists were very much of the moment; their art had an intellectuality and a sense of cool that were in obvious contrast to the neo-Expressionism of people such as Schnabel, Salle, Anselm Kiefer, and Sigmar Polke who had come before it. Koons's contribution to the show included a stainless-steel bouquet of flowers, and busts, also in stainless steel, of Louis XIV and Bob Hope. But the piece that grabbed the spotlight was *Rabbit,* his flawless stainless-steel casting of an inflatable bunny. It was a forty-one-inch-high art bomb that thumbed its nose at the aesthetics of high art and yet at the same time embraced them, a fusion of Pop and Brancusi. With its wit, its physical simplicity, and its characteristically Koonsian reference to sexual symbols and childhood pleasures, *Rabbit* has become one of the artist's most famous and enduring icons. He would say at the time, "I'm making some of the greatest art being made now. It'll take the art world 10 years to get around to it. In this century there was Picasso and Duchamp. Now I'm taking us out of the 20th century." Not the kind of modesty that wins a guy friends. (It's fascinating how Koons's appropriation of the flat Warholian statement began as something that could seem very arrogant and has more recently developed into a paradigm of humility.)

But even with the puffed-up claims, he earned the respect of some major players in the contemporary art world. All over town, arguments were being waged about Koons and his work in a way that happens only when something truly audacious and brilliant occurs in art. For some time he had gone beyond simply appropriating the ready-made icon; he was now performing acts of transformation and transcendence. Kirk Varnedoe, today the chief curator of painting and sculpture at the Museum of Modern Art, is one of many viewers who stayed put when he saw that silver bunny. He recalls, "There are just a few occasions in my art experience in New York where I've been sort of knocked dead by an object instantly. This piece was just riveting. You wanted to laugh, you were shocked, you were planted to the floor. I was galvanized by the object. It has such an amazing physical presence. The swollen nature of it, the preternaturally round head and bulging seams of it, give it a kind of compressed and packed energy you feel instantly when you're in the presence of it. *Uncanny* is the word that comes to mind. There were so many different things going on at once in the piece. It was hilarious, it was smart, and it was chilling. When I looked at the head of the bunny, I thought of the photograph of Neil Armstrong on the moon, with the big, round, reflecting visor. It had that kind of Utopian high-gloss modern clarity to it."

The financial history of that little bunny is its own incredible tale. As is typical, Koons usually fabricates his sculpture in editions of three, plus one artist's proof. After the show, one bunny went to Ileana Sonnabend, one went to Charles Saatchi, and the third was bought by Terry Winters, a painter who liked the piece and who also shows at the gallery. Koons kept the artist's proof (until he had to sell it because of mounting debts). Sonnabend and Antonio Homem, director of the gallery, remember counseling Winters that, with a forty-thousand-dollar price tag, the piece was a good investment. It eventually sold to S. I. Newhouse, Jr., and now that he has promised the piece to the Modern as a gift, it is one of the museum's most prized objects. At "Open Ends," the final cycle of MoMA's millennial exhibitions, the sculpture had a place of honor in an exhibition that included works by Koons's heroes Warhol and Lichtenstein. Meanwhile, the other steel bunnies are among the most sought-after artworks of our time. Sonnabend says she could never sell hers—it would probably go for between two and three million and counting—because so many collectors have asked her for it that she'd end up infuriating many of them; she discusses the piece with such affection that she might just take it with her.

At any rate, soon after Koons pulled his rabbit out of his hat he became an official artist in the Sonnabend stable. The dealer says some people were aghast that her gallery, which had such a solid reputation for serious contemporary art, representing the likes of Robert Rauschenberg and Robert Morris, would consider hooking up with Koons. When he unveiled his next New York show, in 1988, neither those who loved his work nor those who thought it represented the end of civilization were disappointed. For this exhibition, Koons had switched from stainless steel to ceramic, wood, and porcelain and titled his new group of works "Banality." True to his word, he started with a group of icons one would more likely find in a tchotchkes shop or at a rummage sale than poised to enter the canon of high art. In a porcelain sculpture decorated with gold leaf, Michael Jackson, one of Koons's favorite pop icons, holds his chimpanzee, Bubbles, the singer's legs stretched as if he were an odalisque; one of the shocks set off by this piece is the fact that Koons has done his own plastic surgery on Jackson and Bubbles, turning them snow white. (At the time, the real-life Jackson's complexion had lightened only as far as café au lait.) In another piece a blond, busty B-movie type embraces a slightly puzzled-looking Pink Panther, in the process recalling elements of the Baroque and Rococo. This was the exhibition that had the critic Robert Hughes complaining, "The art world is grievously ill at the moment."

But it wasn't just the lowbrow subject matter that stunned people: In "Banality" one sees how deeply Koons understands the power of materials—it misses the point to assume this is one big exercise in kitsch. For this project he engaged workshops in Germany and Italy that had a long tradition of working in ceramic, porcelain, and wood. Their craftsmen were able to respond to his needs, his pushing, and his direction, and the resulting objects have a breathtaking authenticity. Koons himself has been quoted as saying, "I was telling the Bourgeois to embrace the things that it likes, the things it responds to. For example, when you were a young child and you went to your grandmother's place and she had this little knickknack, that's inside you, and that's part you. Embrace that, don't try to erase it."

Koons's next foray into popular imagery would prove to be one of the wildest episodes in twentieth-century art as well as an incredible tale from a human standpoint. Koons says it all started when he saw a picture of Ilona Staller in *Stern* magazine, sometime in 1988. Lightning struck. He recalls, "I was making a billboard for an exhibition at the Whitney Museum. And in the tradition of collage, I thought it would be interesting to put myself with her in a photograph. I came up with the idea of a work called *Made in Heaven,* which would be advertised on a billboard like it's a film. I guess I felt that I was an art star, and I was playing with the idea of becoming another kind of star in our celebrity culture."

He sent her an invitation, via his lawyers, to become a part of his work. She told me that his first correspondence did not exactly have her jumping up and down with excitement. As she remembers it (in her Italianate English), "I never heard the name Jeff Koons in my life—probably because I wasn't so interested in contemporary art at that time. I like so much Dalí. I love so much Marilyn by what's-his-name. But, believe me, I never heard the name Jeff. One day I got the fax saying that Jeff Koons was a very important artist American who wants to meet Ilona Cicciolina. . . . I think maybe this is a very strange thing, maybe best [to say] no. I bring this fax and make trash. But my ex-manager [said], 'No, no, no. We should respond because this artist might be doing good work.'"

Koons's choice of a model couldn't have been more spot-on for him, aesthetically. Staller's persona, La Cicciolina, was like a living readymade for him—her sets and her costumes had a flair for presentation that was Koonsian even before he tuned in to her. Even the plots of her erotic videos have that oddball sense of innocence that is such a big part of his work. She also shares his gift for selling. When I called her recently in Rome she explained, "I am artist because I have my own sensibility. I have my popularity. . . . You know, so many very beautiful young women exist in the world, but so many [of] those young and beautiful women have to disappear because no have talent, or something *significante*. . . . Or *magnetismo*. Now, I know I have every [one of] these things."

Add chutzpah, or the Italian equivalent. Staller, who is forty-nine now, was actually born in Budapest, and was once crowned Miss Hungary. She's likely done quite a bit of creative editing of her own life story, which is told in rather hilarious detail on her website, cicciolina.com. (Minors, beware.) By the seventies she was living in Rome and ended up on Italian radio. Somewhere along the way she also got into pornography (sorting out her story is a bit like untangling Janis Joplin's hair). It was on the radio that Cicciolina, which translates as "little dumpling," was created. In fact, she's more like a French curve than a dumpling, and these assets paid off on her next venture, which proved that all those feminist and postmodern theorists were onto something when they said that "sex is political." When she was voted into the Italian parliament, Cicciolina used her va-va-vavoom power and popularity to push a fairly serious liberal agenda that included animal rights, women's equality, environmental protection, sex education, legalization of drugs, free love, and peace in the Middle East. She didn't encounter much legislative success during her five-year stint—her absences became almost as talked about as her surprising presence. (No Hillary Clinton, she.)

It was inevitable that she and Koons would click on all fronts. When they finally got together to begin to work on the Whitney billboard—he was then thirty-four; she was thirty-eight—Koons was smitten. He would later say, "I met somebody who played a victim to pornography, and I found her at the time to be very beautiful. I found her very innocent. . . . I fell in love with her." But it took the more experienced Staller longer to succumb to this eager American fellow. She describes their first collaboration like this: "I like him, but I not fall in love. I said to him, 'I not love you.' He said, 'I wait—finally you love me.' . . . He have a fascination, no? Not easy to understand. Sometimes when we going and eating, I see him, he see me. We not speak [each other's language], but we look in face. . . . I give a kissing face, but we not have sex in that time."

Eventually though she, too, was a goner, and they began a romantic relationship, one that would turn out to be a momentous chapter in both their personal lives but would also lead to the creation of a series of paintings and sculptures—in porcelain, wood, glass, and marble—that broke taboos that had been firmly in place in Western art for hundreds of years, bringing sex into the foreground of contemporary art as frankly and as shockingly as Robert Mapplethorpe's photographs did.

It was in late 1989—after the whole censorship controversy that had erupted over the cancellation of Mapplethorpe's exhibition at the Corcoran Gallery in Washington—that I received a call from Koons inviting me to go and see some new things he was working on. I had written about the Mapplethorpe brouhaha for *The New Yorker*, but I was not prepared for what Koons showed me: photographs of himself and Cicciolina so explicit and geared to shock that there was no way the work could avoid charges of pornography; in fact, it seemed to invite them. I remember sitting there, looking at the slides that he was projecting on a screen, and wondering what the hell I was going to say when the lights went on. By then we knew each other pretty well, and looking at slides of one of your professional acquaintances naked, with an erection, getting into all sorts of contortions with a porn star, ejaculating, isn't exactly an everyday occurrence for art critics. It would have been stupid to pretend that this was plain old ordinary art. I had also noticed that Koons was very caught up in his physique. He had shown me his weight room—he was like an athlete in training for the Olympics. (This was probably a good idea, considering the acrobatics he and Staller were getting into.) By the way he spoke about her, and because he seemed to have a newfound physical sense of himself, I could tell that there was more going on here than the possibility of a blockbuster show and notoriety beyond what he'd ever dreamed of. It was obvious to me that Koons had a lot more invested in Cicciolina than simply his next body of work.

Before it all fell apart, this couple seemed to be exactly what Koons had titled it in the beginning: a match "made in heaven." On a few occasions I had the chance to witness them together up close. Between her exaggerated sweetness and his courteousness the effect was a bit like hanging out with a Hallmark card. But there were obvious contradictions in play, some of them untenable. Koons may have been willing to exploit Cicciolina's image as a human readymade. ("Ilona and I were born for each other," he said at one point. "She's a media woman. I'm a media man. We are the contemporary Adam and Eve.") But at the same time he wasn't ready to drop all the values that he holds sacred. Recently when I was talking to him, I asked if at the onset of their relationship he'd worried about whether their different experiences of the world—she an "Only in Italy, kids" combination of porn star and politician, he a cutting-edge artist, but one with an idealized, *Father Knows Best* view of family life—might be a source of romantic difficulties. He replied, "I just felt that the art world would be a world where actually, if we were really in love and if she did want to distance herself from her past and not continue to hang on to it, that this could work and that the art world could accept it. So I really kind of blindly went forward."

For her part Staller says she was pleased to be in this new arena: "I am very happy about [meeting Jeff] because I liked so much the idea of being in the art world." She also told me, "I loved Jeff so much. We did good sexually. He very sweet sometimes. He was incredible person. I don't know what happened." That's the thing that makes this story so compelling: Even though their romance played out in some of the most exhibitionistic displays to ever take place between two celebrities (which says a lot), it was painfully real.

When a few of the works that came out of their first graphic photo session were previewed at the Venice Biennale in the summer of 1990, Koons and Cicciolina caused the kind of hoopla with paparazzi that normally goes on at movie festivals such as Cannes. It seemed as though the two of them were well on their way to becoming a whole new kind of first couple of the arts. They announced their intention to marry. There were a few little setbacks—such as the fight that occurred when Cicciolina publicly announced she would sleep with Saddam Hussein if he'd release foreigners being held in Iraq and Koons became a furious jealous boyfriend. Despite such obvious differences in perspective, passion won out, and there was a marriage in Budapest in 1991. The pictures look like some kind of blast from the past—a shy bride and a beaming groom.

What came next, however, was anything but a typical art show. In the fall of 1991 the complete "Made in Heaven" exhibition was unveiled at Sonnabend. By then, word of mouth on this body of work was so strong that the television cameras were lined up outside the gallery on opening day. Koons's mother refers to this exhibition as "The You-Know-What Show," and one can hardly blame her. There were pieces on the walls that were so out there, one could blush describing them. No matter how worldly one was, this show was a real mind bender. I was at the gallery on the Saturday it opened, and I have to say there was plenty that was funny about witnessing the other show: the people looking at what can only be called giant hard-core pornographic paintings on canvas. One well-known collector, who is extremely nearsighted, got up real close to examine a painting titled *Jeff Eating Ilona,* and seemed completely oblivious to its content—she might as well have been examining a Ming vase. Imagine the surprise other collectors had when they walked into Sonnabend's office during that period and found a giant painting titled *Butt Red (Close-Up)* hanging right above her desk. Sonnabend was so cool about it you would have thought she was showing Grandma Moses. Elsewhere in the gallery there were a number of glass sculptures of the couple going at it *Kama Sutra*–style. I pictured Park Avenue maids dusting them and fainting—or quitting. What made the show even more loaded was how Koons wove art history into his blatantly sexual images. To this day he gets dewy-eyed when he talks about two of the paintings, which he titled *Manet* and *Manet Soft*. Imagine *Le Déjeuner sur l'Herbe*—and then some.

Needless to say, this was the best-attended exhibition in the history of Sonnabend Gallery, though the artist's mother could have lived without some of it. She said, "Some of [the work] I don't think was necessary. . . . There were some beautiful things in that show . . . like that huge bouquet of flowers." Those very same flowers were a deciding factor for art historian David Sylvester. He remembers, "I was looking some years ago at one of his flower sculptures and I decided he was a great artist. The Surrealists tried to be shocking. I thought, Koons really is shocking. The intense sexual charge that he gives to innocent or semi-innocent objects was especially palpable in those flower pieces."

Koons's sense of timing with "Made in Heaven" was perfect. He and Mapplethorpe weren't the only artists who had forced the issue of sex into art—for a while, in the eighties and early nineties, it felt like sex and sexuality were the only subjects of contemporary art. This makes total sense. Feminism and AIDS helped to make people understand how important it was to change the subject from a "dirty" one to something that needed to be looked at and talked about and understood—something that was capable of being revelatory. Some of this was little more than faddism, but when the work cut deeper—as it did with Mapplethorpe and Koons as well as Nan Goldin and

David Wojnarowicz—it was an opportunity for real insight. Some of that insight had to do with how we react to sexually explicit work. Koons himself has said, "If there is art to my work it is what the viewer walks away with." From "Made in Heaven" one walked away with a sharper consciousness of, say, the lines we draw between art and life, high and low, appropriate and not appropriate, pornography and art. That was its power—its ability to engage and, as always with Koons, its extraordinary execution.

The critical reaction was divided. Some thought the work daring and illuminating; others said Koons was indulging in shock for shock's sake, and it wasn't easy to sell the work—especially in America, where the puritanical ethos continues to make sex an X-rated subject. But there were other, bigger problems: Koons may have been turned on by the character La Cicciolina, and he may have shared this quite visibly with the world, but now he was a husband and he wanted his wife to himself, becoming outraged when she continued to work and, as he puts it, "not maintain our marriage vows." At one point he told her he wanted a divorce, but when she announced she was pregnant they decided to try to make the marriage work. Their lawyers had finally overcome the objections that the United States Immigration Department had with regard to Staller's visa application, and she was able to move here. The couple found a spot they liked in Manhattan, a thirteen-room town house on the Upper East Side (where Koons still lives). It was chosen for its location—near the zoo in Central Park. On October 29, 1992, Ludwig Maximilian Koons was born at Mount Sinai Hospital at 8:30 in the morning. Koons told me proudly, "I was the first person to greet Ludwig and give him a kiss."

And then the real hell began. Basically, Koons learned that you can't keep a porn superstar down on the farm, even if it is near the zoo. Saying that she needed to return to Rome to attend to some personal matters for a short while in October 1993, Staller left with Ludwig. When they didn't come back to the

States, Koons tried to locate them. He discovered that his wife was actually in Ecuador "on a business trip" and had left his son in Rome. (Koons found accounts in a number of South American newspapers of the erotic stage shows she was doing—this was no Greta Garbo, wanting to be alone.) He hotfooted it over to Italy and brought Ludwig, an American citizen, home to the family residence, and filed for divorce in the Supreme Court of New York as soon as Staller followed them back to the States. Both parties agreed, under American jurisdiction, to have fifty-fifty custody of Ludwig, who was to remain in New York State pending a final decision of the court. It was also decided that for the time being Staller would continue to live in the town house with Koons; during this period they met with court-appointed psychiatrists, who observed them in relation to Ludwig in order to determine which parent was more suitable for his custody. And to ensure that neither party would remove the child from the jurisdiction of the state of New York, a bodyguard was hired. But Staller wasn't Cicciolina for nothing. She asked the bodyguard to do her a favor and get her a pack of cigarettes, and the next thing Koons knew, mother and child were in Rome. A short while later the American courts dissolved the marriage and awarded exclusive custody of Ludwig to his father.

But by then Ludwig was living in Rome with his mother, and for the last eight years, right up until the present, Koons and Staller have been engaged in a tug-of-war for their child. Though Koons's custody has been ratified by an Italian court, Staller won her most recent appeal in Italy and continues to have primary custody; Koons has the right to spend seven days a month as well as summer holidays with Ludwig in Italy, which he does. He speaks often of his fear of the damage that is being done to his son emotionally in his current environment, smack in the middle of La Cicciolina's world. While Koons remains optimistic that he has the law on his side and will eventually win Ludwig back, he also says, ruefully, of both the pornography scene and the Italian legal system, "I did not know the culture."

. . .

Amid all the Sturm und Drang with Cicciolina, and in the wake of the "Made in Heaven" controversies and frustrations, the artist experienced an unqualified success with 1992's *Puppy*, a forty-foot West Highland terrier made out of living flowers, which is probably his most popular sculpture to date. It was first shown near the 1992 Documenta exhibition in Kassel, Germany. Koons hadn't been included in this prestigious international exposition, but he was invited to contribute to a sculpture exhibition that was organized on the periphery of the big event. He showed them! *Puppy* not only stole the sculpture show but it was the talk of Documenta, too. (Since then different versions of the work have popped up in various spots, including the Guggenheim Museum in Bilbao, Spain, and also in New York, where it guarded Rockefeller Center last summer. There's nothing like seeing its tail, which in Bilbao was made mostly of petunias and marigolds, wag in the wind.)

The work that followed *Puppy*, the "Celebration" series, which Koons began in 1993, speaks volumes about what was going on in his life during that period. "I was trying to communicate to my son, when he's older, just how much I was thinking about him all the time," Koons says. Indeed, childhood's iconography—its toys and games and foods, idealized and romanticized—has obviously been his inspiration for most of "Celebration," which is made up of twenty sculptures and sixteen paintings. Much of the work suggests a child's paradise, a hyperintense Disneyland for kids with long art historical memories. How Koons turns various common playthings into art is a lesson in vision. He'll take a party favor, such as a balloon dog that a clown might have made, and seven years later it's an eleven-foot-high stainless-steel sculpture, *Balloon Dog*, that has extraordinary formal and narrative power—and, unlike a child's real plaything, never deflates. When we were speaking, David Sylvester paired some of the sculptures in "Celebration" with Bernini fountains in Rome. "They're both weighty and buoyant," he said. But a piece like *Balloon Dog* can

also be seen as a contemporary equivalent of the mythical Trojan horse. One can imagine it containing Koons's army riding to Rome to bring his son home.

With "Celebration," however, Koons's processes of transformation turned out to be so demanding that they almost did him in. The paintings were complex and took years, but nothing was as tough as the sculpture. No one involved with the project expected it to be so difficult to arrive at these flawless surfaces. An anticipated show at the Guggenheim's SoHo branch, originally scheduled for 1996, had to be postponed four times before it was finally canceled, which led to much talk within the art world that Koons was at best washed up, and at worst seriously unhinged.

At one point, when Koons was attempting to make one of the Guggenheim's deadlines, he had seventy assistants helping on the art. My favorite place to watch what was going on with "Celebration" was in the back studio. Here one witnessed Koons functioning like some kind of Renaissance master, but updated. It was like a giant paint-by-numbers factory—Andy Warhol would have loved it, and there were more color swatches here than in Martha Stewart's wildest dreams. But there was also darkness. Over and over he destroyed what wasn't meeting his standards. I'd stop by and see what appeared to be progress on a work; a few weeks later it was back to square one. One began to hear rumors of how he would trash work that people had spent weeks on, and his reputation as a neurotic madman grew—more than one critic has referred to him as the Orson Welles of art. When I'd go and visit him at the studio during this period, and hear him talk about what he was trying to achieve in the pieces, I had a different image of him. I wondered if he wasn't a contemporary Don Quixote, a romantic figure on a mission to find some impossible ideal.

Eventually, though, the work on "Celebration" stopped altogether. The

Grillo Demo, *Play-Doh, Jeff Koons's Studio,* 1997

money had run out, and from 1996 until 1999 the studio felt like an art morgue. How Koons got to this point is both complicated and simple. Having left Sonnabend after "Made in Heaven" because he felt he wasn't being supported enough, Koons was working with three dealers for this project. They financed the art by preselling some of it, something that Sonnabend had not done with him. When it turned out that it would be much more complex and expensive to get the perfectly smooth, curving, reflective surfaces that Koons was after in the sculptures, he realized there was a large gap between what he had been paid and what the work would cost. Who was going to pay the real costs—the dealers, the collectors, or the artist? A few of his collectors, such as Dakis Joannou, are so committed to his work that they paid what it took (anywhere up to two million dollars) to complete their pieces, but in most instances, finances froze.

When I asked Gary McCraw, who has managed Koons's studio for the last ten years, if he ever saw Jeff ready to quit, I was told, "Jeff regroups. He doesn't give up."

The artist's perfectionism has been a double-edged sword. To some people it makes him a pain in the ass, an artist who is difficult and doesn't obey the demands of the marketplace. To others, like the Modern's Kurt Varnedoe, it is this very perfectionism that separates him from the crowd. Varnedoe says, "Jeff is often described as knowing, calculating, smart, ironic, and strategic. But I've always felt that there's something else. There's something about those surfaces and that degree of perfectionism that goes beyond anything that is necessary. I've always felt that it is that extra surplus of investment in the work, the irrational nature of it, that makes it art. To me it is what makes him an interesting artist, and a singular one."

Obviously he's not your regular guy, even if he dresses and sometimes acts like one—Joe Blow wouldn't go bankrupt trying to perfect a giant balloon dog. And despite his air of reason and control, Koons can be as hot-blooded as Brando in *A Streetcar Named Desire*. At a certain stage in his lawsuits with Cicciolina he destroyed all the pieces that were left in his studio from the "Made in Heaven" series, slashing at the paintings and getting Gary McCraw and some of his other assistants to help him smash the sculptures to smithereens. He and McCraw told me proudly that they were really hard to demolish because they were so well made! (Collectors who did buy "Made in Heaven" works now own very valuable art.)

It was Koons who pulled himself out of the jam he was in with "Celebration." He had taken to dropping by the Sonnabend Gallery, where his old friends and dealers, Ileana and Antonio, would commiserate with him. At one point he brought up a new idea for an art project that was on his mind, and they said, "Let's do it." The resulting work is titled "Easyfun." In 1999, when word spread that Koons had returned to Sonnabend and planned to show a new body of work there, plenty of people said they'd believe it when they saw it. But there were also those who couldn't wait to see what he did. The day the "Easyfun" show opened I popped by the gallery early. The door was locked. After banging on it I was let in. A few minutes later there was more banging. In came Varnedoe. And more knocking. This time it was Peter Schjeldahl, *The New Yorker*'s art critic. The visitors who were after early peeks didn't stop. Soon there was a *minyan* of critics. And when the show finally did open officially, the place was mobbed. Koons slept well that night—he'd been up for four days and nights.

The show was so vibrant one can just imagine the sense of liberation that Koons experienced while he was creating it. After not being able to move forward with "Celebration," he took off like a rocket, creating three new paintings and a series of simple colored wall sculptures that are as reflective as mirrors. The collagelike paintings, which are packed with energy and wit and surprise, forecast the Pop Surrealism that he has been developing ever since. Each work is created from a selection of found images that caught Koons's eye and that are then knit together by a computer. (In fact, these works couldn't have existed before computers.) The paintings are rife with the sexual undercurrent that Koons likes to layer in his work. *Hair,* for instance, includes a bouffant hairdo that overlaps a gooey chocolate-chip cookie dropping into a splash of milk, which, as Koons took pains to point out to me, doubles as a spurt of sperm. These works, as well as another floral sculpture, *Split-Rocker,* which he eventually showed in Avignon, France, seem to have freed Koons from his trap. Suddenly things started to move on "Celebration," too. Slowly but surely he began to complete some of the sculptural pieces. This didn't just happen because they'd figured out how to create the pieces without imperfections— what Koons and his crew call "wobbles"—or because he now had some money thanks to the success of "Easyfun." There was confidence around Koons again.

It wasn't long before art-world gossip had it that Koons was back. All this, coinciding with his recent auction success, put the heat on him again. More exhibitions were scheduled, and the Guggenheim came in with a commission for its branch in Germany, the Deutsche Guggenheim Berlin. It also scheduled a major retrospective for the year 2004, to open in New York and then travel; this act of faith just strengthened the notion that Koons is one of the most important artists working today. The Berlin show, which took place last fall, unveiled seven new paintings entitled "Easyfun—Ethereal," which takes the Pop Surrealism of "Easyfun" even further. Lisa Dennison, who arranged the exhibition and cocurated it with Robert Rosenblum (and who never lost her belief in Koons even during the protractions of "Celebration"), laughed when she told me the story of what had happened the day the work had to be picked up and flown to Germany: "We had people standing outside the studio on Broadway at seven in the morning. They called me to say that no one was answering the door. I phoned Jeff, and he answered, explaining that he was in the back with his assistants just 'tweaking' certain things. He asked for more time. I said, 'Jeff, you must open the door.'"

He did. But what is it that drives him to be so compulsive about his work? Since his need to get it perfect goes beyond anything that I've ever seen, there's clearly something at the bottom of it all that has to do with more than just inspired lunacy or a will to make the best work possible. It has to do with faith in art. In some ways he's like a figure from one of Edward Hopper's paintings of the thirties and forties, a salesman whose product is belief in art. Here's what Koons told me: "When I'm working on something, I'm going to give the bottom of the piece as much attention as the top. A lot of the time artists will work on the visible part of something and then you go around the back and see they didn't spend any time there. I think that makes you lose spiritual trust. All of a sudden you feel let down. I want to create work that always maintains the viewer's trust. I'm looking for friendship through this interaction."

If one asks Koons to pick a favorite work of his own, he will often mention his Michael Jackson sculpture, and it's understandable why the piece would have enormous meaning for him. Although he and Jackson are quite different artists, there is an apt comparison to be made between the two: They both seem to be such lonely figures and both have an epic obsession with childhood, and with maintaining a child's-eye view of the world. So much of Koons's art seems to be trying to make innocence last forever, like that balloon dog, yet at the same time he spikes it all with a heightened sense of sexuality. (Maybe that picture-perfect childhood had some wobbles in it after all.) But as often as he talks about a work's sexuality, Koons will also talk about its spirituality, and as we were drawing our discussions about his life to a close, I thought about something I had read in *The Gnostic Gospels* by Elaine Pagels: "If you do not bring forth what is within you, what you do not bring forth will destroy you."

Vanity Fair, March 2001

The Smithsonian's Big Chill

"The only reason that I was able to do what I did, without people attempting to stop me, is that I was a nobody," says Subhankar Banerjee matter-of-factly. But the freedom to move through the world unobserved is now past for the thirty-five-year-old photographer (whose name is pronounced "Sub-anchor Banner-gee"). Ever since last spring, when his photographs were brandished during a debate in the United States Senate, Banerjee has received a crash course in what happens when images touch a political nerve. A show of his work that had long been planned for the Smithsonian National Museum of Natural History, in Washington, D.C., turned into a circus and became a spectacle of institutional double-talk, foot-in-mouth slipups, and nonsensical, detrimental changes.

Banerjee is certainly not the first artist to produce an exhibition that scared a museum, but what is unusual is that, on the surface, his pictures are tame and sweet. After all, this is not the work of someone who has been sticking hams up his rear end on a government arts grant. He works in a genre—nature photography—that usually has art-world sophisticates looking down their noses while the hoi polloi applaud. While the natural world inspired a gamut of epic photography in the nineteenth century, our time cannot make such claims. Today successful nature photographers tend to produce images that are hackneyed—technically savvy but flat, boring, and mechanically formulaic. As time has gone on and cameras have become as available as candy, with millions of people trying to be their own Ansel Adams, it's a rare nature photographer who has been able to rise above the flotsam. Banerjee may be one of them. His best photographs have an authenticity, a gravitas, and a beauty that more rote imagery is without. Still, who knows if Banerjee's

Subhankar Banerjee, *Caribou Migration I,* 2002

images of frozen and unfrozen landscapes and exotic fauna such as pregnant Porcupine caribou and buff-breasted sandpipers would have won the attention of a larger audience if they hadn't become political hot potatoes.

Banerjee happens to have been working on the coastal plain of the Arctic National Wildlife Refuge, known as ANWR, currently at the center of one of the most contentious issues in Congress—whether to open up 1.5 million of the 19.5 million acres in the sanctuary to oil exploration, a proposal that has been strongly backed by the White House and powerful Republicans in Congress, and just as strongly fought by environmentalists. Banerjee's photographs, shot over a period of two years, beginning in March 2001, constitute the first complete record of the contested area, in all seasons, and the images dramatically contradict the assertion that has been bandied about, especially by proponents of drilling, that it's a blank and barren place with no ecosystem to speak of, a land of endless whiteness and frozen nothingness hardly worth preserving. Indeed, Banerjee's pictures show that the refuge is a complex and possibly fragile world full of polar bears, musk oxen, moose herds, and more than 160 species of birds. And there's the rub.

When the Indian-born Banerjee told friends and family that he was not only quitting his job in Seattle but also giving up his apartment, putting all his stuff in storage, and cashing in his savings as well as his 401(k) in order to head up to the Arctic and undertake a never-been-done photographic project, they thought he'd lost it. First of all, as far as most of them knew he was a scientist, not a photographer. After graduating from Calcutta's Jadavpur University with a degree in electrical engineering, he'd come to America in 1990 on a student visa to attend New Mexico State University in Las Cruces, ultimately receiving a double master's in theoretical physics and computer sciences. But it wasn't what he learned in the classroom that really struck a chord. A backpacking trip through New Mexico's Gila National Forest, and subsequent wilderness treks with the local Sierra Club, changed his view of what he was put on earth to do.

Perhaps it was his outsider perspective that had him falling as hard as he did for this new land and its wildlife (he eventually became a permanent resident of the United States). Along the way he began taking pictures, but on a strictly amateur, hobbyist basis. He had no pretensions about his work, though years ago he'd actually dreamed of becoming an artist—a great-uncle had been an accomplished painter in Calcutta. But he never really considered the idea seriously, despite the photo classes he was taking. "Coming from a middle-class family, you don't really think about that—you go into something that will bring sustenance," he laments. The "real" job that he ended up with was at the Los Alamos National Laboratory, where the atom bomb was developed. The laboratory had gotten a substantial grant for energy research, but when funding was cut in 1996 and the lab's priorities were rejiggered toward areas of defense, Banerjee realized he wanted out. His involvement with the Sierra Club had deepened, his consciousness about land conservation and preservation had been growing, and so the question of where to go next was influenced more by his love for the outdoors than by what would be smart for his career. He chose the Northwest and landed a spot in research at Boeing headquarters in Seattle.

As a city Seattle seemed made for him; it provided him with an instant community, and offered many opportunities for him to pursue his interests. Banerjee's colleagues in a Boeing photography club chose one of his images as "Slide of the Year." And while that may not have been a MacArthur "Genius" award, it did the trick: "I thought, Gee, maybe I could take this interest of mine more seriously. I really wanted to figure out how to combine my interests in art, in the outdoors, and in conservation issues."

He didn't stay long at Boeing, hitting the road with his camera, traveling wherever he was pulled, from Florida to Canada, picking up income here and there from computer consulting work. Then, in October 2000, he had an epiphany. He'd gone to Canada, to Churchill, Manitoba, a popular spot for photographing polar bears. But the site's tourist trappings made the trip a letdown. He remembers, "I would see a bear and then suddenly eight large vehicles would converge on it." He realized he wanted to stand apart from the pack and go where the bears and their environment hadn't been altered and invaded by all sorts of human interests. "I thought, I've got to go to a place where I can actually live with polar bears," he says. A hunch led him to check out the opportunities in northern Alaska, and soon his research led to the U.S. Fish and Wildlife Service in the Arctic National Wildlife Refuge. He struck up a lively e-mail correspondence with some of the biologists who were stationed there. "I'd write, 'What's possible up there?'" he recalls. "I told them I wanted to photograph polar bears living in the wild. They'd write back, 'Yeah, you could do that here.' And they started sending me other reports. I was simply blown away by the diversity of life in this land that had always intrigued me but that I had no knowledge of. I asked how much of it has actually been documented, and the answer was, Very little. I thought, My God, it is the most debated public land in the United States. Every magazine, every newspaper, every TV station has done multiple stories on the place, and yet, believe it or not, while there had been pockets of studies by biologists and botanists, it had not been visually documented in a way that was comprehensive and included all four seasons. I realized I had a tremendous opportunity."

I'll say. He immediately set to work, arriving in the village of Kaktovik, on the northern coast of the Alaskan Arctic, on March 19, 2001, having emptied his savings account (about eighty thousand dollars) and raised some additional funds through loans and grants from various individuals and foundations. (Ultimately, the cost of the project exceeded $250,000, leaving Banerjee currently $100,000 in debt.) Money was one thing. But there were bigger issues, such as how someone with no experience could survive the punishingly harsh winter conditions, which in the Arctic can last until May. What gear and clothing were necessary to help stand up to the weather? Which cameras and lenses could hold up against the wind, ice, and extreme cold? He reached out to the pros for advice. He says his lone respondent was Natalie Fobes, a *National Geographic* photographer; between her input and the advice of Robert Thompson, an experienced Inupiat field guide who had agreed to take on Banerjee and his project, he readied himself.

But nothing could have prepared him for his very first night, when a March blizzard started blowing and the windchill dropped to between eighty and ninety degrees below zero. He and Thompson were on a short snowmobile ride six miles into the refuge. "It was a complete whiteout," he remembers. "The wind was blowing like crazy, and there was this horrendous cold. I felt like I was in a nightmare. I panicked. I thought, What the hell am I doing here? I'm in over my head. I've got to leave. I can't survive, let alone photograph." Thompson and his wife, Jane—both of whom have lived in Kaktovik on and off for more than thirty years—talked Banerjee down, and that was really the first and last time that he thought about throwing in the towel. For the next month or so, Thompson put the photographer through rehearsals, as it were, and after that, even with blizzards that lasted twenty-five days straight, the work became more of an adventure than a trial. Banerjee's faith in his guide was such that he felt he could survive whatever came his way, as long as he and Thompson weren't separated. According to Banerjee, their profound connection carried over to the pictures. He says it isn't just his vision in the pictures but Thompson's, too.

Now that he'd gotten his first photographs, he returned to Seattle and approached Blue Earth Alliance, a nonprofit organization that supports projects that aim to educate the public about endangered lands, threatened species, and related cultural issues. Within days Banerjee got the nod that his project was accepted; the nonprofit status that this accorded him made fund-raising easier. His association with Blue Earth Alliance, combined with the fact that his biggest financial supporters would eventually be Tom Campion, an idealistic businessman who is on the board of the Alaska Wilderness League, and his wife, Sonya Campion, underscores the fact that Banerjee's work was in part sponsored by environmentalists and could therefore be accused of being a propaganda tool. Banerjee is perfectly open about the fact that he began his study with a conservationist bent. He never pretended otherwise, any more than Picasso pretended to be a warmonger when he painted *Guernica,* his antiwar masterpiece. That said, Banerjee was determined to go into the refuge without an agenda. It's one reason why he didn't ever try to get a magazine to sponsor the work. He explains, "I did not want to be influenced by any magazine. I wanted to live in this land on my own terms and learn from the native people how they view it. I didn't want editors or producers telling me what to expect or what to bring back."

Banerjee's pictures are at base a straightforward, unmanipulated visual record of his subject, and the fact that they document such an array of plant, animal, and bird life contradicts notions such as the one put forth by Secretary of the Interior Gale Norton when she famously described the refuge as if it were an object of conceptual art—a "flat white nothingness." It is the "everythingness" that Banerjee's photographs capture that has made them politically explosive. Almost as soon as he had begun to record life in the refuge, word spread that his pictures might be a useful vehicle for the fight against drilling in ANWR, and in July 2001, after the new Republican White House began pushing the issue, he was asked by the Alaska Wilderness League to bring some of his images to Washington. He did, and soon Senator Barbara Boxer of California was hailing his work as a sort of sword against the interests of big oil.

One might wonder whether Banerjee feels exploited by all the politicking around his work. He seems to see it as coming with the territory. Of his many photographic heroes, Ansel Adams may have influenced Banerjee the most, and Adams's best photographs—romantic pleas, really, against building a road through every mountain and every forest—are a continuation of the photographic arguments against indiscriminate industrialization that were begun by nineteenth-century greats such as Carleton Watkins and Timothy O'Sullivan. One day, Banerjee's work may be seen as part of this legacy. Sometimes his eyes get big when he talks about the potential repercussions of taking pictures that are so politically fraught, but he never seems to question whether he should have allowed his images to be factors in the current debate about ANWR. He is like a character from a Frank Capra movie, *Mr. Smith Goes to Washington,* for the nature-photography set. His personality is a curious mixture of innocence and savvy, of idealism and determination, of modesty and ambition.

It was the last quality, and, some would say, a crazy kind of confidence, that drove him to get not just a publisher but also a show at a major museum, long before his Alaska project was even completed. Having wrangled an appointment with Helen Cherullo, the head of Seattle-based Mountaineers Books, on the basis of his first shots of the refuge, he essentially talked his way into a book contract with the nonprofit, environmentally oriented publisher. Cherullo says, "From the moment Subhankar and I met, I knew this book was going to be something special." As for the exhibition, the direct way he got in touch with the Smithsonian is typical of Banerjee—both naïve and ballsy.

After sending an initial letter to the museum, Banerjee checked out its website, called the main number, and got himself connected to Robert Sullivan, a curator who, it turned out, had done anthropological research in the Brooks Range section of ANWR and knew what a hard environment it is to survive in—and what sort of will it takes to come away with photographs of the sort that Banerjee claimed he had. After their phone chat the photographer sent Sullivan a package of images, which were impressive enough that Sullivan agreed to a meeting, after which he promised Banerjee a spot on the museum's exhibition schedule once his work was complete. With all that to look forward to, Banerjee headed back to the refuge, shooting for seven months straight, from March 2002 until the end of September.

Not all of Banerjee's Arctic pictures are standouts, not by a long shot, but those that are succeed both as photographs and as scientific documents. One of his keys is patience. He'll wait and wait for something to happen, perhaps for many days, sometimes meditating. Then, once he thinks he has a potential picture, if possible he'll look at the scene for a long time before beginning to shoot. Perhaps the difficult conditions he worked in—he would ultimately travel about four thousand miles through the refuge, mostly by foot, raft, kayak, and snowmobile—were a blessing, because they forced him to keep things simple. It was hard enough just to get the cameras cranking. (He ended up using old, manually operated Nikons and Mamiyas because, unlike the newer, automatic cameras, their mechanisms work in freezing weather.) Some of his pictures were shot from the air—with the help of Walt Audi, a famous bush pilot in the Arctic who seems to be the point man for anyone who wants to brave the area.

But when you see Banerjee's most memorable pictures, it's not hardship that's evident but beauty. A nonformulaic beauty. Banerjee doesn't try to get perfect Hallmark scenes. While he did shoot the most spectacular, almost neon-like images of an aurora borealis that I have ever seen, he isn't one to milk sunsets. Instead he shows the beauty of ordinary scenes and of the passing of the seasons. He isn't afraid of what others might see as "a mess." He finds the grace in tangled-up branches and unruly weeds. Two of his best pictures—a mountain scene with spruce trees reflected on a lake that has cotton grass running wild in the foreground, and another lake view that includes a chaotic foreground of fall-colored vegetation, some of it dead—could hang beside any great nineteenth-century landscape photograph. His close-ups of animals and birds are less remarkable. They matter because of what they tell us about life in the region but aren't particularly interesting from an aesthetic point of view. Ditto his photographs of the local Gwich'in people and their way of life; they are important anthropological documents, vital social records, not artistic breakthroughs. But Banerjee's landscapes seem epic, and there is something about them that is haunting.

So is the story of what happened to his exhibition at the Smithsonian. Last winter, as the show came together, Banerjee was on top of the world. According to the photographer, Sullivan had been so impressed with the selection of images he'd received that he was hoping to move the exhibition from a smaller gallery to one of the museum's more prestigious and central locations, Hall 10. Sullivan also offered some museum funds to assist in producing the exhibition's prints, an expensive process for large-format pictures. As for the book, Banerjee had managed to get contributions from Jimmy Carter, Peter Matthiessen, David Allen Sibley, and other prominent voices in the conservation movement, once again through a combination of chutzpah, naïveté, and passion. Even though the book had no official connection to the Smithsonian show, the tie-ins were numerous. Banerjee says he had received permission from Sullivan to mention the Smithsonian exhibition in the Mountaineers book, both in the text and on the jacket. The museum even decided to give the show the same title, "Seasons of Life and Land"; in fact, the Smithsonian had also contracted Banerjee's editor, Christine Clifton-Thornton, to help develop the captions that would go on the walls in conjunction with the photos. The agreement letter that Sullivan had sent to Banerjee noted the importance of putting the photos in context: As Sullivan wrote, the exhibition "will not only present spectacular images, but will provide visitors with an opportunity to learn more about the ecology and inhabitants of the region." The show was scheduled to open in May 2003, and short of the champagne corks going off, it looked like a done deal. There had been design meetings on-site in Hall 10 at the museum; there were wall plans for the exhibition, and prints were being made to the resulting specifications. But then, as Senator Richard Durbin, Democrat of Illinois, later told me, "all hell broke loose."

It was a moment that will no doubt become legendary in the annals of photography and politics. On the evening of March 19 of this year, in the middle of a Senate budget debate for the fiscal year 2004, Senator Boxer introduced an amendment to prevent consideration of drilling in the Arctic National Wildlife Refuge from being slipped into a fast-track budget reconciliation bill. The debate that ensued that evening was long and heated, and Banerjee's photographs featured in Boxer's opening remarks. She would go on to display a selection of his pictures, primarily his shots of animals and birds. Many hours and many arguments later, shortly before the vote was taken, Boxer invoked Banerjee's work yet again. This time she urged members of the Senate to look at his book, *Seasons of Life and Land,* and held up an advance copy that had been sent to her by the Alaska Wilderness League. She also encouraged her colleagues to visit his upcoming show at the nearby Smithsonian. The Senate eventually passed Boxer's amendment, keeping proposals for oil and gas drilling at bay for the time being, but the vote was close (fifty-two yeas, forty-eight nays) and there were those who suspected this wouldn't be the end of the matter. Still ringing in Washington's ears was a threat from Alaska's senior senator, Ted Stevens, a Republican who for more than two decades has arguably been the most vocal proponent of drilling in the refuge. With the tide turning against him, Stevens had warned, "People who vote against this today are voting against me, and I will not forget it."

The capital's museums have a history of caving in under political pressure—and, in a way, what came to pass with Banerjee's exhibition is even more frightening than the more famous episode in the early nineties when Senator Jesse Helms led the fight on Capitol Hill against the National Endowment for the Arts and its support of Robert Mapplethorpe's photographic explorations of homosexuality and Andres Serrano's visual critique of the Catholic Church. Helms's position contributed to an atmosphere that led to the Corcoran Gallery's cancellation of a Mapplethorpe show that included some of his most sexually explicit photographs, including his *X, Y,* and *Z Portfolios.*

Of course, Mapplethorpe's work was purposely provocative, as was Serrano's; Banerjee just wanted to shoot a straightforward record that had some aesthetic merit. But when Boxer explicitly linked Banerjee's work to one of the hot-button issues of the day, she changed his life. According to the photographer, Sullivan called him on April 4, two weeks after the Senate vote, and said, "Subhankar, I have good news for you and bad news for you. The good news is that your exhibit is still going on. The bad news is that I have had tremendous pressure to cancel it. I have worked very hard for the last couple of weeks to restore it. However, there are changes that have to be made to the show. The show has to move back to the downstairs gallery—that's one thing. The second thing is that all the captions have been completely expunged."

This wasn't good. But at least it was clear. What came next was a whole different ball game. Banerjee and Cherullo have copies of confusing, intimidating letters they received from Smithsonian lawyers, the first of which implied that the show had in fact been canceled. "Since there has not been, nor is it likely in the immediate future that there will be an exhibition at the Smithsonian, I request that any and all references to the Smithsonian Institution or a Smithsonian-sponsored exhibition be removed from all future printings or editions of the book," the museum's assistant general counsel wrote. Worried, Cherullo made a quick call to Sullivan, who assured her the show was on. But Banerjee and company were extremely upset and scheduled an early-morning conference call with Sullivan, via his assistant, to talk further. Banerjee says the phone meeting never took place, because at the appointed time (six in the morning for the Seattleites) they were told that the curator was unavailable.

In the end, Banerjee's exhibition did go on at the Smithsonian with a run that began in early May and lasted through the summer. But it was essentially buried by the museum, which did live up to its commitment to show the work, but in a transparently ambivalent way. Take the spot where the pictures eventually landed, the Baird Gallery, a glorified corridor with track lighting that serves as a lobby for the museum's auditorium. This was exactly where the show had started out. When I spoke to Sullivan he seemed rather miffed that the media had taken to referring to the Baird space as being in the basement. (If one enters the museum from Constitution Avenue, it's on the ground floor.) But it's hard to buy the claim by Sullivan, and by the Smithsonian's PR office, that the Baird Gallery was in fact the perfect place for Banerjee's work when one compares it with the space at the back of Hall 10, the location the show had been designed for. No contest: Hall 10, which is on the main floor—near the humongous elephant that is the museum's best-known symbol—is more prestigious, more visible, more central. Banerjee still looks at the Hall 10 wall plans ruefully.

And then there were the wall captions, which were drastically edited shortly before the show opened, with any supplemental information completely scrubbed away, leaving only a brief indication of subject and place. What's striking is that none of the original captions took a direct position on the ANWR debate. While Banerjee's book (which, by the way, has sold out in the museum's bookstore) is clearly a partisan product, the exhibition's captions were not. None mentioned oil, or drilling, or even acknowledged the debate beyond making generalized calls for preservation. One caption for a photograph of a buff-breasted sandpiper did note that the bird is among "the top five bird species at greatest risk if their habitat is disturbed." At greatest risk in the Arctic? The United States? The world? And at risk of what, exactly? The caption did not clarify; its problem was scientific sloppiness, not politics, yet instead of being fixed, it was removed. The new caption read simply, "Buff-breasted sandpiper, coastal plain of the Jago River."

More typical of the original captions was the text for a photograph of a willow ptarmigan, a grouselike bird. The text quoted Banerjee: "I would awake in the morning to ptarmigans feeding near our tent, talking to themselves and making noises that sounded like 'go-bek, go-bek' as if to let us know we were trespassing on their territory." Despite the use of the arguably inflammatory word *trespassing,* it's hard to see that quote as anything but romanticization of the sort that comes up over and over again when "the wild" is touched upon; one sees versions of this sentiment so often in Western art and literature, from high to low. But not at the Smithsonian, where the caption was reduced to "Willow ptarmigan, Hulahula River Valley." More innocuous still was this caption for a photograph of a polar bear walking across frozen Bernard Harbor in early June: "The unlikely elements of late-evening light, a dead-calm Arctic coast, a most unusual Arctic mirage in the far distance, and a polar bear offering a perfect reflection combined to create this image, a photographer's dream." New caption: "Polar bear, Bernard Harbor."

The show had originally been set to open with a wall text quoting from Jimmy Carter's foreword to Banerjee's book: "It will be a grand triumph for America if we can preserve the Arctic Refuge in its pure, untrammeled state." This clearly was a no-no, though the idea of using the quote had come from the museum's own staff.

The Smithsonian gets about two-thirds of its budget from the federal government, appropriated directly by Congress. That it can be intimidated is not news. As I got deep into the reporting of this story, I came across a number of fairly recent instances in which the museum ended up acting as if it were an institution in the Soviet Union during the Cold War, instead of a museum founded to promote the "increase and diffusion of knowledge." The photographer Glenn Ketchum has an eerie story regarding a 1994 exhibition at the Smithsonian that echoes what happened with Banerjee. He remembers, "I had done an exhibit on the Tongass rain forest"—another Alaskan wilderness area—"through the Smithsonian Institution Traveling Exhibition Service. Then, a few days before the opening, the Alaskan delegates call the Smithsonian up to say they wanted to review all the texts and change the show. After objecting, the Smithsonian came to me and said, 'They'll kill us in Appropriations if you don't cooperate.' The changes they wanted were completely absurd. It was a tempest in a teacup. One of the changes, for instance, is that when we were talking about old-growth trees we couldn't use the word *primeval* or *ancient.* We made some basic changes but we didn't do all of the big ones." Instead, Ketchum went to the press, and the next day *The Washington Post* ran a story; that ended that. "They realized they were creating a bigger firestorm than it was worth," says Ketchum.

. . .

Senator Stevens has angrily denied putting pressure on the museum in regard to Banerjee's show (though he thinks the museum did the right thing), but it's a matter of public record that he and then senator Frank Murkowski, another Alaska Republican, were the prime complainers about Ketchum's show; this was just one of several occasions on which the senior senator from Alaska has tried to lay a heavy hand on the institution. In 1991, *The Washington Post* quoted the warning Stevens lobbed at Smithsonian officials when he was mad about some museum programs on American history, which he perceived to have a leftist bias. "You're in for a battle. I'm going to get other people to help me make you make sense."

This past May, Senator Durbin and others used a hearing on the Smithsonian's budget to question whether outside influence had been brought to bear against Banerjee's show. The hearing included testimony from Lawrence Small, the head of the Smithsonian Institution, who denied that anything unusual had occurred. But the hearing clearly demonstrated that Banerjee's exhibition was treated differently from another show concurrently hanging at the museum, an exhibition of photographs by Eliot Porter. One picture of a Tennessee landscape included a caption blatantly indicting the environmental effects of strip mining, but the Smithsonian did not flinch. The Porter caption, unlike some of the Banerjee captions, wasn't deemed a potential violation of the federal statute that says the museum must essentially remain neutral about "any legislation or appropriation by Congress."

Would the museum have been so anxious without the fear of crossing powerful politicians? When I spoke to Robert Sullivan he insisted that there had been no pressure from the outside to make changes in Banerjee's exhibition. "As someone who was on the inside," Sullivan said, "I can say quite categorically we never got a call from anyone, we never got pressured. We just went through our normal internal process that we go through to protect our neutrality." On the other hand, Sullivan was perfectly frank about the fact that the drilling debate put Banerjee's show under the gun. He said, "What happened is something we couldn't have predicted, which is that the debate over the ANWR-oil-exploration bill happened right when we were about to open the show. It made us have to be cautious about making sure we couldn't be perceived as advocating for the passage or rejection of that particular piece of legislation. So the timing couldn't have been worse."

The irony in all this is that efforts at suppression can be the best thing for an artist's career, helping to draw a spotlight that might not otherwise have been there. His treatment is in part what motivated Terry Gosliner, the provost of the California Academy of Sciences, a San Francisco museum, to step forward and offer to host another show of Banerjee's work; this exhibition, different from the Smithsonian's, is on view through December and will then travel. The show's captions are exactly as Banerjee wants them—anecdotal and informative. Audiences also have another chance to see Banerjee's work on the East Coast: A show has just opened at the American Museum of Natural History, in New York City, and will run until March 7. It's not a huge exhibition, but here, too, Banerjee's Arctic photographs will be presented with the kind of information that the Smithsonian decided was too political to include. For the American Museum of Natural History's Dr. Eleanor Sterling, who is in charge of Banerjee's show and is also the director of the museum's Center for Biodiversity and Conservation, providing informative captions is not a political issue but an obligation. She says, "That's what our museum does for a living—it tries to share the natural world with people. . . . It's our job to give accurate information on things like reproduction, population size, and conservation status. That's our role as scientists—to inform the public about the entire natural history of an animal, and that includes conservation status."

The Smithsonian episode is a reminder that a museum cannot be true to its mission if it is ruled by a fear of politicians. In fact, the entire issue of "neutrality" that comes up when federal funds are involved can place museums between a rock and a hard place. But whether the impulse to minimize the impact of Banerjee's show came from external pressure or internal panic, or a combination of the two, the result was a loss for the artist, the institution, and, of course, the public.

In its rush to expunge any context from Banerjee's show, the Smithsonian went as far as to invoke some of the old formalist positions on art—that it is form, not content, that matters. But to take the meaning out of Banerjee's photographs and try to build an exclusively aesthetic frame around them is to miss what makes them so vibrant. They are relevant to both art and science; in fact, their strength is that the two ways of understanding the world can't be untangled in these pictures. Their ultimate so-called crime was that they did not depict a wasteland. But the Smithsonian's capitulation, whatever the reason, reminds me of another wasteland, the one T. S. Eliot spoke of in 1921 when he wrote this:

The awful daring of a moment's surrender
Which an age of prudence can never retract.

This lament, like most of Eliot, is, of course, open to interpretation. It was the concreteness of Banerjee's pictures that got them in trouble.

Vanity Fair, December 2003

The Rebel in Prada

Normally fashion folk love the drama of their business's ups and downs, but last year was different. It's no news that by summer the economy had turned bearish—polar bearish—with many clothing companies reporting dips and slides. And then September 11. It will be a long time before the ways in which that day changed the psychic landscape become discernible; but for the economy, the message seemed instant, loud, and clear. Tom Ford, the designer for Gucci and Yves Saint Laurent, put it this way: "On September 11, the 90s ended."

Prada, one of the biggest fashion stories of the nineties, has certainly not been immune to the downturn. At the start of the decade, the company was just beginning to enjoy the cult following that came with its reinvention by Miuccia Prada, who in 1978 took control of the dusty leather-goods concern founded by her grandfather in 1913. The company had once manufactured the finest luggage a traveler could want—Prada's trunks had more compartments than the Orient Express and loads of tortoiseshell toilet articles to boot. By the fifties, all that dedication to design and quality and craft remained, but the products turned mundane. More than twenty years later, with the company in the doldrums, a reluctant Miuccia Prada signed on, despite previously thinking that a life in fashion was like a life in fluff. (Instead, she had gotten a doctorate in political science as well as serious doses of Italian communism and feminism.) By the late eighties, she had moved on from old-world leather and was showing her own collections of clothes and inventive accessories. It took only a few seasons for people to become obsessed with some of her designs, such as the famous nylon backpack, which was the must-have item of the early nineties. This is when Prada began to gain its worshipful following among stylists and editors, when another big-shot Milanese designer, Gianni Versace, may he rest in peace, used to joke among friends about the fashion set's "addiction to their little orgasms"—meaning their Prada bags, their Prada shoes, their Prada outfits. But Prada didn't remain an insiders' phenomenon like, say, the rock 'n' roll urbanism of Ann Demeulemeester; the house continued to expand its inventory and its audience, so much so that in 2000, the most successful year yet in the company's history, it had sales of $1.5 billion.

Another big nineties story was the acquisition battles between LVMH and the Gucci Group, each of which now owns or controls a mother lode of fashion houses. Starting in 1999, Prada began making its own headlines with purchases of, among other trophies, majority positions in style temples such as Jil Sander and Helmut Lang. There was also a partnership with LVMH to buy a controlling share of the Roman fashion house Fendi—Prada kicked in approximately $225 million—and a stock offering planned for sometime in 2001 that, it was predicted, would raise between $6 billion and $8 billion, and that seemed a logical way to retire the $1 billion debt that all this "shopping" had incurred. But the economy's sudden implosion has forced Prada to put aside the IPO until "the right moment" and instead raise money through a bond issue. The company has also had to live through all sorts of bad press and rumors about its tribulations, including speculation about which of its new subsidiaries might be sold off and to whom. This came to a boil in November, when LVMH struck a deal with Prada to take over the latter's 25.5 percent share in Fendi.

In other years, this comeuppance would be cause for lip smacking among rivals. But one gets the feeling these days that even bitter fashion competitors want to read good news about one another, for assurance about their own chances to navigate the uncertain present. So, when Prada let on in late September that the company was forging ahead with its most ambitious project yet, the opening of a revolutionary new store in New York's SoHo district, designed by the Dutch architect Rem Koolhaas at an estimated cost of fifty million dollars, the news was greeted with cheers. Of course, plenty of people also thought Miuccia Prada and her husband, Patrizio Bertelli, the company's chief executive, were nuts.

I didn't put it quite that way when I spent an evening with Prada around that time. But I did mention to her that SoHo was a bit like a ghost town—not a good thing if, like her and Bertelli, you've got a lot of sweaters and frocks and bags and lamé shoes and fox-fur pillows and parchment luggage to sell. I asked if she was nervous about opening at what might seem like a "bad time." She replied, "I know. To put so much work into a shop for downtown New York right now in many people's eyes is a risk. But for me it wasn't even a question of whether to go ahead. It became even more urgent to do it. Of course I'm scared we'll fail. But I'm more interested in putting our money where our mouth is. One's life and passion may be elsewhere, but New York is where you prove if what you think in theory makes sense in life."

Their choice for a collaborator was a fascinating one. Like Prada and Bertelli, Rem Koolhaas is a true renegade. While known as a thinker and writer, he hasn't actually built much, but that will soon change in a big way. Between the Prada commission in New York, two more for Prada stores in Los Angeles and San Francisco, and about a dozen other significant jobs—including the Seattle Public Library, the Los Angeles County Museum of Art, a building for the European Union at The Hague, and a private house in the Bahamas for Jane Wenner (Jann's ex)—Koolhaas and his firm are very busy. He has even become a consultant for Condé Nast, this magazine's publisher. And given his range of interests, calling him an architect is almost reductive. "I always feel that he is a plug and the whole world is full of sockets" is how his wife once described him to *The New York Times Magazine*. But, for all that, Koolhaas has no prior hands-on experience with retail. So when I heard that he had enlisted with Prada, I was intrigued from the get-go. It turned out that the new SoHo store is located in the same building where I work as the editor of *Interview*—so I spent the summer and fall sneaking in to watch the progress.

The shop finally opened in mid-December, and if Versace thought those editors were having orgasms over Prada's products before, he'd really have something funny to say now if he could hear the screams of pleasure. The minute you enter it's clear this is not your typical shop. Think of it as a collision of worlds: The place is part twenty-first-century futurist's daydream, part nineteenth-century Victorian peep show, part personal beauty stop, and, with screens and media installations integrated into the whole, part cinematic spectacle.

Koolhaas, who once wrote movie scripts, seems to have brought his love of scenes and surprising narratives to this job. There are loads of architectural plot twists that give the Prada shop a contemporary dynamism, a sense of motion that has been missing from architecture. First off, there is what is referred to in-house as "the wave"—a clever solution to breaking the old hierarchies among floors. What Koolhaas and his team have done is plunk down a humongous wavelike form through the store's space, swooping from the main floor down to what was a basement and back up. Instead of surf, this wooden wave has steps that can be used to show merchandise or simply as bleacherlike seats. Above the wave is a suspended display system—the so-called hanging city—that can extend throughout the space but can also contract into a solid block. Suddenly, the wave becomes a theater or a cozy movie house, and the entire store can turn into a public space. I've heard Miuccia discussing the idea of free Friday-night showings of independent films (and she means *really* independent films). I've heard her talking about commissioning new plays (as she has done for presentations of her Miu Miu line), or perhaps making the space available for a situationist happening.

The most spectacular use of multimedia installations is to be found below street level, in a warren of rooms that have a feel not unrelated to that of a bathhouse—a secret, private world. Here, there are three stopping points: an interactive kiosk, where you can find out all sorts of facts about Prada; a "peep show" that has a series of small screens running a matrix of images, including shots of Prada factory workers and a dash of fuzzy porn; and a booth with a triptych of plasma screens that falls somewhere between a fashion altar and a confessional. Believe me, Koolhaas's team has had a lot of fun mixing the sacred and the profane. (They wanted to conjoin a shot of praying Muslims with the Pope and a risqué scene from Pasolini, but cooler heads prevailed.)

Without ripping off artists, this project has clearly been informed by contemporary art. One thinks of the mannequin sculpture of Charles Ray, the early happenings of Claes Oldenburg, or the Italian Arte Povera movement when one sees the execution and the span of materials, found and newly invented, that have come together here, including medical gel pads, polycarbonate panels, checkerboard marble, plywood, aluminum, curved mirror, and taped and spackled gypsum board (in pink and Prada's famous green). A massive glass elevator—you can shop in there, too—is an engineering feat that harks back to the radical sculpture of Gordon Matta-Clark, an artist who literally sliced into buildings as part of his work in the seventies and who can be thanked for giving all sorts of architects a whole new perspective on materials and space. The whole shebang is finished off by what appears to be a never-ending expanse of wallpaper. (Koolhaas is a firm believer in bringing in others on a job; the collaborators here have been many, including the design firm 2x4 and New York's Architecture Research Office.)

But all the razzle-dazzle should not let one lose sight of the fact that this is first and foremost a store. For a start, shoppers will have a terrific alternative to fashion's normal seasonal inventory with clothes from Prada collections past. These and items from the current collection can be tried on in dressing rooms that are private one moment and public the next, since the walls go from opacity to translucence at the push of a button. (Can you imagine the inevitable comedies when this happens accidentally?) There are also computers that shoppers can consult to learn everything they'd ever want to know about a product: what it's made of, what colors it comes in, how many exist in the world, what it might look like on you a size smaller. A video screen gives you—this is a big one—an ass view.

When I pointed out to Miuccia that this last feature isn't necessarily a good thing from a seller's point of view—when I saw it myself I ran out of the dressing room—she nodded and laughed. "What we're doing is experimenting with the technological world. We don't know if it will work." At that, she almost looked relieved, saying, "If the technology doesn't work, you can always use the shop without it." An interesting shrug from someone who spent who knows how much on all those buttons.

Everyone involved thinks of the New York shop as a work in progress, and also as part of a bigger story, since it was conceived in relation to the Koolhaas-designed shops that are planned for Los Angeles and San Francisco. *Change* is the operative word in this project.

A few months before the opening, Tim Archambault, a young architect who was one of the job's on-site managers, said, "I hope people love it. I hope they hate it. But it would be sad if everybody just likes it." That's not the kind of attitude that normally makes the retail world go around, but it's perfect for people who believe that consensus isn't necessarily the point of creativity.

"She was always a rebel," an old family friend of Prada's whispered to me last summer in Switzerland. At that particular moment, the "rebel" was wearing what she referred to as her "Heidi outfit," an olive green skirt (from her Miu Miu collection), a white shirt, black ankle socks, and black shoes. On top of the skirt was an apron that she'd pulled from her collection of local costumes; Prada—whose face has long reminded me of a Modigliani—looked as if she were about to burst into a song from *The Sound of Music.* She had organized an idyllic picnic in Silvaplana, near Saint-Moritz, where she had just finalized a deal to buy one of the most soulful pieces of land in the area (it probably doesn't hurt the aura of the place that Nietzsche, Thomas Mann, and Herman Hesse once roamed nearby). The weather was perfect, the fields were speckled with explosions of wildflowers, and you could hear cowbells clanging in the

Photograph by OMA, *The Prada Epicenter in New York,* 2001

distance. Many of her nearest and dearest were there. Prada has a tight band of old friends that do everything together—it's a crowd that's part Fellini, part Antonioni. But she's also big on family, and on this day, up on the mountain, we were joined by her mother, Luisa, and her aunt, Nanda, who are both in their eighties. As her best friend, Nanette, says, "A look at these ladies and you understand everything about Miuccia."

These are the dames who kept the Prada company alive in Milan after Miuccia's grandfather died. Miuccia's aunt, who to this day embroiders the designer's personal linens, has always had a quirky taste that inspires her niece, and Miuccia's mother is a lesson in elegance without stuffiness. When I noticed Mom was wearing the navy skirt and white ankle sock look that Miuccia made popular again in the mid-nineties, I smiled. The designer caught this and joked, "Yes, it's inherited—I invented nothing."

Curious about the way she herself shops, I had earlier asked her to take me to some of the stores in Saint-Moritz that are part of her routine when she's there. There was no wandering. She went straight from store A to store B to store C; inside, she homed in quickly on what she wanted. We dropped in at a butcher's that was so sanitary it seemed like a science lab, at an old-fashioned health-food store, and at her favorite porcelain shop. (She would not let me witness her shopping for jewels—her secret vice.) But the funniest stop we made felt like carrying coals to Newcastle. Apart from some local architectural color—all that Swiss cookie-cutter stuff—Saint-Moritz's poshest shopping street looks like practically every other exclusive commercial district in the world. It has the same boutiques that one finds in rich neighborhoods in Los Angeles, New York, Paris, Hamburg, London, and Dallas. There's Gucci, Armani, Saint Laurent, Vuitton, Pucci, and, naturally, Prada, where the designer dashed in looking for a pair of shoes. The salespeople were very discreet, but as soon as the designer had her back to them, their panic was obvious. They started raising their eyebrows and mouthing her name, but she didn't notice, because she was darting through the store, finally settling on a pair of lace-up walking shoes. She asked if they were black. The salespeople said no, they were dark purple. She laughed and avoided the whole issue by asking for the same pair in brown—which were out of stock. The next day, as we were finishing a five-hour walk to and from the Roseg Glacier, her cell phone started to ring; it was the Prada store in Saint-Moritz trying to find her to deliver the new brown shoes, which had been put in a car and driven from Italy to Switzerland expressly for her. "I am ashamed," she demurred. "I am amused," I answered. "Here's something that will make you really laugh," she said. "My feet have been killing me for the last hour." She had on yet another pair of Pradas. I, feeling very comfortable in my battered old Prada sneakers, winked at her and said, "Next time you go shopping, try your Sport line."

The joke is that shopping is an odd subject for each of us. Having known her for eight years (we became friends after I profiled her for *The New Yorker*), I have always been struck by how "unfashiony" Prada is, so much so that I had no problem confessing to her that I pretty much hate shopping. The last time I did it as a form of recreation was in 1978, when I accompanied my mother to Bloomingdale's and we had a fight going down the escalator about a skirt that she wanted me to buy instead of the leather jacket that I was after. When we finally reached the ground floor we were spritzed by an overeager perfume salesperson. That was it for me. As for Miuccia, even though she's in the business of attracting people to buy, buy, buy, she still has plenty of ambivalence about shopping—which may be why she has been so bent on experimenting with what that activity could mean.

While we were hiking we got to talking about all this, and she said, "It's horrible when people are only interested in buying labels, because it doesn't bring them the happiness they think it will. My friend Nanette says that I am usually so depressed after I go shopping that I should stop doing it! On the other hand, shopping is a part of life, and part of a social exchange. It can be a much wider experience than the terms we are used to thinking about it in. Someone might say, 'Look at that silly woman. All she does is shop.' I am sure it wouldn't be true—that there are many other things she does and thinks about. Many of us grew up with a kind of puritanism against shopping. But shopping can be much more than how it is cast. If you are bored or you have problems, it can be a way of lifting your spirits, by doing something light and superficial. Why not? It can also be a means of learning. When I was younger, shopping helped me discover many new places and many new things. I remember going to London and discovering Mary Quant and the Biba shop and the hippie movement. I learned about hats and furniture from traditional shops in London. And it was when I was shopping for children's clothes for my sons that I made the breakthrough for how I personally wanted to dress."

In terms of her own stores, the Prada concept had always been not to do splashy architects' stores but rather to build simple, spare spaces that work well for selling clothes. The shops the company already has—designed by Roberto Baciocchi—have been home runs, and the plan for now is to keep them as they are. So I asked Prada what was behind her and her husband's decision to break with a winning formula and take a chance on a whole new approach. She answered, "We were bored with the notion that all the shops all over the world had to have the same identity. We thought that the idea of logolike shops was wrong." The company had spent a lot of money buying up new retail spaces around the globe and was now spending still more keeping them empty while it figured out a new direction. "At some point about two years ago, Patrizio said, 'Okay, we have to decide on somebody to be in charge of the architecture of the new stores.'" And how did they land on Koolhaas? "One day we said, 'Okay, we're going to choose someone tonight.' We laid out all the books that we had on contemporary architecture on the floor. I looked at the work of Rem Koolhaas. I didn't know anything about him, yet for me he was the only one. I am very proud of that. I saw something that was different in his work. It was more than architecture. I saw something more complicated. Some of the people around us said that he is too difficult, that he is impossible, that he is too conceptual, a cult architect. We said, 'Probably he is the right one!' "

"A letter from Prada arrived out of the blue," Koolhaas tells me, recalling the beginning of their relationship. "Then Miuccia and Patrizio arrived in Rotterdam almost equally out of the blue, and suddenly we were all sitting in my office. It was all kind of incredibly abrupt, incredibly honest, incredibly brutal, and incredibly clear. Patrizio was talking in Italian, and miraculously I understood, more or less. They wanted a new concept and they wanted some degree of reinvention. I was unsure whether I could do it myself. Wanting to do it was obvious, but being able to was another question."

It soon became clear to both sides that they'd found everything they'd been looking for in a collaborator. Koolhaas had already been grappling with the topic of shopping, thanks to an innovative graduate seminar he has taught at Harvard since 1995. (Students, by the way, with their looser, more contemporary mind-set, are Koolhaas's secret weapon when it comes to oddball ideas.) Each year a different theme is chosen, and in 1997 it was shopping; it's a subject that, Koolhaas pointed out to me in his quiet Dutch-accented monotone, hadn't been the focus of a studio architecture course at an Ivy League university for at least twenty years. Shopping might seem like a light subject to the brotherhood of architectural heavies, who are supposed to be concerned with museums, jails, and science labs. But as Koolhaas says, "The only hope for architecture is to look outside its designated territory."

Koolhaas, fifty-seven, looks like one of those Russian Constructivists photographed by Rodchenko—intense, dynamic, and often at an angle. While he may be very "in" these days, he is a classic outsider. He started his career in journalism, working as both a designer and a writer for a Dutch weekly, earned a pedigree in radical art groups, and co-wrote some infamous (in Holland) film scripts before finally turning to architecture, his grandfather's profession, when he was in his mid-twenties. His firm, the Office for Metropolitan Architecture (OMA), was founded in New York in 1975 but is now based in Rotterdam. It's become a mecca for young architects from all over the world—very few are Dutch—who want to practice their profession in a way that's out of the box. "We are all aliens" is how Ole Scheeren, the Prada store's project leader for architecture, describes the fraternity. When I visited the office on a weekend in November, it was like Santa's workshop, with teams of architects working on deadline for various presentations. But the firm hasn't always been so in demand: Until recently Koolhaas's résumé was composed mainly of critically acclaimed books (including *Delirious New York* and *S, M, L, XL*) and lost competitions. There were many times when OMA struggled economically and one instance, in 1995, when it almost declared bankruptcy.

There were also a few jobs where Koolhaas actually got to build: the Netherlands Dance Theater in The Hague; the Kunsthal in Rotterdam, which is considered his breakthrough building; the Villa dall'Ava, a private house on the outskirts of Paris; and a complex surrounding a train station in Lille, France. Koolhaas is anti Expressionism and against the idea of having a signature style. His work is about taking on issues case by case and then coming up with the best solutions; obstacles are positives for him. But one can say that all his work has a powerful conceptual underpinning and a particular beauty that has to do with movement and using a hybrid of materials, sometimes cheap ones. He can perform with a small budget, too, which makes him unusual. I remember going with him in the early nineties to see the Villa dall'Ava home, with its one-lane rooftop pool that has a view of the Eiffel Tower. The house is like a breath of fresh air in its bourgeois neighborhood. We had tea with Lydie Boudet, who with her husband, magazine editor Dominique Boudet, had commissioned it; you could see how much she respected Koolhaas and how much she loved living in what he'd built. I'll never forget the drive back through Paris with Koolhaas—he was so proud, it was genuinely touching.

It was on that excursion, in fact, that we first talked about fashion. Even back then it was clear that Koolhaas had a fresh perspective on the subject. Here's how he explains it: "I am interested in fashion as perhaps one of the most pure forms of recreation. It's about a maintenance that doesn't require any explanation or argument and that can be completely shameless—and I think it is easier to reach the sublime in fashion than in any other way." And we thought the French structuralists had the patent on intellectual doozies!

Koolhaas will happily say that his clients' input has been pivotal to what he's done with the Prada store. "Of course, Prada was an incredible name—there are certain names that would have had no resonance whatsoever. But what I really like about them is that they have an incredible, instinctual kind of visceral and material intelligence, and it is combined with a real intellectualism. Of course, we are very critical, and some people would find it scary. But I think they find it exciting."

Miuccia Prada is used to sparks; it's part of the dynamic she has with Bertelli, who's known for his volatility. She considers sparring part of a creative exchange. What enabled her collaboration with Koolhaas to click was that Prada was open and undefensive in allowing his team to delve into almost any aspect of the company that they felt was relevant. She did draw the line, though, when the eager young architects asked if they could hook her up with a twenty-four-hour mike and video camera. Otherwise, it seems, the "aliens" were given free rein. The Koolhaas team—including his institutional brain trust, OMA—studied Prada's factories, showrooms, display systems, and existing stores. They came up with proposals for advertising campaigns, major plans for websites, and the irresistible term *Prada vomit*. That refers to the stuff that shows Prada in a more diverse social context, and includes Prada fakes, used Prada on eBay, and the sailors who compete on Prada's sailboat, the *Luna Rossa*. Nothing was considered beyond Koolhaas's purview; so many concepts and notions were generated that they have ended up filling fifty volumes so far. The team's published book, *Prada,* has become a bible for architecture fans. Many of Koolhaas's suggestions—such as including some vintage Prada in the inventory of the New York store—are being incorporated; others remain ideas. Koolhaas remembers, "One of the hilarious things that we proposed was that they sponsor the subway, so that from Bloomingdale's to Prince Street you'd be on the Prada train—and what is astonishing is that Bertelli gave his people an order the next day to investigate the idea."

Beneath all the highfalutin talk, one can be sure Miuccia Prada is not deluded about what they are trying to do here. She's not pretending that it isn't first and foremost a place to sell product. She is also not fooling herself with pronouncements that she will revolutionize fashion with her latest move. She does not miss the fact that one might think that the very idea of spending so much time, money, and creativity on a store could be seen as decadent. But even with that consciousness, she believes that to try new things is better than giving in to the status quo. She says, "If you see a beautiful new place, a more interesting place than the usual stores, that's already something. I am skeptical that one can do more than that. I am realistic. I think the way I can be political in my work is in the way I approach things. The shop, for instance, can become a public space, where everybody can come. We can try to make the most of it."

As to the store's post–September 11 context, Koolhaas is a thinker who has long been dealing with questions of conflict, uncertainty, and reality. His design for the Prada store flows from those issues. As the architect says, "The whole concept was to try and create something which was open to influences from the outside, which wanted to represent the purity of fashion but also the impurity of the world." What he has done, at a time of incredible unpredictability, is create a space that is all about clash and flux. But it also gives great aesthetic pleasure.

One can see consciousness of the history of beauty in Prada's spring 2002 collection for women, which is already in the new shop. One of the ideas behind this collection, whose crudely cut—on purpose—clothes feature a weathered-looking lamé on either the front or the underside of the garments, is destroyed beauty, or the memory of beauty, which goes right to the heart of the current moment. Prada says, "We wanted to use material that is very rich in theory—but that has now been pared down to a basic." And so this isn't just any lamé—it was made on machines that haven't been used in fifty years, and the result is fabric that looks like Baroque foil.

Miuccia had on a number from the new collection one evening in November when we were all in Rotterdam. (She loves to wear her stuff six months before everybody else and always says, "I couldn't resist it.") She, Bertelli, Koolhaas, and I had gone to see the riveting Hieronymus Bosch exhibition that was on view at the Museum Boijmans Van Beuningen. We went our separate ways through the show, individually taking in the images of monsters and demons and hell and comical inventions—the exhibition is a journey into a world of paranoia and madness. When we met up again, we all had the same observation: Our twenty-first-century world doesn't seem that far away from this sixteenth-century vision. I pointed to a drawing by an anonymous Bosch contemporary titled *The Forest Has Ears, the Field Has Eyes,* which is exactly what it depicted: ground covered with peeking eyes, trees with ears hanging from their trunks and branches. I said it reminded me of what Prada has done in SoHo. I wasn't referring just to the way the store plays with voyeurism or to the fact that technology is omnipresent. I also meant that they have established both a world and an underworld. Some of it is breathtaking, some of it is comical, some of it has the quality of mad inventiveness, just like Bosch's work, and some of it is deliciously wicked.

Vanity Fair, February 2002

Nicole's New Light

"My life collapsed," Nicole Kidman recalled recently. "People ran from me because suddenly it was 'Oh, my God! It's over for her now!'" Kidman's leper moment came last year, when her former husband, Tom Cruise, fired her as his wife—that, at least, is how the split came across to the public. But on the day this past summer when she was reliving that moment of reckoning, it all seemed like centuries ago, not only because so much has happened in her life since then but also because we were sitting in a trailer just outside of Poiana Brașov, Romania, a spot as physically and psychologically removed from Hollywood as it gets.

Romania is where Kidman will be through the end of this year, at work on Anthony Minghella's film adaptation of *Cold Mountain,* Charles Frazier's rather turgid best-seller about the Civil War. Although some scenes have been filmed in Charleston, South Carolina, the bulk of this epic is being shot in Poiana Brașov and nearby spots in northern Romania. One quickly understands why: These are places that epitomize the phrase "going back in time." I had arrived in Poiana Brașov a day earlier, in the dead of night. After a hairy mountain ride to my hotel behind an endless stream of horse-pulled carts, and a sleepless night spent listening to wild dogs howl, I was glad to see the morning sun. So was everyone else on the set. It was the first beautiful day after weeks of relentless rain. Suddenly I heard the clippety-clop of horses' hooves, and somebody said, "Here comes Nicole." I spied the actress way up the road in costume as Ada, the book's heroine, all decked out in her corsets and petticoated skirt. She looked the height of refinement, but when she spotted me she let out a hearty laugh. "You made it," she said in her unmistakable Australian accent.

Before *Cold Mountain* is done shooting, Kidman, who stars in the film with

Bruce Weber, *Nicole Kidman, Montauk, New York,* 2003

329

Jude Law, will be on movie screens back home, breaking audiences' hearts with her mesmerizing performance as Virginia Woolf in Stephen Daldry's adaptation of Michael Cunningham's feminist novel, *The Hours.* That movie, which also features Julianne Moore, Meryl Streep, and Ed Harris, and which doesn't betray the profound sense of aloneness that makes Cunningham's novel so moving, is scheduled to be released later this month. And just like last year—when Kidman surprised and won over moviegoers with the one-two punch of her swooningly gorgeous performance as a doomed dance-hall star in *Moulin Rouge!* and her portrayal of a mother on the edge of madness in *The Others*—the studios' release schedules have decreed that she will shortly follow up *The Hours* with yet another adaptation, this time of *The Human Stain,* the tough Philip Roth novel, which has been turned into a movie gem by the director Robert Benton and which will be in theaters next year. Benton's casting of Kidman as the novel's take-no-crap, been-to-hell-and-back female janitor, opposite Anthony Hopkins, is right on the money.

And that's not all. On the heels of her breakup, Kidman spent last winter in Sweden, shooting Lars von Trier's film *Dogville,* which is scheduled for release sometime next spring. Von Trier, the director most recently of *Dancer in the Dark,* wrote this latest film for Kidman, which serves to underscore what has been happening to her career over the last few years. While the world has remained obsessed with "The Tom and Nicole Story," with what their marriage was really like—and especially with what went on between the sheets and with what truly caused the relationship to combust—Kidman has done something more useful: She has shown herself to be a major talent, a remarkable actress who can get in there with the best of them, go toe-to-toe, and come out with her credibility intact. What's more, she's proved herself to be a star with a capital *S,* the one-in-a-generation kind who, like Elizabeth Taylor, is bigger than the Hollywood system, and is also unafraid to be human and real, which only makes her more popular.

Offscreen, Kidman, like Taylor, has a love of life, a strong sense of loyalty, and a madcap sense of humor, and she seems to really know how to be a friend. (Her old buddy Naomi Watts, whose career has only recently taken off, told me, "Nicole was always there with her door open, her arms open, her ears open—just what you need.") Kidman and Taylor know how to live it up, too, and while Kidman may not share Taylor's predilection for carrying really large rocks on her mitts, she's got the rags—closets full of the hippest fashion and vintage clothes. Put this pair in a room and you'll hear two dames who really know how to laugh. In terms of their careers and their craft, there's more than coincidence in the fact that, while Taylor showed the world what she was made of when she walked the razor's edge in Edward Albee's *Who's Afraid of Virginia Woolf?*, Kidman is doing the same thing playing Woolf herself.

I've gotten to know Kidman over these last couple of years, right as her life was falling apart, in my capacity as editor of *Interview* magazine. What struck me initially is that she's a person who doesn't let others down. In one way or another, I have seen her stand by her word and be thoughtful in situations that would likely bring out the worst in other stars. The more one knows her, the less "actressy" she seems. She hasn't undergone the kind of narcissistic transformation that can turn extremely famous people into absolute bores or unbearable phonies. She has gotten used to the attention that comes with being a star, but Kidman is not one of those types that everybody else has to pamper and flatter; instead, she seems to be driven by a feeling that she has so much to learn, and so much to see. She's still curious, still hungry, and will still almost kill herself playing a part. It's like she goes into a trance on set—broken ribs and bloody knees (such as she incurred on *Moulin Rouge!*) or grossly swollen ankles (*Cold Mountain*) be damned.

Nicole's childhood doesn't sound that unusual, but there are a few kinks and clues to suggest that this was a kid with big ambitions. Born in Hawaii in 1967 to Australian parents, Antony and Janelle, she grew up in an upper-middle-class suburb of Sydney, in a family that was close then and remains close today. Both parents worked, her mother as a nurse, her father as a psychologist, and it appears they passed on a strong sense of ethics and social conscience to their two daughters, Nicole and Antonia. As Nicole, the elder, remembers, "My mother would treat us as little adults. We would discuss things. I was raised to think and to question. She wanted girls who were educated, aware of everything, and opinionated. So did my father. They wanted us to be sure of being able to speak out. That's gotten me into trouble at times."

The outside world was less of an oasis, and at times Nicole felt like a bit of an oddball. She says, "My mother was a feminist in a conservative neighborhood, and my father was left-wing. I was Catholic, and most of the kids were Protestant. I looked very different from most of the other people. I was very, very tall"—she topped off at five feet ten inches—"with wild, wild curly hair, which I now try to tame. I couldn't go to the beach, because I was so fair-skinned. One of my most vivid memories is of being a child, sitting in my bedroom, and hearing the laughter from the next-door neighbors. They had a pool and you'd hear them laughing, playing. I remember feeling not included in that, just sitting in my bedroom. . . . I had a huge desire to be somebody else. I would think, I'm not living the life I want to live. I would try to come up with images before I went to sleep, to then try and live the life I wanted to live in my dreams. And I was deeply romantic."

Even today, when friends talk about Kidman they cite her love of losing herself in other worlds. She is an avid reader, frequently seen curled up with a book, oblivious to whatever's going on around her. That started a long time ago: By her teens, novels were a primary means of escape. She has said that it was thanks to characters such as Dorothea in *Middlemarch* and Natasha in *War and Peace* that she began to think about being an actor. She told me, "I wanted to be those women. I would live through them, get lost in them, and be devastated when the books ended."

Nicole also had a definite wild streak. She was hitting the clubs in Sydney by the time she was fourteen, drawn to the bohemian side of life, befriending the transvestites who frequented her favorite joints. Already showing her affinity for avant-garde fashion, she'd doll herself up in a tutu, fishnets, and lace-up black boots, and dye her hair like a rainbow or in even more intense shades of red than her natural coloring. Other nights she'd go vintage.

But of all the pursuits she followed in her teens, it was the drama lessons that from the age of twelve she took on weekends at Sydney's Phillip Street Theatre which really stirred something within her. She got some saucy parts, too, including that quintessential southern belle, Blanche DuBois, in Tennessee Williams's *Streetcar Named Desire,* played by Nicole at the ripe old age of twelve. She's less amused today by the cheeseball Australian films she found herself doing a few years later, such as 1983's teen dirt-bike epic *BMX Bandits* and 1986's *Windrider,* a romance about windsurfing (with the actor Tom Burlinson, a twenty-nine-year-old who became eighteen-year-old Nicole's boyfriend)—but at the same time she doesn't disown them. As an actor, she says, "you're never in a position where you have an enormous amount of choices—that's why I never judge other actors' choices. One doesn't know what's behind them. Why does somebody need to do [a particular movie]? Because they have to pay the mortgage? I've certainly been in that position. *BMX Bandits?* Bring it on. I wanted to own a place. That's how I bought my apartment. After that I always knew, if everything else went to pieces, I had a floor I could crash on." As for the artistic side of the equation, such as it was, no matter how cartoony her parts, Kidman always comes off as a strong, memorable presence—and as killer sexy. Best of all her early Australian films is 1991's *Flirting,* a girls'-school classic in which she plays the alpha prefect who turns nice.

She had begun to work steadily, but at the age of seventeen two events temporarily sidetracked her career. First, she decided to see a bit of the world, bagging high school graduation for an intoxicating few months in Amsterdam and Paris. Kidman recalls, "I was like, 'Bring it on—bring on Europe!'" ("Bring it on" is a pet Kidman expression, a kind of exhortation to herself and others to let life happen.) That same year, her mother was diagnosed with breast cancer and went through chemotherapy. Kidman put everything on hold to be part of her mom's support structure. She clearly respects and loves her dad, but her relationship with her mother seems to have been the more formative one. On more than one occasion she told me, "I still think one of my motivating forces is to make her proud of me." When I asked Kidman to explain that more specifically, she answered, "She once said to me she wished she had had no children, which is a hard thing to hear from your mother. I think I stormed out of the house that day. But I understand what she meant, because she gave up a lot. She would have been an amazing doctor, she speaks French, she plays the piano, she's far more brilliant than me at everything." How many of us feel that same way about our parents' missed opportunities and end up taking on the world in their name?

What set Kidman's career in true motion was a 1987 Australian TV miniseries, *Vietnam,* which suggested she had real acting mettle. She took off in the role of Megan Goddard, an antiwar, anti-Establishment student, got nice reviews, and, out of that success, was eventually cast in 1988, at the age of twenty-one, in the film *Dead Calm,* directed by Phillip Noyce and produced, as was *Vietnam,* by Australia's legendary Kennedy Miller Productions. This was the project that would bring her to America and alter the trajectory of her career. A thriller, *Dead Calm* required her to outfox, outsail, and outfight a psychotic interloper—we see her together, untogether, in the altogether, and her performance never falls apart.

The 1989 film, a smash in Australia and a player in the States, too, came to the attention of the screenwriter Robert Towne, who was then at work with Tom Cruise on *Days of Thunder.* Towne, who is no monkey, showed *Dead Calm* to Cruise. Kidman had already been brought to America for a publicity junket for *Dead Calm,* been signed by ICM agent Sam Cohn, and flown back across the Pacific to Tokyo, where she was doing more promotional chores, when she got a call saying Tom Cruise wanted to meet her. When I asked what her first reaction to the summons was, she laughed, saying, "I thought, Wow! This is America! Tom Cruise wants to meet me. He made *Top Gun* and *Cocktail*—the films I grew up watching." And the fairy tale began. Before she had time to straighten her hair, it seemed, she was in Daytona Beach, Florida, starring opposite Cruise in *Days of Thunder.*

Enter Cupid. Drumrolls. Music. Fireworks! Kidman was smitten: "He basically swept me off my feet. I fell madly, passionately in love. And as happens when you fall in love, my whole plan in terms of what I wanted for my life—I was like, 'Forget it. *This* is it.' I was consumed by it, willingly. And I was desperate to have a baby with him. I didn't care if we were married. That's what I wish I'd done." But that's not what happened. Instead, a few months later, Cruise's divorce from the actress Mimi Rogers came through, and America's most American leading man proposed to Australia's latest hot export.

It's hard to imagine a more dramatic personal and sociological change than the one Kidman experienced the moment she hooked up with Cruise. She went from being an actress who had begun to taste success—and who had always insisted on living on her own, even during her various romances—to a woman inside the engine of the Hollywood machine. As for the first piece of celluloid that came out of their alliance, let's just say that time has not been kind to *Days of Thunder.* Still, it's fascinating to see how Hollywood, led by producers Don Simpson and Jerry Bruckheimer and British director Tony Scott, packaged her raw sexuality, putting a commercial gloss on it.

After *Days of Thunder,* she began working on *Billy Bathgate* for director Robert Benton, who recently teamed up with the actress again. I spent time with them this September on the Paramount lot, where they were rerecording fragments of dialogue for *The Human Stain.* It was quite an eye-opener to watch her work with Benton and the sound technicians. Kidman is a pro, but not a hack. She'll want to keep doing a line or scene until it feels true, but she also seems to have unusually direct access to all sorts of inner emotions, which she is often able to summon in a matter of seconds and articulate with authenticity.

There's a bit of a father-daughter dynamic between Benton and Kidman. When we went to lunch they both cracked up about the old days when Kidman, who married Cruise in the middle of *Billy Bathgate,* would go missing in action. Benton recalled, "One day when I couldn't find her, somebody said, 'Oh! Nicole is skydiving,' and I almost had a heart attack. I thought, God! Like I don't have enough problems." Benton sat his star down and gave her a good talking-to. She solemnly listened and, as Benton laughingly told me, was jumping out of planes again soon after with her new husband. The thrill both apparently get from a sense of danger seems to have been an aphrodisiac for Nicole and Tom, who would also amuse themselves with adrenaline-pumping fun such as spins on Cruise's Harley.

It's clear that the couple's chemistry worked big-time. When Nicole speaks of her years with Cruise she describes a devotion without clauses and without doubt. "I was willing to give up everything," she explains. "I now see that as part of me. I'm willing to do that—I do it when I do a movie, too. I'm willing to go, 'Yeah, bring it on, consume me, intoxicate me.' I want to feel alive—I want to reel, basically. I was reeling with Tom and I loved it and I would have walked to the end of the earth. That meant giving up a lot of things that were very important to me." Kidman doesn't pretend that she was impervious to the glare that came with being Mrs. Cruise. "You're being watched and scrutinized, and that slowly affects you. But it's also deeply romantic, because it feels like there's only the two of you and you're in it together, as if you're in a cocoon, and you become very dependent on each other."

Apart from her role opposite Cruise in Ron Howard's immigrant drama, *Far and Away,* which was a nonstarter when it came out in 1992, Kidman's career wasn't on the front burner during the first few years of the marriage.

Instead of klieg lights, her days were filled with squeals and gurgles, for it was in 1993 that the couple adopted a girl, Isabella. (In 1995 they would add to the family by adopting their son, Connor.) But ultimately the bubblelike existence had to end. This wasn't the Dark Ages. The suffragettes had come and gone, Virginia Woolf had written *A Room of One's Own* decades before, and Kidman, very much a woman of her time and of her upbringing, could not stifle her need to express herself. She started to pursue a number of parts. There was, for instance, 1995's *Batman Forever*, directed by Joel Schumacher, in which she played the love interest, Dr. Chase Meridian.

Schumacher's stories of life on the *Batman Forever* set with Kidman are telling. By that time she had become a certified member of Hollywood royalty, but it seems that that had killed off neither her sense of spontaneity nor her sense of democracy. There was, for instance, the day she got a craving for some kind of iced mocha concoction from Starbucks. As Schumacher recalls, she didn't just order one for herself. "There were hundreds of people working on *Batman,* and, sure enough, an hour later, some kind of truck arrived with all these frozen drinks, and everyone had an iced mocha thingy." But while Kidman helped to put the sass into *Batman Forever,* offering a glimpse of her flair for camp, the performance didn't do much to thaw the ice-princess image that she had by now developed in the media.

In point of fact, Kidman had never been cold or rude to the press, but somehow her perfect behavior as Mrs. Cruise—the couple was famous for their highly controlled public appearances—and the sorts of roles Americans had seen her in, along with the presumption that she was being cast only to curry favor with her husband, all combined to make it seem as if she were high-and-mighty, exquisite, but made of marble. She, too, may have bought into some of that: "I felt I didn't deserve to be there in my own right, and so throughout I wasn't there as Nicole—I was there as Tom's wife."

What finally changed this was *To Die For,* which was also released in 1995.

It was not a part that was handed to her on a silver platter. Even though she had a decent track record by then and was married to such a box-office biggie, she was not considered A-list and had to work to convince the director, Gus Van Sant, that she had what it took to play Suzanne Stone, a woman who is so obsessed with becoming a TV star that she is willing to do anything to make that happen, including seducing a weirdo high school student (Joaquin Phoenix) and persuading him to do away with her lunkish husband (Matt Dillon). Kidman has never been the type to let pride get in the way of work she desires. Even today she'll do the requisite campaigning if she is after a role and she isn't being pursued for it; she has an instinctive grasp of the ebb and flow of fame, of the fact that you have to get up on your board if you want to ride its waves.

Van Sant, whose deadpan way with a story is almost Warholian, recalls, "She got my number somewhere. I don't know if it was hard to find it or not, but she just called me and said hi. She phoned right when Meg Ryan dropped out of the movie, which involved her knowing inside information. Our second choice was Patricia Arquette, and we even had a third choice, Jennifer Jason Leigh. Nicole was somewhere on the list. I had met her a couple of times. When she called she told me that she knew she wasn't on the top of my list, and I tried to kind of say, 'Well, I don't know about that. . . .' But she just cut me off and said, 'Look, you don't have to pretend that I am.' I said, 'Okay,' and then she said, 'But listen, I'm destined to play this part.' That worked really well with me because I believe in destiny."

It did seem as if she had been born to play this knife-sharp black comedy, written to perfection by Buck Henry. She found humor in her character's desperation and yet also made that desperation feel painfully real. She was so wickedly funny that at the time I remember being surprised—as were many others—that there was edge and bite underneath all that Hollywood polish. This was the beginning of her transformation from perfect escort to flesh-and-blood actor. When *Portrait of a Lady,* directed by Jane Campion and featuring

Kidman as the headstrong heiress, Isabel Archer, was released a year later, the project's ambition underscored the fact that Kidman might just become a big deal in her own right—even if the film itself wasn't a breakthrough for anyone.

It was inevitable that performing in these kinds of films would affect Kidman's sense of herself. She says, "I realized I could be fulfilled creatively and that I had given that up. I think this happens to women who reenter the workforce. They go, 'Hold on, there's a world out there, and I wouldn't mind being a part of it.' I tried to deny it because it would have been so much easier for me to be satiated by being a wife. I wish it could have been part of my trajectory, but it wasn't."

Kidman imagined, like millions of women, that she'd be able to fulfill herself through her work and also be a dedicated wife and mother. Her goal was to do a worthwhile project every year or so and still have enough time and energy to give her family its due. For a while the plan worked, or at least it looked that way from the outside. The actress appeared in *The Peacemaker* in 1997 and in *Practical Magic* in 1998 (two films that ended up stiffing) while continuing to show up at her husband's side, always looking like a million bucks, for every important occasion.

And then came an opportunity that seemed heaven-sent: the late Stanley Kubrick's decision to cast Kidman and Cruise in his take on sexual obsession and jealousy, *Eyes Wide Shut*. The couple had a chance not only to work with one of the movies' true greats on a film that promised to be electrifying but also to work together. And so, in late 1996, they picked up their household, moved to London, and dedicated themselves to implementing Kubrick's vision. It was not just a nine-to-five collaboration. Kidman and Cruise's bond with Kubrick proved to be such that their lives became intertwined with his, and the film somehow bled into their relationship.

The two actors, especially Nicole, are known for living and breathing their parts when working; this time their roles were a bored husband and wife who get caught in a web of sexual pretending that then turns dangerously real and winds up threatening their marriage. Sounds like a recipe for an emotional Molotov cocktail that would test many a couple's relationship. On top of that, the shoot, originally scheduled for four months, kept getting extended, and in the end Tom and Nicole would park themselves in London for eighteen months. As Kidman remembers it, "Tom had such a very strong connection with Stanley, and so did I. That resonated through our lives and marriage—it had such a profound effect." Even when the actors and their director weren't actually shooting, they'd spend hours together every day. Nicole says, "Stanley saw Tom and I in the most extreme situations because of the way in which he works. He breaks you down. He challenged all of my concrete, solid bases that I'd set around myself, and basically disturbed them, and made me far more introspective." Nicole does not get literal about how this experience shook things up, but she couldn't be more clear that it did; the couple was also deeply affected by Kubrick's sudden death during postproduction. But she has an artist's acceptance of the entire experience as ultimately valuable, no matter how painful.

When we were talking I was honest with her about my reactions to the movie, which finally came out in the summer of 1999. I told her that, despite the film's visual punch, the prerelease fuss and hype seemed way overblown considering the final product, which to my mind is not the revolutionary work that was promised but rather a bourgeois attempt at titillation, an effort at illuminating truths about sexuality and relationships that have been treated with much more insight by other writers and directors. Nicole responded in a way that is characteristic of her. She was not defensive, but heard me with real interest and openness. She then stood by both her director and her leading man: "I still think Tom was mesmerizing in it, but that's partly because I know what he went through. To me, the themes are so important and so complex—and who knows what Stanley would have done [with it] if he had had more time, if he'd lived."

. . .

In the fall of 1998, Kidman was making new headlines with her performance onstage in London in *The Blue Room,* which required her to be nude for ten seconds. One night backstage, Kidman found a big bouquet of red roses in her dressing room with a note from the Australian director Baz Luhrmann that read something like: "She sings, she dances, she dies, how can you refuse?" Luhrmann was referring to Satine, the doomed heroine of the movie he was planning to shoot next, *Moulin Rouge!* He was following his gut instinct that Kidman would shine in the part of a divinely romantic showgirl who drives folks wild, sacrifices for her art, and dies tragically of tuberculosis on her beloved stage. But Kidman was still perceived by audiences as distant and cold; there was resistance to her from some of the powers behind the project. Nevertheless, Luhrmann and his casting director were passionate about their choice. They fought until the deal was done, and a role that was loaded with risk for both star and director turned out to be the best thing that ever happened to Kidman's career. Not only did it show what a multifaceted talent she is but the part, which had her running off not with the rich producer but instead with the struggling writer, undercut her public image as a cool careerist and plainly rendered her human and warm. Whether she is flying through the air on a trapeze, singing an over-the-top love song with her leading man, Ewan McGregor, or breathing her last breath, her performance is big, bold, vulnerable when called for, and just right in terms of tone.

Like Van Sant, Luhrmann calls Kidman an ally. Recalling the *Moulin Rouge!* shoot, which took place over nine months in Sydney, he says, "She never showed anything but absolute belief in the film, which I've got to say is one of the defining qualities of Nicole. She is absolutely at her best in the worst-possible situations." Little did anyone know how much she would be put to the test on this front. It was during postproduction on *Moulin Rouge!,* sometime in February 2001, Luhrmann remembers, that he got a call from Kidman: "She said, 'I've broken up with Tom' or 'Tom's breaking up with me.' She told me there were helicopters flying over the house, and she was genuinely devastated and shocked."

The public's reaction to the breakup has been a lesson in how the movies and real life can converge. The timing of the marital implosion led into a period when Kidman was also in the public eye because of *Moulin Rouge!* The fact that in this film she died as a heroine passionately committed to her art, a victim of her time and her circumstances, carried over to the perception of her as a victim in real life—a perception to which there seems to be more than an element of truth. My conversations with Kidman about this tumultuous, painful time, which also included a miscarriage, showed her to be a woman genuinely struggling to understand why her marriage failed.

I doubt that legalities are the only explanation for why this couple has been so respectful to each other in public. These are two people who understand good behavior and who are committed to their children's well-being. Even though it looked at first as if they were going to land in an ugly legal battle, the couple settled out of court. Both parties have made it clear that they will not go into the nitty-gritty about what went wrong. But since their split played out publicly in such a bizarre way—with Cruise releasing cryptic tidbits to the press like "She knows why," and Kidman seeming to be in a state of shock—one can't help but still be curious. I asked Kidman point-blank, "Do you know why you broke up?" She said, "I'm starting to understand now. At the time I didn't." So I asked again, "It came as complete news?" She said yes.

Sometimes I got the feeling she'd do anything to reverse events. But I also had the sense she knew there couldn't have been any other outcome, in part, it seems, because of her own artistic needs. It's not clear how these conflicted with the marriage, but what's unusual about her, given her status as a Hollywood institution, is that she's willing to bare the confusion, the contradictions, the regret. She told me, "I didn't have to have a huge career. I would have liked to be able to make a *To Die For* occasionally and things that could stimulate me. And this makes me sad, but I still would probably choose a marriage and an intact family over my career." When I pointed out to Kidman that the beauty of living in the twenty-first century for women is that, one hopes, they don't have to choose between work and family, she replied, "But I think I had to choose. I think [the marriage] would have come down to it. I suppose it wasn't meant to be. What I see now is a nine-year-old little girl who [the divorce] affected and I see a seven-year-old boy, and see my duty as a mother. It means for the rest of my life I have to do things to protect and help them and make it up to them. That sounds so old-fashioned and strange. I don't know why that's in me, but it is."

While it's not unusual to worry about the kids in a divorce, Kidman is clearly wearing a kind of hair shirt; after all, she was raised as a Catholic. This leads to the role of religion in her marriage—specifically Scientology, which, as everyone knows, is Tom's thing. When I asked Kidman about her ties to the organization, she said, "Tom is a Scientologist. I'm not. I was introduced to it by him, and I explored it. But I'm not a Scientologist. I told Tom I respect his religion. I said to him, 'It is what you believe in, and it's helped you.' "

One of the most fascinating aspects of the entire story is how intrigued people are by the couple, even those who aren't normally into tabloid-type gossip. The marriage remains a kind of blank slate upon which we can all project our own ideas; people have floated so many theories, from unfaithfulness to the fallout from prenuptial agreements to who knows what. The speculation was endless—and still is. This sense of mystery goes way back: The marriage had always been surrounded by whispers about the couple's sexuality and questions about just what kind of transactions were taking place between them.

When I decided to face these issues directly with Nicole, she laughed at the awkwardness with which I brought them up, and then asked, "Do you want to know if I had a real marriage?" Even though I thought it was my duty as a good reporter to poke around in there, I was embarrassed by having to be so nosy. So I circled the issue of the relationship and brought up the fact that Cruise seems to call the lawyers whenever the *g* word is thrown at him (and I don't mean *garter*).

This time, she grabbed the bull by the horns and said, in a serious tone, "Look, the marriage was real. The marriage existed because it was two people in love. It's that simple. They've said I'm gay, they've said everyone's gay. I personally don't believe in doing huge lawsuits about that stuff. Tom does. That's what he wants to do, that's what he's going to do. You do not tell Tom what to do. That's it. Simple. And he's a force to be reckoned with. I have a different approach. I don't file lawsuits because I really don't care. Honestly, people have said everything under the sun. I just want to do my work, raise my kids, and hopefully find somebody who I can share my life with again, or, you know, have a number of different people at different times who come into my life. I don't know what my future is. But I really don't care what anybody else is saying."

On the same day that Kidman and I had this conversation in Los Angeles, I happened to visit the producer Lynda Obst. Philip Roth's masterpiece *American Pastoral* is on her plate as her next film project. Kidman's name came up as a possible lead. Obst and I then fell easily into the inevitable who did what to whom Tom-and-Nicole conversation. Has anyone in America *not* had this conversation? After a minute we laughed at ourselves and Obst pulled out a copy of *American Pastoral* and read a passage that says it all. The subject is "other people":

> *You never fail to get them wrong. . . . You get them wrong before you meet them, while you're anticipating meeting them; you get them wrong while you're with them; and then you go home to tell somebody else about the meeting and you get them all wrong again. . . . The fact remains that getting people right is not what living is all about anyway. It's getting them wrong that is living, getting them wrong and wrong and wrong and then, on careful reconsideration, getting them wrong again. That's how we know we're alive: we're wrong. Maybe the best thing would be to forget being right or wrong about people and just go along for the ride.*

. . .

Kidman's willingness to stay on life's ride, even when it feels like a roller coaster, is proven. She doesn't deny that doing so was hard at first after the marriage fell apart. She even told me a story about being so upset that she was lying on the ground in the fetal position, weeping, while her parents, who had arrived to help her get through the whole circus, were trying to make her snap to. "That's enough now—get up!" her mother said. She did. There were other issues to deal with, such as how the divorce was going to affect her career. Kidman remembers, "At the time, it felt like the work was going to be taken away from me. I had more things that I wanted to give, do, participate in creatively, and to have had that denied prematurely would have been awful." She saw to it that none of this happened, and she had people who were true-blue behind her. One of them is Baz Luhrmann, who spent much of the first year of the breakup's aftermath with Kidman promoting *Moulin Rouge!* Luhrmann had told Kidman that, under the circumstances, he'd understand if she bowed out of the promotional duties that can make a movie live or die. Instead, she stood by him and their work as though their lives depended on it. Luhrmann recalls, "I saw her realize the motto of the film, which is 'The show must go on.' She absolutely embodied its spirit."

Between *Moulin Rouge!, The Others,* and even the rather kooky thriller *Birthday Girl,* released last February (Kidman plays a Russian con artist with a throat-scraping, Moscow-ready accent), she made people take her seriously. As Anthony Minghella says, "Each film is so different and distinctive. They make you feel like there's an enormously rich instrument there." When Kidman received a Golden Globe and an Academy Award nomination for *Moulin Rouge!* as well as a Golden Globe nomination for *The Others,* one could feel how happy people were for her. She was finally getting recognition for who she was, not who she was with. It really didn't seem to matter to her that she didn't win a prestigious statue on Oscar night. Stepping out onto that red carpet with her sister as her date, she was a class act in a pink Chanel gown.

When *The Hours* comes out this month it is bound to cause a sensation. It's hard to imagine a finer cast of actors interpreting this remarkable book, which covers three eras—the beginning of the last century, the 1950s, and the 1990s. How appropriate that it is Kidman's job to play Virginia Woolf at the time she was writing *Mrs. Dalloway* and looking for reasons to live as she struggled with thoughts of suicide. The meaning of the role is not lost on the actress. She says, "I truly believe characters come into your life at certain periods of your life for a reason, and Virginia came into my life to help me." Her performance is nothing short of astounding. Much will be made of the aristocratic prosthetic nose she wears, which makes it difficult to recognize her. But even more amazing is the way she seems to transform herself in every possible way, from the lids of her eyes to her soulful mouth to her bony elbows to the crack in her voice, which is fragile and strong at the same time. Her portrayal of Woolf, accent and all, is so convincing it's hard not to conflate the two women's lives. When I told Kidman this, she smiled and made reference to a scene in the movie in which Woolf is sitting on a bench at the Richmond, England, train station, having escaped what she saw as the suffocations of her country household. Her husband, Leonard, comes running up, afraid that she has tried to do herself in again. Virginia finally lets it all out. "The scene at the train station was the reason I wanted to do the film," Kidman told me. "It is about a woman saying, 'This isn't what I want to be. I have the right to make choices for my life that are going to fulfill me.' I loved Virginia. I just love when she says, 'I'm living a life that I have no wish to live. I'm living in a town that I have no wish to live in.'"

These were the exact lines I had written down in the dark when I first saw *The Hours*. They seemed to get at the essence of what Kidman's life has been about these last few years, a period in which she has become not just a bigger star, not just an actress who deserves to be taken seriously, but a truly daring artist. Ann Roth, the costume designer who worked with Kidman on *The Hours* and who, with Conor O'Sullivan, perfected the soon-to-be-famous nose, said it perfectly: "It is like she is in a new skin. She is on her own satellite. She is all alone out there and it's something you want to watch. It's as if she's an amazing piece of art."

Who knows if this would have happened if she hadn't gone through all her marital difficulties? When someone turns a potential calamity into something great we cheer. In Kidman's case, she has moved people not only because she has done that but also because of who she's been. She's shown her feelings. She's asked for help. She hasn't come up with a bunch of phony escorts to make her life look good. She doesn't seem to mind that we can see that her life may be as messy and flawed as the rest of ours. She's even been ruefully witty, as when she remarked to David Letterman, "Now I can wear heels" (a reference to the height gap between her and her ex).

On my last night of talking to her for this article, I went over to her house in Pacific Palisades for a glass of wine. It's the same house that she lived in with Cruise, which embarrasses Kidman. She says that her friends keep saying, "Sell it! Sell it!" but that she prefers things to be done gently, not in a rushed way. She's proud, however, that she finally bit the bullet and got a place in Manhattan in the West Village. When I went by the house in L.A., it happened to be September 11, the anniversary. The kids had made a fire, and Kidman was sitting with them in the den watching the news on TV, a rerun of the day's memorials and events. When it was time for them to go to bed she said, "See, everything went okay today. Nothing bad happened," and turned off the TV. Relief for all of us. She came back downstairs after tucking Isabella and Connor in. We went into the living room and I noticed art, such as paintings by Ben Shahn and Milton Avery, on the walls, and photography books on the table. There was a clear sense of shared lives and interests—it felt like a home, not a set. I thought about another line from *The Hours:* "I don't think two people could have been happier than we have been." For a while.

Vanity Fair, December 2002

How Fashion Left Me Speechless

No doubt many of us have been rendered speechless by fashion at one point or another. Maybe something unbelievably beautiful did it. Maybe it was something so loony, or hideous, or so offensive that words failed. Or then again, maybe it was something from left field, something as simple as an overactive air-conditioning system. That's what got my tongue last fall at the spring shows in New York. The gusts of air were absolutely arctic, and by the next morning I had come down with a rotten case of laryngitis.

After a few days of croaking like a frog over the insanely loud music that is now a feature of most shows, my voice was totally gone. I wound up at the doctor, who told me that my vocal cords had hemorrhaged. The prescription? Two weeks of total vocal rest. No whispering, no cheating—total silence. What made this remedy particularly challenging was that I was due to go to Europe the next day, to Milan and then Paris, for the next leg of the collections. My doctor thought about it and said, "Go ahead. Just write everything down. Don't speak."

So off I went with a miniature blackboard, several Magic Slates, and an assortment of Day-Glo markers. I have to admit that the people I always share a car with, to get from one show to the next, immediately saw the silver lining. They luxuriated in their newfound peace and quiet. They also had even more entertainment than usual, which is saying a lot, because the whole experience of going to the fashion shows—of magazine editors, stylists, print and TV reporters, buyers and, of course, guest celebrities traveling from city to city in this kind of circus caravan—is a riot at times. Fashion is full of some of the most fascinating personalities in the world and can really be seen as its own tribe. Robert Altman tried to capture it in *Prêt-à-Porter,* but he failed miserably because he worked with the same old clichés. While he was onto the competitiveness, the currying of favors and the silliness, he missed the humor, the passion, the loyalty, the drama, and even the genuine creativity that is very much alive and well in fashion. That's what keeps the real fashionistas coming back season after season. The shows are a cross between being in the trenches and being spoiled rotten. One minute you're being elbowed and shoved by a bully of a guard; the next moment they're handing you flutes of the best champagne.

And then there is the talk.

Sure, the shows are visual, since one is ultimately there to look, but they are also verbal. Very. Talk is a vital ingredient of the collections: from small talk to big talk to opinion-mongering to gossip to the sharing of information and, naturally, to that age-old ritual of editors going backstage after a presentation to congratulate the designers. Think reception line at a wedding. You need to keep moving so that the person behind you can have her chance to communicate with the stars of the day, too. So, right off the bat, at the first show in Milan, I caused an embarrassing traffic jam backstage with my miniature blackboard and Magic Markers. Not only did I have to write my message out while everyone watched; then the poor designer had to read it, and my handwriting isn't the greatest.

By that time, word was out that I had been forbidden to speak, and I was getting all sorts of sympathetic, if sometimes kooky, reactions from my colleagues. My blackboard contraption was like a perfect setup for that old TV show *Candid Camera*. The funny thing was how many people seemed to get their wires crossed about what was going on. Many seemed to think I'd lost my hearing, or my mind, not my voice. One editor came over and held my hand. A photographer gave me candy. There were many attempts at sign language, which were more like games of charades. A number of people would turn to whoever was sitting beside me, tell them a whole long story, and then ask them to explain it to me—when I'd heard it perfectly well. Karl Lagerfeld, always attuned to fashion's next big "thing," wryly observed, "How chic. Silence. I think I'm going to have a dinner party where no one speaks. I'll give all my guests pens and pads instead of the usual table conversation."

But probably my most interesting encounters occurred backstage with the designers. In Paris, I saw John Galliano after his dynamic Dior presentation. I'd left my board in the car, so I just pointed to my throat as if to say, Sorry, I can't speak. And a colleague explained the situation. Galliano reacted sympathetically. A few days later I saw him again; this time it was after the show he'd done for his own John Galliano line. Part Bollywood, part Art Meets Fashion, it was absolutely mad and inventive. Even though it was the end of a long day, it felt right to go back and tell him what a fabulous experience it was. By that time, my two weeks of voice rest were almost up. (There was one day to go; I also must confess that I wasn't always 100 percent compliant with the doctor's orders. Every few days I couldn't resist doing little test runs to see if my voice was coming back. I'm happy to say it did.) Anyway, by Galliano's show I had writer's cramp from scribbling so much, so I spoke. "Wow!" I said. Someone screamed, "She talked!" Galliano, never one to miss a moment of high drama, said in a mock-tragic voice, "Aha! So you don't have laryngitis. You can speak. You just didn't like Dior!" Fortunately, by then, I could laugh.

The New York Times Magazine, January 26, 2003

Ruben Toledo, *Ingrid,* 2018

Rosenquist's Big Picture

"When things become so peculiar, so frustrating or strange, I think it's a good time to start a painting," said James Rosenquist recently, while we were watching the news together. By his criteria, then, this should be a golden age for art. We'll see. In the meantime, what's certain is that this is once again a moment in which people are hungry for Rosenquist's work after a period in which it has felt as if he were on the periphery rather than at the center of the action. The painter himself seems almost amused by the vicissitudes that come with being an artist. As he says, speaking from the vantage point of his sixty-nine years, "It's not an uphill grind. It's up, down, up, down, et cetera. That's what makes it interesting. It's not like you're climbing a hill all your life—not like in some corporations, where you might end up at the top, only to get fired."

Rosenquist's "comeback" is due to a variety of factors. Pop art itself is enjoying yet another major renaissance in the art world and the culture in general. (There's even a new fashion magazine called *Pop*.) The new Pop-aholism—most subversive in the work of the brilliant multimedia artist Takashi Murakami—is omnipresent not only in galleries and on runways but in music videos, interior and graphic design, the look of television, and (welcome to the hall of mirrors) advertising itself, which was part of Pop's original subject matter. As with the first go-round, some of these impulses may be a response to prosperous times (or, in the current instance, recently prosperous times); once again there seems to be a desire among artists and other creators to make commerce work for one rather than against one. And so the resurgent interest in "the founding fathers" of Pop art. (Although plenty of women are part of the current landscape, the story of sixties Pop—or at least of the stuff that made it to the surface—is a male-dominated one.) Andy Warhol is more copied, more quoted than ever. Roy Lichtenstein's comic aesthetic is all the rage in the world of graphic design. As for Rosenquist, his art is reverberating with the Zeitgeist in a whole bunch of ways. People haven't always acknowledged it, but his work's influence on several subsequent generations of artists, from Jeff Koons and David Salle to Damian Loeb, is obvious. For other artists, who are looking for a way out of the apathy that has been so pronounced in recent times, Rosenquist's history of integrating politics and sociology into his art is also inspiring. But that's not all. There are veins of abstraction, Surrealism, and photo-realism in his work—areas that are also of high current interest. Quite a few roads taken by younger artists lead back to Rosenquist.

All this and more renders the timing of the new Rosenquist retrospective—organized for the Guggenheim Museum by the curators Walter Hopps (who knows this story inside out, since he was there from the beginning) and Sarah Bancroft—just about perfect. The exhibition opens this May in Houston, at both the Menil Collection and the Museum of Fine Arts. After that it is scheduled to travel en masse to the New York Guggenheim in October, and then eventually to the Guggenheim Bilbao. The show, which includes never-before-seen preparatory collages, will offer a chance to assess Rosenquist's place in art history beyond the usual one-dimensional categorizations; among other things, it will allow viewers to see his connection to abstraction rather than perpetuate the idea that his work was a total rejection of it.

Rosenquist was never a laid-back kind of guy. Whereas Warhol and Lichten-stein were cool and ironic, sometimes even opaque, Rosenquist was always hot to trot. He was hard-living, jazzy, and, when he arrived in New York City in the mid-fifties, ready to turn the town on its ear. (As a leftover from the old days he still says, "You dig?") He is hilarious on the subject of the "What will the neighbors think?" attitude that is such a characteristic of today's careerist artists. (First question at a typical panel discussion: "How do I get a gallery?") "I'll tell you what I've encountered," Rosenquist told me. "I've gone to cocktail parties with successful young artists and nobody says a peep. It's like *shhh,* hush, hush. I remember going to a party with Bob [Rauschenberg] and his boyfriend. They'd shout, 'We can't leave the party yet! Because if we leave, there won't be any more party!' The artists in my group weren't afraid to make fools of themselves. Young artists today are so careful to seem smart, and they don't want to let their hair down."

Rosenquist, an artist who has spent his life getting under the skin of images, feels no such need to protect or inflate his own—which makes him not only a gust of fresh air but inspiring and touching. As he knows only too well, he is one of the last of a legendary generation. When he talks about this, one feels how much he misses his deceased contemporaries: "I used to say that my old friends are libraries of worthless information to keep my sanity. But I can't call them up for a recipe anymore. Roy Lichtenstein's gone. Andy. Donald Judd. Dan Flavin. I guess it happens to everybody. Who do I go to for stuff like 'How do you make rabbit-skin glue again?'" (The reference is to a traditional method of coating stretched linen canvases with a glue literally derived from rabbit skins; John Singer Sargent's paintings are a good example of how this rather stinky process can enrich a sense of depth.)

It's a long way from Grand Forks, North Dakota, where Rosenquist entered the world in 1933, to the life he made for himself after he moved to New York. In the flush years right before he was born, his parents, both pilots, had had schemes for the family to start a small airline business that would fly the mail route between Grand Forks and Winnipeg. This went the way of all Dust Bowl dreams when the Depression hit. After that, Rosenquist's father tried to eke out a living working a string of jobs that included pumping gas. The family was constantly having to pick up and move. Rosenquist, an only child, became his mother's favorite date, whether going with her to movies and stage spectacles or just staying home and listening to the radio. But there was nothing Rosenquist liked better than drawing by himself, covering long rolls of cheap wallpaper with crayoned war scenes. (One sees this pleasure played out over and over on an adult scale in the vast horizontal paintings that have been such an important part of his art.)

. . .

The family eventually put down stakes in Minneapolis, where his father had found employment at Mid-Continent Airlines during the war and where Rosenquist finished high school and went to the University of Minnesota. But the curious young man wasn't about to stay put for long. In the summer of 1951 he answered an ad in the local paper for a traveling sign painter and got the job— and therein lay the seeds for a whole new chapter in art history. First, though, Rosenquist would live an adventure that sounds like a cross between *I Am a Fugitive from a Chain Gang* and *Lust for Life*. Painting signs on grain elevators, gasoline tanks, and billboards by day, and whooping it up by night, Rosenquist and the rest of his itinerant crew (many of whom were ex-cons) worked their way across Minnesota, Wisconsin, Iowa, North Dakota, and South Dakota. He remembers, "I had some very starry, strange experiences out there." The job (which included painting Phillips 66 signs and Coca-Cola ads) allowed him to save enough money to head to New York in the fall of 1955, having earned a one-year scholarship to the Art Students League. His first eyeful of midtown bustle, following a night at the YMCA on Thirty-fourth Street, made a real impression: "I had breakfast and then I stuck my head out the door. I thought, Whoa! I'd better have another cup of coffee before I go out on the streets here!"

After that second shot of caffeine he marched over to the League and declared, "I'm here now!" I asked him if the place erupted in cheers, and he laughed. Even though they hadn't exactly been waiting for him, soon the new guy was getting everything he could out of this longed-for opportunity; Hans Hofmann, the famous teacher of abstraction, was gone by then, but Rosenquist learned from many other renowned faculty members, including George Grosz, Will Barnet, and Edwin Dickinson. But he was broke by spring and his scholarship was up. He became a kind of boy Friday for a while before going back to his earlier trade—sign painting. First, though, he had to join the International Brotherhood of Painters and Allied Trades union. "They asked,

'Whaddya wanna join this union for? There's no jobs for yew,'" Rosenquist recalls, slipping from his ever-so-slight Fargoese accent into a broad New York patois. "I got up and made a speech. I said, 'I'm ready to recognize the rights of all the older gentlemen here, and I'm willing to take my turn.' They replied, 'All right, kid, bring your initiation money around Thoisday.'"

The artist was basically on his way. For the next three or so years, he worked painting billboards and marquees, mostly around Times Square, often at dizzying heights. (His assignments included giant likenesses of the stars of the day, including Gregory Peck and Jean Simmons; for an audition, he had had to render Kirk Douglas's head.) At night and on weekends—whenever he could—he did his own work. He also joined a drawing class organized by a couple of new friends who were eager to take art in new directions, Jack Youngerman and Robert Indiana, whose name was Bob Clark at the time. Claes Oldenburg, who would also be counted as an important early Pop artist, took the class, too.

For Rosenquist, the question of what to do in his own work was the big conundrum, as it is for many artists starting out. One leg up: Thanks to his day job he had free paint, bringing home rejected mixes. "I'd take the billboard colors that were considered wrong—the paint that was thought of as too dirty for the neck in an Arrow shirt ad, for example, or for beer. I'd paint a big glass of beer and the salesman would come in and say, 'We can't accept it. There's not enough hops in that glass.'" Rosenquist, never one to miss an opportunity for irony, called the resulting work the "Wrong Color" paintings. These canvases are mostly abstract, but there's also evidence of the artist's experience as a sign painter. In one of the strongest works from that time, 1959's *Astor Victoria*—named after a theater, the marquee of which Rosenquist had often painted—most of the letters *E* and *W* boldly enter the pictorial space. This transitional work is surprisingly powerful.

While Rosenquist was trying to find his voice as an artist, he was also soaking up a lot of atmosphere. There were favorite hangouts along the waterfront—

including a bar known as Keller's, where Rosenquist and his pals would go to get "blind." Sometimes after work, Rosenquist and a few buddies would check out the gallery openings on Fifty-seventh Street, where there was plenty to look at (and also plenty of free wine). And then there was all the action downtown. The first time he made it to the Abstract Expressionist gang's famous "Friday Night Club," he walked into Jackson Pollock's boozed-up wake. "People just kept getting up and saying, 'Jackson Pollock will live with us forever.' Finally, de Kooning gets up and says, 'Goddammit, *no*! He is dead. He is six feet in the *ground*!'"

Rosenquist wasn't an art snob. When he first got to town he would often stand on line to try to get into some of the TV shows that were being taped around Times Square. He has fantastic stories about what he saw, including Elvis three times on the Jimmy and Tommy Dorsey show. Rosenquist's favorite anecdote, though, is about Jack Kerouac's appearance on *The Steve Allen Show*. The artist recalls, "They announced, Ladies and gentlemen, tonight we're going to have the so-and-so dancers, the so-and-so jugglers, and Jack Kerouac of the Beat Generation. This guy comes out of the wings with a three-day growth of beard and a long overcoat and a curl in his hair and he sits down. Steve Allen says, 'Tell us, Jack, what is the Beat Generation?' Kerouac says, 'Nothing.' And he left and never came back. He was so cool."

Rosenquist is one of the great raconteurs, and by all accounts he always has been. He's a true charmer, and a looker, and no doubt these attributes served him well as he tried to invent a life for himself as an artist in the big city. (As a young man he looked like he could have starred in the road company of *Oklahoma!*—tall, blond, and fit as could be.) He seems to have gone everywhere, met everyone; he even scored a job modeling for a Volkswagen ad. Of all the people he came across in the early days, it was Jasper Johns and Robert Rauschenberg, both a few years older than Rosenquist, who made the biggest impression. He gives them the most credit for his evolution as an artist because of the way in which their work empowered his own experiments. Johns and

Rauschenberg were, of course, ahead of the Pop curve, and some of their art—Johns's flag and target paintings, Rauschenberg's three-dimensional *Coca-Cola Plan,* for instance—had already been causing a major stir by the time Rosenquist came on the scene. He remembers the two artists, who were a couple back then, being friendly to him. They, in turn, have vivid memories of their first Rosenquist sightings. "I first noticed him on the street," Rauschenberg told me. "He looked like such a unique person. He was absolutely not outfitted for Wall Street, and he looked like a blond angel. I stared at him a little bit and then went on my way. The next time I saw him he was knocking on my door."

This was 1960, and Rosenquist was wandering around the waterfront in lower Manhattan searching for a place to rent. A man who worked at a sandwich store directed him to the building where Johns and Rauschenberg lived and worked on different floors. Tips were shared, including a connection to another plugged-in guy at another local store, and soon Rosenquist made a deal to take over Agnes Martin's loft in Coenties Slip, a seaport neighborhood where a number of other artists had found cheap pads, including Indiana and Ellsworth Kelly. Rosenquist had just quit the sign-painting business to focus on his own work—like Warhol, he'd also picked up some quick cash creating window displays for Bonwit Teller, Macy's, and Tiffany & Co.—and the pressure was on. "I didn't want to reiterate what was being done, like a second-generation abstract painter," he says. Instead, he pushed himself and broke through with *Zone* (1960–1961), one of his first paintings to incorporate the types of techniques, perspective, and content he'd been working with on his commercial jobs. It took him a long time to arrive at the approximately eight-by-eight-foot canvas's final composition, which featured a woman's face, taken from a cosmetics ad, and a huge gray tomato; Rosenquist says that if curators x-rayed the canvas they'd find, among other painted-over images, "three cows and someone committing suicide."

I asked Jasper Johns if it had seemed unusual at the time for an artist to earn his living as a sign painter. Johns, always thoughtful, answered, "What was unusual was that he was an artist and a billboard painter, someone who was within two worlds, someone who came from both positions, who introduced one into the other." I asked Johns about the perspective and scale of Rosenquist's work. "He was seeing something—I think it was a result of the billboard painting—that was different from what the rest of us were already seeing. Of course, one relates some of it to other artists, too. Others had brought up the idea of wishing the viewer to be so close to their work that they couldn't see the whole thing, or to have the work so large you couldn't see the whole thing. That idea emerged more or less from several positions at the same time. It wasn't just Jim's idea. Other artists, like Barnett Newman, had some similar feelings. It must have been in the air, or about to be in the air. It certainly manifested itself very strongly." Johns gave me a kind of bottom line on Rosenquist: "At the time those works occurred, what was surprising wasn't how they related to other things. It was how they didn't."

The seeds of Rosenquist's signature approach were actually planted several years earlier, thanks to an epiphany. "In 1957," he says, "I was painting Schenley whiskey bottles on every candy store in Brooklyn. One day, after painting about fifty bottles, I got tired of filling in the label, which was supposed to say 'This spirit is made from the finest grains,' in script. Instead, I started to write, 'Mary had a little lamb, her fleece was white as snow' on the damn labels. From the street you couldn't tell what it said, but when they took the ads down, they asked, 'What the hell is this kid doing?' That's when Pop art occurred to me. That's when I asked, What is this bombardment of advertising that's driving you nuts? . . . I thought, How can I use this method to show the emptiness and numbness of all this? I wondered how I could make a mysterious painting in which I painted huge realistic fragments of things, the largest of which would be recognized last. That was

Following spread: Bob Adelman, *James Rosenquist Working on "Fahrenheit 1982 Degrees,"* 1982 my idea at that time. Many of my fellow students were just copying de Kooning's calligraphy. I didn't want to be like everyone else, even if they laughed."

Many did laugh, or grumble that Pop art signified the end of civilization. (At a later symposium on the subject at the Museum of Modern Art, the opening speaker said, "Tonight we're going to bury the Pop." Rosenquist, who was there, remembers Marcel Duchamp in the back row, taking it all in with his overcoat pulled up over his ears.) For Rosenquist, 1960 and 1961 were busy years. He hit upon his mature style of painting, got married to Mary Lou Adams, a textile designer he met while at work in Times Square, and received many important visitors at his studio, not only artists but practically every dealer with good antennae, including Allan Stone, Ileana Sonnabend, Ivan Karp, Leo Castelli, and Richard Bellamy, who became Rosenquist's first dealer. Henry Geldzahler of the Metropolitan Museum of Art came by for a look-see, as did Robert Scull, the owner of one of the city's biggest taxi fleets and the collector who would be the first to buy a work from Rosenquist. A one-man show at Bellamy's gallery in January 1962 really propelled Rosenquist into the limelight. (It also sold out.) That fall, G. R. Swenson, one of the era's most perceptive critics, wrote his landmark essay, "The New American Sign Painters," which first grouped Rosenquist, Lichtenstein, Indiana, Jim Dine, and "Andrew" Warhol.

Two years later, in a famous 1964 interview with

Swenson in *Artnews,* Rosenquist explained his approach this way: "Commercial advertising . . . is one of the foundations of our society. I'm living in it, and it has such impact and excitement in its means of imagery. Painting is probably more exciting than advertising—so why shouldn't it be done with that power and gusto, with that impact."

Both at home and abroad, the media were now all over Pop art, and many galleries and museums wanted to give the new hot artists group or solo shows. As one of Lichtenstein's paintings put it, "POW!" The Pop art "movement" was really an explosion of work by many artists in both America and Europe, with roots in all sorts of art from earlier in the century, including Cubism and Dadaism. There are other obvious antecedents, such as Marcel Duchamp's appropriation of everyday objects (for instance, his famous 1917 urinal sculpture) and Stuart Davis's paintings of commercial products (including his 1924 rendering of a bottle of Odol disinfectant). And then there's the role of photography—the work of Walker Evans, for example—which is intrinsic; without photography, there could be no Pop. But, as often happens, the mass media, historians, and even critics cut out a lot of the history that led to this new art and reduced it to a clean package. (The actual term *Pop art* has been credited to the critic Lawrence Alloway, who is said to have used it sometime around 1954, but he has written that he doesn't know exactly when it was first uttered. He speculates that he probably used it in conversation in the mid-fifties in the context of popular culture and work by a group of English artists that included Richard Hamilton, whose 1956 collage, *Just What Is It That Makes Today's Homes So Different, So Appealing?,* is such a hoot.)

One of the best books on the subject to date is Lucy R. Lippard's *Pop Art,* published in 1966. In it she makes a critical stab at listing who really counts, telling the reader that "the New York five" are Warhol, Lichtenstein, Rosenquist, Oldenburg, and Tom Wesselmann. Apart from some quibbling here and there, this judgment has pretty much held up in the intervening years (as has the idea that Johns and Rauschenberg were vital precedents for American Pop artists).

Rosenquist had met Oldenburg in the late fifties, but he, Warhol, and Lichtenstein didn't get to know each other until Pop had already become a noteworthy phenomenon; though each was tapping into the Zeitgeist with works that would later be connected by critics, they were doing so independently. When the core group finally did spend time together they seem to have gotten on like a house on fire. None of the old macho Abstract Expressionist fisticuffs for this group; while they were competitive, they amused one another, too. Rosenquist tells a funny story in this regard. He'd run into Warhol, who'd remark in his slightly ironic, famously flat tone, "Oh, you're the greatest artist." Rosenquist would reply, "No, Andy, *you're* the greatest artist." And the two would continue to josh each other this way until one gave up. (Rosenquist also enjoyed seeing other artists take Warhol's droll compliments seriously.)

Now that nearly four decades have passed, it's hard to believe that up until recently Rosenquist, Warhol, Lichtenstein, and the others were lumped together so definitively. The differences of vision, of style, and of content are enormous, even when they paint the same subject. Warhol's Marilyns, for example, are plainly iconic and glamorous, whereas Rosenquist's treatment of the actress is almost a deconstruction. He has also painted straightforward pictures, but Rosenquist's work often accumulates, morphs, and layers disparate images; the final results can be real head scratchers. He seems to like the fact that his work is so open to interpretation. In fact, he initially chose commercial images because he wanted a kind of blank slate. He told G. R. Swenson: "If it were abstract, people might make it into something. If you paint Franco-American spaghetti, they won't make a crucifixion out of it, and also who could be nostalgic about canned spaghetti? They'll bring their reactions but, probably, they won't have as many irrelevant ones."

Rosenquist clearly believes in art's ability to affect consciousness. When I visited him recently in Aripeka, Florida, a marshy, unspoiled hamlet north of Tampa, where he has produced much of his work since 1976, he said, "I want people to get my art, but I want to put them in a new mind-set." This isn't just talk. You can witness it in action in Rosenquist's strongest works. Perhaps the most famous example is *F-111,* an eighty-six-foot-long multipaneled masterpiece, completed in 1965, that melds domestic, commercial, and martial worlds—a little blond girl under a hair dryer that resembles a soldier's helmet, a resort umbrella providing shade from an A-bomb blast. The painting, which has often been interpreted as Rosenquist's statement against the Vietnam War, has also been called the *Guernica* of the sixties. The artist's own description is more Rosenquistian, equal parts poetic and blunt: "It's a life-size painting of a bomber flying through the flak of consumer society; and a statement on all the money and power that buys war weapons to supply this society." The sheer ambition and thrill of this massive painting, even without the evocative imagery, make it a showstopper, a work that displays all of Rosenquist's talents, not least his mastery of drawing and painting—*F-111* would not succeed in the way it does without Rosenquist's sophisticated palette, his facility with perspective, and his willingness to experiment. With *F-111,* the sign painter had made a masterpiece out of signs.

When the work was first shown at the Leo Castelli Gallery (which Rosenquist had joined in 1964), it caused a major ruckus. Speaking for skeptics, the critic Hilton Kramer called *F-111* an "irredeemably superficial" work that "leaves the spectator feeling as if he ought to be sucking on a popsicle." The controversy didn't hurt: *F-111* was soon traveling from museum to museum in Europe. By then Rosenquist had established himself as a true original, a highly conceptual painter who could perform a kind of alchemy with images. One sees this combination of mind and matter in unforgettable paintings such as *Blue Sky* (1962), *Air Hammer* (1962), *Promenade of Merce Cunningham* (1963), *Joan Crawford Says . . .* (1964), and *Growth Plan* (1966). Sometimes his work reminds one of the Surrealists, in particular Magritte. What's interesting is how Rosenquist does and does not conform to the typical Surrealist strategies, where the imagery may be strange but there's still some sense of traditional perspective, as if one were looking through a window. Rosenquist, on the other hand, often wants to explode the frame.

By the late sixties, he had become one of the most in-demand artists on the contemporary circuit, and he used his success to help causes he believed in, as well as to have fun—including a nutty project commissioned by *Playboy*, a kitschy take on pregnancy that featured strawberry shortcake, a large sour pickle, and giant breasts with "surprised" nipples. As for the money that came with all this success, as Rosenquist now ruefully says, "Everything went for peanuts." His point is well taken by the standards of today, when Pop art is being sold at auction for staggering prices. *F-111* sold originally for fifty thousand dollars, of which Rosenquist got half. In 1996, it was bought on behalf of the Museum of Modern Art for a reported $5.5 million. But even in the sixties, sales of his work were healthy enough to allow Rosenquist to move his family—he now had one son, John—to East Hampton, where he lived for ten years, joining a long tradition of East End artists, including Pollock and de Kooning; like them, Rosenquist was drawn by the area's luminous light, a by-product of all the surrounding water. He was extraordinarily productive in his first years there, and when both the Whitney Museum in New York and the Wallraf-Richartz Museum in Cologne announced that they would put on retrospectives of his work in 1972, the future must have seemed set.

But before the celebrations could begin, Rosenquist's family went through hell and back. He was driving in Florida with his wife and son, who was now six, when their car was involved in an accident, injuring all three and putting his wife and child in comas for months; hospitalized in Tampa, they both eventually recovered, but with permanent reminders. The retrospectives went forward, but these were painful, difficult times for the artist. As he says, the medical expenses alone put him under intense pressure; the emotional costs, of course, were even worse. In 1972 he was also arrested in Washington for protesting the Vietnam War. (While in jail he conceived of a couple of paintings that feature nails neatly lined up in rows, as if counting by hatch marks. "The idea was, Am I doing time or am I marking time?" Rosenquist recalls.)

The exhibitions kept coming and the work continued, but Rosenquist himself seemed to move more into the background by a certain point in the early eighties. You couldn't read about a big night out on the town without coming across Andy Warhol's name; Rosenquist had become a wallflower by comparison, though he did have a few high-profile friends. (He once told the actress Liv Ullmann he was working on a painting that would express "the sound of all the world's souls after the Earth has blown up." "Oh, *ja,*" she blandly replied, as if such concepts were commonplace. "She had been with Ingmar Bergman too damn long," Rosenquist says today with a laugh.) He had gotten divorced in 1975 and soon afterward started to build his modest compound in Aripeka. Since then he has spent much of his time working in Florida and commuting to Manhattan and, more recently, Bedford, in Westchester County, where his family lives in a white clapboard farmhouse down a dirt road. (In 1987 he married Mimi Thompson, a painter, writer, and curator who had also been an assistant editor at *Vanity Fair;* the couple has a thirteen-year-old daughter, Lily.) In the intervening years, Rosenquist has been industrious, working on commissions for all sorts of venues, including the Four Seasons restaurant in New York, a restaurant at the Stockholm Opera, the Palace de Chaillot in Paris, and, currently, a Starwood hotel in downtown San Francisco. And even though Rosenquist's art of the eighties and nineties has shown less obvious evidence of his old occupation as a sign painter, he has remained true to his complex pictorial approach.

Some of his most dynamic pictures of the early eighties, such as *Star Thief* (1980) and *Fahrenheit 1982 Degrees* (1982)—with imagery that includes symbols of glamour such as lipsticks and a fingernail that's been manicured to look like the tip of a fountain pen—have the visual sock-in-the-face quality of his sixties work, but with more of a sense of mystery. Other paintings are infused with palpable emotion, such as *Through the Eye of the Needle to the Anvil* (1988), a response to his mother's death, in 1986, or *Gift Wrapped Dolls,* a group of oils about AIDS created in the early nineties. Quite often, though, his intentions have remained difficult to read. But even if he's no longer causing furious debate the way he once did, Rosenquist's love of painting, his understanding of scale, and his fascination with the space between abstraction and realism have never left him. (In this regard, he reminds me of Gerhard Richter, the German artist of the same generation whose paintings also have this constant swing between the two genres.) *Joystick* (2002) is a monster-size work, seventeen feet by forty-six feet, that has objects sticking out of the picture—there's a clear plastic rod with two ropes tied to a trapezoidal mirror. Altogether the painting evokes feelings of being high above the ground, perhaps like a child on a swing, or a passenger in a small plane. (When I asked Rosenquist why he enjoys painting such enormous pieces, he answered, "Because they're a big workout." And for the most part he completes them without the help of assistants.)

Among Rosenquist's most ambitious recent works are the three paintings, each titled *The Swimmer in the Econo-mist,* that he created in the late nineties for the Berlin branch of the Guggenheim Museum. They're much more intricate than the sixties work, but they remind me of it. In addition to classic Pop iconography such as lipsticks and household products, there are direct references to *F-111* as well as to Picasso's *Guernica.* These are bold, colorful, dazzling paintings—fascinating, too, in the way one passage flows into another with real verve. Here you see Rosenquist using different perspectives, warping space with the kind of innovation that made certain early Cubist works so astounding and memorable. These paintings must have been challenging to pull off, but then Rosenquist likes that: "A real artist has to get a bigger and bigger kick out of his or her idea."

·　·　·

That's one thing Rosenquist is: a real, old-fashioned artist. I guess because he's been a big deal for so long I wasn't quite expecting the man I found at the Tampa airport—standing alone, waiting to pick me up. In this age of famous people being impressed by themselves and wanting to impress others with their material success, the mere fact that Rosenquist didn't dispatch an assistant to fetch me makes him unusual. This personal quality defined our time together as it defines his work. What makes both Rosenquist's art and the man himself so compelling is that each contains contradictory elements. Like painters of centuries past he'll work only with natural light, yet his subject matter has often been the fake. As Rauschenberg says, "He is always a surprise." The down-home and the futuristic coexist in Rosenquist's world, and spending time with him can be like landing in one of his paintings. One morning he baked us corn bread and scrambled some eggs; the night before, we'd driven to dinner at a local mall in his brand-new electric hybrid Toyota.

When Rosenquist is in Aripeka, having left his family up north in Bedford, he is there to work. Apart from excursions to the nearby general store, where he likes to get the news from the locals, he seems to relish his isolation, painting by himself or maybe going out alone on his boat. In order to feed himself he's become the Edward Hopper of the strip malls. Practically every meal we ate was at one or another mall, and all of the people at these joints seemed to know him. But chitchatting with the owners of the Golden China restaurant seemed to be the extent of his socializing. I got the feeling that when he's there all his energy is saved for painting.

His office is a riot. I have never seen a table with more piles of papers on it. For a while Rosenquist's mother ran things, and after she died it took him some time to hire someone else. Beverly Coe, his main assistant, who has worked with him for seventeen years, laughs that her résumé got lost under a pile of papers and it took a couple of years before he finally came across it. Granted, when I was there, they were in the midst of preparations for the upcoming retrospective, but I had the sense that a perfectly organized business is not one of Rosenquist's priorities. At this point he doesn't even have an official art dealer. As for studio assistants, there were some fellows hanging around the large prefabricated studio, but they were tinkering with old cars—a Chevy and a Lincoln—that are parked right in there with the paintings.

Being with Rosenquist, I found myself thinking about something I might have expected had I been visiting an old Abstract Expressionist, but not one of the founding fathers of Pop art: the romance of painting. Rosenquist has a great story about his first show in Paris, in the early sixties, which caused a fight between an artist and a poet: "Edouard Jaguer said I was a Surrealist. Then Pierre Alechinsky said no, I was a New Russian Realist. They kept arguing, and finally Alechinsky popped him in the jaw and knocked the guy over. I thought, Wow, Paris is a fantastic place, because they sock somebody for an aesthetic." Clearly art is his air—he lives and breathes it. Consider this description of what it's like for him to do his work: "When you start a big painting, it's like a little ant climbing up a hill. When you get to the middle of it, you can see that it's coming off, that it doesn't look too bad. Then when you're sort of finishing it, it's like a sleigh ride. It's downhill and you're very happy. It's like, 'Hey, this is gonna come off, this might even be a painting.' You rush to finish. Bing. Bang. Boom. Then it's done to that point. But you look at it for a long time afterward. This is different than a lot of contemporary people who just throw paint at the canvas and send it to a museum or to an art gallery. Centuries ago, I believe, painters even had a system. They painted something, looked at it, then they painted it again and again until the paintings achieved a deep chiaroscuro, not because of varnishes or anything else, but because the paint could run deep. . . . I do that to a degree."

Sounds like a hell of a way to spend the day, doesn't it?

Vanity Fair, May 2003

Image Maker

"I come from long-lived stock, and expect at least forty years after forty to practice what my education will have presumably taught me," wrote the photographer and curator John Szarkowski in a letter to a college buddy fifty years ago. "As a crusty octogenarian, I shall hobble about and point with a trembling, Elon-stained finger toward the direction in which my carrying-boy should set up the camera. And all the while chuckling quietly at the unreasonable beauty of things." At the time, Szarkowski could not have known just how prophetic his words were. All that's off about his prediction is the physical part; though he's a year shy of eighty, Szarkowski remains sure-footed and still carries his own tripod and view camera. His hands, too, are steadier than Tom Cruise's in *Cocktail,* a fact that is especially noticeable when Szarkowski is mixing up and pouring one of his beloved perfect Manhattans.

At the time Szarkowski wrote that letter predicting his future, he had already begun to make his name as a photographer. He'd received his first Guggenheim Foundation Fellowship and had good reason for faith in what was to come. But even before the kudos started, his writing had that sense of romance, and that feeling of destiny, that surrounds people who end up as legends. Still, even he would have never guessed that, while putting his own cameras away for almost thirty years to run the department of photography at the Museum of Modern Art, he would turn out to be the man who made the medium really matter. Before Szarkowski, the main line of defense for photography was that it could be as artistic as the other arts. But Szarkowski won photography respect for being itself. Other people might be flattered to hear that they had played a vital role in making photography valuable— literally, now that pictures are going for hundreds of thousands at auction. Not Szarkowski, whose interest was the medium, not the market. He says,

"People threaten to give me medals for turning photography into what it's become! God, what if it's true?"

Whether he likes it or not, Szarkowski, whose tenure at MoMA lasted from 1962 to 1991, is the single most important curator that photography has ever had. He can fairly be said to have "discovered" or "legitimized" the work of Diane Arbus, William Eggleston, Lee Friedlander, Chauncey Hare, André Kertész, Jacques-Henri Lartigue, Daido Moriyama, Garry Winogrand, and so many more. By the end of the seventies, he had been responsible for a staggering array of exhibitions and books, the by-product of which was to make it clear that photography was as intellectually rich and as visually exciting as any of the other arts. That notion may not seem like such a big deal nowadays. But ever since the medium was invented in the 1830s, it had largely been viewed, despite enclaves of enlightenment, as a sort of second-class citizen of art. Not that curators at other museums hadn't put up a good fight for photography before, but they hadn't had Szarkowski's rigor and deep understanding of the medium from the inside out.

Richard Benson, a friend, fellow photographer, and dean of the Yale School of Art since 1996, sums it up this way: "John defined photography. He stated a case for a certain kind of photography that had to be intellectually responsible. He said photography is about intelligence, not warm, fuzzy feelings. He was so smart and such a forceful personality that for the duration of his time at the Modern he shut everybody else up."

Szarkowski's story is a tale that falls into three distinct chapters, culminating in his return fifteen years ago to the life of a working photographer. In contrast to the fame he won as a curator, his photographs, as a body of work, are really unknown to all but the field's insiders. That will change dramatically this February when the San Francisco Museum of Modern Art opens its John Szarkowski retrospective, which will travel to the Milwaukee Art Museum and MoMA, in New York, and then on to various institutions around the country over the next few years. This show promises to be a revelation about Szarkowski, his pictures, and photography itself.

The charm that practically knocks you down when you're with the man is clearly intrinsic to his DNA. Whether he's wearing his country barn jackets or his worn in-town tweeds, he is old-fashioned-movie-star beautiful, though not a pretty boy; he's as masculine as Gary Cooper—and as feminine. Or, to compound the Hollywood metaphor, imagine the slightly aristocratic air of an American Laurence Olivier blended with a Jimmy Stewart character's preference for the plain over the pretentious. Top that off with a big baritone voice and a bartender's way with a yarn and you've got a pretty good picture of Szarkowski. "It's not exactly sex appeal," says the photographer Judith Ross. "It's life appeal."

Speaking of yarns, the story of how he met Arbus is a good one, and one that tells a lot about Szarkowski. It was during the summer of 1962, his first at MoMA. Back then, part of the museum was in a town house on West Fifty-third Street, and the photography department was on the ballroom floor. Arbus brought in her portfolio; Szarkowski wasn't impressed. "Technically the pictures were kind of grainy and in a fairly ugly tonal scale," he recalls. "They looked halfway between Robert Frank and William Klein, but they were frontal and static. I didn't like them very much. We'd never met. But when she came to pick up the portfolio, I happened to be walking out of my office. It was the end of the day, and my assistant, Pat Walker, said, 'Oh, Mr. Szarkowski, this is Diane Arbus.' So I *had* to meet her." He laughs. "I just instantly liked her. After a few minutes she asked, 'Well, what did you think of the portfolio?' If I hadn't already decided that I liked her, I probably would have said something evasive and found some way to get out of it. I don't know what words I used, but I made it clear that I hadn't liked the work very much. And she said, 'Well, why is it?' I replied, 'Well, I think the pictures don't look like what it seems to me you're interested in.'"

Szarkowski's point—that the grab-shot look of those particular photographs didn't match their ceremonial nature—seems to have engaged Arbus. Szarkowski brought up August Sander's archetypal portraits of early-twentieth-century Germans, which lent gravitas to bakers and bricklayers and even artists. "I remember absolutely clearly that she said, 'Who's Sander?' That same day I showed her a lot of Sander, and I thought she was like Saint Paul on the road to Damascus, she was so impressed. By this time we were buddies. Everybody else had gone home an hour ago." Not all the Arbus scholars like this anecdote, which so clearly suggests Szarkowski's influence. But Arbus did soon switch from a rectangular format, shot with a Leica, to the famous two-and-a-quarter-by-two-and-a-quarter square negatives that are now such an important part of twentieth-century photographic history.

I myself first got to see Szarkowski close-up when I spent a year or so in the department in the seventies, on a National Endowment for the Arts curatorial internship. I was twenty-five and had been out of college for a few years. I'd had one job that was the equivalent of working in an art-world sweatshop. I'd also made a brief appearance in the public-relations department at the Guggenheim Museum, but that ended quickly because I'd had to wear a skirt. (I ended up throwing my one gray corduroy skirt in the Hudson River and swearing that I'd never take a job again where I felt like I couldn't be myself.) In comes Szarkowski. I had sent him a letter with some examples of my writing, but I never really expected to hear from him. Instead, I got the biggest break of my life—an appointment in his office. I remember sitting down anxiously. There were a couple of eight-by-ten Ansel Adams photographs on a ledge. My immediate impression of Szarkowski himself was of a man who was doing something of consequence, something he profoundly believed in. What a relief! The truth is I have no idea what we talked about, until the end. That was when Szarkowski explained that he was counting on an NEA grant that the department had had for the last few years to come through again, and that he'd like to give it to me. He said that he thought it would take about nine months and that he would telephone me as soon as it arrived so I could start work. Elated, I said I'd see him then. It all felt so unreal that by the time I got home I thought I'd imagined it. After a few days his promise seemed just like a nice dream—nothing that could actually happen. I found other work. But exactly nine months later, the phone rang, and I heard Szarkowski's unmistakable boom. "Well, are you ready?" he asked. When it was time to go home after my first day at the museum, he was sitting at the big table the staff used to view portfolios and discuss them. I waved good-bye. He said, "Good night. And, by the way, welcome home." And that was how I felt: home, finally.

The atmosphere around the department was very professional, but also with its share of familial goings-on. Szarkowski had no patience with bureaucracy, and he certainly wasn't curating for the money. There was a famous meeting at the museum which had been called to figure out how to pay staff authors for their work on catalogues. After a lot of chitchat Szarkowski came up with his hilarious suggestion: that staff writers be paid a flat fee for any museum text, *minus* five cents a word. With a great sense of irony he told me his idea would strike a blow for art criticism.

During a recent conversation we talked about what it is to live one's life as a photographer. He quoted me that gut-wrenching line from Arthur Miller's *Death of a Salesman:* "He's a man way out there in the blue, riding on a smile and a shoeshine." For more than three decades Szarkowski was the guy giving the smiles back when certain photographers rode into MoMA (though if he thought a portfolio was hopeless he tended to stay out of sight in his office). As the photography department's senior curator, Susan Kismaric, says, "When John got to the Modern, photographers weren't given much dignity in the world. There was Lee Friedlander in a tacky jacket. There was Garry Winogrand in

John Szarkowski, *Garrick (Schiller) Theater, Chicago,* 1954

those blue denim work shirts that everybody wore in the sixties, with lots of pockets, walking the streets, walking, walking, walking, and nobody had lent any dignity to them or to photography itself—unless it was Steichen's highfalutin stuff. One of the things that I've observed with John and always respected was his respect for photographers, partly because he was a photographer himself. There wasn't just understanding, but a sympathy for their trials and tribulations and all of the stuff they go through. John created a persona that gave photography that dignity. It has to do with his writing, his eloquence. I don't know who else could have done it. Steichen did it in his fashion for his era. John was perfect for his."

Szarkowski's rise to prominence is as American as can be. His parents, Rosella and Julius Henry Szarkowski, both descendants of Polish immigrants, did everything in their power to make a decent life in Sioux City, Iowa, where they were living with their two young daughters, Georgianna and Mary. Soon, Julius moved the family to Ashland, Wisconsin, to be closer to his mother. Once there, he was "retired" from his job as the town postal inspector for refusing to pander to a local congressman who had decided he was such a big shot he could break the postal rules. Julius eventually found employment again with the post office, but this time in a lesser position, as assistant postmaster; it's hard not to see this incident in terms of Szarkowski's strong moral center.

Apart from playing the clarinet and trout fishing, only one other childhood hobby counts in Szarkowski's formative years—photography, something that started up because his parents gave him a Kodak Baby Brownie camera when he was about eleven. As his nephew John Henry Childs says, "If you're creating a biography of a boy who grows up to do something great, you can't do better than the stories of John building a darkroom in the cellar of the house, and of him taking his camera out there in the family canoe, striking out for days at a time, photographing and, of course, fly-fishing, too."

Szarkowski's single most important learning experience while attending the

University of Wisconsin occurred when a teacher advised him to pick up a copy of Walker Evans's then recently published *American Photographs.* After he got it home, Szarkowski was completely stumped. At the time, his taste was oriented toward more immediately artful pictures, such as the best Steichens or Dorothea Lange's evocative 1938 photo of a woman in a funeral cortège looking out a car window—pictures he still loves. Of the Evans book, he remembers, "I couldn't make heads or tails of it. Was this guy pulling my leg? All the pictures were sharp! It was facts, just facts. But I'd paid four dollars for the book, and I wasn't going to throw it away. Gradually I began to see some virtues in it."

After Szarkowski graduated in 1948, he got a job at the Walker Art Center as museum photographer—shooting whatever was needed. For Szarkowski, this was definitely the right place at the right time. Back then, the Walker, which has always been a unique American gem, was more of a family venture, attracting a dynamic staff and supporting avant-garde projects such as the *Everyday Art Quarterly,* to which Szarkowski contributed photographs of objects from Tupperware to Greek pots. The implicit idealism and the social orientation of this publication mirrored the concerns and conversations that were such a part of the dreams of the day. In fact, many of Szarkowski's views on photography—his intrinsic belief in its democratic nature, his connection to books that use the medium intelligently, his antipathy toward preciousness—can be traced to his roots in classic mid-century socialism.

During this time Szarkowski, already a fan of Frank Lloyd Wright, also became intoxicated with the work of Louis Sullivan and the architect's uncompromising, truly radical, but also absolutely democratic approach to building. The obsession started when his friend Arthur Carrara introduced Szarkowski to Sullivan's most unconventional book, *Kindergarten Chats.* With its pedagogical conversations between "master" and "student," its idealism, its humor, and its strong, clear vision, the book found a perfect mate when it fell into Szarkowski's hands.

Knowing the time had come to venture out on his own, Szarkowski quit the Walker in late 1950, but not only did he have no plan for what he might do, he didn't even have any prospects. His letter home conveyed this double feeling—of excitement and uncertainty. "Well I finally did it," he wrote. "As of the first of the year or so I am a free agent—free to make a million dollars, starve, do some really important photographs, or get into the baby picture racket, as the case may prove to be."

He eventually took a two-year teaching position at the Albright Art School, in Buffalo. The general point was to have a job, but an added incentive was that Buffalo was where Sullivan had built the Prudential Building (initially called the Guaranty). By the time he saw it the building was not in great shape, but at least it still existed, unlike Frank Lloyd Wright's Larkin Building, which Szarkowski had also expected to find in Buffalo, but which had been torn down months earlier. Who knows if Szarkowski would have ended up doing his first book, *The Idea of Louis Sullivan,* a brilliant elucidation, in photographs and text, of the meaning and importance of the architect's work, if Wright's building had still been standing; but with only one game in town, Szarkowski focused on the Prudential Building, photographing it repeatedly. Between that, teaching, and visits home, he was fully occupied, but he did take a small side trip to nearby Rochester, where Beaumont Newhall was curator of the George Eastman House. Newhall, who had been the first head of the photography department at MoMA, was a major force in what was then a small world. He was impressed with Szarkowski's pictures, trumpeting the news in a letter to Ansel Adams. "First photographic find in my four years here," he wrote. "A chap named Szwarkowsky [*sic*] . . . brought in twenty-three pictures—he hadn't more than shown them when Oscar and I asked him for a show—they go up week after next."

Szarkowski's next stop was Chicago. The city was home to enough buildings by Sullivan—the Garrick Theater, the Chicago Stock Exchange, the Getty Tomb—that he was able to break the back of the book he'd decided to do on the architect. Money remained an issue, but even when he was out of work or broke, Szarkowski kept his humor. "I am freelancing," he wrote once when he'd gone back home to live with his folks. "Freelancing (in northern Wisconsin) is a euphemism for sleeping late and being supported by one's parents. I tell my friends among the local tradesmen (who look askance at the slothful, purposeless life) that I am working on a book. This immediately puts them on unfamiliar ground, and in self-defense they steer the conversation back to trout fishing, where it belongs."

Little by little, the Sullivan work proceeded, and after a while Szarkowski, who'd had a number of small shows by then, developed enough confidence to send his Sullivan project around to some of the period's most influential figures. He also asked some of them, including Newhall, Edward Steichen (Newhall's successor in MoMA's photography department), and Wright himself, for recommendations—not bad for a beginner!—to accompany his application for a Guggenheim grant, which he received in 1954. The sum, three thousand dollars, allowed him to get far enough with the pictures that he started to look for a publisher for the book.

On a visit to New York he struck out with various publishers, but Szarkowski laughs at what happened the day he was walking in midtown and, with nothing to lose, got it into his head to give Walker Evans a buzz. He recalls, "All I knew about him was that he allegedly worked at *Fortune* magazine. I phoned him from the street—this was when street telephones still had telephone books on chains, if you can imagine. A lady answered, '*Fortune*.' I said, 'Good morning. Does Walker Evans work for you?' She replied, 'Just a moment.' The telephone rang and somebody said, 'Evans here.'" The next thing they both knew they were sitting together in Evans's office. (Years later Szarkowski would find out that Evans was already aware of his work thanks to Evans's role as a Guggenheim Foundation committee member, but the older man gave no clue that day.) Szarkowski was shocked by Evans's appearance. He'd expected some version of Abraham Lincoln, but that's not what he found: "Here's this dandy little Connecticut commuter with his polished cottons and his English handmade shoes and his half-glasses." The older photographer was very complimentary about the dummy for the Louis Sullivan book that Szarkowski had brought along. Thus encouraged, Szarkowski put in a plug for future assignments. Evans answered, "This place, Time Inc., isn't the right kind of place for people like you and me."

Finally Szarkowski hit the jackpot. Helen Clapesattle, director of the University of Minnesota Press and the author of a popular book of the time, *The Doctors Mayo,* believed so wholeheartedly in the Sullivan work that she seems to have published it without diluting Szarkowski's vision. So many photography books are just ordinary exercises in getting from beginning to end, mechanical and unthought out—they could just as easily be a pile of papers or a PDF file on a computer. Not so here. The final product demonstrates just how electrifying a visual book can be if one understands the opportunities presented by the sequencing of images, their accumulation, and the way this can extend meaning. The underlying concept—that photography could be a type of architectural criticism—was itself new, and the pictures themselves are a tour de force of description, though, perhaps more important, Szarkowski's photographic voice is also clear and present. With visceral intelligence the pictures capture Sullivan's genius for ornament and mass, his understanding of shadows and light and space. At the same time, these images lie far outside the European tradition of photographing ruins. Szarkowski insisted on the importance of capturing the lives behind, around, and in these buildings, and did this not just through his pictures but also by mixing in a fantastic variety of texts: conversations with the architect's clients and collaborators; newspaper articles, reviews, and editorials of the period; writing by other architects, including Wright, Sullivan's most famous pupil; poetry by Walt Whitman; and fragments from Sullivan's own books, adding up to a story of inspiration, achievement, and ultimately tragedy. It's all in there—the victories against impossible odds, the struggles between art and commerce, the betrayals, and the fall into loneliness and the bottle. The end of Szarkowski's introduction is one for the annals of bitter, dissipated genius: "[Sullivan's] cutting tongue did not fail him, and this offered some comfort as he saw his life run out, and his work forgotten."

Even before the positive reviews came in, Szarkowski was up and running with his next book project, *The Face of Minnesota*, courtesy once more of Clapesattle, who proposed the idea to him one night at Harry's, a Minnesota hangout. Szarkowski's approach here was just as ambitious as it had been with Sullivan, and the result was once again unique. The printed object is a lesson in the beauty of black-and-white photography—in the gorgeousness of black tones especially. No matter how dark the images get, they are never dead. *The Face of Minnesota* is a quieter book, though, and more obviously personal than its predecessor. After all, the focus is the midwestern rural culture that Szarkowski was a part of and knew so well. Much of it is dedicated to daily community life, though the pictures never fall into clichés or empty monuments to the so-called folk. Szarkowski was not trying to create pictures with a message, as some of the Farm Security Administration photographers were when they were sent out into the heartland by the government to bring back images of the Depression— Szarkowski was well schooled in much of that body of work, but he imbued his own pictures with a sense of his personal experience, and his subjects always remain individuals. Similarly, his landscapes and views of the countryside convey intimacy rather than the grandiosity of, say, an Ansel Adams epic vista. Looking at them, one feels a sense of place and of home, rather than of awe.

Despite the time pressure he was under while making the book, Szarkowski remembers, "I never had such a good time." Nobody expected news to be made with *The Face of Minnesota*. When it landed on *The New York Times* best-seller list in the summer of 1958, Szarkowski wrote to a friend that, in the words "of the Minnesota Press publicity director, [this] was a hell of a commentary on the state of the book business."

MoMA's courtship of Szarkowski began with a July 1961 missive from Monroe Wheeler, then the museum's director of exhibitions and publications, that was so courteous and so vague and so pregnant with the belief that the museum was the center of the universe, it really is a hoot. At the end of his note Wheeler wrote, "It has occurred to us that you might like to talk with us about our future and perhaps yours. . . . Have you any plans for coming to New York in the near future?" Szarkowski had no clue what was on their minds. Maybe they were going to offer him a show, he thought. About to plunge into a series of wilderness pictures for his next Guggenheim Foundation project, and probably not exactly flush enough to take a casual trip to New York, he wrote back an equally polite letter, explaining that unfortunately a visit to the city was not in his immediate plans but maybe that would change in the fall. In any case, when all was said and done, and the museum had managed to declare its intentions more forthrightly, Szarkowski was anointed as the director of the department of photography. The actual changing of the guard occurred in the summer of 1962, when Steichen officially stepped down and Szarkowski seized the reins.

Szarkowski likes to tell a story that encapsulates the Modern back then: "After it was decided I should be offered the job, somebody realized that I hadn't met Alfred Barr, the director of the museum. There was a crisis. It was horrible manners for the museum to appoint somebody to a curatorial position without Alfred's at least passive knowledge of it. So it was decided that Alfred, Steichen, and I would have tea at five o'clock that day in the penthouse of the museum. Steichen and I went up and Alfred was already sitting at the table. Steichen said, 'Alfred, this is John Szarkowski.' He replied, 'How do you do?' We ordered our martinis. Nobody said anything. I thought, I'm not going to stick my nose in this, so I sat there sipping away. It seemed like five minutes. Finally Steichen put down his drink and said, 'Well, Alfred, it's a risk!' Which was brilliant. Steichen had the ability now and then to tell the straight truth at the right time. What he said was unanswerable. Of course it was a risk. Alfred kind of laughed, and that was it."

But, apart from Szarkowski's risking the end of his life as a working photographer—something that he hoped would not happen—was his appointment such a risk? A genuine outsider, he was also clearly a star. His old friend Richard Benson has this take: "My theory is that Steichen felt his legacy was safe if they got some hick from the Midwest to take over the department. So he brings in this tall guy with a curlicue mustache from Wisconsin." If he's right, the irony is that the opposite happened. While Steichen took many remarkable photographs himself, his talents were not those of a visionary curator. Most of the shows he oversaw were broad, and he had a predilection for rather sweeping themes. While his most popular blockbuster exhibition, "The Family of Man," had some perfectly fine pictures in it, ultimately the sentiments behind the show were not much better than those in a parade of Hallmark cards. The exhibition's universalist thesis—that all people are the same—may have been a crowd-pleaser, but the effect was to bunch photographers together in meaningless ways.

Szarkowski's intentions were just the reverse, and he put them on the table right from the start with his first exhibition, in 1963, titled "Five Unrelated Photographers." The show, which included the work of such disparate figures as Garry Winogrand, Jerome Liebling, Minor White, Ken Heyman, and George Krause, was actually Szarkowski's statement of purpose. Instead of creating connections among these figures, Szarkowski showed the individual ways each of them used photography as an expressive medium. He says, "I didn't mean to be rude, but I wasn't talking about a family." What he was talking about was ways in which one could think about photography. "It seemed to me that nobody had really thought about that very hard," he recalls.

Nineteen sixty-three was indeed a big year for Szarkowski: He met Jill Anson, an architect; they married in London and honeymooned in France—his first trip to Europe. (The couple eventually had three children, two girls and a boy; the son died in childhood.) The next year he unveiled one of the all-time great photography exhibitions and books, *The Photographer's Eye*—the beginning of an unforgettable string of museum publications under Szarkowski's direction. His achievement with this project, which plumbed the breadth of photographic history, was twofold. It's astounding how many of the pictures included—Berenice Abbott's 1927 portrait of Jean Cocteau's hands, Henri Cartier-Bresson's 1933 picture of Spanish children playing in ruins, Richard Avedon's 1958 portrait of Ezra Pound—have been ingrained in our consciousness. The point, however, wasn't just to spot first-rate photographs. It was also to provide a theoretical basis for thinking about the medium, which Szarkowski did when he spelled out the choices and decisions a photographer has to make when taking a picture, whether you're Amateur Annie or Annie Leibovitz. But in addition to being one of the most sophisticated how-tos ever written, *The Photographer's Eye* conveys a visceral sense of excitement about the medium. "Like an organism," Szarkowski wrote, "photography was born whole. It is in our progressive discovery of it that its history lies."

As the decade went on, he was responsible for a series of thoughtful one-person shows focusing on a wide range of photographers, including Jacques-Henri Lartigue, André Kertész, Elliott Erwitt, Dorothea Lange, Brassaï, Harry Callahan, August Sander, Bill Brandt, Duane Michals, E. J. Bellocq, Berenice Abbott, Walker Evans, and Barbara Morgan—many of them unknown then. Perhaps the most prescient show, though, the one that ultimately had the most reverberations and that only Szarkowski could have done, was "New

Documents," an exhibition that he curated in 1967 and that included the work of Diane Arbus, Lee Friedlander, and Garry Winogrand.

No museum had given these photographers the time of day before. Szarkowski not only took their work seriously but championed it. He recalls, "I wanted to do a show about what I thought was the most interesting, most advanced work being done. What was considered the most avant then"— showy work by people such as Robert Heinecken or Naomi Savage—"was not what I thought was the most challenging work." Not everyone agreed. To some eyes it looked as if Arbus was a loon who was taking advantage of other people's misery, Friedlander was a snore who shot boring things such as switched-on TV sets in hotel rooms, and as for Winogrand, why, he couldn't even hold the camera straight. When one considers the reputation of these photographers today, and the massive, even pervasive influence they've had, the scathing reviews that came out when the work went up at the Modern serve as a reminder not only of how far audiences have come but also of how powerful and persuasive Szarkowski was.

The show is now legendary, but at the time, other than critics' getting riled up—as Szarkowski remembers, "Lee wasn't quite so much abused, but certainly Garry and Diane were badly abused"—there doesn't seem to have been much public reaction; back then, the audience for photography was tiny. All three photographers would remain important to Szarkowski, both professionally and personally. Up until Winogrand's death, in 1984, the two men were tight; Szarkowski gave one of the eulogies at his memorial. As for Friedlander, the two have worked together often and are still very much in each other's lives. Since the late nineties, they've gone on yearly picture-taking expeditions together, accompanied by Benson and Childs. With all of their stuff packed into the biggest four-wheel-drive station wagon they can find to rent, these trips around the country sometimes sound like photography's version of *The Odd Couple.* Friedlander is big on "early to bed, early to rise"; Szarkowski is not.

Lee Friedlander, *Garry Winogrand and John Szarkowski, New York City,* 1975

Friedlander wants to shoot as much as he can without thinking; Szarkowski thinks much more than he shoots.

The story of Arbus and Szarkowski doesn't have as many chapters. But by the time Arbus killed herself, in 1971, right before Szarkowski opened her one-woman show at the Modern, which they had worked on closely together, a lot had passed between the two of them. No doubt her suicide added to the seriousness and the mythology surrounding the work, but this time viewers were ready. Szarkowski recalls, "The vitriol had really died down. In the exhibition, going from picture to picture, people were so quiet it was as if they were going to Communion." Arbus had died without a cent, and with a closet full of unsold pictures. Szarkowski godfathered a deal so that Aperture published the book for the show at a higher royalty rate than the museum would have offered; that way her children could make some money, and many editions later, sales are at least at the half-million mark. The help that Szarkowski gave in this instance was not an isolated incident. Earlier, when Arbus was still alive and the two of them were planning her exhibition, he found out that she was going through a rough patch, financially and otherwise, so he offered her a research job on another upcoming exhibition, "From the Picture Press." It was a show right up her alley; in fact, the plan to do it had grown out of conversations they'd had about news photography. Arbus seized upon the chance to visit the picture morgues at places such as the *New York Daily News* and dig up photographs of crimes, disasters, weird happenings, political shenanigans, and other goings-on; one can imagine how absorbed she must have been.

Szarkowski says that his next triumph, the book *Looking at Photographs,* was the application of the theory he proposed in *The Photographer's Eye,* and if any publication can be said to have been pivotal in creating a general audience for photography, it is *Looking at Photographs.* The simple format—spreads juxtaposing photographs with Szarkowski's sparkling short descriptions and in-tune interpretations—was an instant winner.

But there were also rare occasions when Szarkowski lost his Midas touch. The "Mirrors and Windows" exhibition, which opened at the beginning of 1978, was one of those fascinating failures that really whipped up the art and photography communities. Szarkowski's position was overtly reductive, to say the least. Basically, he claimed that there are two kinds of photography—one being photography about photography, and the other being photography about the world.

But underneath the theorizing Szarkowski was throwing down a gauntlet. What was happening was that photography, which had almost always been relegated to its own, segregated galleries, was suddenly "in" at art galleries—not so-called straight photography but rather works where the medium was used as a basis for art, as a tool in conceptual or performance art, or even as a way to create sellable product out of otherwise ephemeral undertakings. For Szarkowski, most of this stuff was a waste of time. Plus, he was put off by its marketing; some pieces had begun to get inflated art-world prices, which offended the curator to the core. All these issues were swirling in the background of "Mirrors and Windows."

In contrast to his earlier big shows, which, though eclectic, had been powerful and convincing, half of this one was much more a grab bag. His view of photography's true purpose was so strong and evident in the "Windows" section that one pitied the pictures in the less cohesive "Mirrors" part of the show, even if some of them were standouts. The exhibition manifested just how human he was: It suggested he was farsighted when looking at work that fit his belief system, but not always so when work didn't. There was fallout: As time went on, the Modern missed the boat on some major acquisition opportunities, such as Cindy Sherman's complete "Untitled Film Stills" series or Jeff Wall's light-box pieces, both of which the museum paid an arm and a leg for after Szarkowski left. (The Sherman series, which reportedly went for around a million in 1995, could have been had for less than twenty thousand dollars in the early eighties.)

"Mirrors and Windows" proved to be a blip, eclipsed by shows such as the

Modern's humongous series of productions—including four books, which Szarkowski coauthored, and four exhibitions—devoted to the work of Eugène Atget. (In the seventies, with the help of Berenice Abbott, Szarkowski had arranged for the museum to acquire thousands of glass plates by the largely unknown photographer, who had died in Paris in 1927 as an out-of-work actor without a centime.) And even though Atget took center stage in terms of Szarkowski's focus, the department continued to knock out one terrific show after another in the eighties, and with the 1984 Irving Penn exhibition, Szarkowski demonstrated he still had surprises up his sleeve. He hadn't exactly shown a predilection for fashion photography, so the interest in Penn's work was unexpected, but when the show went up it helped establish Penn as a photographer who counts.

That exhibition pinpoints why Szarkowski was such an interesting and powerful curator: Just when plenty of critics thought they had him pegged, he showed he was still his own man. Then again, he sometimes continued to give fodder to the notion he had blinders on. Such was the case with the exhibition that was expected to be the crowning glory of his career, "Photography Until Now," which opened in 1990. By then his impending retirement was public knowledge, and though he still had a few other exhibitions on the schedule, this was supposed to be the big kahuna, the one that would sum up what he'd been about all these years.

That's not quite how things worked out. Most of the show was genius. As the century's early decades unfolded, history came alive, and the story he set up was electrifying. Szarkowski's choice of imagery was beyond reproach, and his installation was flawless, as usual. But as one veered toward the messy, complicated present, the show went bust: From the mid-seventies on, the view was cloudier. It felt like Szarkowski had only grudgingly included certain photographers and artists who worked with photography, and this ambivalence showed in the weak choices of their work; again, Szarkowski's antipathy got in the way of his eye.

At the time of the show, I was the photography critic for *The New Yorker*, and I was asked to weigh in on the exhibition, and on his career in general. It was thought that I'd have a unique view as I knew the story from the inside. This was a complicated matter for me, since I felt, as I still do, that I owe him a huge debt for teaching me how to live inside a photograph, how to get in there and breathe the life that's been captured between its four edges. On the other hand, as someone who'd argued the merits of the work of people such as Cindy Sherman and Robert Mapplethorpe with him on more than one occasion, I knew all about Szarkowski's strong opinions. You can just see us at lunch at his favorite restaurant, Chez Napoléon. There I am, going on about the importance of looking at Sherman's work in the context of the history of images of women, and there he is, telling me authoritatively that that sort of thing (feminism) has nothing to do with what makes a great photograph. Another Perfect Manhattan with an orange twist, please. I don't need to tell you what happened when I brought up the fact that I thought the Modern should buy Mapplethorpe's controversial *X, Y,* and *Z Portfolios,* because I believed these would have enormous historic significance one day. Make that a double Perfect Manhattan, please.

So there I was, now at *The New Yorker,* trying to write a fair and honest summary of his career. Despite our different viewpoints, we still got along like a house on fire, but what stopped me wasn't the personal connection. (I had planned to write about it, as I do here.) No, what prevented me in the end from writing about Szarkowski was that I felt I had only half the story. The other half is in the photographs that he has been taking for the last fifteen years. Now it can be told.

When he took over the department, in the early sixties, he had hoped he could somehow keep doing his own photography, too. "In 1969 we found this place upstate in Columbia County, and I would load up a few holders in the summer when the days were longer and take a picture or two," he says. "It just got to be less and less and finally almost nothing." In addition to being consumed by museum work, there was another reason he dropped the ball: He was conscious there were many potential conflicts of interest. As Peter Galassi, Szarkowski's successor at the Modern, says, "John was extremely honorable. He essentially took his whole identity as an artist and put it in the closet for twenty-nine years."

It isn't surprising that, after he packed up his things at the Modern and the noise of his nearly thirty years there started to dim, Szarkowski returned to where he'd left off: photographing the land. This round, however, it was land he knew like the back of his hand—his own. All of Szarkowski's pictures are seamless combinations of simplicity and sophistication, and those of his barn are a great place to start. At first these images seem so familiar that they appear to be nothing. Look again and they become everything: architecture, sculpture, but also fragments of an eloquent America. And it's no surprise that Szarkowski turns out to be the greatest photographer of apple trees the world has ever seen. Apples, after all, are a near-lifelong obsession of his. In the fall, after a weekend in the country, he would sometimes walk into the department and pull fresh Baldwin and Winesap and Northern Spy apples out of his pocket, and we'd all sample them. In one way or another, photographs of apples were also present in many exhibitions, and when he produced *Looking at Photographs,* he included an intriguing color picture postcard with oversize apples and the caption "How do you like them Apples, Annie?" The subject would also come up in speeches that he gave. I remember one in which he likened the job of a curator to having an ability to know which apples to pick at which time. (It's interesting, by the way, that toward the end of his time at the Modern, Steichen became obsessed with delphiniums, even crossbreeding his own varieties and photographing them. For his part, Szarkowski has spent years grafting his own apple trees.)

As for the apple photographs themselves, they are testimonies to the pleasure of looking at the world, and the pleasure of looking at photographs. The more time one spends with these knotty images, the more one is rewarded: the light coming and going, the thickets of leaves, the tangle of branches bearing the weight of apples, which seem to miraculously find their way through the darkness out into the open. There's a depth to these images that seems to reflect Szarkowski's working methods. He explains, "I don't have a schedule. I just take my camera outside. Some days I go to the pond and some days I don't. Some days I look at the apple trees, and some days I find other things. I love it even more now, because these are my trees. I planted them. I've walked around all one hundred and fifty acres, so when I walk around again I can see what's changed. As you get older you're not so much interested in seeing things for the first time, but in seeing how they changed."

One night when we were talking about his adventures working on *The Idea of Louis Sullivan,* Szarkowski said, "I think Americans were more interesting then. It makes me want to cry to say it." Looking at his photographs created over the last fifty years makes me want to weep myself. They are truly American pictures; one feels his desire to show not just what America was but what it still can be. And whether they're describing the democratic ambition of Louis Sullivan's buildings, Minnesota's communities, his barn, the Sonoran Desert in Arizona in the 1990s, or his apple trees at the beginning of the twenty-first century, all are riveting.

A few years ago Szarkowski wrote this in a letter about his return to being a photographer: "I will make those disrespectful middle aged friends (who say that I have locked the door after the horse is gone) eat their words. But perhaps not immediately; I may keep them in suspense for a while . . ." The suspense is over.

Vanity Fair, January 2005

Artist in Residence

The artist Julian Schnabel is famous—too famous—for possessing such a big ego that he thinks he can do anything. The list of job titles attached to his name—painter, sculptor, furniture designer, filmmaker—keeps getting longer. But what if he really is that rare being, a true Renaissance man? The latest clue is a stop-you-in-your-tracks work of architecture he's just now finishing up in Greenwich Village. Plunked smack on top of the early-twentieth-century factory building where the artist has long lived and worked on far West Eleventh Street is a Pompeii red palazzo, stuccoed on the outside, with five huge residences, plus a studio for Schnabel, some serious exhibition space, and a swimming pool fit for Citizen Kane. The place looks as if it began life in Venice on the Grand Canal, somehow floated up the Hudson River, moored on the West Side Highway, then hoisted itself atop its three-story "pedestal." The building even has a fanciful name, announced on its front: Palazzo Chupi, after the nickname of Schnabel's Spanish wife, Olatz.

Incredibly, much of the construction and interior work, which went on for well over two years, was done while Schnabel was shooting and editing his latest film, *The Diving Bell and the Butterfly*, in Paris and Berck-sur-Mer, and then taking it on the film-festival circuit. At first, faxes with questions, comments, drawings, and images were sent from New York to the set, where Schnabel would work on this "side" project between takes, communicating mostly with Brian Kelly, a musician who started out as the artist's assistant twenty-five years ago and who led the charge on the building in New York.

Construction had begun in September 2005, and, like a lot of Schnabel's projects, it was initially controversial, drawing the ire of a Village preservation group, which staged protests. The cries of "there goes the neighborhood" hurt the artist, but they didn't stop him. He said at the time, "In principle the protesters are right, but they're wrong about me and this building." (And he told his team to offer the demonstrators the use of his bathroom when the need arose.)

Robert Polidori, *Interior, Palazzo Chupi, New York City, New York*, 2008

It's not wrong to think of the whole fifty-thousand-square-foot object—and that includes the original building, which has been completely reconfigured on the inside, as well as the new addition—as a huge sculpture designed for living. And that's some living! With 180 generous windows, balconies galore with all kinds of spectacular cast-stone or bronze railings, and the largest terraces I've ever seen in this town, the building is one of a kind. Each of its residences—a triplex, two duplexes (one of which is occupied by Schnabel and his family), and two single-floor homes—has the larger-than-life quality that defines Schnabel himself. Everywhere one experiences pleasure in materials and the presence of the hand. One sees it on the walls, in how the plaster is applied; on the ceilings, with their unfinished timber; in the surfaces of the fireplaces, which are themselves sculptures. The sheer thickness of the walls—they range from one and a half feet to four feet—is monasterylike, and provides the same kind of quiet. Tiles are used abundantly and to fantastic effect: Cement tiles from Morocco, clay ones from California, and handmade terra-cotta tiles from North Carolina—all coexist as if they'd never been apart.

Within Palazzo Chupi, Schnabel has found an original way to reference and meld many of the architecture-related experiences that have affected him, informed him, and inspired him over the years. In fact, one could view the building itself as a sort of architectural autobiography. The grandness and craftsmanship betray the memory of a little boy who was nuts about his parents but felt debilitated by the small scale and lackluster materials in their Brooklyn home. "Everything was fake, except them," he remembers. "It was the feeling of limitations." (Neither of Schnabel's parents are alive, but I'd still say this place is for them.) Then there's the epiphany he had as a young artist walking through a huge wooden door into a courtyard in Mexico City and being wowed by the sense of privacy that people could have in the middle of a teeming urban world. That revelation is reflected in the interplay between indoor and outdoor spaces that is such a big part of Palazzo Chupi's effect and in its no-holds-barred views of the Hudson River.

· · ·

But the place that has had more influence than any other over Schnabel is the Scrovegni Chapel, filled with frescoes by Giotto, in Padua, Italy, which, when he first saw it in 1977, at the age of twenty-five, led to his most important artistic epiphany. "It was the complete experience that I knew must have been there but I hadn't seen before, where the architecture of the place and what was painted on it were inseparable," he recalls. "What I came to understand there was that I needed my paintings to be walls. I needed to build an architecture to support whatever pictorial language I was going to invent."

Of course, Schnabel's West Village building is an entirely different kind of *Gesamtkunstwerk,* or total artwork, but it is born from the same fervent attitude that makes Giotto's blue-backed frescoes so unforgettable. It also owes a huge debt, which Schnabel freely acknowledges, to two American architects: Addison Mizner and Stanford White. Schnabel's experience with both architects' work is personal and direct. He has rented a Mizner house in Florida in the past, and owns an 1880s fishing "cottage" by White in Montauk, on Long Island, where Schnabel spends lots of time painting and surfing. The West Eleventh Street building abounds in nods to both architects, all of them put through the Schnabel strainer. He'll take a Mizner fireplace, for instance, and create a pumped-up version by, in his words, "putting some balls on it." Likewise, the kitchens in each of the Chupi residences—with their board-and-batten wooden ceilings, emerald green terra-cotta tiles, and cast-concrete countertops dyed chromium-oxide green—are straight out of Schnabel's Montauk house, though retuned. None of this is simple mimicry. What's interesting is how Schnabel mixes these references to White and Mizner into a global iconography, including Moorish, Turkish, and Venetian touches, motifs the architects were attracted to themselves.

In 1987, Schnabel was introduced to the original building—which in previous lives had been a stable, a perfume factory, and a water-sampling plant—by the artist Roy Lichtenstein. They'd run into each other and, as artists like to do, started talking real estate. Schnabel asked, "Did you find your dream loft?" "I did, but it's too big for me—it's right for you," replied Lichtenstein, who knew his customer. At first, Schnabel just rented some space for a studio, but after he split from his first wife, Jacqueline, he set up camp there in a womblike cubicle he built in a mezzanine, just above the studio, which he called "the Monkey Room." (The label was a nod to the stuffed simian residing within.) He covered the walls with red velvet, brought in a few favorite possessions, including Picasso's *Femme au Chapeau,* ran *The Godfather* on his VCR twenty-four hours a day, and painted his way out of his hole, eventually remarrying, buying the building in 1997 for $2.1 million, and creating a home there for his family.

A few years ago, when Schnabel decided he needed more elbow room, he naturally thought he'd take advantage of his right to build on the roof. He started sketching out ideas, which evolved from a simple rooftop cottage to the deliciously bonkers notion of putting up a palazzo on the dour block. Soon it was time to bring in an architecture firm, Hut Sachs Studio, from New York, which figured out how to pull off Schnabel's vision. Since then, the team responsible for the finished product has included a whole range of artisans and artists as well as the usual construction crews.

Now that it's finished, Palazzo Chupi has gone from being a neighborhood pariah to a place that people point at and *ooh* and *aah* over. Isn't that the way with art, when it's good? First there's the outrage; then comes the pedestal. We'll see how it does in the marketplace. Bono, Johnny Depp, Martha Stewart, Hugh Jackman, and Madonna have all checked out the remaining residences for sale, at prices ranging from $27 million to $32 million. (Schnabel declines to reveal his overall construction costs.) So far two units have sold: a single floor, for $15.5 million to Credit Suisse executive William J. B. Brady; and the other single floor to Richard Gere for an undisclosed sum. There's a funny anecdote about Madonna looking out at a neighboring Richard Meier apartment building on the West Side Highway. As the story goes, the singer remarked that its cool modernism reminded her of a housing project in comparison to Schnabel's Venetian splendor.

Meanwhile, as his new film racks up awards and Oscar nominations for best director and adapted screenplay, Schnabel and his wife and fourteen-year-old twin sons, Cy and Olmo, have settled into life in Palazzo Chupi. Schnabel will have to accept the way each eventual buyer finishes up his or her place, but he has decorated his own home the way he always does—alive with color, full of art and surprises. A photograph by Luigi Ontani hangs above a massive "elephant leg" cast-stone fireplace in the living room, which also has works by Francis Picabia, Man Ray, and Schnabel himself. Here the walls progress from turquoise green to faded mint. In the master bedroom they're fuchsia—which makes the intense greens of Picasso's *Femme au Chapeau* look even more vibrant. Two of Schnabel's greatest paintings, *St. Sebastian* and *Procession for Jean Vigo,* also hang in the bedroom, together for the first time in ages.

If you know Schnabel, one thing that's fascinating about Palazzo Chupi is that it's really just a big-time expression of an impulse he's always had. For decades now, he has been rejiggering rooms he's found himself in, from simple tweaks to total reconstructions. (His abilities in this arena have been public knowledge since the August 2006 opening of the newly renovated Gramercy Park Hotel, where Schnabel designed the public spaces as well as much of what went into them.) We've been friends since the early eighties, and I've witnessed this obsession with physical equanimity up close. Once, in the late eighties, we shared a hotel room in Florence, and when I checked in, I found he'd already moved the furniture around and taken down the standard-issue art reproductions, replacing them with some drawings that Cy Twombly had given him the day before. He wasn't being cute; it was just something he needed to do. The chambermaid was horrified by the scribbles that had been Scotch-taped up on the walls. Maybe Schnabel should send her a plane ticket so she can see Palazzo Chupi.

Vanity Fair, March 2008

Calvin to the Core

Five years ago, when Calvin Klein was in the process of selling the fashion and design company that bears his name, family and friends were worried. "I thought, Oh my Lord! Is he going to be depressed?" says Bianca Jagger. "Will he regret that he sold his business? How will he react? I've had a few friends who have sold their businesses and it's almost as if their life is over, despite the money they have acquired. How wrong I was." Klein's daughter, Marci, a TV producer, couldn't imagine her father without his label. "I was like, *What?*" she remembers. "What are you talking about? Like, you're a workaholic. Like, you can't *not* work. I thought about when Johnny Carson left. I remember thinking, What's *he* going to do? What are we going to watch?"

There was also reason for concern on a more personal level. Those who were closest to Klein had for some time been anticipating a D-day on the substance-abuse front. It had become obvious to his intimates that Klein was once again battling demons that he had first wrestled down in the late eighties. There were "morning after" phone calls among insiders reporting of antics, kept just among friends out of protection and love for him. Miraculously, his work hadn't suffered—which says a lot about Klein's extraordinary sense of responsibility to his company—and, for the most part, neither had his public image.

But then, on March 24, 2003, less than six weeks after Klein and his longtime friend and business partner, Barry Schwartz, sold their company to Phillips–Van Heusen, picking up $400 million in cash for themselves (plus approximately $30 million in PVH stock, along with future royalties), the designer set jaws dropping, tongues wagging, and headlines screaming across New York. The setting was Madison Square Garden, a game between the Knicks and the

Bruce Weber, *Calvin Klein, Ghost Ranch, Santa Fe, New Mexico*, 1984

Toronto Raptors. Most people sitting courtside don't get up and breeze over to say hi to one of the players, as Klein did with the Knicks' Latrell Sprewell while the player was trying to inbound the ball at mid-court. According to tabloid accounts, a "stumbling . . . off-balance" Klein grabbed Sprewell's arm and started to chat him up, until a friend and two security men escorted Klein back to his seat. "I didn't know that was him," Sprewell said after the game. "I wasn't nervous, but I was surprised. I was like, Is security going to come over here at some point or what?" Adding to the embarrassing public nature of it all, the New York City Council soon passed a "Calvin Klein" bill, which increased the fines for unruly fans who interfere with games; one of the most powerful names in fashion was now associated with streakers and bottle throwers.

For all his celebrity and off-and-on notoriety, Klein the man is extremely shy, so private, such a paragon of discretion, and so old-fashioned and correct in the department of manners that this episode must have been agonizing for him. I've known him well for about six years, and casually for twelve years before that, and I can just picture him playing the scene over and over in his head the next day, torturing himself. Fortunately, it wasn't long before he was out of the public eye and far from the madding crowd, just another human being who fucked up, the way we all do, trying to put himself back together in the safety of rehab at the Meadows, a clinic in Arizona.

When he talks about that time today, he sounds like someone at peace with the idea that he can't always be perfect. This recognition had to have been hard for a man who is so obsessed with perfection—in the clothes he designed, in bodies, in colors, in photographs, in houses, in the suits he now wears (made by Caraceni, once Gianni Agnelli's tailor)—that he has spent much of his life in pursuit of it; the rigor of that pursuit is one of the things that define him as a designer.

I found Klein's acknowledgment of his substance-abuse relapse all the more moving because confessional speeches go against his grain. "I crashed after

I actually did the deal," he says. "I think I was overwhelmed with what was going to be next—the future. For a number of years, I was preparing for this. I knew that I was looking for other challenges or maybe other things. I had made so many collections. I had done everything I wanted to do. I was ready to let go. But when it actually happened I just went completely crazy. Then, once again, I dealt with getting my life together. Since then, it's been the best time in my life."

We began our conversations for this piece in the summer of 2006. Our first taped session took place in Southampton at his large, turreted Gothic mansion, which sits on one of the best sites on Long Island, facing both the ocean and Shinnecock Bay. The designer had recently finished temporary renovations, removing every arch, squaring off planes, getting rid of all the pink and black and gold—wiping out all traces of the monstrous renovation executed by a previous owner—and coating the whole place in a Calvin-approved shade of white (it's never *simply* white), so he could bear to live in it while he figured out what to do with the joint. For the next six months or so we continued our talks in New York City, meeting when the mood struck, or where the story took us. We spent informal time together, too, which included dinners at Klein's two other new homes, in New York and Miami. He was always the first one to get to our appointments, always in good humor, and dressed like Calvin Klein—impeccably, but never in a show-offy way.

It hasn't really been possible until now, five years after his last collection, to fully measure what Klein accomplished as a designer and a businessman—jobs that were for him completely intertwined. While some designers look down their noses at bottom-line concerns, or at least pretend to, Klein, because he had this double perspective, was able to nail the Zeitgeist with precision time and time again; often, in fact, he nudged the Zeitgeist forward. In that way, he has been a great and canny pop artist, like Andy Warhol or Madonna.

Klein says he was never "snobby" about his role as a designer, never wanted to limit his audience to the elite. "Some people are motivated by money, some by power. I think what motivated Calvin was to do something that had never been done before," says his friend Sandy Gallin, the former talent manager.

Another thing that set Klein apart in the fashion world was the utter seriousness with which he took his job—sometimes at the expense of the business's social niceties. After a show, for instance, there is always the protocol of going backstage to schmooze the designers. It's almost a tribal rite practiced by most of the big shots in the business. And it was clearly something that Klein despised. Once, after a menswear show in Milan in 2000, he just turned his back on me and marched off. I brought this up with him during our talks, and he laughed. He said that he hated the idea that people at shows would feel pressured to give him a lot of phony baloney. He also explained how deep his investment in the work was. "You want to talk about how crazy I am?" he asked. "You could go and do an article on that. I'm not a normal person. I know it. In one sense we were appealing to Wall Street, trying to be a real business, where you'd say, 'It's a business that's not emotional—it's all marketing, it's all figured out. You don't have to worry.' But let me tell you, it's very emotional, it's very personal. And I cared a great deal. By the time [a show] was over I just wanted to go home and be by myself."

This is a reason that Klein's name has transcended the field of fashion: For all its commercial savvy, his work has, indeed, been highly personal, a product not just of its times but more specifically of the way the times influenced the designer. Klein himself has been a human weather vane. What went on in the mid- to late seventies—when he became an international celebrity hanging out at Studio 54, a designer who reinforced America's arrival as a fashion force and set the retail world on fire with Calvin Klein jeans (and his controversial commercials featuring a sexed-up teenage Brooke Shields)—is the most extreme example of this interplay, but it has really been true of his entire career. By the time he was done with his company, more than three decades after he founded it, people's ideas about fashion had radically changed.

His life began humbly. Klein, who was born on November 19, 1942, grew up in a Jewish immigrant family in the northern part of the Bronx, near Riverdale. He rarely mentions his older brother or younger sister, but they all lived in very close quarters in the apartment where he spent his entire youth. Right from the get-go, Klein saw what it meant to work hard. His father, Leo—who'd arrived in the States from Budapest at age five—was often absent because of the long hours he put in at the family grocery store on Lenox Avenue in Harlem. Calvin, a mini merchant in training, would visit the store and remembers lots of conversations about the cost of things, a subject that interested him even then. "I would see grapefruits in the fruit and vegetable department, and some of them were twenty-nine cents a pound and others were forty-nine cents," he recalls. "I'd ask, 'What's the difference between the two?' My father said, 'Some people like to pay twenty-nine cents and some like to pay forty-nine cents.' I thought, Hmmm. I learned later that that's the fashion business to a great deal. You pick the spot where you want to be, where you want your products to be. Many people think just because it's more expensive it's better. That isn't always the truth."

Klein doesn't talk about a happy childhood. Instead he describes it as secure and serious. But he does light up when he describes the countless afternoons that he and his mother, Flore, known as Flo, whiled away on Bainbridge Avenue, hanging around the dress and alteration shop that his grandmother Molly owned. It was a tiny, jam-packed place. Still, for Klein it was like a *Wunderkammer*. His grandmother had once worked for Hattie Carnegie, the pioneering American sportswear designer, and Flo, who liked to sketch fashion, couldn't get enough of talking about it or, apparently, of buying it. ("Every time I get crazy about clothes I think about my mother spending all of my father's money during the war," Klein has said.) Hanging around with these two—what better training could the young boy have had about what women want and don't want out of clothes? Years later he said, "I spent the first ten years of my life designing beige, cream, white, brown, because those were all the colors that [my mother] loved. She would line her jackets in fur, she would do all of these outrageous things considering that we came from what you would call a very middle-class family in the Bronx." The talk at Molly's wasn't only about fashion. Klein remembers that his mother would often tell him how ashamed she'd been as a child that Molly was divorced, so humiliated that she'd pretended her father was dead. One wonders if this is the root of the concern for appearances that Klein has; it's a surprising anxiety when one thinks about how much *épater*-ing he has done of bourgeois tastes and beliefs.

Klein early on expressed his own interest in fashion, sketching his designs and throwing himself into special art classes at PS 80. When he learned that a friend's mother had been a designer, he was over the moon. "I don't think I was more than ten or eleven, but I glommed on to her, showing her my sketches and ideas, and talking to her about them all the time," he says with a laugh. His intimates always talk about Klein's drive and ambition. As Barry Diller, his friend of some thirty years, says, "In any place, in any business—in anything—Calvin would succeed. With him it's a force of curiosity and willfulness." At the beginning, there was also impatience. Klein says, "I couldn't wait to get to high school so that I could get out of the Bronx. As soon as I got to school, I couldn't wait to get to work. I was always in a rush, and I was always thinking about the next step and the future." This was not a kid who played hooky. "I was always in art class," he remembers. "But I knew at an early age that I wasn't going to be a painter in a studio working with a canvas. I was interested in design, in clothes." His fashion and design education—New York's High School of Industrial Arts, in Manhattan; extra classes at the Art Students League; college at the Fashion Institute of Technology, from which he graduated in 1963; a string of garmento jobs—was solid but basic. From high school through college the routine was pretty dull: wake up, go into Manhattan on the train for classes, take the train back home to the Bronx at night, get the homework done, go to bed, and start all over again the next morning. But his ability to give it his all was in the blood. "I came from a family in which all they did was talk about work," he says.

Socially, Klein didn't run with a big gang in school. As has been true throughout his life, there were only a few intimates. "I've always had that since I was a child," he explains. "Because my sister and brother are so far apart in years, we were just never close as a family. I felt somewhat alone." (He once told Warhol and Bianca Jagger in an interview that his brother used to refer to him as "the king," which says everything about his position in the family.) To fill the void there were the long days of studies, the hopes for the future, and a few close friends, principally Jayne Centre, who lived nearby and had gone with him to PS 80, as well as FIT, and Barry Schwartz, Klein's best friend since age five.

Klein started seeing Centre, a New York knockout, in junior high; they were two green-eyed kids from the Bronx, both dreaming of a much grander existence. The early years of their courtship involved the usual dating rituals, a movie and a bite. Centre was smart and artsy (she became a textile designer), and they both wanted some kind of artistic life. They were married in 1964 (she was twenty, he was twenty-one), at the Hampshire House hotel, on Central Park South. Their lives had officially begun. Picture *Barefoot in the Park,* but with a divorce on the horizon.

It was Calvin's relationship with Schwartz that had the glue. They would stick together, through thick and thin, for fifty-six years (Schwartz is six months Klein's senior). This was one of those celebrated, nothing-can-tear-them-asunder partnerships in the fashion world, like that between Yves Saint Laurent and Pierre Bergé, or Valentino and Giancarlo Giammetti. To look at the relationship in the simplest terms, what Schwartz did was provide the business structure to help make Klein's vision real. (People say he could do numbers in his head quicker than a calculator, and in the company's early years, especially, he had a reputation as a super-tough bargainer.) "It was the ideal partnership because we didn't compete," says Schwartz. Since the sale there's been a drift in the relationship. That makes its own kind of sense, for the two men were really opposites, their differences growing more pronounced as the years went on. A list could fill up this page, but let's start with the obvious. Klein has had two marriages and seen a lot of other action, while Schwartz, to quote the designer from a 1984 *Playboy* interview, "lives a very straight, normal, family kind of life. He hates being in New York and wants to go home to his children, wants to be on the farm, looking at his horses. We have to understand and be tolerant of each other." At the start, though, when they were becoming friends at five, who knew from such things? They began their first business venture around then, selling cups of water, which they got for free, from Molly's shop, on a nearby street corner. By age nine they had a newspaper business, selling the *New York Daily News* and the *Mirror* at a markup. Klein once remarked that dividing up the money they'd made was like sex to Schwartz; he also remembered that Schwartz would always push the extra penny over to Klein's side.

"I always believed in him," Schwartz says, "but it was pretty easy to believe in him, because he's a pretty impressive guy." Whereas Klein's mission was to become a designer, for Schwartz—whose father was also in the small-supermarket business in Harlem—it was business, business, business. He got his chance to flex his muscles at it faster than anyone had imagined. In 1964, Schwartz, then twenty-two, was away in the army but rushed home after his father was murdered on the job; as the only son, he had to step in. This sudden responsibility eventually led to a kind of crossing-the-Rubicon moment for Calvin, as well. A few years later, he remembers, "I was at a terrible job making inexpensive Dacron dresses, and Barry said, 'Why don't we go into the grocery business together? We'll open lots of stores. We'll have a chain and make lots of money.'" Klein was torn. After all his striving, the supermarket business? But he was married now, had responsibilities—Marci, his daughter, was born in 1966—and certainly wasn't thrilled or inspired by the depressing work he was doing. To him it was drudgery, not design. As he considered Schwartz's offer, he went to his folks for advice—one of the few times he'd ever done that. He expected a difference of opinion, that his practical father would tell him to go with Schwartz for the financial security that this plan offered, while his mother would want him to continue with the fashion thing. What Klein heard shocked him. His mother was silent; she really didn't have to say anything, because his father advised his son to stay the course and see his fashion vision through. Otherwise, Leo Klein said, he'd be sorry. Calvin recalls the conversation as the best advice anyone has ever given him. "What he was really telling me is it's not about money," remembers Klein. "It's about being happy and feeling good about what you're doing. I just sailed out of there."

Schwartz's response to Klein's "I just can't do it" was to siphon cash out of the register at the family's supermarket and hand it over to his best friend so he could begin to be a fashion designer for real. The sum was ten thousand dollars. (He later added another twenty-five thousand.) When Schwartz had given his buddy the money, he meant it as a show of faith and support and did not expect anything but a thanks. Klein would have none of it, and insisted they were now partners. Klein used the money to create a handful of ensembles that could serve as a selling platform. The focus was on coats—with dresses or skirts and blouses underneath. (This would lead to Klein's being slotted as a coat designer for the first five years of his career.) He held on to his day job, too, as a kind of safety net, continuing to work on clothes that left him cold. But now he had an outlet for his own stuff, which he put together at night and on weekends. He'd sketch out his designs and then pass them on to others he'd befriended on jobs: a pattern maker he'd found on Long Island, and then a special sample tailor from Coney Island. There was a lot of running around, but Klein wasn't about to let up. Then the boss found out about his double life. "It became a really unpleasant scene," remembers the designer. "I felt terrible. I had a contract with them, and I was close to one of the owners, and I betrayed them. They asked me to leave immediately, and I did." In March 1968, he leased room 613, a cubbyhole of a space at the York Hotel, on Seventh Avenue, where other manufacturers had modest showrooms, too. ("That number stayed with us for a lot of years," says Schwartz. "It's always been our lucky number. The first plane that we bought, the Gulfstream, was 613CK.")

The alliance between Klein and Schwartz was cemented on April 4, 1968, a date imprinted on our national consciousness. When word spread that evening that Martin Luther King, Jr., had been gunned down while standing on the balcony of the Lorraine Motel, in Memphis, Klein and Schwartz were at a hockey game at Madison Square Garden. Klein remembers his friend predicting that there would be a riot in Harlem that night, and there wouldn't be much of the family store left in the morning. He was right. The next day, after Schwartz made his way uptown and surveyed the damage, he phoned Klein and told him to get there pronto. Schwartz then made a remarkable proposal. Klein remembers, "He asked, Why don't we just run up and down the aisles, knock everything down that's still on the shelves, and then go outside and throw the key into the street and never come back?" One can only imagine the combination of pain, fear, and liberation that the two young men felt as they acted out these primal motions of letting go. I don't know what the Schwartz family made of all this, but Klein now had company at the York Hotel: Schwartz, a newly free man with time on his hands to start planting the seeds for a business that would grow into an American legend.

Perhaps it's only fitting that the house that became Calvin Klein, Inc., was born out of this brew of changing times, changing lives, and cultural revolutions.

Change seems to be in the company's DNA. Right from the start Klein wanted to clear away the cobwebs. "In design school, believe it or not, we were taught how to make above-the-table dresses," he recalls. "It means when you're seated at a table there has to be something happening from the waist up. I would think, Who on earth thinks like this? It has to be such an antiquated way of creating clothes for a modern woman." The young designer had a much more contemporary view of women—as more than simply creatures of reproduction and decoration—which was evident from the rack of samples, his first collection, that he was getting ready to present at the York Hotel. He so nailed the way that women in the late sixties wanted to dress that when Donald O'Brien, Bonwit Teller's general merchandise manager, got off the elevator on the wrong floor and accidentally landed in Klein's showroom, something instantly attracted him. What he saw included mid-calf-length coats in a variety of pale colors and simple high-waisted sleeveless shift dresses. The fabrics had a lot of body, and the clothes had been steamed and molded within an inch of their lives. Today, Klein refers to them as "bulletproof" and "architectural," and says they all could have stood up by themselves. "I thought American women needed to be more streamlined," he says. "They moved faster, they were working, they were raising kids. It was that time when rules were changing. They were busy—they didn't have time to change. They went to work, to the theater, to a restaurant. That was my inspiration. What I didn't know at the time is that there were people all over the world who were thinking the same way."

Clearly, O'Brien was on that wavelength. He dispatched a buyer from Bonwit's to second what he felt he'd discovered, and then arranged a face-to-face for Klein with Mildred Custin, the store's president. The next part of the story is firmly entrenched in fashion lore. Instead of taking his goods in a taxi, which might have led to the clothes' becoming creased, he put everything on a rack and wheeled it himself from Seventh Avenue and Thirty-seventh Street to Fifth Avenue and Fifty-sixth Street—a distance of nearly a mile and a half. "This way everything could be perfect," he remembers. (*Perfect* is a word that comes up a lot with him.) A wheel broke on the way, but determination won out. Klein left Bonwit's that day with a fifty-thousand-dollar order. Better yet, he outfoxed Custin, who ruled high-end retail back then—only Geraldine Stutz at Henri Bendel counted as competition—on the question of whether the store would have his line exclusively. It wasn't easy to win on this point, because Custin may have spoken in a little-girl voice, but she meant business. Klein didn't cave, and kept the right to sell to others. The key to his fearlessness? "I saw my father not being assertive enough in business," he says, "and that disturbed me. I watched him give up at a certain point when he was in his middle fifties. It just killed me. I thought, Why doesn't he fight?"

Now came the tough part: the challenge of actually producing the outfits in a way that would keep their quality and still get them delivered to the stores on time. Klein remembers, "Every aspect of this was an adventure—from the banks to the fabric houses, to trucking." After turning cartwheels to get it all done, day after day, long night after long night, Schwartz and Klein came through—with help from their mothers, who sewed the Calvin Klein labels into the coats and dresses. Not only did the clothes make it to Bonwit's on time, they sold. The buzz about Klein began.

This success of these first few years was due to many factors, not just the way Klein's designs hit a nerve. The partners did their own PR, cold-calling buyers, other fashion people, and that era's retail bible, the *Tobe Report*. As Klein says, "The great thing with fashion is that word travels fast." Besides, Schwartz knew exactly how to play it, and Klein himself was a lure. He is down-to-earth, direct, and has an easy sense of intimacy. He also has a seductive boyishness that has nothing to do with age, not to mention good looks, cool, and a magnetism that attracts both sexes. (When I was interviewing people about him for this piece, I was struck by how many men and women confessed that they once had a crush on him.) None of this hurts when you're trying to make your way in the world, especially if you also have promise, which Klein did, winning him the support of an established designer, Chester Weinberg, and the editors who ruled the fashion press. At *Vogue,* Klein could count on Baron Nicolas de Gunzburg, a man whose family had supported Diaghilev and the Ballets Russes and who was then at the height of his fabulousness. He moved in the same circles as Cole Porter and Noël Coward, was full of stories about Coco Chanel, and worked under Diana Vreeland, the most inspired nutter in all of fashion-magazine history. The September 1975 *Vogue* trumpeted, "If you were around a hundred years from now and wanted a definitive picture of the American look in 1975, you'd study Calvin Klein."

It is de Gunzburg in particular whom Klein credits with helping him when he was first developing his fashion voice, in the early seventies. Klein says, "I just worshipped him. I was so thrilled that he would look at what I was doing and tell me honestly what he thought, whether it was good, not good, whether I could do better." Later, Klein would end up hiring de Gunzburg when Condé Nast put him out to pasture, around 1975. But in the early days, when he was on top, their conversations stimulated Klein's vision of what he was creating and helped the young designer formulate the big themes that would carry through the decades that followed. "He saw that I was doing something that he felt was relevant and American," remembers Klein. "He kept referring to that all the time. He'd say, 'It's American, it's pure, it's not fake, artificial, decorative.' Not any of the stuff that he disliked."

Klein's timing couldn't have been better. Even though Europe still regarded the States as a fashion backwater, the American industry was coming alive. Anne Klein (no relation) was in her heyday, and thanks to her and others (including Yves Saint Laurent, across the ocean), the enormous possibilities of what was called "luxury sportswear" were becoming evident. Calvin didn't miss his chance: In 1973, he changed the direction of the company from coats to sportswear. "It was Calvin's call," says Schwartz. "He was the visionary. I just executed what he wanted done."

The other predominant strain in American fashion was a new kind of democratized glamour, most evident in the work of Roy Halston Frowick. Halston had begun as a hatmaker, turning out Jackie Kennedy's famous pillbox (ironic, when one considers his nonmedicinal use of cocaine), but he was a font of talent, with a wide range. His tailored suits, crêpe evening dresses, and signature Ultrasuedes were coveted by fashion hounds of all stripes, from Texas oil wives to the era's boldfaced names. Klein, ten years his junior, wasn't yet in the same league. But the look of Klein's clothes—the focus on simplicity, subtlety, and a clean cut—and the philosophy behind them were similarly rooted in a casual American style that went back to the forties and pioneering designers such as Claire McCardell. Merchants and editors tuned in to what Klein was doing before fellow designers, some of whom were downright condescending. For Klein's part, his early years in business were so consuming that he didn't have time to worry about what people were saying behind his back.

He also didn't have much time for Jayne and Marci, which did not help his marriage. The family had moved to Forest Hills, Queens, and there was many a night without Calvin. The days were long—eighteen hours was not unusual—and Klein often slept at the West Thirty-seventh Street showroom, along with Schwartz (the floor and a convertible couch came in handy). Klein's regret about the life he missed with Marci is visceral. He and Marci are fiercely close these days. Her childhood memories humanize the sense of finished product that is Klein's public image. "They were young parents from the Bronx," she says. "They were still living in Queens when I was born, so I remember my dad before he was famous. There were canvases around and he was [still] painting. *Hippies* is not the right word for them, but they were artsy. The apartment didn't look like other people's. It had white wood floors and all white walls. They weren't like anybody else's [parents]." Calvin and Jayne would stick it out for Marci's first six years, divorcing in 1974. Ultimately, it doesn't seem to be the work that busted up the family. Klein once analyzed it thus: "We were kids. We grew in different directions."

He began making a name for himself as a man-about-town, with a list of consorts that eventually included both women and men, but he was continuing to give work his all. An old friend, Lizzette Kattan de Pozzi, now the Honduran consul in Milan, shared a "love shack" pad with Klein on the Upper East Side for a few years after he split from Jayne. She remembers that period vividly: "He would just collapse on the couch at the showroom and fall asleep and wake up the next day, and he would still be trying to get the perfect cut or the perfect sleeve until he had it. The man drives on perseverance until he gets it, looking for that right touch. I spent endless nights with him doing that, whether he was drawing or we spent, I think, maybe two nights trying to get the right cut on a bathing suit once. He doesn't give up."

This perseverance paid off. In just ten years the partners had created a $100 million business. Klein, thirty-six in 1978, had already won the Coty Award, a prestigious honor in fashion circles, three times. Meanwhile, his apartment, on the forty-sixth floor of the Sovereign building, between Sutton Place and First Avenue and designed by Joe D'Urso, was emblematic of his new life. The look was a composite of white walls, gray industrial carpet, and black leather, which was the dominant motif; among its features were a platform bed covered in black leather and a black leather hammock in the living room.

Klein's creative team from this period is famous in fashion circles. That is one of his great talents: He has an instinct about whom to bring on and when. He'll go the extra mile to get them, too. In the nineties, when he was looking for a new company president to revitalize the label's image and make it more global, he set his sights on Gabriella Forte, who had worked beside Giorgio Armani for ages. When he couldn't reach her directly, he waited outside her house in Milan so he could make her an offer. Guess where she ended up working? Back in 1976, he brought on Frances Stein, an editor at *Vogue* (she had also been in Halston's inner circle), to be part of his creative team. Over time Klein would hire a cluster's worth of star talent, including Grace Coddington from British *Vogue,* in the eighties, and stylists Tonne Goodman and Melanie Ward, who went on to become editors at *Vogue* and *Harper's Bazaar,* respectively. One often hears from fashion old-timers that the Stein era represents a high point in Klein's career. As many others have pointed out, that period, which went from 1976 to 1979, was when the designer really found his voice and started to articulate the vocabulary that we now think of as his: sexuality, sensuality, and classicism, with the key words being *attitude* and *gesture.* Stein wasn't with Klein for long—she would go on to serve Chanel as an accessories designer for more than two decades—and the fight between her and the designer on her last day is said to have been a humdinger, but those who were around the label then always remark on the way that Stein keyed into Klein's personal style, and to what was going on in his private life, and used those insights to help clarify his voice as a designer.

Like others, John Calcagno, who worked for Klein during that period in the design studio, credits Stein with helping to put the undercurrent of heat into the label. "I don't think it became really sexy and sensual until Frances arrived," he says. But he also flips the whole thing back to Klein himself: "I remember what Calvin wore in those years. It was these heavy tweed suits, not unlike what the Duke of Windsor would wear, or what Ralph [Lauren] would wear or do. But because of Calvin's body and the length and slouchiness of it"—Klein is a skinny six foot one—"the whole thing changed. Of course, what he did was wear it with a T-shirt, which also made all the difference, which is exactly what Frances must have seen. I've never forgotten this: the way he wore his thick socks, because I think he felt he had skinny ankles, with these heavy shoes, and the perfection of the way the jeans sat on his body, the way he looked at himself in the mirror and adjusted them, the oh-so-perfect T-shirts that he bought by the hundreds. The way the clothes draped on his body, there was a kind of sensuality, which I think Frances picked up on and somehow translated into the clothes we did at that period, which I think really was a change."

Klein didn't always have that much on. There's a hilarious story that Calcagno tells about working with the designer on the first menswear collection, which launched in 1978. Calcagno had gone off to Scotland to pick out tweeds with Zack Carr, the very talented head designer who would work beside Klein off and on for more than twenty-seven years (and Calcagno's partner at the time). The two men needed to consult with Klein regarding the final choices. It was summertime and the designer was out at the house in Fire Island that he shared with fellow designer Giorgio Sant' Angelo, so Klein told the team to come on out and bring the Scottish textile man who was going to supply the tweeds. They took a seaplane to the Pines and found Klein and Sant' Angelo sunning themselves on the beach in charmeuse bikinis. "There we were," Calcagno remembers, "picking out tweeds with them all oiled up, with this conservative Scotsman, and it was just unforgettable."

But it was in women's fashion where the label really began to innovate. The designers discarded the stiffer fabrics and more structured designs with which Klein had made his name and started to use softer materials they thought were sensual, such as crêpe de Chine, thin cashmeres, charmeuse, satin, linens, and layers of silks (minus anything underneath). As Calcagno says, with these clothes, "everyone took notice." Instead of making the shapes or structures of clothes the focal point, the designers found magic in the drama of what happened when they put together different textures. Klein recalls, "To me the contrast between rough fabrics and satin fabrics against a woman's body was really sexy. That's how I started doing slip dresses in the very beginning. They were under something that was more tailored and strong. It's the combination that has always intrigued me. The contrast between soft and hard." The designer had also begun using the natural palette that he would explore for the rest of his career. ("All my staff had training on color names from Calvin himself," remembers Nian Fish, the creative director at the public-relations firm KCD, who worked with Klein beginning in 1990. "White was not white. It was chalk, or it was Dover, after the white cliffs of Dover. One would never say beige. It was sand. And black would be coal. It's like how the Eskimos have all these different names for snow.")

There was something else, too: a discipline that kept the clothes focused on a few strategies. By the late seventies, the art world may have considered *minimalism* old hat; in fashion, however, the term would not be in common usage for another ten years or so. But at the time, Klein and his collaborators hit on some of minimalism's fundamental principles and translated them into their own kind of fashion vocabulary.

It was in 1977 that Calvin Klein the man became Calvin Klein the icon; you can pinpoint it in the press coverage, in the paparazzi shots of him and Bianca Jagger and Liza Minnelli and Andy Warhol and everyone else who was hanging out at Studio 54, the era's defining nightclub. Klein was made for the place, which opened in April 1977, and the club, where the creativity and license that were coursing through the 1970s flowered, seems to have been made for him. For a few years, the disco was the nerve center for New York's fashion, art, and entertainment worlds. As Klein says, "Who wanted to be lunching with a socialite? I wanted to be part of a whole new era that got inspired by what was happening in the world. It was an amazing time in New York City. Everyone from all walks of life, from any part of the world—at least I had the opportunity to meet them and get inspired by the way people looked or by what they did. I was there. Studio 54 was our El Morocco, our Stork Club."

For many of those who frequented the club, their time together seems to have either made them never want to see one another again or bonded them forever. Although Klein and Barry Diller had met some years before, at a lunch at Ali MacGraw's house in Los Angeles, Studio 54 is where the two became true friends. As Diller remembers it, "There was a group of us who would go to Studio all the time. There was a ritual in our lives, which was we would go to Calvin's. We would go at eleven or twelve at night and hang around. Some of them were doing drugs. I didn't know from drugs. It was Steve [Rubell], Halston, Sandy [Gallin], David [Geffen] if he was around, and maybe a couple of others. Andy Warhol wasn't part of this group. He was somewhere where people were paying for dinner. We would then go to Studio."

With the music blasting, the topless waiters shimmying, and shenanigans in every banquette and bathroom, the club's vibe was the opposite of a staid boardroom's, but for Klein it also happened to be the place where one of the biggest business opportunities of his life presented itself. There he was one night in 1977, dancing up a storm just before daybreak. "I ran into this guy at Studio 54 at four o'clock in the morning who said to me, 'How would you like to put your name on jeans?' " recalls Klein. The music was deafening, and no doubt Klein had more than Perrier in his system, but he got the potential impact of the offer. The entire concept of "designer jeans," such a given today, was in embryo form back then. Fiorucci, a store near Bloomingdale's that was more like a nightclub than a retail environment, offered a pop riff on the classic Levi's, with examples in gold and plastic. Gloria Vanderbilt had launched her eponymous line of jeans in 1976, and Jordache would bring out its upscale jeans around the same time Klein's hit stores two years later. But that night at Studio 54, this was still something of a lightbulb idea. The man said he was speaking for a friend in the fashion business, and asked, "How would you like to make a million dollars?" "I heard him loud and clear," the designer remembers. "When it's about the work and the business, I don't miss it. I thought this could really be interesting. My mind was going. I always liked the idea that I would be able to reach more people. That's why the jeans interested me. The jeans gave me the opportunity to get the message across to the masses. They gave me an opportunity to create in another way."

Klein was leaving for Frankfurt later that morning, planning on sleeping on the plane. When he got to the airport he phoned Schwartz to give him the low-down and the contact. The rest is history. It turned out that the company that was involved in the deal, Puritan Fashions, had made only dresses before, but they were ready to jump into the jeans market. This was really the first big deal Schwartz made for the label, and he negotiated it with real smarts and vision. He got royalties on every pair of jeans sold (one dollar per), with a provision for a cost-of-living increase. It wasn't long before Puritan was shipping 500,000 pairs of Calvin Klein jeans a week. (As Schwartz remembers it, the jeans cost $19.75 to make and sold for $40 a pair.) The ongoing business meant that Schwartz worked closely with Carl Rosen, whose family owned Puritan, and after five years Calvin Klein, Inc., ended up purchasing Puritan for $68 million; by then the company was selling about $500 million worth of jeans a year.

The playing with fabrics and their erotic possibilities that was so critical to the ready-to-wear fashion also cropped up in the marketing of the jeans—Klein's first masterstroke of many as an advertiser. "The first thing we did were those Brooke Shields commercials," he says, "and they caught on like crazy." I'll say. It's difficult to think of another series of ads that kicked up as big a brouhaha as did Richard Avedon's 1980 TV commercial featuring a fifteen-year-old Shields looking directly into the camera and asking, "You want to know what comes between me and my Calvins? Nothing." Nearly thirty years later it's not difficult to understand why this ad—in which Shields was dressed in a loose charmeuse shirt, which Klein describes as "the color of liquid," and a pair of his jeans—created such a kerfuffle. This was an early iteration of the fashion world's now perennial theme of the girl-woman, both innocent and sexual. (The fact that Shields had played a prepubescent prostitute in Louis Malle's film *Pretty Baby* a couple of years earlier surely added fuel to the fire.) The other commercials in the series continued to pivot on double entendres—in one, Shields recites a monologue about genes; in another, she defines what it means to be "Calvinized." All of that imagery became "indelible," as Shields herself says. "There was an iconic tone to it," the actress notes. "I don't think you can really know that at the time, because it feels like that type of vision is after the fact. But [the response] was immediate. It was me and the jeans. We were inseparable. I didn't do a television show without that being in my bio. I didn't go on the street without somebody saying, 'Got your Calvins on?' People still come up to me and mention it."

The images and the surrounding controversies got both actress and designer on the cover of *People* magazine in 1982; the designer took her for a celebration party at Studio 54. She remembers him being very protective of her.

He was less careful about himself in those years. While Klein walked away from the Studio era a much more famous, wealthy man, he also walked away with a taste for more than H_2O. These days he is comfortable talking about how that period has a role in the etiology of his history with addiction. Klein remembers, "I was experimenting during that time. I didn't think it was bad. I didn't know I was doing something that could really be damaging. We would tell each other, 'In South America they always do cocaine'—silly things like that." During another of our conversations Klein returned to the theme of his carefree youth. "I burned the candle at both ends. When you're young you can do that to a certain degree. I learned that I could not do it. I learned the hard way, and I paid a price. It was all new. I just didn't know any better." He pauses, then offers a kind of explanation, both for himself and for his set. "The thing is we were successful. We managed to be very high-functioning people. So that was a source of denial."

When he says he was high-functioning, he isn't kidding. No matter the chemical alterations to his system, he remained fully in charge at the company.

"The thing that really connected me to Calvin is I knew how much he loved his work," says Bruce Weber, the photographer who has shot so many of the label's most memorable ads. "He could be out all night and might not go home, but he was in that office, on time, ready to go. That made me want to have that same drive for his work." Klein's ability to motivate people created not just a pride in the company—in the fashion, the campaigns, the new product lines—but an atmosphere of seductive excitement surrounding the designer himself. "We were all in love with Calvin," says Calcagno, "as were all the editors. He was the most seductive person. You wanted to please him. Men, women, everyone."

Klein certainly made good use of his charms. "He was one of the first designers to be treated as a movie star," says Weber. "We used to hear all these stories about him. He'd be dating one of the girls and then some guy he met. He was really open about himself. He didn't hide things. And that's likable." Indeed, this sexual ambiguity shows up loud and clear in the erotically charged imagery that Klein and Weber created together—which is what made the pictures reverberate so much with the times. Klein says, "You can see a photograph that Bruce Weber did which said a lot about my life. It was in 1985 for the fragrance Obsession, and [the model] Josie Borain was in it. I was obsessed with her. She was such an interesting woman and not an obvious sexpot, androgynous in a certain way but so fine and classy. In the ads there are arms and hands and all of these body parts all over her. You didn't know if they were men or women. You didn't know how many of them there were. But it got your mind going. That was a period of time when sex was everywhere, as were drugs. Not for everyone, of course. I've experienced—and I've said it before—a lot of my fantasies. I've experienced sex with men, with women. I've fallen in love with women. I've married women. And I have a family. I have experienced lots of things that have influenced my world. I am for good or bad a real example of whatever I've put out there. [The imagery] really is a part of me. And it happened because I was either observing or living in a certain way, or desiring to. It's not something where we tried to say, Well, let's outdo the other people and see if we can be more outrageous. It was real."

Klein's way of discussing his personal life—and entwining it with his work life—is emblematic of him. He's not someone who kisses and tells; he'll talk about the gist but not the details. As he told *Playboy* in 1984, "I think it's more fun if you have the reputation and people don't know everything—a little mystery isn't so bad." I believe there's more to this, and it has to do with an incident that reinforced Klein's fundamentally discreet nature. Thirty years later he still describes the day in 1978 that Marci, then eleven, was kidnapped as the worst day of his life. The actual event sounds like something out of a frightening movie: Marci tricked off a school bus by a former babysitter, who had set up the scam with two accomplices; Calvin dropping off the $100,000 ransom, then going to rescue his child from the apartment where she'd been held (and, before it was over, being mistaken for one of the kidnappers by a huge FBI squad). Marci remembers, "All of a sudden I hear him screaming my name. I hear him banging, banging, banging on all these doors." Klein was in the hallway of the building where Marci had been left, but the kidnappers had given him the wrong apartment number. "I ran out and I saw him and I jumped into his arms. I've never felt so safe in my life." Marci says they didn't talk about what happened for years, and when they finally discussed it, her father welled up with tears. For his part, Klein remembers, "That was a nightmare that changed our lives a great deal." It certainly made him hyperconscious of the pitfalls of being a public person and having one's life on display. "Let's face it," says Marci. "This is a guy from the Bronx. This was not what he thought was going to happen in his life, which has something to do with the way he is."

By 1981 a new arrival had been added to the team. Kelly Rector would become an integral part of Klein's life as his partner, wife, and, now, intimate friend, but she started out as an assistant who'd been very aware of him as a nighttime glamour-puss as well as a happening designer. Rector, then twenty-three, had received her training in the design studio of Ralph Lauren and had observed Klein out and about at various hot spots, including Studio 54. She had interviewed with Klein a few months previously but didn't get the position. Then they'd run into each other at Studio 54 and he'd called her at seven the following morning with a start date: the next day.

Eventually their professional and personal lives would merge, and out of that came new creative and business ideas. Kelly, for instance, is the one who came up with the idea of appropriating the men's underwear for women. She remembers saying, "There's something sexy about wearing your boyfriend's underwear." There was a gold mine in this offhand thought: seventy million dollars' worth in 1984 sales alone. More significantly, Kelly became the ne plus ultra of the designer's "muses," the basis for what we think of as the Calvin Klein woman—the woman who will go out in a perfect-looking thin cashmere T-shirt evening dress, not the one who's all glittered up in a va-va-va-voom number. In hindsight it's hard to believe that their relationship was ever doubted. But, boy, were there a lot of raised eyebrows when their hookup went public in the early eighties. I remember when they married, in Rome in 1986 (and went fabric hunting the next day). I wasn't personally acquainted with either of them; at the time I barely knew anything about the fashion world. But I sure heard the gossip that the union was some kind of marketing-driven "marriage of convenience." Because of the open way that Calvin had displayed his attractions to and relationships with men, it was assumed he was strictly gay (his earlier marriage being seen as some kind of aberration). Maybe none of us is immune from a desire to define people narrowly, and in the area of sexuality it's a virtual reflex. "That person's straight." "This person's gay." "This is normal." "That isn't." But life doesn't come in neat slots; it is full of surprises, if one is lucky. Kelly says, "When you fall in love with someone, all the rumors that you hear fall away. My whole life changed with Calvin." Their romance happened on the job. She remembers, "He would walk into the room, and it was just like the lights went on. The movie started every single day. I was so much more special when he came into the room."

"Everyone who knows me would ask what happened at that moment," remarks John Calcagno. "It was some kind of magic. He fell in love with her and she madly with him. They didn't care who was around. They showed it, kissing and holding each other and having fun and cuddling."

Klein's personal income in 1981 was said to be around $8.5 million; the following year independent retailers and Calvin Klein boutiques pushed $750 million worth of product out the door. By the mid-eighties, Klein ruled American fashion, along with Ralph Lauren and Donna Karan. Each of "the big three" had a distinct voice, but each was also inherently American. For Klein, there were occasional misses, such as when the women's ready-to-wear line got uncomfortably close to what Yves Saint Laurent was doing. But Klein's clarity and directness, his emphasis on trick-free fashion and natural fibers—he once said, "That damn polyester killed the whole country"—won him a devoted following. The house had a reputation in particular for turning out some of the best pants in the business, and its trench coats became a must-have item.

Not enough credit has been given to how on point Klein's fashion was in the eighties, because the subject of his brilliant marketing seems to have eclipsed all else. He has struck gold often in his advertising campaigns, and with a lineup of photographers that would make any museum—that knew what it was doing—envious. Call it commerce or call it art, it doesn't matter: the list, with only a few exceptions, reads like a who's who of twentieth-century fashion photography: Irving Penn, Richard Avedon, Bruce Weber, Steven Meisel, Steven Klein, Mario Sorrenti, Juergen Teller, and more.

It used to be that if one was a "real" photographer one wouldn't sully one's "integrity" or "art" shooting fashion campaigns. Klein is one of a handful of designers who helped change that. He gave photographers such a visible forum for their work—shot in the spirit of his universe, of course—that it became prestigious to shill for him. There were Avedon's taboo busters with Shields, and unforgettable images by Penn of models draped in opulent mixes of fabrics that made them look like members of some kind of new, ultrastylish tribe. But the photographer who captured (and helped define) the combination of polymorphous sexuality and physical wholesomeness that was such a big part of Klein's imagery was Weber. (His ability to serve successfully as the photographic messenger for both Klein and Ralph Lauren—two fundamentally different designers—throughout the eighties is a subject worthy of its own article.) Weber's big break came when he got the call from Klein's people to come up to the office to discuss a jeans campaign. On his first assignment in 1981, with a model named Romeo—who'd been discovered by Calvin pushing a clothing cart on the street, just as the designer himself had once done—he created an instant pinup. The money shot, the one that was chosen for a billboard in Times Square, as well as for magazine ads, presents a figure who is part Adonis, part toughie. With the sleeves of his T-shirt rolled up, biceps rippling, one arm raised, cradling his head the way a Roman or Greek marble sculpture of a god might be posed, and the other arm grazing his abdomen, fingers just under the waistband, Romeo looks like the progeny of a marriage between James Dean and Elvis Presley, before the fried peanut butter and banana sandwiches. (According to others who were around at the time, Romeo's charms were not lost on Klein.) I asked Weber if he'd realized he had a hit with the picture. With a laugh, he said, "There was so much yelling. Frances was screaming at Romeo because he kept eating pizza and was wiping his hands on his pressed white T-shirt."

One of the subsequent Weber shoots, a ten-day affair in 1982 on the Greek island of Santorini that would produce images for an array of Klein products, was one of the wildest in advertising history, which is saying something. Twenty-six years later the people who were there still talk about it. The group included the label's creative director, Rochelle Udell; her assistant Sam Shahid (who would eventually become Klein's creative director); Zack Carr; John Calcagno; models galore (Iman and Christy Turlington among them); Nan Bush (who has been Bruce Weber's partner for thirty years); and Klein himself. Even the accommodations were memorable: a hotel where the rooms were literally caves—"very cold caves, which is why people kept getting in bed together, to warm up," says Weber with a laugh.

Of all the pictures that were taken, it was the series of photos of Tom Hintnaus, a Brazilian-born Olympic pole-vaulter, that struck Klein as *the* images. Weber's shots of Hintnaus arching his naked torso against a white wall in Calvin Klein underwear—his "package" competing for its own gold medal—were chosen for billboards and bus-shelter posters. I was on a crosstown bus in Manhattan early one morning right after they'd been put up. When we passed a shelter almost everyone on my side of the bus swiveled his or her head to get a better look at the image, which was basically shoving the man's physicality down the audience's throat. I was so curious about it that I got off the bus so I could see it properly. I must admit I was wary. Was this some newfangled version of what Leni Riefenstahl had done for Hitler with her so-called perfect Aryan images? In retrospect, Weber's and Klein's prescience about the cult of the body, which would start to sweep across our culture a few years later, was the real story.

Unfortunately, a big part of that story was AIDS. With the fashion world, as with the art world, one cannot recount this period without dividing it in two: before and after the virus. Once the crisis started, the list of the fallen grew long with lightning speed. Now there were voids where before there had been excitement and competition in the industry, carefree days replaced by fear of the next piece of bad news. The impact of AIDS on fashion itself can't be measured in a literal way, but it clearly affected creativity as well as business. The fear of the disease and the reality of loss after loss, of course, impacted everyone who was touched by this modern plague. Sometimes it set up the old witch-hunting dynamic. There was a dramatic moment in Klein's *Playboy* interview where he insisted that the tape recorder be turned off, because the writer asked him about the rumors going around that he had AIDS. (The interview eventually resumed.)

One could see the disease's impact on the culture at large in the mid-eighties advent of the gym lifestyle, replete with newly bulked-up physiques. Klein's own physique went from slim to pumped. It was as if people's bodies had become a kind of metaphor for the time. The collective subconscious: Let's fight! And in the mid- to late eighties, Klein's collections—like those of many other designers—accommodated the new silhouette, with bigger shoulders. Some, though not Klein, trafficked in a kind of Amazonian proportion. No wonder the supermodels were warrior-scale. They were yet another example of the decade's bigger-is-better psyche—bigger offices, bigger houses, bigger paintings, bigger art galleries—which flourished before the flush eighties economy imploded.

The most momentous development in Klein's personal life during this period, aside from his second marriage, was his decision to go into rehab. "There came a certain point when I knew that this was no longer fun," he says, "and I couldn't stop drinking or using recreational drugs. Then I had to do something about it." He entered the Hazelden clinic in 1988. When I asked Klein if he was worried about the impact that undergoing treatment and the attendant publicity might have on the business, he said, "Betty Ford had changed all of that. She was the most courageous woman, and for her to do what she did at that time was really a breakthrough. That was a turning point. I was never concerned about Barry not understanding. I thought, If I don't deal with this, we will really have serious problems with the business. I just won't be able to work. So I had to do this. It wasn't an option."

"We were an established company," Schwartz says. "There were people who could fill in until he got himself straightened out. It was strictly a case of protecting him, because there are a lot of nasty, vicious people out there."

Klein had another advocate on his side, of course—Kelly. And it was during this period, as his personal life stabilized, that she had her greatest effect on Klein's vision and marketing, tempering the label's hothouse sensuality with a new classicism. Kelly's main surrogate in the shows and in the ad campaigns was Christy Turlington, the most genteel of the era's supermodels, who became the face of the Eternity fragrance when it launched in 1988. The choice was most purposeful. "I always felt her intelligence came through in photographs," Klein says. "At the time there was a lot of vulgarity and that didn't interest me. It's easy to go there. People respond to it. But I was looking for something more. And Christy is that person." For her part, Turlington understood the personal semiotics. "Calvin and Kelly were sort of this American royal couple," she says. "I think that's what I was fulfilling for them. I was stepping in as the Kelly character. The Eternity fragrance was about this ladylike setting. *Puritanical* wouldn't quite be the right word, but very serene. It was a new life for Calvin." Their Camelot was their classic Shingle style "cottage" on Georgica Pond, in East Hampton.

The peace wouldn't last. This is fashion, after all, and the pressure to evolve, to remain on the cutting edge, is a never-ending spur. That Klein managed to keep pushing his clothes forward, while also pushing the envelope with his advertising, fragrances, and other products, is testimony to his fierce focus. The pressure to grow the business was a parallel challenge, and Klein and Schwartz would face having to dig themselves out of a financial hole in 1992, when the eighties culture of financial excess came back to haunt the company. The partners had gotten themselves tied up in junk bonds, and when the jeans market plunged, they were stuck with enormous interest payments on their debt. The troubles ballooned, and the company found itself facing a serious cash crunch. "I took my daughter for a walk on the beach in the Hamptons," Klein remembers, "and said, 'I really think we might have to sell everything.' It was a terrifying moment." Instead, the designer's buddy David Geffen bought $62 million of the company's outstanding debt at a sizable discount and told Klein and Schwartz to pay him back when they could. (They did, a year later.) As Klein says, "David helped us out with the financial part of it until we could straighten it out with the banks, which we were able to do in a short period of time. But the work was that I had to fix what was wrong with the company, with either the marketing divisions or management or design. I may have gotten complacent. We think things are good and all of a sudden you turn around and it falls apart. So that was a hard lesson. I didn't think of selling at that moment. I thought, I've got to fix it and I will fix it. I knew I could do it, or I'd die trying."

The nineties backlash against vulgarity and big everything suited him just fine, and soon another muse entered the picture: Kate Moss, whose English schoolgirl look (not the fancy boarding school variety) was the absolute antithesis of the glamazon look that had been representing beauty in the fashion business in the eighties. Despite the storm that erupted over Kate Moss's thin and "unshapely" physique, which some critics called borderline anorexic—complex issue, wrong target—she found a champion in Klein. He went one better than simply hiring her for a new Obsession campaign; he gave the photography gig to Mario Sorrenti, then a young unknown who was Moss's boyfriend. The couple went off to a desert island, alone with a camera. The resulting campaign, with its intimate and emotional imagery, took the concept of personal in advertising to a new level. Making Moss the symbol of his company was a radical move even in a business known for skinny malinks, but, to put it squarely, she moved product. "With advertising, people respond very quickly, and you can measure it very easily," says Klein. "We just saw the sales take off. They were sick of fake boobs." As a counterbalance to Moss's grace, Klein chose her opposite for the men's side of things—Mark Wahlberg, then a cocky rapper beauty of a man-child.

· · ·

All together the nineties played out for Klein as a breathtaking renaissance, including the invention, in 1993, of an entirely new business: CK, the lower-priced, youth-oriented line, inspired by Marci, who was about to take her first job out of college, at *Saturday Night Live,* and told her dad that his clothes were too expensive and not on-message enough for either herself or her generation. With the economy coming out of a recession, CK was such an instant hit that the late Amy Spindler, a normally acerbic critic for *The New York Times,* said "it looked like an incubator for everything exciting in street-level fashion."

The company had very few creative bombs in the nineties, but one, a series of ads from 1995 shot by Steven Meisel for CK, blew up big-time. The TV spots, with an offscreen interlocutor putting questions to young models sitting against a wall of knotty-pine paneling, were meant to be a humorous simulacrum of an open casting call, but the grungy rawness of the spots and their insinuating edge suggested to some viewers a porno shoot with underage models. Not only was there a media firestorm but the Clinton White House got involved. In a fund-raising speech Bill called the ads "outrageous," and Hillary wrote that they "push[ed] the envelope of gratuitous sex and exploitation of children." The Justice Department even launched an investigation to see if child-pornography laws had been violated. (*Adweek* has since listed the campaign as one of "the lowest moments in advertising.") Klein pulled the ads—a first—after three weeks. He wasn't about to stand on a freedom-of-speech soapbox. The company was opening its first store in New York, a John Pawson renovation of a Greek Revival building on Madison Avenue, and the last thing anyone wanted was a picket line.

The other big business drama of the nineties, after the cash crisis, was the company's war with the manufacturer Warnaco and its CEO, Linda Wachner. Klein had met her in late 1993, when her reputation for turnarounds—she had revived Max Factor—was at its height. It wasn't long before she cut a $62 million deal for Klein's underwear business. (Most of the money went to pay back Geffen.) A roaring success at first—within a few years annual sales had jumped from $50 million to $300 million—the relationship soured after Warnaco also acquired the jeans license through a third party, over Klein's objections. Klein accused Wachner of making shoddy products and dumping them in price clubs and other low-end stores, sullying the label's reputation. A lawsuit filed in 2000 by Calvin Klein, Inc., seeking to void the jeans license, was accompanied by public name-calling—Schwartz told *The New York Times* that Wachner was "a liar," and Klein decried her "abusive . . . disgusting" language. Much to the disappointment of fashion-industry bystanders, however, the suit was settled the morning it was scheduled to go to trial, with Warnaco retaining the jeans business and Klein gaining a strong say in distribution.

It was during the late nineties, with the economy going gangbusters and newly minted moguls cashing in left and right, that Klein and Schwartz, who had never gone the IPO route, began to explore a possible sale of their company. Rumors were flying that Klein and Schwartz were asking for as much as one billion dollars. But no buyer materialized. "The only reason we didn't get it was because of our alliance with Warnaco and Linda Wachner," says Schwartz. "There were a number of interested people, but they were all afraid of her." A sale would have to wait until 2003.

The fragrance that Klein launched in 2000, Truth, would be his last as creative head of the company. He has always said that the names he picked for his fragrances were a reflection of what was going on in his life at the time. And a moment of truth was upon him. There had been upheavals in his personal life: In 1996 he and Kelly had separated (though they walked away from each other as close as ever), and at some point he began struggling anew with his substance-abuse issues. Soon the company would be in new hands, and with that change would come the question: What to make of Klein's creative legacy?

The influence of the "unfashion" aspects of his repertoire—the jeans, the underwear, the fragrances, the advertising, the cross-branding into other areas such as products for the home, the marketing of it all—has been acknowledged ad infinitum. Things get trickier when it comes to the "fashion" side of his career; for the most part, insightful illumination of Klein's place in fashion history has been elusive. In the early nineties, there was criticism that his clothes were appropriating ideas from Giorgio Armani, Helmut Lang, Miuccia Prada, and Jil Sander, and this gave momentum to the notion that Klein was a copier more than an inventor, that he was a skillful brander but not a real designer in the old-fashioned atelier sense. (Not that Klein had any interest in being old-fashioned.) If one were to pick at various collections, one could definitely find examples that fit the accusation, but this view really obscures the big picture.

Stored in Klein's vast archives in the basement of the company's Garment District headquarters are hundreds and hundreds of outfits from collections he presented over the thirty-plus years he was running his label. When we were at the archives, Klein could tell I was overwhelmed by the thousands of outfits hanging on the racks; stored away like this, they just looked like old stuff. He knows how fashion has to come alive on a body if we are to understand what it's about, so in true Calvin style he organized a mini presentation, with every detail under his purview and flawlessly executed. He called up the very in-demand Natalia Vodianova, who had been his last featured model, hired the best hair and makeup artists, consulted with Melanie Ward (the editor at *Harper's Bazaar* who worked closely beside him in the nineties), and showed me Calvin's Calvin. What was striking about the selection was that it didn't feel dusty; there was also a clear through-line in what he showed me, from the seventies and the nineties and up to his last collection, from 2003. (Intriguingly, he skipped the eighties.) Every single outfit—there were forty altogether—shared a softness, a subtlety, and a sensuality. The palette was as American and as warm, rigorous, and nature-based as Frank Lloyd Wright's. Among my favorite designs: a rose-print crêpe de Chine V-necked T-shirt and pajama pants from 1978; a sand-colored, bronze-studded wrap dress from 1979; a heather gray cashmere crew-necked T-shirt and mineral-colored straight skirt from 1998; and a cream chiffon jersey-styled long gown from 2003 that looked as easy to wear as your favorite old T-shirt.

While I was working on this piece I attended a New York University communications class where Klein was sitting in as a guest teacher for a friend, Jean DeNiro. He told the students that "repetition is reputation." It's an idea that artists from Warhol to Donald Judd (whose stripped-down, what-you-see-is-what-you-get work Klein has said inspired him in the nineties) have demonstrated for decades. With Klein it goes deeper than an obvious truism about branding, and cuts to the essence of his voice as a designer. Think of the paintings of Agnes Martin, who basically returned to the same endeavor every day for forty years, drawing or painting horizontal lines on canvas. The record of her hand—sometimes steady, sometimes wavering, sometimes in pencil, sometimes in subtle color—is about as moving as art gets. Think of the paintings of Robert Ryman, who for fifty-five years has also returned to the same strategy with almost every work: strokes of white paint on top of more strokes of white paint on an otherwise nude canvas. It's the almost imperceptible evolutions and setbacks that tell all. Both of these artists, of course, are minimalists. And their paintings were on my mind when Klein put on his little show for me. (Marci Klein even uses the *m* word about the man himself: "I think it describes how he fathers and what kind of a person he is; he doesn't add shit on.")

But, again, fashion doesn't hang on a wall: The real action is the alchemy between clothes and wearer. Nan Bush sums it up: "I think his fashion sensibility was so subtle that a lot of people maybe didn't get it. He had a definite point of view. The thing I always liked was that his designs let the person come through. When you saw them you didn't necessarily say, Oh, look at that fashion. He let the person be the star." Or as Jean DeNiro, who worked in sales at Bergdorf Goodman in the nineties, puts it: "His clients had complete confidence that not only were his clothes beautiful but that they could count on him. When [other designers] were sort of scaring them, or they couldn't fit in the clothes, they were like, you know, 'Give me Calvin. Help.'"

As part of the sale to Phillips–Van Heusen, Klein remained a creative consultant to his old company, where his duties had him advising on the collections and campaigns through 2006 and launching one more fragrance, the tellingly named Euphoria. (The company is now in the creative hands of Francisco Costa and Italo Zucchelli, both of whom had worked under Klein and were essentially anointed by him as successors.) Now that he is largely his own man again, Klein has been enjoying his freedom like nobody's business. The first thing he did was turn his new homes on Long Island and in New York and Miami Beach into projects that he could put his all into. The one in New York, a triplex on Perry Street in one of the fabled, troubled Richard Meier buildings, is a modernist masterpiece, with a gravity-defying stone staircase that looks like a waterfall. John Pawson's description of the apartment as "a bit like a flying carpet or a glass house in the sky" is apt. (When Klein was deciding whether to buy the place, before the building had gone up, he hired a helicopter, taking a hop with Meier to check out the view from the proper altitude.) The house in Miami Beach, which Klein finished renovating in 2006, is where one really sees how his fashion voice carries over into his living spaces. It is both a monastic and fantastic place, with decorative details stripped down to nothing, so that what *is* there—the understated lighting, the plastered, almost Rymanesque walls, the "simple" but extraordinary furniture—is exquisitely heightened. At night, a bamboo allée over the pool offers an unforgettable romantic peek across the bay at the lights of Miami Beach. It made me think about Klein as a young boy, dreaming of his life-to-be in Manhattan. And given his talent, his drive, and the fact that he has some serious cash in his pockets, I have a feeling there are some dreams still to be dreamt.

Vanity Fair, April 2008

Kith, Kin & Khaya

David Goldblatt is a true misfit in the history of photography: a standout whose commitment to the medium is epic. He is one of a kind, and his images of South Africa, taken from the 1940s and still going, will only be more reverberative as time goes on. For me they have become a life jacket of the forty-plus years I missed, when my family, like so many others who could not tolerate the policies of the apartheid, got out. Like many South African exiles, we made a new life, elsewhere, but there was always something missing. Goldblatt's pictures fill the void. He is among the ones who stayed to tell the stories.

I trust the work because it is not sensationalist, not exploitative, not shallow. In fact, Goldblatt's inability, or was it unwillingness, to, as he puts it, "photograph riots and policemen bashing people in the head" made it hard for him to get published in the early days. He remembers an editor telling him he didn't have a shtick, and he had better get one if he wanted to make it as a photojournalist. What the young Goldblatt, the son of Lithuanian immigrants, did have, though, is something much more meaningful: good old-fashioned idealism. He remembers:

> *It came out of the necessities of the situation we were in, with apartheid, and partly out of the struggle against it. In 1948, when the Nationalists came in, that was a cataclysmic event. People like my mother and father, and many quasi-liberals had assumed that at the end of the Second World War against fascism, we would see a turn in South Africa towards more liberalization. But the contrary happened. With the Nats all that was kaput. Among them were those who had been interned during the war as Nazi sympathizers so the feeling was that you couldn't really stay in this country. It was going to be a police state, a fascist state, an anti-Semitic state, and of course a racist state.*

436

David Goldblatt, *Cup Final, Orlando Stadium, Soweto,* 1972

For a time I thought I was a missionary with a camera, because there was no attempt internationally to tell the world what was beginning to happen in South Africa.

In fact, this sense of isolation, of being far from the action of the world of photojournalism, which was at its apex at the beginning of Goldblatt's journey in photography, seems like a gift in retrospect. It allowed Goldblatt, who is not the type to look over his shoulder anyway, to truly find his own way in the medium. That, plus a bit of inspiration from local photographers like Jürgen Schadeberg (the influential picture editor of *Drum* magazine), Peter Magubane, Ian Berry, and a few others, as well as an endless supply of will and determination, and a little help from a technical book he picked up from the Ansel Adams Basic Photo series. These touch points and characteristics, and a few committed collaborators, editors and publishers whom he has worked with over the years, were Goldblatt's tools to build a body of work that is now a real gold mine of imagery. Oh, and one can't forget Lily, Goldblatt's wife of fifty-five years, and the motorcycles and campers that have often been his companions as he has gone on his photographic expeditions. I was a passenger in his latest Rube Goldberg version of a camper recently—he referred to it as his "submarine"—and indeed in it, and with his cameras, he goes to the depths.

A highly sophisticated, even strict, sense of aesthetics, combined with a rigorous moral stance about what it means to take somebody's photograph, is what sets Goldblatt's work apart. He traces his respect for his subjects, and also for the clients and corporations who have sometimes employed him, to his training in his dad's clothing shop in Randfontein. (Make no bones about it, if Goldblatt has any hesitations about a job, he just doesn't do it.) "I think my father's way of valuing customers probably rubbed off," he says. "We were never allowed to ask the customer what size he was. It was our job to know." And in the same way, Goldblatt's knowledge of his subjects and themes—be it the life around the mines, the Afrikaners, the Bantustans, the citizens of Boksburg, the changes of Johannesburg, or the structures of all kinds that express the South African experience—comes through loud and clear in his photographs.

While Goldblatt's photographs sometimes resonate with images that have been done by European and American photographic legends—from Dorothea Lange to Walker Evans, from Helen Levitt to Garry Winogrand, from August Sander to Bill Brandt, from Diane Arbus to Eve Arnold—I defy anyone who really looks at Goldblatt's pictures to say that they are derivative or to peg them into a neat slot. You can't. That's because the glue that holds this broad body of work together is a mix of Goldblatt's highly attuned eye and his razor-sharp mind. His photographs are objects of thought as much as they're objects to behold. Before Goldblatt chose the camera he spent some years studying economics. While his professor wrote him off when the young man spoke of his intention to become a photographer, not all was lost. Goldblatt explains, "In a peculiar way I would vindicate myself with that professor although he would never know about it. What I learned in his economics classes became the nub of what I wanted to probe in photography. It has to do with an analytic approach to human action and values."

These days there are photographers who have become such superstars of the art, fashion, advertising, and magazine worlds that the inventors of the medium wouldn't believe their eyes. The shoots of these superstars can be as high-budget as a movie, and the lives and perks as glamorous as a Hollywood fantasy. That's not Goldblatt—who has portrayed his homeland, with all its complexities, contradictions, and conundrums, for sixty-plus years—by any stretch of the imagination. Goldblatt couldn't be more different. He comes

David Goldblatt, *Baby with Child-Minders and Dogs in the Alexandra Street Park, Hillbrow,* 1972

from the other side of photography's tracks, the side with the history that is peopled by loners, who rough it, risk it, and do it, not for the rewards but for something else, something that is becoming ever more rare in this world: an authentic desire to understand and capture what is in front of him. What's striking about Goldblatt's pictures is that they never preach; the photographer is allergic to the cheap shot. This has meant that he has been criticized, on the one hand, for not taking sides, and, on the other hand, for doing pictures that are "too tough." But Goldblatt is not in the business of pleasing. He has spent a life trying to know his country, looking and seeing—whether this has been during the apartheid years or after that ended and the freedom came, and with it the new South Africa and its new struggles.

Here's an anecdote that says it all. When Goldblatt decided to make a trip to North America in the mid-seventies to catch up with a number of friends and meet up with a publisher and curator or two—he's not big on networking—he brought his bicycle along on the plane from Johannesburg. After stopping off first in Toronto, and then in a village in Pennsylvania to see a pal, next up was New York. Drumrolls: Out comes the bicycle. He made it as far as the first bridge to Manhattan. As he was about to make his two-wheeled entrance onto the island the trouble began. Picture him covered in sweat, the city that Salvador Dalí compared to a ripened cheese melting and shimmering before him. "As I remember it, three major streams of traffic converge at a certain point. That's where a policeman stopped me. He shouted, 'You can't enter here!' It was a mess, and then a guy in a van stopped to offer me a lift." Did he take it? Of course not. Goldblatt diverted to the George Washington Bridge, continuing under his own steam and staying true to his journey, as he has always done with his photography.

Kith, Kin & Khaya: South African Photographs, 2010

Living Large Is the Best Revenge

"In 2008, I was saying, 'I'm going to be broke,'" confessed Jean Pigozzi, an Italian automotive heir who had further to fall than most, having topped off the millions his father left him by investing his way to his own sizable fortune. Of course, in 2008 a lot of people were worried about going broke, but Pigozzi was unusual in that he faced ruin with curiosity and even something approaching zest. "I was kind of intrigued," he told me. "I thought, Everything is going to collapse and I will be selling apples in the street with Ronald Perelman." As Pigozzi happily pointed out, that didn't happen. But when he raised that Depression-style scenario, his ample frame settled on a green, luxuriously long couch in his New York City apartment—designed, like most of his seven homes, in the irreverent, historically conscious, color-savvy style that might now be called "classic postmodernism"—and with the north light glancing across paintings by Francesco Clemente and the African artist Chéri Samba and photographs by Cindy Sherman, Seydou Keïta, and Malick Sidibé (the latter two African photographers), the funny thing was, I really could imagine Pigozzi on a street somewhere selling his wares. Not apples, though; I can't see Pigozzi bagging the Fujis, Macouns, and Granny Smiths. Too pedestrian. But one of his passions is photography, both his own and others', and what I could envision was Pigozzi in front of a PICTURES FOR SALE sign. Every day, he says, he worries about losing all his money, but I could see him hawking photographs and having a good time, liberated from obligations, business meetings, and worldly possessions, all of which he has many.

In a way, it's how we first met, some thirty years ago. We were both in our midtwenties; he'd been out of college only a few years, and I was new on the job as the editor of *Artforum.* Pigozzi had been recommended by the artist Sol LeWitt as the guy we should hire to take pictures of an upcoming trip to China that a group of art-world luminaries was planning. Who knew Pigozzi was the heir to a serious car fortune? Though LeWitt did mention he could afford to pay his own way. More important, LeWitt said, Pigozzi was a young guy to watch and could be counted on to come back with photographs of the group that we'd want to run. They'd be lively. And they were. I was pleasantly surprised that it all went so smoothly—and Pigozzi and his photographs have been surprising me ever since. This fall *Catalogue Déraisonné* (Steidldangin), his first book of photographs in nineteen years, was published, a collection of portraits, landscapes, travel photographs, and party pictures—though that latter term doesn't do those images justice. Rather, they can be seen as a diary of his life and times, as if Pigozzi were a camera-toting Pepys. (The book's release also coincides with a November–December exhibition of his photos at the Gagosian Gallery in New York.)

"Johnny is one of the world's greatest characters," says Elton John, who is not part of Pigozzi's inner circle but has a friendly relationship with him. "I don't really know what he does, though, apart from always taking those pictures." This is a refrain echoed even by his close friends—"I don't actually know much about him," more than one supposed intimate told me—but everyone in his orbit marvels at his ability to be seemingly everywhere and to know seemingly everyone. As his unlikely partner in the apple business, Ronald Perelman, says, "You never know who the fuck he's going to show up with." Pigozzi spends a lot of time sailing the world's less charted waters on his boat, the *Amazon Express,* an ex–fishing trawler converted into an unforgettable pastel-hued pleasure and adventure boat; it is bigger than most yachts, smaller than an ocean liner. (And for shorter excursions on water, he has two former military tenders.) The *Ama-*

Following spread: Brigitte Lacombe, *Jean Pigozzi, Villa Dorane, Cap d'Antibes, France,* 2010

zon Express is also a metaphor for the man: colorful, big, and always on the move. As another friend, Lord Jacob Rothschild, puts it, "Johnny doesn't want to tether himself. He's a kind of ambient human being in every sense."

From Wall Street to Silicon Valley, Hollywood to Paris and London, Planet Pigozzi is better connected than Verizon. *Large* is the operative word. Large guy, large portfolio, large art collections, large inventory of homes (apartments in New York, Paris, London, and Geneva; a fantastically situated villa in Cap d'Antibes, in the South of France; and a brand-new acropolis in Panama), large Rolodex, large "little black book," large sense of humor, large fan club of loyal friends . . . a very large life. Another thing that's striking, though, is how little he has been written about. Pigozzi has been clever on that score, mostly keeping himself out of the press other than as a peripheral figure, a sidekick to the people who run, or sex up, the universe. There he is with Steve Jobs, Jann Wenner, Arki Busson. Now he's off with Rupert Murdoch, or out with Bono, or hanging with Roman Abramovich and Larry Gagosian at one of the art circus's big-top events. Or laughing it up with Michael Douglas in Cannes, or some grande dame in London, or a politician in Paris, a princess in Panama, a knockout date in New York—enough of the latter to make Hugh Hefner look abstinent.

Because Pigozzi's own photographs are often of his famous friends, at play and at rest—and sometimes he's in them, too—there has been an assumption by those who know him only as a picture taker that he's a dilettante paparazzo, a second fiddle to the main players. Not so. A sharp investor with a keen eye for culture and a restless intelligence, he has lived the kind of improbable life that his favorite directors, Federico Fellini and Stanley Kubrick, might have wanted to steal from for their movies. "If I had done what I was programmed to do," Pigozzi told me, "I would now be sitting in a car factory looking at the sizes of wheels, or wondering how to get credit to start a new factory in

Russia." Instead, with his fingers in almost too many pies to count, and not all of them purely for profit or for fun, he goes his own way. For instance, he has amassed a unique collection of contemporary art from sub-Saharan Africa, the largest such personal collection in the world, and he just finished construction on a state-of-the-art scientific facility on an island he owns in Panama that has oceanographers drooling. Part twenty-first-century Renaissance man, part contemporary caveman, Pigozzi is a living exception to the supposed rule that "they just don't make 'em like that anymore."

There they were: magisterial, magnificent asses, just like in Rubens's or Botero's paintings. But these asses were dressed in the latest threads, size twelve to twenty-six, including newspaper-print leggings (fifteen dollars), flower-patterned short shorts (twenty-two dollars), T-shirt dresses (twenty-four dollars), and "skinny" jeans (thirty-four dollars). Jean Pigozzi was in heaven. He had invited a group of us to join him on an excursion to Bay Plaza, a mall in the Bronx, for the grand opening of a new Fashion to Figure store, part of a fast-growing clothing chain in the New York and New Jersey area geared to women who need bigger sizes than can be found on most racks. Pigozzi signed on as an investor a couple of years ago, and the minute we walked in it was clear he knew he was onto a good thing. The excitement was written all over his open face—a face that is up there with Chaplin's, Laurel's, and Hardy's for expressiveness—and it was catching.

Pigozzi himself is no toothpick. He is six foot four and lately takes a size XXL (down from XXXL after a recent diet). So he knows something about walking out of regular stores empty-handed because he can't find anything that fits him. It was probably out of necessity, and not just desire and taste, that Pigozzi found his own signature look. Let's put it this way: He hasn't landed on any best-dressed lists yet. A queen of New York society whispered to me, incredulously, "You know he dresses the way he does on purpose!" He veers toward a sort of collage of styles, a blend of Africa, prep school, hip-hop, and Peter Pan (the attitude, not the collar). For dress-up, he is not a stranger to a tux, and they've known him for decades on Savile Row. He is also a big fan of Jimmy Jazz, a store on 125th Street in Harlem, where the X's in the XL's multiply exponentially and, he explains, "you can get your name written on a belt that lights up."

The day before the Bronx opening he'd told me about a conversation he'd had with Tom Ford, and just conjuring the visual of the two of them—Ford crisper than a potato chip in his usual black and white; Pigozzi comfier than a goose-down pillow in, say, a custom-made long-sleeved lavender J. Crew polo shirt and booger green cargo pants—made me laugh. Pigozzi reported, "I said, 'Tom, I went to your shop. I walked around. I couldn't buy a handkerchief. Nothing!' Tom said, 'You know why? I don't want big fat guys like you in my shop.' I said, 'Okay, that's fine.' But I think he's making a mistake, because big guys like me have the money." Pigozzi has been putting that money where his mouth is, not just by investing in Fashion to Figure but also by making like a designer and launching his own menswear line, LimoLand, for which he serves as creative director.

Pigozzi says his inspiration for LimoLand was making clothes "for my peers, myself, my clan, the people I've been with for the last thirty years." Which is probably why his original slogan for the brand was "Street Wear for Rich Old Men." I loved that tagline, because it had humor and self-awareness, which is unusual for fashion, but the safer, vaguer, more commercial "Live to Create" has replaced it. LimoLand, which opened its first store in the States this past summer, in the Meatpacking District in Manhattan, has evolved into a company that wants to appeal to a broad range of sizes and ages and types. When Usher—rich but definitely not old—dropped by the new store, Pigozzi sent me a proud e-mail.

I watched Pigozzi work with a fitting model while putting together the fall collection. Though backed up by some real pros, Pigozzi was no slouch when it came to knowing what worked and what didn't in the clothes. The details—the line of the seams on a pair of pants or the way a collar sits—are important to him. So is a sense of flash and wit: One of the line's signature colors is magenta, and one of the house prints, named "the Hedge Fund," is made up of symbols for various global currencies.

Back in the Bronx, Pigozzi was certainly getting a lot of enjoyment out of the scene at Fashion to Figure. He liked the fact that the shopping experience provides its customers with a genuine sense of relief and satisfaction. With glee he pointed to the changing rooms, which are around twice the size of the norm, and have extra-large mirrors. You wouldn't have thought we were in the middle of a historic recession: This joint was hopping. The local pizza place delivered a mountain of pies. Gone in a gulp. That you don't see at Hermès. *Ka-ching* went the cash registers.

The brains behind the outfit, the brothers Nicholas and Michael Kaplan—who also happen to be the great-grandsons of Lane Bryant (née Lena Himmelstein), the godmother of "plus size" fashion—were kvelling that Pigozzi was so pleased. He happily observed that "usually you hold your stomach in, but here you can put it out."

This is not a guy who is easy to pigeonhole. Perelman offers this explanation of Pigozzi's success as an investor, which also speaks to who he is as a social creature: "Johnny's got good judgment and a sense of what makes sense. And he's got a lot of friends. If somebody offers him a deal to make chocolate pudding in Nigeria, he can pick up the phone and in two calls get to the minister of food and agriculture in Nigeria and find out if there's a market for it. It's a combination of his own sense and intuition and gut and judgment coupled with his ability to get to the source of an answer faster than anybody else."

He has another natural advantage, which attracts people to him: As Brett Ratner, the movie director, puts it, Pigozzi is "pathologically happy." This wasn't always so. Pigozzi's early life, while comfortable, sounds wretched. He grew up in Paris as the only son (along with two sisters) of Henri Théodore Pigozzi, a dominating, tough father from Turin, who worked his way up the car-business ladder, selling Fiats in France, until he hit the jackpot by launching the Simca car company in the early 1930s. Decades later, the homely Simca, no longer in production, looks like a cartoon of an automobile, but there was nothing funny about its Everyman popularity at its height, in the 1950s and 1960s. (The name was an acronym for a boring corporate parent: Société Industrielle de Mécanique et Carrosserie Automobile.)

"It was hard to argue with my father," Pigozzi remembers. His mother, Loisette, also from Turin, upheld the father's rule, so there was no place at home to hide. She oversaw a household that was a paradigm of French bourgeois tastes and manners, Sisleys and Renoirs included. School was no fun, either. The Jesuits who ran the Saint-Louis-de-Gonzague school, one of the best in Paris, clearly failed the young boy. "The first tongue I ever had in my mouth was a Jesuit priest's," he says today with a shudder.

As an adult, Pigozzi sees his dyslexia as a tool that has enabled his mind to wander productively from project to project, but it didn't serve him well at school. "They said I was lazy. The head of discipline beat me with his cane on my ass, and it really hurt." At home there was more hell to pay. He remembers, "My father was a powerful businessman in France by then, and in my same class was the son of the minister of industry, who was a much better student than me. My father would come home and say, 'How could you not do well? It's embarrassing for me!'"

In 1964, when Pigozzi was twelve, his dad dropped dead of a heart attack; the youngster was shipped off to boarding school in Normandy, which he hated just as much as the Jesuit school. He ultimately earned his French baccalaureate from the Lycée Janson in Paris, and then he had the last laugh. He got into Harvard. The story is fantastic. He explains, "I did terribly on my SATs. But I had an interview with a very nice man who ran the Irving Trust Bank in Paris. I went to see him in his big office, and I had my little suit on. He asked, 'Oh, Mr. Pigozzi, where do you come from in Italy?' I said, 'I come from Torino.' 'Okay,' he says, 'I'm going to ask you two questions. If you answer these two questions properly I'm going to get you into Harvard. What is the best restaurant in Torino?' I said, 'It is probably Gatto Nero, the Black Cat.' 'Okay. And when is the season for truffles?' I said, 'October–November.' He said, 'Okay, I'll get you into Harvard,' and I got into Harvard because of truffles. So I always respect truffles."

On his first day at Harvard, in the fall of 1970, he hit a snag. Due to a lost-in-translation error, he'd been registered instead at Radcliffe, as Miss Jean Pigozzi. Once that was sorted out, life got a lot more interesting for him. At Harvard he discovered his own artistic sensibilities, and the transformation of "Johnny," as all his friends call him, began. Paul Josefowitz, an old college chum, remembers Pigozzi as an initially uptight, old-world character: "He was the only guy out of a class of sixteen hundred to wear a jacket and tie to class—it's hard to believe looking at him today." Maybe it was Pigozzi's dyslexia that led him to choose Visual and Environmental Studies as his major, and as a means to find a niche at school and in life, one that was far from his father's. (Sports—no way, not then, not now, apart from swimming.) He became a fixture in the film department; he had also brought his old Leica along with him—given to him at age twelve by his father, shortly before he died—and began using it to document his daily life. "He would record everything that entered his mouth," Josefowitz says. "So it would be the pizza, the pizza in his mouth, the plate with the left-over pizza—every single meal, every little snack, was recorded."

It was all in perfect sync with the experimental, conceptual art that had gained attention by the late 1960s, work focused on the body and identity. This personal approach became a foundation for Pigozzi's pictures, and it's what separates them from the snaps of party photographers or paparazzi. Pigozzi's pictures have a vivid, vital energy; they're real fly-on-the-wall stuff. Elton John, who is frequently captured by Pigozzi's camera, calls him "an upscale Weegee." The comparison with the *New York Daily News* photographer, who was so obsessed with photographing crimes, accidents, and fires that he'd chase ambulances, police cars, and fire engines, gets at the rough-and-tumble, "scene of the crime" spirit that Pigozzi brings to his work—a traffic-accident pull that can be hard to look away from. Other Pigozzi pictures draw you in with their charm, such as his 1994 image from Venice of Gianni Agnelli and Jimmy Goldsmith, both mentors of his, wrapped up against the weather in their winter coats and shooting the breeze like two yentas. My favorite is a photograph taken on Pigozzi's boat in St. Barth's in 1991, of Larry Gagosian, Charles Saatchi, and Leo Castelli lounging in bathing suits and looking conspiratorial. Talking art-world domination?

Another touchstone for Pigozzi's work, as his friend June Newton (Helmut's widow) notes, is Jacques-Henri Lartigue, the French photographer who at the turn of the last century so casually yet perceptively captured the leisure classes at play along the Côte d'Azur with their cars, their prop planes, their toys, their sense of entitlement, and their optimism. Pigozzi covers the same beat on a global scale and, like Lartigue, is playing with his camera more than working with it. The mystery surrounding Lartigue was how this untaught young boy, who snapped many of his most unforgettable pictures by age twelve, could have taken so many all-seeing images. Pigozzi is not untaught, and he is not unsophisticated—he's the exact opposite—but he has maintained a sense of fun and play in his work and life. Sometimes he even sounds as if he's a kindred spirit to the pubescent Lartigue, as when we were chatting about the fact that we'd both recently lost weight and improved our respective blood pressures. He added, "You know? My little thing works even better." And, yes, by "thing" he meant his penis. Charming self-deprecation is one of his specialties.

Back in college, Pigozzi says, he was "no lady-killer." Nor was he content to hang around Cambridge and do the kinds of things that college students do. Rock 'n' roll, yes, but no drugs or booze; thirty years later this is still true, apart from a baba au rhum here or there. What he's addicted to is charismatic people, and he found plenty of them in New York City, where he'd often head during his Harvard years. His crash pad, the Lexington Avenue apartment of Delphine Rattazzi, an old friend from Europe and a fourth-generation member of the Agnelli clan, had lots of hipsters milling around and gave him a head start—it wasn't long before he'd become pals with the likes of Jann Wenner and Lorne Michaels. "Johnny had this charisma," remembers Josefowitz. "I think we were still in college and I was visiting him at the family residence in Cap d'Antibes. I'd arrived a day earlier. Johnny gets there and says, 'I met John Lindsay'—who at the time was New York's Mayor Lindsay—'on the plane, and he's coming for lunch tomorrow.' And he did. Lindsay was a busy, mature man, and yet Johnny had this strange ability to make people want to be with him."

Naturally, Pigozzi was drawn to Andy Warhol's Factory, a hub of all things cool and creative. Warhol thought Pigozzi had a lot of potential in the dating department and tried to fix him up with his favorite transgender star, Candy Darling. Pigozzi remembers, "I'd say, 'Andy, you have to have a limit.' Andy would go, 'Oh come on, she's so sweet!'" Warhol may not have succeeded in getting Pigozzi to squire Miss Darling out and about, but he did show the younger man how to be free about taking photographs, and that you could navigate life with a camera around your neck. Like Warhol, Pigozzi, for all his skill as a schmoozer, has a fundamental shy streak, and the camera is a great icebreaker.

Another mentor, and perhaps a more serviceable one in the dating department, was Ahmet Ertegun, the cofounder of Atlantic Records. He took Pigozzi under his wing in New York, and the two hit the town together, from fancy dinner parties to strip joints. Ertegun taught Pigozzi that business can be fun, but it was his lessons in the birds and the bees that brought out the Don Juan in Pigozzi. "When we were kids we thought if a woman sleeps with you it's an incredible sacrifice," Pigozzi says. "Ahmet said, 'Forget about it. They like it as much as you do'—which was a huge eye-opener for me." And Pigozzi's eyes have been open ever since.

When he turned twenty-one, in 1973, he received a portion of his inheritance and immediately began proving his mettle as an investor. (The inheritance was structured so that Pigozzi's money would come to him in stages.) Josefowitz recalls, "He was one of the first guys, if not the first one, to put together a little fund of funds for himself, of hedge-fund guys. Nobody was talking about hedge funds, and Johnny was right in there from the beginning." By the eighties, he had found his way to the center of the financial labyrinth, one introduction leading to another. He started off well by handing $250,000 to George Soros to invest around 1977. Another guru was Intel's Max Palevsky, who helped Pigozzi with lucrative high-tech investments in the eighties. Paul Tudor Jones, Louis Bacon, Stevie Cohen, Bruce Kovner—you name them, Pigozzi eventually invested with them. (I asked him flat out how much money he had to play with when he started investing, and he told me, "Somewhere between five and ten million dollars.") Odyssey Partners, led by Leon Levy and Jack Nash, performed particularly well for Pigozzi, giving him a 20 percent return for five years in the 1980s, and really secured his fortune. Ben Rosen's venture partnership, Sevin

Rosen, which backed high-tech companies such as Lotus, Compaq, and Silicon Graphics, helped to multiply it. Of course, all roads in the new technology led to Steve Jobs, whom Pigozzi encountered by the early 1980s, when Jobs was just getting Apple off the ground. Decades later Jobs and Pigozzi are still talking, texting, and getting together. (Pigozzi's friendships are marathons.)

In the early nineties, Pigozzi made another adventurous foray, this time into publishing, when he and his friend Charles Saatchi bought *Spy* magazine, the brash satirical monthly cofounded by Kurt Andersen, Tom Phillips, and Graydon Carter, the editor of this magazine. As Susan Morrison, another *Spy* editor (now at *The New Yorker*), remembers it, "We were a bunch of scrappy public school kids, largely middle-class. When Pigozzi appeared on the scene, none of us had ever really seen anything like it. He was this languorous European dressed in pajama tops with all these houses everywhere, so we had to keep track of what felt like dozens of different fax numbers for him." If anything, Pigozzi was precisely the kind of over-the-top character that *Spy* liked to poke fun at, so it was either brave or clever of him that he was drawn to the magazine. Unfortunately, this was one investment that didn't pay off: *Spy* shuttered in March 1994 (though it was later published under new ownership for a few years before closing again).

While Pigozzi took a bath in 2008 like everyone else—and blames his own greed—he is not one of those investors who ask no questions. He does his homework and sweats the details. (At *Spy*, that meant offering a retroactively hilarious, exacting faxed critique of Sharon Stone's lighting, makeup, and upper anatomy as displayed in a cover photo.) He always keeps up with new technologies and concepts. To apply an art-world term to business, he's an avant-gardist. Newer investments have included Facebook and Second Life. Also recently added to his e-mail address book is Jack Dorsey, the cofounder and chairman of Twitter. Dorsey told me, "I have a lot of conversations with people around new ideas and technology. Johnny was instantly comfortable enough to show his excitement, which is rare."

Pigozzi always credits two other mentors—both of whom, like Ertegun, he befriended when he was in his twenties—for showing him that, while no detail is too small to worry about, life should be lived as large as possible. One was the stylish, patriarchal head of Fiat, Italy's Gianni Agnelli, he of the wristwatch-worn-over-the-shirt-cuff fame; the other was the British tycoon Sir James Goldsmith, he of the famous bon mot "A man who marries his mistress creates a vacancy." Although they were both billionaire businessmen, both Renaissance men, both busy in the women department, and both old enough to be Pigozzi's father, they were very different types, and they imparted different passions to Pigozzi. For Agnelli the top of the list would have to be a love of boats and art. For Goldsmith, unorthodox domestic arrangements and a commitment to land preservation and the environment.

"I spent years laughing with Jimmy," says Pigozzi. "I was a junior partner in some investments we had together. We'd go to a meeting and afterward in the elevator he'd ask, 'Did I look too Jewish? Did I scream too much?'" That self-consciousness mixed with humor would appeal to Pigozzi. Some of his friends believe that he is a snob, but the Pigozzi style is relaxed and easy; what he looks down his nose at is pomp. "For me to be pompous is the most horrible thing in the world. It's like putting a wall around you. It screws you up. You'd better be willing to change your views or adapt and be modern."

He talks about modernity, but when it comes to his taste in design, he could be a postmodern poster child, as evidenced by his seven homes (including the *Amazon Express,* on which he spends a few months a year). Each of his apartments—in Paris, London, New York, and Geneva (his official residence for tax purposes)—is situated in a historically significant building (among them the Hotel des Artistes in New York and the Albany in London), but the interiors and furniture, designed or overseen by the late Ettore Sottsass, flirt and play with tradition. A friend of Pigozzi's who is not sold on the aesthetics of the Memphis design group, of which Sottsass was a cofounder, describes Pigozzi's homes in New York and London as "how a twelve-year-old would decorate if he had money." Sottsass would have taken that as a compliment, and if ever there was an ideal client for Sottsass's postmodern vision, it is Pigozzi. The profusion of styles and periods, the embrace of a broad color palette and pattern, and the emphasis on play, which were integral to the Memphis philosophy, are in perfect accord with Pigozzi's ADD brain, multifaceted lifestyle, and youthful taste. He's also a boy who likes his toys. Each of his homes has drums and keyboards at the ready. One can just picture the folks upstairs yelling, "Turn it down!" Marco Zanini, an architect who worked on many of Pigozzi's houses, offers a bit of armchair psychology: "Everything was forbidden in his horrible childhood. So when he grew up, he said, 'Screw you. I'm going to buy all the toys in the world.'"

In a similar vein, Ronald Perelman notes that "the house in Antibes is Johnny's most lavish toy," and in one way it is a key to the man. The house, known to the locals as "La Dorane," was originally built by Pigozzi's father, in 1953; stocked with rote antiques, it had the same well-mannered, bourgeois look of the family home in Paris. Johnny took years to give it his much lighter spin. Zanini recalls, "When we first started to work on La Dorane, Johnny's mother was still alive and he wanted to be careful about not upsetting her by doing these crazy things to it. He wanted her to live there in peace."

Loisette died in the 1990s, at which point the transformation of La Dorane began. Until then Pigozzi had focused on renovating the guesthouse. The symbolism is rich, if one is aware of the secret to his upbringing; one might say he understood only too well the semiotics of being a guest. The plot twist is like something out of a grand nineteenth-century novel, and it is something that Pigozzi himself only discovered when he was about eleven years old. Henri and Loisette had brought Johnny up as their own, but he learned that his biological mother was his father's mistress, the daughter of a distinguished, wealthy *notaire* (a lawyer-notary), who lived in the city of Versailles. (Pigozzi says his father had mistresses all over the world.) Pigozzi's biological mother was around eighteen years old when she gave birth to Johnny. Loisette was unable to bear children so the mistress became the childbearer for all three Pigozzi kids. It was Loisette who laid out these facts for Johnny, before his father died—one can only imagine the young boy's complex feelings. Today he says, "It's true, and I have no shame whatsoever." (This is the first time he has discussed his birth mother publicly.) He only met his biological mother, who he says died about ten years ago, three or four times. "She was good-looking, very distinguished," he adds. Maybe in our age, when the discussion of surrogate birth mothers is so much more open, in part thanks to gay couples who want children, stigmas about these sorts of things will start to ease up, but when Pigozzi was growing up his parentage was very hush-hush. Mistresses were fine. But if a woman could not have children it was treated like a blot on her reputation.

It's hard to know whether Pigozzi's own amorous goings-on with women are new or old, modern or postmodern, or fodder for Freud. One person who has worked with him describes him as "an Italian Pepé Le Pew." One woman who is no longer a paramour said that many of his exes form a kind of sorority: friends with one another, and still close to Johnny—Delta Delta Pigozzi. The lovefest isn't unanimous, though. There were those who said they "just didn't get it." One such woman e-mailed about her "relationship" with Pigozzi: "One date. He said he would like to date me again but I would have to give up smoking and drinking—a no-brainer, from my POV. . . ."

Pigozzi is open about his rules and regulations: "I don't like dirty. That's why I hate cigarettes. A little bit of alcohol is okay, but no drugs. And I like to sleep alone because I wake up, I walk around, I bring my computer with me to bed, I have a great time." But what if that offends a partner? I wondered. "Once they've slept a couple of nights with me, they hear me snore, they're happy to move" to a guest room.

I was struck by the individualism and intelligence of many of Pigozzi's exes, which says something about the man. His intimates cite Princess Olga of Greece as the woman who has come closest to being Mrs. P. The couple dated in the early 2000s, but "the angels wept the day they went their separate ways," says a close friend. Pigozzi himself admits, "We were soul mates." The consensus seems to be that the relationship imploded because, for Pigozzi, there were to be no trips to the altar and no baby carriages. (Princess Olga subsequently married and has a family; the two remain friends.)

Some of his pals do worry that Pigozzi has not tied the knot—yet. "Why is he fearful of getting married?" Martha Stewart asks. "I've told him he should get married. For a while I even harbored the idea that he'd be a fun son-in-law. I could have pruned the trees [at his home] in Antibes. Oh my God, they need it so desperately!" Other friends, such as Mick Jagger, are amused by, and amusing about, Pigozzi's confirmed-bachelor status. When I asked Jagger which of Pigozzi's personality traits is most surprising, the musician laughed and imitated the voice and tone of a scandalized old biddy: "'Never married!' That's what they used to say in people's obituaries in England when they were gay"—one of the few things Pigozzi is not. Speaking of which, I bat on Gertrude Stein's team, and love my partner, so the following point is not to be taken too personally, but it makes sense that women fall for the guy. His frankness about his own foibles makes him so human in a European or Woody Allenesque way.

That, and how much fun he can be (as he himself would admit, the money doesn't hurt, either), is a key to why so many people, of all sexes, enjoy him.

Others in Pigozzi's circle are in awe of his approach to dating. The director Brett Ratner, no sluggard in this department, says, "When you're a single guy, Johnny's the ultimate guy to enjoy your single life with."

It's a status he appears to guard very carefully; he certainly was intent on making sure that I wrote nothing in this article to suggest he was closed for business. This e-mail, for instance (I've concealed names to protect the innocent):

Dear Ingrid:

It's come to my attention that you are under the impression that [attractive young woman No. 1] is my girlfriend. While I'm very close to [attractive young woman No. 1] and greatly admire her many talents, [attractive young woman No. 1] is not my official girlfriend. For the record, I have many "great lady friends" and many "old lady friends." I do not have an official girlfriend at the moment.

Yours,

Jean

A few days later I received a sequel:

Dear Ingrid,

Yesterday I got a panicked phone call from [attractive young woman No. 2].

She heard through the grapevine that supposedly you are saying she is my girlfriend in the *Vanity Fair* article and she got very panicked.

[Attractive young woman No. 2] is a very good friend of mine, as is [attractive young woman No. 1], and many other girls in my life, and I do not have an official girlfriend.

I hope I'm not being pushy, but I would really like this point to be accurate in this exciting article.

Yours,

Jean

Wealthy globe-trotters typically cross paths with eager bevies of potential "great lady friends," and Pigozzi insists that his is a discriminating eye: "A lot of these girls have a goal in life to find a rich guy. I can smell it from a mile away. They won't catch me! I know what they look like. They come with their little Kelly bag and their Rolex and the Louboutin shoes that are slightly too sexy. Shove off! Do you think I'm going to be the next sucker here?"

Like Howard Hughes, a kind of avatar for Pigozzi—Hughes was big on women and memos, too—Pigozzi has an obsession with "cleanliness." For one thing, he avoids door handles in public toilets like the plague. Apparently this germophobia was inherited. Pigozzi says, "I remember my father in his bathroom. He used to rub his entire body with alcohol, including his penis, which I tried doing. It burns beyond. I had to jump in the shower!" And you thought you were going to read about just another rich guy.

His friends like to dish about Pigozzi's parsimony. You will never read about his spending an obscene amount of money on an artwork, and when it comes to food, diners are just fine with him (apart from the trauma of those bathroom door handles). When in Paris he drives his 1974 gray Volvo—no air-conditioning, no electric windows, just a wave from every doorman at every restaurant in town; they all know Pigozzi. He can be generous with friends, but he can also be tight. Brett Ratner was so amused by the sign on the refrigerator on Pigozzi's yacht that he photographed it: MR. P BOUGHT JUST ABOUT ALL THE FOOD IN THIS FRIDGE FOR HIS CONSUMPTION ONLY.

One of his nearest and dearest made me promise not to attribute this quote, but said, "He can be mean to the help. If he asks for something and it doesn't come in time, he doesn't tolerate it." But the same friend points out how quickly Pigozzi will snap out of a fit; after all, he is Italian.

It's not just staff who have been on the receiving end of Pigozzi's short fuse. Chris Blackwell, the founder of Island Records, who is as close to Pigozzi as anyone, experienced his impatience firsthand in the early eighties, when the two of them started a little software business. Blackwell remembers, "I had no grasp of what we were doing, and it was difficult because he was very impatient. It was a miserable experience for him, and for me. We stopped it. But there was no lingering fallout or bad vibes." I've noticed, too, how good-natured Pigozzi is about fights. Still, another acquaintance adds this warning: "He's fun and he's good company, but you don't want to be downwater from him."

I had asked Blackwell what it is that really drives Pigozzi. Money? Women? Power? Creativity? Blackwell replied, "I would say he has the desire to make a mark." In fact, he may end up making a few. Perhaps the first sign that Pigozzi was in it for something lasting was the ambitious collection of African art that he started to build in the early nineties, after he saw the "Magiciens de la Terre" exhibition of non-Western art at the Pompidou Center, in Paris, in 1989. The show so impressed him that he hired André Magnin, who had curated it, to help him put together a collection. The deal was that Magnin would be the scout (germophobes don't "do Africa"), finding the work and then presenting it to Pigozzi, who would give the thumbs-up or -down. The collection, at present made up of ten thousand–plus pieces, most of which are stored in Geneva, has become widely renowned; portions have been exhibited in museums in the States and Europe. It was built during the years when the boundaries around European and American art were coming down, and people in the Western art world were realizing that they'd better start learning about what was happening in China, India, and Africa. Diane von Furstenberg, a close friend of Pigozzi's, says, "Johnny's African collection is the only collection in the world that I wish I had thought of." Some critics complain that the collection is too superficial and, in some choices, clichéd. (There was also a lawsuit over ownership issues involving family members of the deceased Malian photographer Seydou Keïta—whom Pigozzi helped to make famous—which is now settled.) Regardless, as with his incursions into Silicon Valley, Pigozzi was unmistakably ahead of the game, although some pals joke that he really got into African art because it was a bargain compared with the Basquiats, Koonses, and Warhols so coveted by Pigozzi's art-collecting billionaire friends. (And if he ever wants to sell off his African works, he could now turn a nifty profit.) Lately he has been training his eye, and bargain hunting, in a whole new direction—contemporary Japanese art, another undervalued corner of the art world. Not for long.

Having started out as such a rotten student, Pigozzi has certainly made up for lost time. He says he likes to learn something new every five years: "I learned about hedge funds. I learned about leverage funds. I learned about the Internet. Now I'm learning about fashion, and I'm learning about ecology." To the latter end he has made a contribution to the field by building Liquid Jungle Lab, the scientific facility in Panama, at the bottom of a mountain atop which sits his just-completed futuristic home. The location is an idyllic jungle-covered island of around 270 acres that was originally part of an estimated 6,000-acre purchase of land along Panama's Pacific coast that Pigozzi made in the late 1990s, originally with Daniel Wolf, a private art dealer. Pigozzi's whopping construction project, ringing up at around thirty million dollars thus far, started out as a collaboration between Marco Zanini and Simón Vélez, a Colombian architect who has a way with bamboo. Vélez walked after a couple of years in a bust-up with Pigozzi, leaving Zanini alone at the helm.

Liquid Jungle Lab—which is run in collaboration with the Woods Hole Oceanographic Institution and the Smithsonian Tropical Research Institute—has been configured like a small village, including lab, dormitories, and infirmary, all under a humongous, breathtaking bamboo roof. It presents an extraordinary opportunity for scientists to explore the forest and the ocean and their interdependency because Pigozzi's spot in Panama is even richer than the Galápagos in terms of eco- and biodiversity. But Pigozzi has made it clear he's no Medici: The deal was that he would build the lab and occasionally fund individual projects, but, in general, the scientists have to make it a self-sustaining enterprise, getting their own grants and paying their own way.

Dave Gallo is the director of special projects at Woods Hole and one of the scientists involved with Liquid Jungle Lab. A heavy hitter in his field, he is thrilled by his working relationship with Pigozzi. He confessed, "I thought it was going to be a perfect storm: Pigozzi, who's impatient and demanding and driven; and science, which is plodding. But one day Pigozzi said, 'I have to tell you, every day I'm with these people I learn something new.' Holy cow! I had felt a little responsible bringing these young researchers down there and leaving them in the hands of the monster. It turned out they grew to love the monster, and the monster grew to love them. Forever we've been looking for the next Cousteau, the next person who can win the confidence of the public and the money guys, whose passion is deep, and I see that in Johnny Pigozzi." Will the wet suit be by LimoLand?

The mountaintop Panama house—more like a personal acropolis—is, in its way, just as impressive an achievement, a testament to Pigozzi's imagination, will, and bank account. The compound, featuring sweeping, generous spaces, many of them shimmering with color, measures around sixty thousand square feet and includes a main pavilion, a personal pavilion for Pigozzi, three guesthouses, and a separate kitchen building. The primary construction materials—steel, concrete, glass, and bamboo—are not necessarily ground-breaking, but putting them all together at a remote location required feats normally reserved for pharaohs building pyramids—twenty-first-century pharaohs, since the builders had to install two monorails to schlep materials up the 450-foot mountain. But now that the compound is finished, the construction saga has become legend among the locals. The fact that the complex changes colors at night, thanks to the LED lights in the polycarbonate walls, only serves to give it even more of a science-fiction, otherworldly vibe.

Pigozzi's Panama project is in some sense his answer to the extraordinary hideaway and visionary conservation effort created in the eighties by his old mentor Jimmy Goldsmith on Mexico's Pacific coast. The Panama complex has triggered the imaginations of Pigozzi's friends, too. Christian Louboutin loves the idea of his pal as a character in a James Bond film. He says, "The first time I went [to Panama] I thought, This is very *Dr. No.* I would not be surprised one day to hear that something was hiding in the belly of the island, and that Mr. Johnny Pigozzi was trying to perfect some sort of weird thing to save the world." Pigozzi himself compares the saga of building his new home to Werner Herzog's classic 1982 film, *Fitzcarraldo.* In it, a huge steamboat is dragged on land over a mountain so that the partly mad, partly visionary title character can fulfill his dream of building an opera house and bringing Enrico Caruso to perform in what had been an impenetrable Amazonian jungle. Pigozzi says that when he saw Herzog's film he laughed. "Oh my God, that's me! I'm the same idiot." Can Pigozzi's future houseguests look forward to a night when the monkeys are howling, the iguanas are watching, and Jagger and Bono take it away? Hey, it's Pigozzi, so let's throw in Lady Gaga, too, and maybe a couple of plus-size shoppers from the Bronx. Keep an eye out for the photo.

Vanity Fair, December 2010

A Man of Darkness and Dreams

"What makes me so sad about Lee's killing himself is that there are so few people with that kind of talent mixed with that fury of originality. Now we have one less of the few who are amazing. Why did he have to go and do that?" wondered Sam Taylor-Wood, the British artist. She was throwing out the big question that has consumed the fashion world since the suicide of her buddy and sometime subject Alexander McQueen, the forty-year-old designer, known to his friends by his given first name, Lee. His body—a physique that he'd worried over and tried to sculpt at the gym—was found at 10:30 a.m., February 11, hanging in his wardrobe, by his housekeeper in the apartment he'd been renting in London's Mayfair, a far cry (and six or so miles) from the working-class East End neighborhood where he'd grown up. The tragedy was compounded in that it came just a week after the death of his beloved mother, Joyce, who at seventy-five had succumbed to an undisclosed illness. But even though McQueen's brutal act of self-annihilation ultimately did not surprise those who knew him best, and were aware of his dark moods and inner agonies, plenty about his death didn't add up.

After all, he'd been busy preparing for his autumn-winter ready-to-wear show in the days just before the tragedy. He'd been tweeting and texting his nearest and dearest, and apart from his obvious sadness about his mum, there wasn't anything particularly unusual about his actions or his messages. In retrospect, some of his pals say they see portents in how loving his greetings were, but even they caution that they may be reading too much into this. The photographer Steven Klein, who was close to the designer for years, found him to be in good shape at the lunch they had in London at Christmas. "He was very together, in great form," says Klein. "We made plans to do several new projects together."

McQueen had even put in a surprise appearance at a dinner for Tom Ford,

Derrick Santini, *Lee in His Studio,* 2006

given by *Vanity Fair*'s editor, Graydon Carter, at Harry's Bar in London on February 1. McQueen, who lived nearby, popped in uninvited; he sat at the bar, had a drink, chatted with Ford, and split. Ford had initiated the purchase of a majority stake in McQueen's label in 2000, when Ford was the guiding force at the Gucci Group, owned by the French luxury-brands company PPR, and thus was McQueen's old boss. So there was plenty of symbolism in this encounter. But then again, symbolism is everywhere in this story, as it was in the presentations of McQueen's collections.

At their best, these shows were feats of magic, drama, and the sheer beauty of high fashion. McQueen was a traditionalist and an avant-gardist both. He liked to provoke with his ideas and shock with his ability to create unforgettable, original, sometimes extremist, often breathtaking clothes. He designed for both sexes, and in between, but soared highest with the women. His signatures were strong shoulders, strong tailoring, and a love of the corset. His collections were so specific, so true to himself, and so visceral that they are easy to remember. It helps, too, that they earned nicknames nearly as evocative as the clothes themselves—"the Shipwreck Collection" (spring-summer 2003), "the Chess Collection" (spring-summer 2005), "the Hitchcock Collection" (autumn-winter 2005). Among the most memorable was the now iconic "Highland Rape Collection," from autumn-winter 1995 (one of his earliest shows, when he was starting out with his then-shoestring label), which mixed flesh-baring see-through material with eruptions of tartan, the clashes and juxtapositions intended as condemnation of England's historic bullying of Scotland. (The folklore: One model hit the catwalk with a visibly dangling tampon string. To this day McQueen's intimates aren't sure whether that was accidental or intentional.) The rawness may have been polished as time went on, but it never went away. "The *They Shoot Horses, Don't They?* Collection" (spring-summer 2004) was presented as if in a Depression-era dance hall, a marathon where the models had to dance till they dropped in dresses that started out as perfect specimens and ended up in tatters. "The Wolves Collection" (autumn-winter 2002) was shown at the Conciergerie, in Paris, where Marie Antoinette had been held before she was sent to the guillotine. The opening model came out in a lavender hooded leather cape, walking a couple of trained wolves on leashes. (I think I only imagined their howling.) McQueen was the king of metaphor.

The immediate reaction to his death reinforced the notion that his wasn't just another name on a label. Beyond the front-page stories and worldwide headlines, beyond the reports of his clothes' selling out in department stores, there were Diana-like tributes. Students, artists, and fans left farewell notes and bunches of flowers outside his boutiques in London, Milan, Los Angeles, and New York, all of which were shuttered after the news broke. (The designer Diane von Furstenberg was spotted adding a bouquet to the ones that had already been dropped off at his shop on Fourteenth Street in New York's Meatpacking District.) McQueen's death also coincided with the opening of New York Fashion Week, and there were nods to him in a number of the shows, including the beautifully elegiac opening of the Marc Jacobs presentation. No question: Alexander McQueen had become a name for the ages, the James Dean of fashion.

To call someone an artist in this milieu is tricky, because that can connote pretense, a rarefied air, a certain preciousness—all things that were not true of McQueen. But fashion has produced genuine artists, designers with deeply iconoclastic visions such as Charles James and the painter and sculptor Lucio Fontana, who made clothes and jewelry for a short while. Although McQueen was very much a fashion person, working with a fashion vocabulary, his clothes and presentations had a true art streak. He even behaved like an old-fashioned artist, never letting the fact that he worked for giant, powerful fashion corporations—first for LVMH, where he was installed in 1996 as the designer of Givenchy, and then for PPR—curb his creativity or freedom. This wasn't someone who'd suck up to the bosses or important editors or celebrities. Elton John, who befriended the designer and respected his talent, says,

"McQueen was never anybody's boy. He was never going to bow down and kiss ass to anyone, which made him rare in that world." He was freakish in terms of his natural abilities, too. Mark Lee, the highly respected former president of Gucci and Yves Saint Laurent (also owned by PPR), remembers, "Besides his eccentric vision, he really knew how to make and cut clothes. All the seamstresses, technicians, and product-development people who were around from the Gucci Group would talk about it all the time. He would just take a bolt of fabric and, in front of their eyes, would cut the pattern for his clothes. People said it was like watching Edward Scissorhands. There are not many designers around who can do that." Similarly, McQueen often displayed a fearless, tour-de-force way with materials. There was nothing too fine or too common for him: neoprene, plastic, crocodile, paper, rose petals, antique lace, lamé . . . there was no stopping him. The finale of his autumn-winter 2006 collection, a pale gray organza spiral ruffle dress, worn by Kate Moss, was as dreamy as it gets. That was highbrow McQueen; for lowbrow, look to his witty "bumster" pants from 1993—a feat of anatomical engineering described by one aficionada as "as low as you could go without having your trousers fall right down."

McQueen used to call himself an East End bloke, which was code for saying he was not born into the world of caviar, champagne, and fine cloth. On a couple of occasions I had what he called "a proper English lunch" with him (I remember picking out the kidney in my steak and kidney pie), and each time he wanted to discuss the painter Francis Bacon. The combinations of gruesomeness and beauty, of raw flesh, homoerotic desire, and highly sophisticated execution that Bacon brought to his painting are not so far away from the concerns and approaches of McQueen's work. There are personal parallels, too. I think of Bacon's predilection for sex with men who were streetwise and of his finding refuge in the old London gay subculture. I think of the fact that his lover took his own life in 1971, on the eve of the opening of Bacon's big retrospective in Paris, at the Grand Palais. (Camping it up, Bacon is supposed to have said, "Oh my dear, she's gone and committed Susan-cide.") For McQueen, too, a vociferously open gay man, there was an unforgettable combination of tough and fragile that was intrinsic to his emotional makeup. By all accounts, the designer's childhood, growing up in the 1970s and early 1980s, was like something out of *Billy Elliot*. His dad, Ronald, a taxi driver, reportedly had plans for his youngest child to become an electrician. (The designer had three sisters and two brothers.) McQueen, though, had fashion dreams, and as if that didn't already make him a misfit in his environment, he had to put up with early torture about his sexuality; in his later life he often spoke about having been taunted with the nickname "McQueer" when he was young. Throughout, his mother was his shield, his advocate, the parent who eventually turned up at his shows, believing in his talent and adoring him unconditionally. Their bond was unbreachable from beginning to end.

McQueen's formal education and professional rise are now part of fashion lore: the old-school tailoring training on Savile Row, where, as he later admitted and denied in equal measure, he had scrawled a punk-style slur—I AM A CUNT—inside the lining of a jacket being made for Prince Charles; the graduate fashion school training at Central Saint Martins College; the meteoric trajectory of his career as a designer, which saw him going from overnight sensation after his last student collection to taking the reins for his bumpy five-year tenure at Givenchy, to finally having a house of his own, as Virginia Woolf might say, and really stretching his wings as a designer, to the sad, sad end.

The search for an answer as to why McQueen decided he'd had enough is really a struggle to find meaning in an act of nihilism. But as an old friend of his said to me, McQueen's life was like an onion, and you have to peel away the layers to get to the center; it's a process that can sting and bring tears. There was the loneliness, no doubt made all the more visceral by his mother's death. Despite the surrogate family that McQueen created with a tiny clutch of fiercely close and protective friends—including Shaun Leane, the jewelry designer; Philip Treacy, the milliner; Daphne Guinness, the heiress, editor, and most daring dresser in fashion; Annabelle Neilson, a sort of sidekick; and Sam Gainsbury, who produced nearly all of McQueen's shows—he had no long-term Mr. It. People remember how he'd say he was unlucky in love: He'd had a failed marriage to George Forsyth (Kate Moss was a bridesmaid at the 2000 wedding), and in the last years he seems to have had on-and-off liaisons with men, some of whom he met online. (Word is there was at least one porn star, a so-called Mr. Stag. There was also an older East End gangster he had a longer romance with.) Then there was his well-known history with drugs, especially cocaine. He was open about his substance abuse, and I wouldn't be surprised if the autopsy told the same story when the results are released.

But it is my belief that all these traits were symptoms of something else. McQueen loved and collected art, and it is no coincidence that one of his favorite photographers was Joel-Peter Witkin, whose bleached and scratched images of masked figures, transsexuals, hermaphrodites, and corpses occupy a sometimes grim, sometimes joyous netherworld. The more one talks to those who knew McQueen, on and off the record, the deeper one goes, the clearer it becomes that what friends refer to as his "darkness" is where the truth of his death lies. Virginia Woolf and her struggle with depression is a kind of specter here. Sam Taylor-Wood says, "Lee would just sometimes go into this void, and we'd wait for him to resurface."

He was not the only one in his circle to have terrible bouts with deep depression. Isabella Blow, his over-the-top, born-to-the-manor-but-without-a-pot-to-piss-in pal, who had an unlimited clothing allowance at his company and was often credited with discovering McQueen when he was in art school, also committed suicide, with weed poison, on her third attempt.

When Blow died, in May 2007, McQueen dedicated his next show to her, but some say he was angry at her for taking her own life. The rub is that he leaves behind a similar sense of frustration. There was a suicide note—what McQueen wrote hasn't yet been disclosed—but it's likely no one will ever know his whole story. Some have speculated that he may have felt he was done in fashion, sure of his legacy, and that his suicide was a kind of deliberate statement to that effect. Or was it something more uncontrollable? Sam Gainsbury says, "I appreciate that some people who were close to him think it was purposeful. But I think Lee got to a really dark place and could not get out of it. It was in that instance on that night. On another day maybe he would have gone to sleep and gotten out of it."

People have commented on how, as the years went on, McQueen would disappear with lightning speed after his shows, rather than sticking around for the ritual backstage congratulations. "It always made me think of J. D. Salinger," says Kerry Youmans, one of McQueen's publicists. His suicide is perhaps the ultimate version of that impulse to withdraw. But PPR has announced that the McQueen business will continue. Fashion insiders have raised their carefully shaped eyebrows at the notion of replacing someone with so strong and individual a voice. McQueen's friends remember his infectious laugh, and I wonder, Could he be out there somewhere laughing now—maybe at the prospect of what will surely be a hard, hard search to fill his shoes? Or maybe in happiness that the line will go on?

I'm reminded of a show that McQueen did for autumn-winter 2007. It was known colloquially as "the Witches Collection" and was inspired by the fact that his mother, a genealogist, had discovered a relative who'd been a victim of the Salem witch trials. Like so many of McQueen's presentations, this one had a high element of performance art to it—and a theme of death. The venue was very dark, people had difficulty finding their seats, the show started very late, it was raining outside, and there was an all-around bad mood in the air. Editors, who normally worshipped at McQueen's feet, were yelling, "Who the fuck does he think he is? How dare he keep us all waiting like this?" The way people feel today, they'd be happy to wait for a much longer time to see one of his spectacles again, and they'd probably pay almost anything for his clothes.

Vanity Fair, April 2010

Hollywood's Rebel Belle

*I shambled after as usual as I've been doing all my life after people that interest me,
because the only people that interest me are the mad ones, the ones who are mad
to live, mad to talk, desirous of everything at the same time, the ones that never
yearn or say a commonplace thing . . . but burn, burn, burn like roman candles
across the night.*

—From the original manuscript of *On the Road,* by Jack Kerouac

There aren't enough of those kinds of mad ones these days. Not on the screen,
the stage, the page, or the gallery walls. Instead, watch the bowing down to
fame, money, and power, the capitulation to status. So rarely do we witness
a young artist, singer, or actor who wants to burn, burn, burn, to set off on a
new path that will inspire future generations, but who is also willing to suffer
the rod that comes with saying no to things as they are.

But this is not a cry for the good old days; there was no such thing anyway. It
is a call to remember what matters. Happily, every new generation still has a few
misfits who have sworn their own declarations of independence. One is Kristen
Stewart, the restless twenty-two-year-old actress best known to tens of millions of
fans as Bella Swan, offbeat heroine of the *Twilight* series. But Stewart will ingrain
herself even deeper in the public's consciousness in 2012 as she appears in a trio
of movies, beginning with this month's wham-bam *Snow White and the Huntsman* (Hollywood's second take this year on the old fairy tale) and continuing
with an adaptation of the hipster bible, *On the Road.* Topping them all, at least
at the box office, will be this November's grand *Twilight* finale, *Breaking Dawn 2.*

En route Stewart has gotten herself a bad rap for making the lives of talk-show

Hedi Slimane, *Portrait of Kristen Stewart,* Los Angeles, 2015

hosts, red-carpet photographers, and interviewers hell, because she can't, or won't, play the usual movie-star game. "Kristen doesn't know how to be in a popularity contest," says Sean Penn, who in 2006 directed the then sixteen-year-old actress in *Into the Wild*. Penn has nothing but praise for Stewart, whose brief performance in his film is unforgettable; he compares working with her to having a perfect day—blue sky, blue ocean—walk in the door. And when it came time to publicize his brave and beautiful film—a heartbreaking adaptation of Jon Krakauer's nonfiction book of the same title, about a young man's doomed search for an alternative to the commerce and corruption of modern life—Stewart did her best to rally and help shill the picture. But as Penn explains, "You can see Kristen generously trying to join the popularity contest when a movie is being publicized. She'll try to get on board, but her body language has a whole different dynamic." In other words, she's not about to get any Saleswoman of the Year awards anytime soon.

Stewart certainly isn't the first performer to take issue with the sideshow that comes with Hollywood success, but she's definitely the least afraid young female superstar to be so outspokenly critical of the system. Since the dawn of cinema, there's always been a pressure for movie stars to project the right image, especially the women, but the demands have gotten much more intense over the last twenty-five years, to the point where looking good at premieres and awards shows has become a nearly full-time job, with the performers often mere mannequins for product placement. And sadly, the actors and musicians often go along with it, against their own instincts, for fear of media retribution, such as landing on some dreaded worst-dressed list. God forbid. Not Stewart, who has gotten so used to her reputation as a snarler that she even laughs about it. She says, "My dad will be like, 'Oh, you could have smiled a little more.'"

Even that might not help. "People have decided how they are going to perceive her," says Robert Pattinson, her red-lipped Romeo in the *Twilight* films. "No matter how many times she smiles, they'll put in the one picture where she's not smiling." It's true, though, that despite her ravishing looks, she is not a ray of sunshine on the red carpet. Think thunderstorm, bolts of lightning. "I have been criticized a lot for not looking perfect in every photograph," she says. "I get some serious shit about it. I'm not embarrassed about it. I'm proud of it. If I took perfect pictures all the time, the people standing in the room with me, or on the carpet, would think, What an actress! What a faker! That thought embarrasses me so much that I look like shit in half my photos, and I don't give a fuck. What matters to me is that the people in the room leave and say, 'She was cool. She had a good time. She was honest.' I don't care about the voracious, starving shit eaters who want to turn truth into shit. Not that you can say that in *Vanity Fair*!"

For all that unease on the red carpet and at photo shoots, she has learned to love great fashion—"I never saw that coming," says Pattinson—especially when the designs represent true creative expression, or are, in her terms, "some cool shit." If she wears it, you can know she loves it. So, I wasn't surprised when I heard she'd become the "face" for Balenciaga's upcoming new fragrance. In fact, we sat down to talk for this article shortly after running into each other again at the Balenciaga fall 2012 fashion show, this past March, in Paris. (We had first met in 2006.)

A basket of bread and a plate of snails were plunked down at a corner table in the back of Le Duc, the restaurant where Stewart and I met for a lunchtime conversation. I had chosen the place, a Parisian institution with the freshest fish in town, because I thought the clientele would be way too snooty and advanced in age to know or care that Bella Swan was in their midst. (Also, I'd been dreaming about Le Duc's feather-light langoustines drowning in garlicky butter.) But neither of us was expecting an offering of snails from the waiter, and neither of us, as it happened, was an aficionado. Stewart gave me a wary look of "You go first." I confessed, "I'm a bit scared. You?" She rose to the occasion. "I feel like I have to go for it. I'd feel rude not to," she said. She had on jeans, a black tank top, and a drop-dead-gorgeous black leather Balenciaga jacket, but I'd say it was more Lady Sybil from *Downton Abbey* opposite me, the manners were so gracious. A (large) gulp of white wine, a tear of bread, and down the hatch slipped Stewart's first snail.

And her last. "Pretty good," she declared. "Though I just don't want to eat a whole plate of them." I laughed. Throughout our conversations for this piece, there was something so endearing, so human, about her combination of bravado, kindness, self-preservation, self-assertion, and revved-up fierceness that I found her cheering. Of course, her idealism and drive to tell it as she sees it—the voracious, starving shit eaters be damned!—could be just a product of her youth. She could grow up to be another narcissistic Hollywood snore, but my sense is that's not in the cards here.

One might think Stewart would be down with the package-oriented ways of the entertainment business, since she's a homegrown Hollywood product. Her mother, Jules Mann-Stewart, is a respected script supervisor who has just directed her first film, about sexual politics in prison. Kristen's father, John Stewart, is also in the business, having worked as a producer and stage manager on TV specials and reality shows. Her brother, Cameron, is a grip—a lighting and rigging technician.

Stewart, growing up in the San Fernando Valley, learned the drill about a life in film and TV early, and just as early caught the bug to do it. Her dutiful mother schlepped her to auditions but was not gung ho. She'd tell Kristen, "I work with these kids—they're crazy people. You're not one of them." In fact, Kristen's earliest stabs at job hunting were a misery. "I wasn't doing anything but smiling for the camera," she remembers of trying out for commercials when she was eight. "You can feel that the adults aren't getting what they want no matter how old you are."

Stewart, who shunned girlie-girl outfits, didn't fit in in a lot of casting offices—or anywhere, for that matter. Finally, her perseverance and true-to-herself behavior paid off; in 2001, at age nine, she snagged a "tomboy type" role in Rose Troche's movie *The Safety of Objects*. She loved being part of something bigger than herself, and relished being heard. A few other roles followed in projects that failed to reach much of an audience. Then came her big break: David Fincher's *Panic Room,* released in 2002, in which Stewart, then eleven, had a lead role, opposite Jodie Foster.

Fincher's pairing of Foster and Stewart, as a mother and daughter who are the targets of a terrifying robbery in their fancy new Manhattan town house, was uncanny. They were born to share the screen—complementing each other both physically and temperamentally. Foster remembers, "Kristen was incredibly mature in some ways and grounded and very calm under pressure. She was an incredible listener, but then she'd say something so childlike that you'd be like, That's right—she's only eleven." Foster, who knows a thing or two about being a child star, remembers a conversation she had with Stewart's mom. "She was not helicoptery at all. She wanted [the film] to be Kristen's thing, but wanted to make sure she was well taken care of, and not overworked. One day she came down [to the set] for lunch, which I think is very smart. I said, 'Kristen doesn't want to be an actress, right?' 'I'm afraid she does,' she replied. 'Believe me, I would love to talk her out of it, but it seems she's really into it and really focused on it. And it seems like she wants to do it for the right reasons.'" As Foster says, "Kristen does not have the traditional personality of an actress. She doesn't want to dance on the table for Grandma and put a lamp shade on. She doesn't want to do voices and be the center of attention. If anything, she's uncomfortable with that. She approaches things in a very analytical way. She is conscious."

All that awareness and independence made for some tough years in school; at fourteen, Stewart officially quit and signed on for home schooling. "I hated school so much," she says with a shudder. "Look at a picture of me before I was fifteen. I am a boy. I wore my brother's clothes, dude! Not like I cared that much, but I remember being made fun of, because I wasn't wearing Juicy jeans. I didn't even think about it. I wore my gym clothes. But it's not like I didn't care that they made fun of me. It really bothered me. I remember this girl in sixth grade looked at me in gym and was like, 'Oh my God! That's disgusting—you don't shave your legs!'"

Just in case there is anyone left on earth who hasn't seen the films that made Stewart famous, a brief *Twilight* primer: Stewart's Bella is the new kid in town, with an eye for fellow outsiders and a heart ready to be given; Edward Cullen, played with Byronesque flair by Robert Pattinson, is the high-haired high school beauty who just happens to be a closeted vampire; Jacob Black, played by Taylor Lautner, is the buffed-up, frequently topless third point on this romantic triangle, who also, on occasion, turns into a wolf. With this cast the films' swoon factor is off the charts, but there is something deliciously dorky about the series, too, especially the high-flying sexual tension. But ultimately the power of the narrative, across the five films drawn from Stephenie Meyer's four novels, is how it recognizes our need to bond with others; we humans are tribal creatures, even when sucking blood.

It was Sean Penn who suggested to Catherine Hardwicke, the director of the first *Twilight* movie, that she give Stewart a shot. The director signed on because she believed in Stewart's ability to embody the feelings of longing that drive the original book. There were a few actors still in the running for the part of Edward, and Hardwicke was smart enough to involve Stewart in the final decision making. "Chemistry reads" are a long-standing ritual for testing whether two actors will work well together on-screen, but it sounds as if Hardwicke was experimenting with explosives the day she had Pattinson, a young British actor then best known for playing Cedric Diggory in *Harry Potter and the Goblet of Fire,* show up at her house to run through some scenes with Stewart, in the bedroom no less. "Honestly, I was nervous," the director remembers. "I saw they were so attracted and Kristen was underage. I said, 'Rob, we have a law in this country under eighteen. Don't get in trouble here.' I felt I was in the presence of something strong and powerful." When Pattinson left, Stewart said, "It's him." Hardwicke listened but wanted to be sure that their charisma and visceral connection translated onto film. "Not everybody makes it all the way through the screen to our hearts and souls in the movie theater," the director says, "but these two did. It was electrifying."

Stewart was fully engaged on set. She is open about the creative tensions that developed. "Me and Rob got into a lot of trouble," she told me with a smile. "We wanted it to be not so polished. Catherine was all for that. But we were getting notes from the studio. They wanted me to smile all the time. They wanted Rob to be not so brooding. We were like, 'No! You need to brood your ass off.'" A worldwide box-office take of almost $400 million certainly proved that the audience was ready for an unsmiling Bella and a brooding Edward. The fact that emotionally involved fans have taken the films so personally has only increased the sense of responsibility Stewart already felt to her character, to the point where Bill Condon, the director of the last two installments, affectionately calls her the "*Twilight*-book Nazi," because of her commitment to staying faithful to the novels.

As for some of the feminist critiques—that Bella is a throwback heroine because she sacrifices so much for her man—Stewart strongly disagrees. "In fact, you have someone who is stronger than the guy she is with, emotionally. Fight for the thing you love—you are a remarkable person if you do it. It's a cop-out to think that girl power is all about gusto and ballbusting." Her comments seem particularly pointed now that *The Hunger Games* has come along and outgrossed any of the *Twilight* films with its take-no-prisoners heroine, Katniss Everdeen, played by Jennifer Lawrence. One might say that swords will be drawn when Condon's grand *Twilight* finale, *Breaking Dawn 2*, hits theaters at the end of the year. Don't kill me, but I've seen it. And don't worry—I won't give anything away that the novel's readers don't already know. But let's just say that Simone de Beauvoir would approve.

I asked Stewart when she fully realized that *Twilight* had changed her life. "You can Google my name and one of the first things that comes up is images of me sitting on my front porch smoking a pipe with my ex-boyfriend and my dog. It was [taken] the day the movie came out. I was no one. I was a kid. I had just turned eighteen. In [the tabloids] the next day it was like I was a delinquent slimy idiot, whereas I'm kind of a weirdo, creative Valley Girl who smokes pot. Big deal. But that changed my daily life instantly. I didn't go out in my underwear anymore."

Between making successive *Twilight* installments, Stewart has shot a number of mostly smaller films. The one that should have been a keeper was *The Runaways,* a biopic of the pioneering all-girl L.A. glam-punk band. Stewart (as Joan Jett) and Dakota Fanning (as Cherie Currie) did their all to bring life to the film, but in the end the direction was obvious and it fell flat, lacking any kick. (Jett and Stewart, on the other hand, got along like a house on fire when they met during filming.)

After each of these more independent productions, it would be *Twilight* time again—Old Home Week for Stewart. She says that in retrospect she sees the *Twilight* sets as the equivalent of the high school she never attended. As you may know, her offscreen relationship with Pattinson has drawn enormous attention, but she is publicly mum on this one. That the two are a couple is not something they seem to want to hide; it's just that they like their privacy. A friend who knows Stewart very well says, "This is something that she wants to keep for herself."

Stewart is definitely a director's actress: She loves them and vice versa. Condon sees Stewart as a sort of trailblazer. "She has a strong sense of creating a new path. She's got the thing that people describe with Jack Nicholson in the beginning, that sense of danger, and the sense that you'll always be surprised," he says. Rupert Sanders, Stewart's director on *Snow White and the Huntsman,* describes the actress's relationship to her work with a survival metaphor. "She's one of those people who's got that creative spirit and exists by having to output it," he explains. "She's like a kind of copper wire. She's got this incredible electric energy and she just has to find a ground to discharge some of that power. Otherwise I think she'd explode."

In his out-there *Snow White* film, Sanders highlights Stewart's capabilities as an action star, and it's fun to see her make use of her natural physicality. "To me Kristen is at her best when she is in fight-or-flight mode," Sanders says. "The perception of her is that she's 'awkward,'" says Pattinson. "But it's funny knowing her. It's the absolute opposite of what people think. She is insanely confident." And sometimes insanely brave. Sanders still shivers when he remembers shooting a scene that involved Stewart taking a twenty-foot leap into filthy brown water in a tank at Pinewood Studios in the freezing cold of December. "Her performance before she jumps is sublime," says Sanders. "You see the hesitancy in her stomach, where she must have been thinking, I don't want to jump!" After she did the stunt, Sanders found the actress in her trailer in soaking clothes hovering in front of a tiny heater. He was worried she'd get hypothermia if she did it again. But there was no stopping her.

A different side of this fearlessness is what makes Stewart's performance in *On the Road* so memorable. Adapting a beloved, even sacred book is always tricky, but when director Walter Salles (*The Motorcycle Diaries*) decided to take on Kerouac's 1957 novel, he set himself an unusually hard task, because the text—about a group of young people (based on Kerouac's circle, including Allen Ginsberg and Neal Cassady) trying to escape the conformity of their time—is so full of spontaneity and commitment to living in the moment that too much planning would have rendered it dead on arrival as a film. Thus Salles felt he needed actors who could improvise and who truly understood what Kerouac's adventure book was all about: the essence of experience. He was sharing this with two old friends, the composer Gustavo Santaolalla and the director Alejandro González Iñárritu (*Amores Perros*), when they both said, *Stop! Don't even start looking for the part of Marylou*—the Cassady character's sometime lover and fellow traveler, a woman hell-bent on following her own path. Both men told Salles that Stewart was his Marylou. He followed up and learned that Stewart (who'd placed a copy of *On the Road* on the dashboard of her first car, that's how much the book meant to her) was so passionate and insightful about the character that he never even auditioned her for the part. (The top-notch cast also includes Amy Adams, Steve Buscemi, Garrett Hedlund, Kirsten Dunst, and Viggo Mortensen.)

Stewart made sure she knew her stuff before filming started, spending hours talking to the daughter of LuAnne Henderson, Neal Cassady's first wife and Marylou's real-life counterpart. Her director calls Stewart "a great partner in crime," and her performance has the qualities of a jazz riff; it is alive with freedom and a sense of beat (small *b*). "The desire to really live an authentic life seems to me very, very strong in her," Salles says.

A few days after we'd had lunch together in Paris, I watched *On the Road* with Stewart at a screening room in the Bastille section of town. She showed up in a red plaid shirt, jeans, the same Balenciaga black jacket she'd had at lunch, and sneakers: your all-American girl on a trip to Paris. As much as she loves this film, and is proud of it, I could feel Stewart squirming in her seat and hear her "yeeooow" when things got intense on-screen. My favorite moment was during a beautifully uninhibited sex scene between Marylou and Garrett Hedlund's Dean Moriarty (the Cassady character). I could have sworn I heard Stewart mutter, "For God's sake!" Her publicist was sitting between us and had thoughtfully brought along some French "muffins" that were like fancy doughnut holes. I popped a few into my mouth to cover my gulps. After the screening was over, I had to run, because I had an appointment, so I couldn't stay to discuss it with Stewart. I was almost glad, because watching the movie had been such an intimate experience—which is, of course, the power of the film, but still. So, I took off in a car, and she went her way.

Departures came to signify Stewart for me. After the lunch we'd had at Le Duc, earlier that week, when we finally got ready to move on, Stewart peeked out the door at something and then went over to the bar, where I noticed a testosteroned-up marvel of a guy, clearly a bodyguard, with whom she had a few words. Stewart didn't say anything to me when she returned to the table but was ever so slightly flushed, and there was a subtle clenching of her jaw. I looked out the door myself. "Oh boy," I said. The paparazzi were posted; it turned out they'd followed Stewart, who had traveled in an inconspicuous black van from her hotel to the restaurant. Just a few minutes before, she had summed up the conundrum of the kind of fame she's been living with. "It's not the fans that are scary," she said. "Each one of them is different. But large groups of people are scary—there's no individual there. It feels like it's just an enormous body of water, like a wave that's stronger than you. And it's loud like water, so it is all-encompassing. You'd have to be a sociopath not to be penetrated by the human energy that's, like, cumulatively being hurled at you from every direction."

We decided to try to wait out the cameras and keep talking, though I worried that meant that we'd end up spending far more time together than had been allotted on her schedule. She didn't care. "I'm not doing anything," she said. "I was just being protected by people that do that job. I have nothing to do." (She is not someone who is intent on proving how wanted she is; the paparazzi do that job whether she wants it or not.) Hours later, when we finally made our respective getaways, the paparazzi were still waiting for their fifty-thousand-dollar candids. (Make that seventy-five thousand dollars if they get her angry, and one hundred thousand dollars if they get the prize: a shot of her and Pattinson.) I hung back while Stewart and the bodyguard drove off, with the pack of photographers on their trail. I pictured her wishing she were anywhere else, perhaps heading off in the open blue pickup truck, a proud possession of Bella's police-chief father in *Twilight*, which she'd bought and driven home, from the location in Portland, Oregon, to Los Angeles, when filming was over. "But," as Kerouac wrote, "no matter, the road is life."

Vanity Fair, July 2012

"I still don't know exactly who I am," wrote Gordon Parks about his **Hats Off** multiple creative identities. "I've disappeared into myself so many **to Karl** different ways that I don't know who me is." Of course he knew exactly who he was. He defied categorization and was a boundary-busting, barrier-breaking beacon. If ever there was the perfect recipient for a Photographer's Award in Gordon Park's name, on a night when creativity is the theme, it is Karl Lagerfeld—the man who wears more hats, or fascinators, than they just had at Kate and William's wedding.

Here's an abridged list of some of the ways that Lagerfeld gets more out of a day (and often it's the night, too) than anyone I know. Creative director and resident genius fashion designer, at Chanel for twenty-nine years, Fendi for more than forty years—a world record—and Lagerfeld, the house that bears his name. Artist who sketches with the natural ease of a true talent. Author who writes with the knowledge of the world's libraries. Publisher who helps keep alive the art of bookmaking. Film-maker, who is creating the glamorous version of a Cassavetes-like atmosphere by casting his friends and chosen family. Actor-ex-Warhol superstar and current leading man in the many Lagerfeld documentaries that are popping up. Wit—who is every interviewer and writer's dream, he is so quotable, and deliciously wicked. Collector, who has an eye for design that is as sharp as they come. Interior designer—who makes most of the professionals look like sheep. Letter writer—who would have impressed even Elizabeth Bishop, one of his favorite authors. Advertising's go-to secret weapon—one who shoots the campaigns for not just his own houses, like Chanel and Fendi, but the competition too, and he also gets a Warholian kick out of creating an aura for all things popular—from Coca-Cola to ice cream. Tired yet? Karl's not. He'd modestly say he's just getting started. And if you congratulate him on any of it, he'd answer, "But that doesn't make the next one."

Which leads to his bond with photography. It is his lighthouse—he always goes back to it, whether it's architecture, landscapes, portraiture, fashion, still life, et cet-era. When other fashion designers are kicking back after a day's work, a show, or a long season, Karl is almost always off doing a photo shoot, for an underground magazine, or a powerful glossy, or a campaign, or a personal project he has assigned to himself. We became friends over our mutual obsession with photography. He had looked at every photography book that had ever been printed and still does.

Our first conversations were a long time ago—when Karl had just begun to pick up the camera for real. What was striking about his first pictures was that they had an instant sense of weight, probably from all the looking at photographs he had done over the years, and they also had his own voice. Mountains of books, stories, assignments, and campaigns later, this is still true. Watching Karl photograph says it all. I have been with him on shoots in the streets of New York, Paris, Los Angeles, and Tokyo. Each time enormous crowds have gathered, and traffic jams have clogged up matters, with fans gaping at the ponytailed icon with high white collars and sunglasses, calling out, "We love you, Karl." Always polite and always slightly startled by his fame, he looks up and thanks them, but then gets right back to work. Nothing can break the spell.

Karl doesn't just reserve the sense of magic for his own work. Last night when he arrived in New York we had dinner together with some friends. He immediately wanted to show us a rare portfolio, from 1914, that he'd just tracked down in France, designed by Paul Iribe, with text by a number of writers, including Auguste Rodin and Jean Cocteau, and photographs by Baron de Meyer of the ballet *Prelude of the Afternoon of a Faun,* starring Nijinsky. There are only six copies of it left in the world. After we'd all looked at it and marveled over its sophisticated design, the beauty of the graphics, the tenderness of the paper, the printing of the photographs, and the romance of the photographs, we got into a debate about whether a facsimile should be made from it. Karl said, "I love it so much that I can't bear to be without it—even for the hours it would need to be out of my hands." One day there will be people out there saying the same thing about Karl's photographic work. In fact, they are already.

Karl Lagerfeld introduction, Gordon Park Awards Dinner, June 1, 2011

Rene Ricard

For the life of me, I can't remember exactly when or where I first met Rene Ricard. But it had to have been sometime in the spring of 1981 that our editorial bond was forged. Bets are I hooked up with Rene, in one way or another, through Edit deAk, the first writer I'd brought to *Artforum* when I stepped in as editor with the February 1980 issue; back then, deAk's antenna for changes and breakthroughs in art and the discussions around it, particularly in the contemporary American-European nexus, was like lightning's attraction to metal. She could zap it like no one else. "A Chameleon in a State of Grace," her wide-ranging piece on Francesco Clemente, published in the February 1981 issue of *Artforum,* caused a buzz, especially among younger artists; of course, the reigning establishments were horrified. Not Rene. DeAk's article was the first thing that Rene and I talked about. He said we needed to go on the record about Julian Schnabel's work next. Note the *we,* as if we were already partners, when I had just met him minutes ago. No matter, I was in.

How could I not want to go on a dangerous mission with him? Eyes with sensory and electrical impulses that always reminded me of a camera's aperture. One minute you saw something light-filled and charming in them; the next they were darting around, globes in a skirmish with life. By the time I met him, his Factory days were over, but Rene's charisma was not lost on Andy Warhol, who cast him in *Kitchen* (1965) and *Chelsea Girls* (1966), among other films. For my money, though, this poet, critic, painter was born to play a thief and a priest. He could fake other people's art almost convincingly, and had a definite moral compass. From the moment we pledged to do the Schnabel piece, we were glued together by the work. It was only a matter of

Francesco Clemente, *Rene Ricard,* 2006

days before Rene started showing up with the bits and pieces he was building into the article, which would eventually be called "Not About Julian Schnabel" and would be published a couple of months later, in the summer of 1981.

Rene's independence was fierce and never for sale; it and his red Olivetti typewriter, a proud possession, his few artworks that he'd received as gifts, and his poems were pretty much all he had. He put his time in at the Chelsea Hotel, but during the period when he wrote for the magazine, he lived here and there in borrowed flats, mostly thanks to the respect and affection of close pals. Rene's *Artforum* pieces were not written in order for him to climb any academic ladders, or get tenure, or for the usual career enhancements. I quote from one of my favorite of his poems:

All you sycophants and grant hustlers.
I will never chase the rich again. Let me starve.
I will never apply for a grant. Let me starve.
I must look out for my biography. After all,
I may be a pariah but I am still and always
Will be a living legend. I'd rather starve.

I hold sacred what goes on between a writer and an editor during the process of creating a work, and I will never spill what happens in that "room of our own." But I can say that Rene's critical essays were constructed the way he might lay out a poem: not necessarily in chronological order, eventually put together the way a builder might go at a house, brick by brick. The two best-known essays from our period of working together at *Artforum* were written barely a year apart: "The Radiant Child," starring Jean-Michel Basquiat, Keith Haring, graffiti, that moment, van Gogh, and so much more, was published in December 1981; "The Pledge of Allegiance" appeared in the November 1982 issue, which bore a camouflage logo and a picture of an industrial typewriter on its cover. Here Rene was making a pledge to an attitude, as well as to artists including Futura 2000, Basquiat, and the poet Duncan Smith, and also to Patti Astor's Fun Gallery. He meant it. I quote from his pledge: "I have made my liaisons in print and as these artists' fortunes rise and fall so do mine. I will be forever in league with them, and if they slip I'll look like hell. I have championed them. I've pledged allegiance, I've signed my name, and there my reputation sits."

Rene could be wild. There was one patch while he was working on "The Pledge of Allegiance" when he basically asked me to save him from himself. He wanted to hunker down and write but was worried that when the sun went down, temptation would get the better of him, and he'd hit the clubs, taking God knows what while he was at it. So he gave me the keys to the apartment he was borrowing, and I'd show up every day to check on him. Our exchange: He'd hand over whatever paragraphs or pages he'd come up with, and I'd bring a little feast for him to celebrate his progress. I'm sure I got the better end of the deal.

There was only one time that Rene scared me; it was my fault. I'd been asked to choose a group of *Artforum* writers to speak at a little symposium on art writing at Books and Company, then a mecca for meetings between New York's literary world and its art world, and only a few doors down from the Whitney Museum of American Art. Rene was among the panelists that evening. I could tell he was amped on something, maybe moonshine, maybe something more illegal, or perhaps just pure Ricard juice, before he went on, so I cautioned him to watch what he said. *Big* mistake. He went on to insult a number of people in the room, including calling an art dealer who was present by her primate nickname. I should have known better than to try and tame him. I had never attempted to before, and I never did again. Why mess with his refusal to censor himself? It was a gift.

Artforum, May 2014

Galliano in the Wilderness

Might as well face the worst of it right away, so here it is: the transcript of a cell-phone video of an encounter at La Perle, a bar in Paris's Marais district, which stunned the fashion world, and millions of people outside that world, with its mix of inexcusable anti-Semitism, childish bile, and outrageous obscenity. The video was first posted on the website of the British tabloid *The Sun,* on February 28, 2011, and immediately went viral:

> Woman: "Are you blond?"
>
> Man: "No. But I love Hitler. People like you would be dead today. Your mothers, your forefathers, would all be fucking gassed, and fucking dead."
>
> Woman: "Oh, my God! Do you have a problem?"
>
> Man: "With you? You're ugly."
>
> Woman: "With all people. You don't like peace? You don't want peace in the world?"
>
> Man: "Not with people that are ugly."
>
> Woman: "Where are you from?"
>
> Man: "Your asshole."

The fact that this spew came from the mouth of John Galliano, fashion's most irrepressible showman—and back then the creative director of both the luxury giant Christian Dior Couture and his own, namesake house—was all the more shocking because he had consistently made a point of tolerance and inclusion in his career. This was perhaps most famously expressed in the spring/summer 2006 ready-to-wear show he did for his Galliano label, sim-

Annie Leibovitz, *John Galliano, Saugerties, New York,* 2013

ply titled "Everything Is Beautiful." The runway had featured models of all shapes, heights, sizes, colors, ages, and ethnic origins. Giants and dwarfs welcome. Members of the cross-dressing and transgender communities, too. It was a joyous call to respect one another, no matter how different—just the kind of sentiment that the Nazis would have declared "degenerate."

Thus, when the cell-phone video surfaced, fashion insiders were so gobsmacked that to this day they'll tell you where they were when they first heard about it. "I'll never forget," says Ronald Frasch, president of Saks Fifth Avenue. "It was Milan Fashion Week. I was at the Dsquared show. One of the folks had the download on their iPad. I was completely shocked. We were all leaning over the iPad. The immediate reaction was 'Jesus Christ!'"

Awful as it was, the video was only the final nail in Galliano's professional coffin. His public troubles had begun four days before the video surfaced, on the night of February 24, 2011, when cops had been called to La Perle, his neighborhood watering hole, because of an unrelated confrontation between Galliano and a couple, Géraldine Bloch and Philippe Virgitti, who lodged an official complaint against him. Bloch claimed Galliano had insulted her hair, her "ugly eyebrows," and her "cheap thigh boots." Nothing for Galliano, then fifty years old, to be proud of, but petty. Unfortunately, there was also some more really, really bad stuff. The couple said that the designer had hurled anti-Semitic insults at Bloch ("Dirty Jewish face, you should be dead") and anti-Asian threats at Virgitti ("Fucking Asian bastard, I'll kill you"). Galliano had his own side of the story, claiming he had been verbally harassed, that his look was insulted, that he was provoked and physically threatened with a chair—an account that was supported by observers (though plenty of people are provoked and threatened without resorting to ethnic slurs). In a moment of pathos, Galliano had reportedly struck his signature runway pose—a bow with a touch of flamenco in it, one hip jutting out, stance ever so proud, albeit wobblier than usual because he was drunk as a skunk—and mumbled, "I am the designer John Galliano!"

Anti-Semitic and racist remarks are a criminal offense in France. As news of Galliano's run-in with the police broke on Friday, Dior, whose parent company is LVMH Moët Hennessy–Louis Vuitton, suspended him from his five-million-dollar-a-year position. That weekend, another complaint was filed against Galliano, alleging a similar anti-Semitic incident, again at La Perle, the previous fall. On Monday, as the video went viral (its provenance and context remain unknown; it had clearly been edited and was reportedly shopped to the French media long before Galliano's arrest), Dior announced it had dismissed the designer. Sidney Toledano, the chairman and CEO of Christian Dior Couture, was quoted as saying, "We unequivocally condemn the statements made by John Galliano, which are a total contradiction to the long-standing core values of Christian Dior." There was nothing else the house could have done; hate speech has no place in a civilized company, and Galliano, genius or no, had to go.

The day after his firing Galliano issued an abject, if nuanced, apology that included a denial of the specific claims made against him; a condemnation of prejudice, intolerance, and discrimination; an apology for unstated behavior on his part that had caused offense; and an explanation that he had begun to get help. "I only have myself to blame and I know that I must face up to my own failures," he stated. That September, after a brief one-day trial in June, he was found guilty of "public insults based on origin, religious affiliation, race or ethnicity," but it was clear the court knew that Galliano's behavior was more complicated than a "normal" hate criminal's. There was no jail sentence; Galliano, who had apologized to the plaintiffs in court, was ordered to pay court costs and given suspended fines totaling 6,000 euros (about $8,400).

Evidence had been given on Galliano's behalf that he was suffering from barbiturate poisoning—the result of a combination of painkillers, Valium, sleeping pills, and alcohol. A toxicologist testified that the medications and liquor (particularly red wine) in Galliano's system could—to use nonclinical language—drive someone out of his mind.

Galliano's conviction has since been "spent," a European legalism meaning it can be ignored in many circumstances. But the stain will be with him forever. That he was in the acute stages of an untreated disease that millions of others suffer from has engendered sympathy in some quarters. But the video and accusations had already destroyed Galliano in the court of public opinion. He has been busy during these last two and a half years of public silence, however, learning about what he has to do to keep his illness at bay, facing up to what went wrong in his life, and doing everything he can to atone. He has also begun taking baby steps to reenter the world of fashion. My prediction: Get ready for his second act. But first the truth about his life so far.

Aside from his post-scandal statement and testimony in court, the public has not heard from Galliano—until this article, for which we met over several days at his Paris apartment. Galliano had never invited a journalist into his home before, and there was something else unprecedented: He told me ours was the first interview he had ever given sober.

The first afternoon I arrived at his building, March 1, 2013, was exactly two years after Galliano had been fired from Dior. It was ghostly quiet on the street. La Perle is only a few doors down, and it surprised me that he had chosen to continue to live so close to the scene of the crime—a reminder every single day.

We spent most of our time talking in Galliano's salon. His boyfriend, Alexis Roche, told me that in the old days every surface would be covered with the flotsam of Galliano's research for whatever designs were gestating. "Each centimeter was a shrine to a collection—it was his laboratory," explained Roche. Now there is order, but the room is still full of objects and works that have inspired Galliano. In particular I noticed: African artifacts, photographs by Steven Klein and Guy Bourdin, high-caliber early-twentieth-century drawings by the likes of Modigliani and Morandi, contemporary abstract paintings by Jorge Galindo, and a big flat-screen TV integrated into the gallery-style hanging of the art. During each visit incense was burning and candles were flickering. The large, low table around which we talked was always set for tea, with different brews simmering in teapots of different sizes and patterns. English, Turkish, green tea, a mix from Mariage Frères, the fancy tea emporium. Some nibbles—chocolate-covered orange peel, maca-roons, and pyramid-shaped colored jellies—had been carefully arranged on a couple of pretty porcelain plates. Books lay about in small piles near our feet.

"I'm a bit rusty—I haven't given an interview for two years," Galliano acknowledged. His voice—deep, English-accented, but not a toff's—seemed tentative at first. He was obviously shaky. I wasn't so confident, either. We both warmed our hands on our teacups. Later, he told me that he had prayed right before he walked into the room. But when he finally talked, boy, did he talk.

"I was going to end up in a mental asylum or six feet under," he said of his drinking and drugging in the years leading up to the scandal. As he had testified in court, he told me he had no memory of the incident at La Perle during which he was filmed—he had blacked out. He told me about the days immediately after his firing, when he was still in a chemical fog. "When everyone came over to tell me that I had done these terrible things," he said, "I was walking round and round and round not really knowing what had gone down. My assistant told me about the video. When I saw it, I threw up. The feeling was like I was about to take a step out onto the street and a bus or truck whooshed past me and the blood was drained from my legs. I was paralyzed from the fear."

Though he was delving into highly personal and emotional issues, Galliano never spoke with a melodramatic air. Rather, he was matter-of-fact. When someone is trying to spin a story, my antennae (or stomach) usually go on red alert. Not here.

After the preliminaries, we started in on his unidyllic childhood. Juan Carlos Antonio Galliano Guillén was born on Gibraltar in 1960, the middle child between two sisters. His father, a policeman turned plumber, wanted a better life for the family, so he moved them all to London in 1966. It didn't feel like an upgrade to a six-year-old boy. "We came from this sunny clime, blue sky, a mix of cultures and religion and flamenco and spices and smells," he explained. "We moved into a very poor South London suburb called Battersea. Now it's called Ba-tar-*shay*—it's terribly chic, my dear. But when we were there it was rough, rough, rough. Gray thunderous clouds, wet chalk. I felt like an alien."

I wondered what kind of rough ethnic language Galliano may have absorbed in his youth (a possible clue to his litany at La Perle). "South London saw the first immigration of Jamaicans, Indians, Greeks," he recalled. "It's funny—when this all first happened I was like, I can't be a racist. I *can't be.* I grew up in South London, in a melting pot. But I did hear awful things. I remember a lot of the insults that were thrown backward and forward."

And right at him, too, hitting the bull's-eye. *Poofter,* and worse. "I don't need to say the words. If I didn't already sense that I was different, I certainly was reminded, whether by my parents or by the other schoolkids," he said. "Not just reminded. *Told.*"

It likely didn't help that he was obsessed with dance and won medals at it—not just the flamenco he'd grown up with but also the rumba, cha-cha, and fox-trot. Photographs of Galliano as a youth make plain he was not a toughie. Looking at a picture of him feeding a flock of pigeons, probably around age five, or another of him as a teenager looking adoringly at a godson, you can just feel his sensitivity. I asked if that made life difficult. "I was made to believe it wasn't right," he said. "If I went a little bit too off—*slap!* It was Dad's upbringing and it was Victorian, and that's the way he was."

At school, the taunts and bullying didn't stop him from putting his own spin on his drab uniform. "At a very young age I would doctor or customize it." Here, too, Galliano paid a price for his individuality. "Oh, I developed cunning because of it," he told me ruefully. "I would work out what earlier trains to get and what carriages to ride in to not be beaten by the boys. Hiding the bruises, hiding the cuts, going home and not being able to talk about it, because if I did, I would get another good beating."

A rich fantasy life—one that would eventually bring a sense of magic to Galliano's fashion—was a kind of life jacket for the young man. "I made up stories in my head, because it was a really nice place to be," he said. "It was my space, my secret garden." Of course, lies are the poor relations of stories, and Galliano's experiences on that front, sadly, are not unusual. "I was never honest. My father died, and I had never said to him, 'I'm gay,'" he admitted. "I knew what I was, but I had to pretend not to be that to avoid the beatings." Galliano, like so many other gay people who live with guilt and shame, learned how to survive with secrets and lies.

Eventually, once he made it to Central Saint Martins, London's highly respected art and design school, in the early 1980s, he was rewarded for the very same eccentricity that he'd previously been punished for. "I was meeting people like me," he recalled. "Creative peacocks. We talked the same language." Galliano also found a soul mate, a fellow student named John Flett, who died of a freak heart attack in his twenties, in 1991. When Galliano talked about Flett, who was Jewish, it was with the sweetness and sadness of a first romance remembered—"the love of my life," he said.

Galliano worked hard at Saint Martins. He worked hard outside of school, too, augmenting a tuition grant with a number of jobs, including one he was crazy about—as a dresser in the theater. You still feel his amazement that he was allowed to help actors such as Judi Dench, Nigel Havers, Martin Jarvis, and Bill Nighy prepare to cast their spells. "I learned so much," he remembered. "Going to the wardrobe department, watching how they treated the fabrics to produce the emotion they were after. Witnessing how the clothes helped the actor bring out the character." In hindsight it's almost uncanny how much of what Galliano picked up backstage—an education in period costume, dealing with high-strung personalities, creating miracles under pressure—turned out to be defining characteristics of his career in fashion.

Student life wasn't *all* work. London's early-eighties nightlife is justifiably mythic today. Boundary-breaking, gender-blending characters such as Boy George and Leigh Bowery set a high bar. Clubs such as Taboo and the perpetually moving Warehouse parties were environments where the more creative you were, the more appreciated you were. "It was an amazing, inspiring, tingling time," Galliano remembered. Tasty Tim, the doorman at Taboo, was famous for holding up a mirror to prospective clubgoers and asking, "Would *you* let you in?" In other words, if you looked boring you went home. The door was never slammed in Galliano's face.

In fashion studies, as in art school, if a student's graduating show becomes the talk of the institution—which is exactly what happened with Galliano's 1984 senior project—chances are a serious career is in the offing. The theme of Galliano's show was "Les Incroyables," the dandies and fashion plates of the French Revolutionary period. No small ambition here. Galliano dipped ribbons in treacle and pulled out some of the tricks of the trade he'd learned at the National Theatre. "I couldn't find enough bathtubs to stain blouses with tea," he told me with a laugh. Altogether there were only about eight outfits. But the impact! Joan Burstein, the owner of Browns, one of London's most important fashion emporiums, bought the entire collection. "It was sensational," she recalled. "There was a freedom of spirit. I wanted to show this young man's expertise—his dreams." As soon as the clothes arrived, Galliano's first customer was Diana Ross, who bought a coat.

One day Galliano was in school; the next he was in business, running his own, eponymous label. It was shortly thereafter that he met Lady Amanda Harlech (at that time Amanda Grieve), a junior fashion editor who was restless at *Harpers & Queen*. A friend told her about Galliano; she looked him up and was instantly hooked: "I sacked myself from *Harpers* and I started working freelance for John. No money. Everybody doing it out of belief. We probably had the sense that if we weren't going to jump on the ship it would sail without us, and you wanted to be on that incredible galleon crossing the sea of fashion with him and all the adventures."

Part of what turned Harlech on is what has always thrilled Galliano's audiences: His clothes didn't come out of nowhere. They always had an implicit story, a beyond-just-spectacle theatricality in which Galliano invested each garment with the sense it had been designed not for some abstract size four but for an actual, specific woman, a character drawn from history, art, culture, or his imagination—sometimes all at once. As Harlech said, the narrative was woven into the cloth. This extended to Galliano's work with models. He became their Hitchcock, their Minnelli. "We weren't just walking down the runway when it was John," said Naomi Campbell, who modeled for the designer for more than twenty years. "I was not Naomi when I did his shows. I was whoever the character was that he wanted me to be. We took it very seriously. We had to bring the character—and most importantly the dress—to life."

One triumphant show after another sealed Galliano's local reputation in London as a wizard of cutting, a master of layering and materials, and a brilliant showman. Malcolm McLaren used to ask the designer when he was going to start charging for shows, they had become such hot tickets. But the hand-to-mouth financial reality was grim. In 1992 Galliano moved to the potentially more lucrative environs of Paris, where he eventually settled in the Bastille district in a workspace that had seen better days. The balance sheet finally perked up after the spring/summer 1994 "Princess Lucretia" collection, which somehow mixed thirties-style evening dresses, pajama suits, and kilts. (The story: A royal heroine escapes Russia—in her crinolines, naturally—and takes a trip through fashion that no travel agent could plan.)

Vogue's creative director André Leon Talley flipped for the collection, and if you were looking for a booster who could broadcast your fabulousness and get all the right people to your shows in the early 1990s, you couldn't do better than Talley. He also happened to have the boss of bosses in his editor in chief, Anna Wintour. "Probably rather naïvely, I hadn't realized how hand-to-mouth John's existence was at that point," Wintour told me. "It wasn't until I talked to André about John's need for financial investment that I realized. I think it's a peculiarly English thing how these very inventive, creative, brilliant designers can create this magic with nothing. . . . I was more than happy to help because it's very unusual to see a talent of that magnitude. We wanted to get his work out there."

Wintour's and Talley's introductions carried enormous weight; the Paine Webber banking group was found as an investor, and Galliano was finally on sure footing. Talley's matchmaking for Galliano included a lunch with São Schlumberger, the famed Paris hostess. She was charmed—and Talley pounced. How about lending John your *hôtel particulier* for his next collection? he asked, not really asking. The resulting fall/winter 1994–1995 collection, which Galliano put on at Schlumberger's mansion, has become part of fashion lore. A hush of concentration bonded the audience as the models—Linda Evangelista, Naomi Campbell, Christy Turlington, Kate Moss, Michelle Hicks, Carla Bruni, and others, all working for free, no less—wowed. Galliano was offering a new perspective on the East-West dialogue that had become such a staple in fashion. He pulled off the entire show with basic rolls of black fabric, using both the matte and the shiny sides. Models came out in jackets that morphed into tiny kimonos with floral-patterned obi sashes. There was a shot of pink at the end, which underlined the electricity that was in the air.

"What was it—sixteen, seventeen pieces? But one was more remarkable than the other," Wintour recalled, "and it was one of those times in fashion that you realize everything is changing. There was a simplicity and a heart to that show that was a very emotional moment for all of us."

One by one, the most sought-after grandes dames in the rarefied world of couture clients—Schlumberger, Dodie Rosekrans, Béatrice de Rothschild, and more—showed up at Galliano's door. "That's really how the job at Givenchy started," said Galliano. "I think they were bemused with the fact that they had heard these amazing ladies were coming to this rickety studio in the Bastille and looking amazing in my dresses." When LVMH offered Givenchy to Galliano in 1995, there was some grumbling—an Englishman, *there?*—but mostly there was anticipation. By then he'd established his signature "bias" cut. When women wore these dresses made out of satin-backed crêpe and their body temperatures got hotter, the material would mold to their form. His "slip" dresses didn't stretch or shrink or drop too much—which can happen when clothes are cut on the bias—and they sold.

Galliano had been at Givenchy only fifteen months when, one Friday afternoon, he got a call with the message that Bernard Arnault, the chairman and CEO of LVMH, would like to see him. "I had a bad-hair day, bad nail polish, the wrong red—what a time to be caught!" he confessed. "A car was sent and I get in and then go up in this lift to his office at the top of the building. It was all very James Bond and intimidating. The lift opens and there stands this elegant man, Monsieur Arnault. He starts talking about Dior and then pops the question. Would I? I nearly fell off my chair." (As part of the deal, LVMH also agreed to get behind the designer's own company, John Galliano.)

By this time he had most of his core team with him, among them: Steven Robinson to head things up in both the Dior and Galliano studios, Bill Gaytten as the linchpin for the actual execution of the clothes, Jeremy Healy to pull together the music for the shows, Michael Howells for the sets, and Stephen Jones for the hats. Camilla Morton would eventually come on board as an outside "voice" for the designer. (One person who didn't make the move to Dior was Harlech, who felt her earlier willingness to work for next to nothing was taken for granted during the deal making and went on to join Karl Lagerfeld at Chanel. The move initially enraged Galliano.)

Galliano's early days at Dior were heady. Suddenly, he had access to the house's extraordinary ateliers, with all their expertise. He dedicated himself to learning about Dior's fashion codes and reinterpreting them for the present. For instance, the famous bar jacket was such a critical part of Christian Dior's original vocabulary that Galliano knew he had to figure out a way to both honor it and give it a new spin, season after season, year after year. It's one of those staples—like Coco Chanel's tweed jackets, which Lagerfeld has so ingeniously kept updating for the last thirty years—that a fashion house depends on. Galliano's reinterpretations and deconstructions of the bar jacket were constantly evolving and are an example of his ability to take a shape and really sculpt with it.

Often Galliano's themes were ambitious—even if they were occasionally expressed in the superficial way that can be an occupational hazard in fashion. Take his Dior Haute Couture Collection for fall/winter 1998–1999, which took on the weighty topic of Christianity's seventeenth-century mission to convert a millennia-old Native American culture and then essentially reduced the issues to: color versus stark black and white; "Pocahontas" fringe versus ruffs and ecclesiastical collars; loose shapes versus strict silhouettes. The clothes were gorgeous, but outside the fashion hothouse the pseudocultural commentary might have seemed laughable. Sometimes Galliano's socially minded themes backfired, as with the collection that the press dubbed the "Clochard" (hobo or tramp) collection, shown first in January 2000 for the spring/summer haute couture. Protesters gathered around the Dior shop on Avenue Montaigne. (Riot police added to the drama.) Galliano's intentions had been well meaning: an homage to the homeless men and women he'd seen sleeping alongside the Seine wrapped in layers of newspapers. With added inspiration from Charlie Chaplin and Diane Arbus, the collection was a triumph of graphic sophistication and technical wizardry but also very easy to find patronizing. One model came out in a waistcoat and baggy, oversize pants, silkscreened with the fashion pages of the *International Herald Tribune,* the trousers defying gravity, thanks to an embroidered belt that looked like rope. Another accessory: a scarf made out of a sock held together by a giant safety pin. (Ironically, the subsequent ready-to-wear collection that expanded upon these ideas was a hit, made more desirable when Sarah Jessica Parker wore one of the newspaper-printed silk-jersey dresses on *Sex and the City.*)

The excitement that Galliano brought to Dior never really subsided. The house grew and stretched every which way, becoming a model for the global expansion that has characterized the fashion industry for the last fifteen or so years. Galliano had a brilliant, capable boss in Sidney Toledano, who took over as CEO of Dior in 1998. This is a man who understands the needs and quirks of creative types, and by the time Galliano self-immolated the two had been standing at the apex of an organization that had sales in 2010 of more than one billion dollars and was producing not just couture and ready-to-wear but bags, shoes, baby clothes, you name it.

Galliano's personality affected everything that took place at Dior. Retrospectively, some of it—such as the fragrance Addict—now seems rather ironic. But there are plenty of charming stories, too. Whether it's apocryphal or not, I've always loved the tale of how another one of the company's fragrances, J'adore, got its name. Galliano, probably self-conscious about his language skills, didn't use much French at the beginning. His answer to many questions in French was *"J'adore." What time is it, John?* "Oh, *j'adore." Would you like lunch?* "Oh, *j'adore."* Now comes a meeting for a new perfume that was being developed. *John, what would you think if we . . .* "Oh, *j'adore."*

All this success masked a growing problem: Galliano had become a highly functioning addict, relying on an almost lethal mix of alcohol and pills to stay on top of his game. As Naomi Campbell, who has been there herself, told me, "Those of us who know how to cover and who are active are the most dangerous to ourselves." Like many addicts, Galliano slipped into his disease slowly, over the course of years. "I never drank in order to be creative, or to do the research," he explained. "I didn't need alcohol for any of that. At first alcohol was like a crutch outside of Dior. Then I would use it to crash after the collections. I'd take a couple of days to get over it, like everyone. But with more collections, the crash happened more often, and then I was a slave to it. Then the pills kicked in because I couldn't sleep. Then the other pills kicked in because I couldn't stop shaking. I would also have these huge bottles of liquor that people got for me. Toward the end, it was whatever I could get my hands on. Vodka, or vodka and tonic. Wine, in the belief it would help me sleep. Wrong. I did manage to stop the voices. I had all these voices in my head, asking so many questions, but I never for one second would admit I was an alcoholic. I thought I could control it."

Galliano suffered a serious blow in 2007 when Steven Robinson, who managed Galliano's studios and who had become his chief confidant and right-hand man, died at the age of thirty-eight. The cause was listed as cardiac arrest but cocaine was later reported to be involved. The loss struck Galliano to the core, and it was around this time that his dependency on alcohol and self-medication really sank its fangs in. He never lost his passion for the work, but his sense of burden increased. He even stopped getting a kick out of his famous runway bows—crowd-pleasing performances that had him dressing up as a sailor, a matador, Napoléon, the Marquis de Sade, Madame Butterfly's Lieutenant Pinkerton. "What had started as self-expression turned into a mask," Galliano said. He was always charming and polite when I saw him then, but I noticed that his throne had gotten bigger, metaphorically speaking. "I lived in a bubble," he said. "I would be backstage and there would be a queue of five people to help me. One person would have a cigarette for me. The next person would have the lighter. I did not know how to use the ATM."

Galliano did know on some level that he had a substance-abuse problem. He couldn't help noticing he'd lose days to bouts of drinking. "Not having washed, I'd be covered in sores and humiliated," he recalled. But then he'd start up another round of pills. "I had the tremors. I wouldn't sleep for five days. I would go to bookstores and get some self-help books, but I was in denial. I'd throw myself back into the gym. I'd be careful about what I ate. And, of course, the whole cycle would start again."

Professionally he was still functioning at a very high level, but Galliano's demons were no secret within his innermost circle. By 2010 those closest to him were bracing for disaster. He would let friends down. He would go MIA for days. Jeremy Healy, his musical collaborator, watched the downward progression along with others whom Galliano trusted enough to see him at his worst. "It started when we were twenty-year-olds," Healy told me. "It was a laugh then. He'd be in a restaurant and stand on the table and sing a song and everyone would love it." As time went on, though, the acting out grew less charming. "When you're still drunk two days later, it's not fun," Healy said. "John would become a monster. He'd go on for days and days."

Healy and a few other pals became so concerned they thought they should go to the bosses at LVMH and ask the company to suspend Galliano until he cleaned up, but in the end no one wanted to betray him. And, anyway, after a drinking binge he'd seem fine again, so his intimates would think, Oh well, maybe he'll be all right—the usual dance of an addict and those who love him or her.

A tipping point seemed to come in November 2010 when Galliano visited New York for work but instead went on a bender. He retreated to his room at the Mercer hotel, worrying an assistant to the extent that LVMH had to step in. Alexis Roche, his boyfriend, was dispatched to bring Galliano back to France. That Christmas, the couple went to Thailand, and when Galliano returned in January he seemed rested, with a new lease on life. Everyone breathed a sigh of relief, but Toledano wanted to grab the moment. He took his star designer to lunch and said he needed to get help. Galliano turned the tables and suggested that Toledano should change his diet and eat more healthily.

In the end, Galliano had a productive January, creating couture and menswear collections and giving a presentation to several hundred worldwide Dior executives where he appeared dressed as a torero. But there was a second confrontation that month—a scene so outrageous as to be almost funny. Bernard Arnault and Toledano called Galliano in for a heart-to-heart and told him that he was going to die if he didn't do something about his problem. Galliano's response: He tore off his shirt to reveal a gym-toned torso, then asked, "Does this look like the body of an alcoholic?" (Because of complex ongoing litigation between Dior and Galliano involving compensation, executives at the company were unable to speak for this piece. But all the details about the designer's employment have been confirmed by both Galliano and well-placed sources at LVMH.)

It was soon after the meeting with his bosses that Galliano found himself on front pages, newscasts, and websites worldwide—and holed up in his apartment, still boozed- and pilled-up, with the media thronging outside. Some friends and colleagues washed their hands of him, but others rallied. Naomi Campbell was on the phone arranging for a bed at a rehab center in Arizona, where Galliano would eventually spend six weeks. Jeremy Healy packed the designer's bags. Camilla Morton pitched in. Gerrard Tyrrell, his lawyer, was working to contain the explosion that Galliano's behavior had caused. On Tuesday, March 1, they sneaked him out of his home. Twenty-four hours later he was in Arizona under medical supervision.

In rehab, there would be no coddling and no funny business. Pretty much everything Galliano brought along was taken away. Even a book he had, Keith Richards's *Life,* was confiscated as (maybe no surprise) "inappropriate reading." After a few days, he was allowed his first two-minute call and tried to reach Bill Gaytten back in Paris. The Galliano show was nearly under way, and, still passionate about the collection, he wanted to tell the models what they should be thinking about as they walked. The call didn't go well. "Bill said, 'Do you realize what you've fucking done?' " Galliano remembered. "And I said, 'Kind of.' But I still didn't. I couldn't say yes. I just couldn't. And those were the last words we shared. That's someone I've known for thirty years. Even now I'm still learning every day how many people I hurt."

When the first visitors' weekend rolled around, Linda Evangelista was the sole friend to make the trek. "I just didn't want that weekend to go by without anyone reaching out to him," she told me. She'd spent years living with a yellow silk tulle ball gown she'd worn in Galliano's spring/summer 1995 "Pin-Up" collection—her favorite dress of all time, she said. She kept it in her bedroom on a mannequin so she could see it every day when she woke up, until she finally donated it to the Metropolitan Museum.

With the start of the Paris collections having coincided with Galliano's exit to Arizona, pity the lesser-known designers who were trying to get editors' and critics' attention; there was only one subject on people's minds, and it wasn't whether pants were back. D-day was at the end of that week, on March 4, when the Dior fall/winter fashion show was to be held in a tent in the gardens at the Musée Rodin. There had been a question about whether the show would actually occur, and also whether the Galliano label would have its own showing. But the decision was made to go forward, on both counts. Dressed in an impeccable, serious-looking suit and tie, Toledano stood on the Dior runway and made a pre-show announcement. His words were well prepared and well aimed, returning the spotlight to the label and Monsieur Dior's original mission to bring out the beauty of women, to give them confidence and dreams. Toledano was also direct in his condemnation of Galliano's behavior, even though he did not name the designer. Toledano is Jewish; one felt his pain, believed it. Not hiding his emotions, he ended his speech by crediting all the hardworking, usually anonymous seamstresses and craftspeople—*les petites mains*—as the real stars of the show, "the heart of the house of Dior, which beats unseen."

Galliano says he has been sober for more than two years now, approaching recovery the same way he used to go about creating a collection—throwing himself into it with all he's got. But perhaps the most difficult part of the process has been his realization that he may never have all the answers about those lost evenings at La Perle. One addiction expert who saw Galliano as a patient told him he may never find out why he said what he did; he will wear a permanent hair shirt. He insists he is not an anti-Semite, or anti-Asian, and none of the dozens of friends and colleagues I spoke to said they had ever heard him express any views that could even remotely be called prejudiced. And yet his words were his words.

"It's the worst thing I have said in my life," he told me, "but I didn't mean it." Later he added, "I have been trying to find out why that anger was directed at this race. I now realize I was so fucking angry and so discontent with myself that I just said the most spiteful thing I could."

I spoke to quite a few addiction experts and each time began with the notion that I had heard so often when the scandal erupted: If Galliano said these things, he must have somehow meant them; if they came out of his mouth, they were part of who he is. I would mention the old saying *In vino veritas*—In wine, there is truth. If only the human mind were that simple, I was told in response, over and over. Dr. Harris Stratyner, a psychologist, addictionologist, and vice president of the Caron Treatment Center in New York, one of the largest and oldest rehabilitation programs in the United States, said that in a blackout state "things can come up that are the complete antithesis of who you are. In terms of the saying 'In wine, there is truth,' that comes from the fact that initially, when you drink, alcohol is a mood disinhibitor. There is a tendency for people to say things because they feel disinhibited. But it doesn't actually have to be the truth. It could be something that is going through somebody's stream of consciousness because they saw something on television, for instance. Let's say Mr. Galliano—who I have never met and never treated—was coming into a bar and saw Hasidic people. That could have triggered something. That does not mean he is an anti-Semite. He certainly could be anti-Semitic, but he may also love Jewish people. The thing to know is that in the *Diagnostic and Statistical Manual of Mental Disorders,* alcohol dependence is under the rubric of being a mental illness. Pills can cause the same thing—the brain is going, to use a layman's term, haywire."

Ex-addicts themselves have stories galore about going haywire. I was talking to Elton John, who has been sober for twenty-three years, about Galliano, and he said, "I still hear stories from the people who had to put up with me when I was an addict. I'd been up for days on a bender in a London hotel during the worst of my days. I was trying to get some sleep but couldn't because it was so windy outside. I phoned my office and told them to call the meteorological office to demand they turn the wind down *now*! And I was serious."

While struggling to overcome his addictions and atone for his actions, Galliano has also had to cope with being a pariah. The instances when people have offered a hand to help him climb a little further out of his abyss have been monumental for him. When Kate Moss contacted him a few weeks into his recovery and asked him if he would design her wedding dress, which they had been discussing while he was still at Dior, he felt it was a gift for him. As he told me, "Creating Kate's wedding dress saved me personally because it was my creative rehab. She dared me to be me again." Galliano may not have had his old resources, but he created one of the finest, most beautiful, most tender dresses of his life. His boyfriend, Alexis, was his fitting model. "It was absolutely gorgeous," Moss said, "a diaphanous 1920s-type dress, romantic, with gold sequins in the shape of the phoenix—as if he was saying he would rise from this."

The wedding in July was the first public appearance Galliano had made since he'd gone into treatment. He was terrified at the prospect, not knowing whether people would snub him or cause a scene. They didn't. Moss: "When my dad gave his speech, he thanked everyone and then he referred to the genius of Galliano, who made his daughter's dress. Everyone stood up and gave John a standing ovation. It was the most moving thing, because suddenly John realized he wasn't on his own."

Before the wedding, Galliano had called Jonathan Newhouse, chairman and CEO of Condé Nast International (part of the company that owns this magazine), whom Galliano knew professionally, and talked to him about the scandal. He had slowly begun to do this with other people, too, both close to him and members of the larger fashion community, as part of the process of making amends that is so important for any recovering addict. Newhouse was perfectly frank with the designer about the hatefulness of his remarks. The two spoke for a while and, after they saw each other at Moss's wedding, kept in touch. Newhouse gave Galliano books on the Holocaust, including *The Last of the Just,* by André Schwarz-Bart; *Night,* by Elie Wiesel; and *Survival in Auschwitz,* by Primo Levi. (I noticed these books, and many more about Jewish history, when we were talking in Galliano's apartment. Some of them were quite dog-eared.) Eventually, when Newhouse was convinced of Galliano's remorse, he decided to help build some bridges between Galliano and the Jewish community, particularly in London, where Newhouse lives.

I had known that Newhouse admired Galliano's work, but since the kind of help he offered goes beyond the call of professional courtesy, I asked Newhouse (whom I work for directly when wearing my other hat, as international editor for the *Vanity Fair* European editions) why he had stuck his neck out. He answered, "Start with the fact that the man in the video is clearly suffering from acute addiction, an AMA-recognized disease which impairs the mind. Over the past two years John has courageously taken the steps to recover from the illness and to confront honestly the moral issues that were raised by his conduct while in its grip. He's done the hard work, from going to meetings to reading the books, to meeting with Jewish leaders. He has actively looked for meaningful ways to make amends. In the throes of disease and despair, at his lowest point, he resorted to a school-yard racist taunt. Must he pay his entire life for this mistake? I asked the chief rabbi in Britain what to do about John. He said if someone who does wrong sincerely wants to atone, then we have to welcome this. My focus is not on his moral behavior but on my own. A person I care about was lost, sick, and in trouble. What kind of friend would I be if I turned my back on him?"

Not everyone has believed it to be appropriate to have Galliano in their midst. Gilles Bernheim, the chief rabbi of France, rejected requests to meet with him, I was told by several people with knowledge of the situation. They also recounted another episode, when the designer was invited to visit the Shenkar College of Engineering and Design, in Tel Aviv, to teach senior students one-on-one; Galliano had his plane ticket, but at the last moment the invitation was rescinded, supposedly because a wealthy board member threatened to withdraw financial support of the school if Galliano appeared. On the other hand, Rabbi Barry Marcus, of Central Synagogue, one of London's oldest Orthodox synagogues, has begun a dialogue with Galliano. The designer attended a service one Saturday morning with Newhouse, wearing a tallith and *kipa* Newhouse had given him. Not surprisingly, he was anxious, as he later wrote in a present-tense e-mail: "I am dressed appropriately but still attracting silent glances so I bury my head in the Prayer book, but it's in Hebrew so I feel stupid. Some Elders approach me and at this point, even though I am a guest of Rabbi Marcus, I'm convinced they are going to boot me out. I'm busted, not Jewish, a fraud. 'Shabbat Shalom,' they greet me. A wonder is taking place as I am warmly greeted by all." It happened to be a Bar Mitzvah, and afterward Galliano and Newhouse went on to the kiddush, the Bar Mitzvah boy's celebratory lunch. The boy's mother thanked Galliano for coming and said she would have invited him personally if she'd had his phone number. The best response, though, was from a kid who tweeted, "Saturday my mum met John Galliano in synagogue. Why am I in Cardiff?"

When I spoke to Marcus, it was the simplest thing he said that stayed with me: "As a Jew and as a rabbi, if anybody makes a mistake—and we all make mistakes—built into Judaism is the concept of giving a person another chance, or forgiving. So much of who we are and how we operate as human beings is built on that very principle."

A looming question for Galliano is whether the rest of the world will be as forgiving as Rabbi Marcus so that the designer can go back to work. Galliano certainly has his champions in the fashion community. One of them, Oscar de la Renta, took an enormous risk last winter when he invited Galliano to spend a few weeks as a sort of guest artist in his atelier while he was preparing his collection for fall/winter 2013. The collection was shown in February and was the most newsworthy thing to happen during New York Fashion Week. It's not as if Galliano had designed the collection; de la Renta is perfectly capable of that himself. But Galliano's touches were evident. The designer stayed discreetly in the background and went home just thrilled to have had a chance to be back in an atelier.

Not for long. The very next day, there Galliano was again, on the cover of the *New York Post* under the headline SHMUCK! The outfit he had worn to the de la Renta show—a black suit, a broad-brimmed black hat, black silk knickers, and braids that looked vaguely like *payess*—was taken to be a mockery of Hasidic dress. The reactions were furious, and in some cases oddly gleeful, and it took Abe Foxman, the head of the Anti-Defamation League, to calm the waters by speaking up for Galliano. When I talked to Foxman, he said, "Every time Galliano's head surfaces, people dredge up that he is an anti-Semite. Never mind what he's been trying to do [to atone]."

In fact, what Galliano wore that day had nothing to do with Hasidim. Galliano was wearing clothes that have long been a part of his personal fashion vocabulary: a plush-velvet homburg hat of his own design, an Edwardian Crombie coat, a Dolce & Gabbana waistcoat, satin plus fours. "It was not my intention to upset anyone. I thought I looked chic," he said. "I felt awful when the papers came out, for the people who had supported me. It was maybe silly of me to go there that way. I probably should have been more conscious of how I could be misunderstood." No doubt. Still, it would be a sad day if he felt forced to rein in his highly personal mode of dressing—the equivalent for him of the "room of one's own" that Virginia Woolf said every artist needs. When he and I first talked, he had been wearing an eclectic mix of layers—a United Nations of different kinds of clothes—and when I asked him exactly what he had on, he bristled a bit, as if I'd struck a nerve. *Not you, too,* he seemed to say.

Perhaps Linda Evangelista put it best: "If John walks in with nothing interesting on, I'm going to know something's wrong. I don't want to see him arrive with a short haircut wearing a polo shirt and jeans. No thank you."

All in all, the response to Galliano's guest appearance at de la Renta was positive. The show got good reviews and it was the first sign the tide may be turning for Galliano. For his part, de la Renta told me, "John is one of the great talents of our times. It's always great to have another eye challenging you, and we had a wonderful time working together. I think he deserves a second chance, no question about it. If you ask me the question, Would you like to have him again? *Yes.*" This, from de la Renta, is more than just a nice word or two. The question of succession at the house has been in the air—de la Renta is eighty—and it is not a great leap to imagine that when de la Renta is ready he might tap you-know-who.

But the real key to Galliano's professional future, if he is to have one, is how customers will react to him. LVMH protected the Dior business for the short term with its assertive actions in the immediate wake of the scandal, and for the long term with a well-chosen successor to Galliano: Raf Simons, the Belgian designer who has been running his own label for eighteen years and who is doing an excellent job bringing his voice to Dior. The Galliano label is a different story. Bill Gaytten stepped in as creative director, but the company was hit hard by the scandal. A few executives, such as Galliano's old pal Joan Burstein, of Browns, stuck by the label. But others had almost no choice but to dump it. Ronald Frasch, president of Saks, recalled, "We started getting e-mails from our stores about it, saying, 'Hey, guys, what are you doing over there? Our customers are livid.' It was a very easy decision for me. We couldn't have the Galliano brand in our stores at that time."

Some leaders of the retail community, including Frasch, agreed to meet with the designer in New York this past May to see what he had to say. Others don't seem to be there yet. Rumors were buzzing this spring that one key department-store executive was trying to assemble a coalition of retailers that would not support Galliano if he returned to the business. The biggest elephant in the room is an apology from Galliano to his former bosses at Dior and LVMH, human-to-human, for the hurt his words may have caused them personally. When that moment comes—it hasn't yet, perhaps for complex reasons—a lot of people will exhale. My hunch is that most will forgive but not forget. The designer Diane von Furstenberg, president of the Council of Fashion Designers of America, a powerful lobbying group, is very supportive of Galliano. She said, "As a daughter of someone who was in the death camps, I feel like I should be most offended by the remarks he made. But I know the kind of person he is. To portray him as anti-Semitic is completely not true."

. . .

As I was reaching the end of interviews and research for this article, I was talking to Galliano's crony Jeremy Healy, who casually mentioned something that might be a clue to the designer's state of mind those fateful evenings. He recalled that the timing of the famous cell-phone video coincided with a period in which Galliano must have been thinking about the Galliano menswear show for fall/winter 2011. "It was a mixture of *Fiddler on the Roof* and the Rudolf Nureyev story," Healy said of the show's theme. "That is probably what was in his head at the time. It was basically Russian, Jewish, turn-of-the-century style, big coats and furry hats and all that, mixed in with seventies Nureyev." But Nureyev wasn't just an extraordinary dancer; he was also known for making offensive remarks about Jews. Some people said he was an anti-Semite, and other people said he wasn't. Galliano was well aware of this debate, as it had come up in his research. Could it be that all this Jewish history was in his head and got scrambled and twisted as all the chemicals in Galliano's body were affecting his brain? We will never know.

What we do know is that, while Galliano deeply regrets what he said, he does not regret the last two years. I could also feel how ready he is to get back to work, and in recent months I've gotten an equal sense that many people are eager to see what he might now create after two and a half years of silence and a trip to hell. His name keeps coming up among artists, actors, all sorts of people, when fashion is being discussed. As Anna Wintour said, "We need the dreamers. We need those designers who create a magic moment, a world that changes the way you look at clothes."

And Galliano himself has clearly started to dream again. He told me, "I know it sounds a bit bizarre, but I am so grateful for what did happen. I have learned so much about myself. I have rediscovered that little boy who had the hunger to create, which I think I had lost. I am alive."

This made me think about my own brother, Mark. He was a brilliant judge who worked in Scotland; unlike Galliano, he did not come through to the other side, and died an alcoholic. During that Paris fashion season two years ago, on March 6, 2011, the day of the Galliano fall/winter women's ready-to-wear show, I couldn't be there because I had flown to Edinburgh to be at the stone setting for my brother's grave, which is in the Piershill Cemetery, in a section designated for Jews, which is what our family is. It was drizzling, cold, miserable. When I got back to Paris that night, the people who had been at the Galliano show, earlier that day, reported that it, too, had seemed funereal, there was such a sense of pain about Galliano's fall.

Somehow my private grief and the public sadness that was so visceral all that week dovetailed in a way that seemed right to me. When Sidney Toledano got up on the runway at the Dior show, it wasn't just to handle a PR emergency. It was to address the collective pain and also the personal pain he felt—as if something horrible had happened to a family member, which essentially it had. That Galliano had catalyzed such intense feeling was sadly, ironically appropriate, because emotion in fashion is a subject he stressed from the beginning; it's why people have cared so much about his clothes.

In fact, he was preparing to teach a four-day workshop on the subject to students at Parsons in New York this past May. He had already taught a similar class in March at his alma mater, Central Saint Martins—a grand success. But at the eleventh hour the Parsons class was canceled. Some students had begun petitioning and protesting against Galliano's appearance, and so the school asked him to submit to a mass question-and-answer session in the school's auditorium. It had the potential to turn into a show trial, and his publicist—correctly, I thought—refused to put the designer through that. Galliano's trial should be over. Now it's time for him to get out the scissors. And ribbons.

Vanity Fair, July 2013

Jeff Koons Is Back!

If the walls at Manhattan's Frick Collection could talk, they would have been uttering tiny gasps of shock and awe this spring at a lecture given by Jeff Koons for a small, mostly professional art-world crowd. Koons was sharing his ruminations on the Renaissance and Baroque bronzes from the Hill Collection then on view in the galleries, and it was one of the artist's classic performances: No opportunity was missed to point out breasts, testicles, and phalluses, both in the bronzes and in his own work. This way of seeing and talking about art is his specialty, and the crowd ate it up, many of them getting the droll underlying humor of the situation as a deadpan Koons busted taboos in snootsville. But not everyone was happy about it. The very idea of Koons's being invited to speak at this old-world institution apparently put someone's nose out of joint enough that he or she had sent the museum postcards featuring drawings of poop.

The Frick isn't the only important institution to embrace Koons. The Whitney Museum plans a retrospective, curated by Scott Rothkopf, opening to the public on June 27. It will be historic in many ways. Spreading out just over 27,000 square feet—in all the museum's exhibition spaces save the fifth floor, which holds selections from the permanent collection—it will be the biggest show devoted to a single artist that the Whitney has ever done. Furthermore, it will be the last show, for now at least, that the Whitney will put on in its current home—Marcel Breuer's bold, unconventional gray granite and concrete modernist structure at Seventy-fifth Street and Madison Avenue. After the Koons exhibition, the museum will reopen downtown, in spring 2015, in a much larger space designed by Renzo Piano, smack at the southern end of the High Line, in the Meatpacking District. The museum, which can't afford to erect a new building and keep the old one operating at full throttle, has leased the Breuer building for eight years, with an option to extend, to the Metropolitan Museum of Art, which has never had a sympathetic exhibition space for its collection of twentieth- and twenty-first-century works. Now it does.

First, though, the prospect of the Koons show is revving things up in the art world. "Jeff is the Warhol of his time," proclaims Adam Weinberg, the Whitney's director. The exhibition's organizer, Rothkopf, adds, "We didn't want to leave the building looking backward and being nostalgic, but we wanted something very bold that was new for the Whitney and Jeff and New York."

It is a banner year for Koons in general. *Split-Rocker*, 2000, the artist's second live-flower sculpture, will be shown in New York for the first time, at Rockefeller Center, under the auspices of the Gagosian Gallery and the Public Art Fund, to coincide with the Whitney show. With its references to Picasso's Cubism, to my eyes it is even more multilayered and pleasurable than Koons's other megahit, *Puppy*—which also has its own soil and internal irrigation system to take care of the flowers. Meanwhile, at the Louvre, in January 2015, Koons will install a selection of his large-scale balloon sculptures, including *Balloon Rabbit, Balloon Swan,* and *Balloon Monkey,* in the nineteenth-century galleries.

The last time I wrote about Koons for this magazine, in 2001, he was in a very different place, having just gone to hell and back, not only in the effort to pull off a fiercely ambitious project, "Celebration," which he had begun in 1993, but in his personal life as well. He'd basically lost everything except his faith in his art. At the time, I thought how unruffled Koons was, how most people would have been hysterical in his situation. But as Gary McCraw, Koons's loyal right-hand man, says, "Jeff does not like being stuck—he figures out what needs to change." Koons's cool paid off. He extricated himself from a number of business relationships that clearly weren't working and returned to his original home at the Sonnabend Gallery. He took a detour from the struggle to complete his "Celebration" sculptures and paintings, and created several new

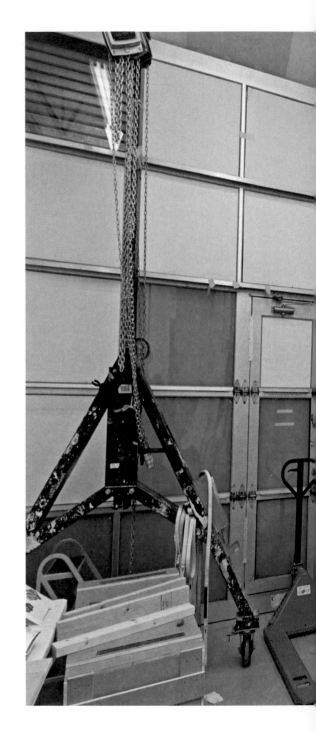

Annie Leibovitz, *Jeff Koons, New York City*, 2014

series, including a couple of painting shows and animal-shaped reflecting wall reliefs ("Easyfun" and "Easyfun-Ethereal"). Skip ahead a dozen or so years, to today, and the change in Koons's circumstances is almost beyond belief. He is a superstar for a consortium of three powerful galleries—Gagosian, David Zwirner, and Sonnabend—each of which works with him independently, and, astonishing as it may sound, his earlier high prices now sound like flat-out bargains. A few examples of his auction sales prices, totaling $177 million over the past year: $28.2 million for the mirror-polished stainless-steel *Popeye*, 2009–2011; $33.8 million for the stainless-steel *Jim Beam–J. B. Turner Train*, 1986; $58.4 million for *Balloon Dog (Orange)*, 1994–2000, the highest price ever paid for a work by a living artist.

How Koons managed to go from obscurity to white-hot to near ruin and then back again to the pinnacle is a classic American tale of self-invention, ingenuity, and unbreakable will, not to mention a genius for salesmanship and spin.

The artist comes by his talent for salesmanship honestly. When I visited him this spring at his farm in south-central Pennsylvania (which had once been owned by his maternal grandparents, Nell and Ralph Sitler, and which he bought back in 2005, as a country place for his family), Koons took me to the cemetery in nearby East Prospect, where his mother's side of the family is buried. Parked in front of a row of headstones with the name Sitler carved into them, Koons read the first names and told me what each of his male relatives had done. Most were merchants. His uncle Carl Sitler had a cigar business; his uncle Roy Sitler owned the general store; and on it went. The artist's father, Henry Koons, was an interior decorator whose business catered to the most affluent citizens of York, which back then was thriving as a small industrial hub.

The young Koons fit right in. In addition to helping his dad—even making paintings that would end up in his furniture store—he loved selling ribbons and bows and gift wrap door-to-door and also Cokes at the local golf course.

"Everyone else would sell Kool-Aid, but I would sell Coca-Cola in a really nice jug," Koons recalls. "I would lay out a towel and stack up all my cups, and really try to make it a nice, hygienic experience." (The artist has a sensitivity to hygiene and odors that is almost comical.)

Koons's early art heroes were those who had personal meaning to him, such as Salvador Dalí, whose work he knew from a book his parents had given him, his first art book. While at art school in Baltimore, Koons tracked down Dalí at the St. Regis Hotel, in New York, and the next thing you know they had a memorable date—the boy who looked like he had popped off the back of a cereal box (he still does) and the man who defined Euro-decadence. The subsequent nods in his work to Dalí's famous mustache are fun to pick out.

Similarly, Koons was so knocked out by a show of Jim Nutt's paintings at the Whitney in 1974 that he decided to spend his senior year at the School of the Art Institute of Chicago, in the city where Nutt belonged to a loosely connected collective of artists known as the Chicago Imagists. There, Koons ended up working as a studio assistant for one of the key Imagists, Ed Paschke, whose nightmare palette and netherworld iconography still pack a punch. Paschke recalled how Koons was such a dedicated assistant that his hands would bleed from trying to stretch the canvases to be perfectly taut.

Once he made it to New York, Koons landed the perfect, for him, position at the Museum of Modern Art, manning the membership desk. I was working at MoMA back then, too, on a National Endowment for the Arts fellowship in photography, and I often spied him in the lobby in his eye-catching outfits and attention-getting accessories, such as paper bibs, double ties, and store-bought inflatable flowers around his neck. These shenanigans made for some hilarious anecdotes, such as when the museum's then director, Richard Oldenburg, politely asked Koons to pull a Houdini and disappear till the coast was clear. Oldenburg was acting at the behest of William Rubin, the humorless head of the painting and sculpture department, who was bringing a delegation from Russia, as Koons remembers it; Rubin was hoping they would help fund an exhibition or two, and he worried that Koons's antics might be a turnoff. (I recounted this story to the architect Annabelle Selldorf, who has worked with Koons, and she observed, laughing, that those collectors are now the ones buying his work.)

Koons's job at MoMA gave him the opportunity to immerse himself in the history of modernism, in particular the ideas of Marcel Duchamp, who changed art history by showing how everyday objects, or "readymades," could be elevated into the realm of art, depending on context. Duchamp's theories were a revelation to Koons. While at MoMA he started to fool around with a bunch of cheap inflatables, blowups of flowers and bunnies, riffing on Duchamp's idea of readymades and propping them against mirrors in his apartment. "The sexual power of the imagery was so intoxicating to me visually that I had to have a drink," he remembers. "I went to Slugger Ann's, Jackie Curtis's grandmother's bar."

The reference to Curtis ties Koons to the last true avant-garde—a pedigree the artist likes. Curtis, who refused to be called a drag queen, was a pioneer of the LGBT movement and, like Candy Darling, was made famous by Warhol. Koons clearly relishes the fact that he and Warhol are often discussed in the same breath these days, but in fact, as artists and personalities, they couldn't be more different. Warhol had a double whammy of an outsider perspective: The American son of Slovak immigrants, he was gay at a time when it was a very different proposition from what it is today. Koons, on the other hand, grew up in the embrace of community, with a secure sense of belonging. Warhol liked to have young folks around him at the Factory, but he didn't want to actually spawn any. Koons has enough kids of his own (eight) to start a touring company of *The Sound of Music.* Warhol was almost Zen in his grasp of the light touch in making his artworks and getting them out into the world. Koons goes through a ring of fire for each work, so much so that his finished output is actually quite slim. "We average six point seventy-five paintings and fifteen to twenty sculptures a year," he told me. (He is always very exact.) Warhol was practically monosyllabic with art critics, dealers, and collectors. Koons is the opposite.

Actually, if there is anyone the artist seems to be inspired by at this point in his life, it is Picasso, whom Koons refers to a lot. Koons, at fifty-nine, has already begun a strict exercise and diet regimen so that he will have a shot at working undiminished into his eighties, as Picasso did. He hits his upstairs gym every day at around noon when he is in the studio, then eats a lean lunch. For the rest of the afternoon he dips into an assortment of nuts, cereals, fresh vegetables, and Zone bars. Once in a while he'll apologize for an odor if he's eating broccoli.

What Warhol and Koons do have in common, though, is an uncanny ability to nail an image or an object so that it catches the Zeitgeist. The first time Koons landed on such an idea was in 1979, around the time he left MoMA. He had been experimenting with kitchen appliances, such as toasters, refrigerators, and deep fryers, attaching them to fluorescent light tubes. These gave way to the artist's first fully realized series, "The New," which included never-used vacuum cleaners and rug shampooers, often presented in clear Plexiglas vitrines and illuminated by fluorescent lights. "I thought of them as eternal-virgin-type situations," says Koons.

By then he was selling mutual funds to get by. The artworks got some buzz in the downtown art community, and for a minute Koons was taken on by the dealer of the moment, Mary Boone. As he whispered to trusted fellow artists, he was excited to become a "Booney," but it didn't work out in the end. Another dealer returned a vacuum-cleaner piece. Broke and heartbroken, Koons called a time-out and spent six months or so with his parents, who had moved to Florida, where he saved money from a job as a political canvasser.

What came next, upon his return to New York, was the game changer: his "Equilibrium" series. He was working once again in the high-pressure world of finance, this time trading commodities, but by night he was cooking up what would turn out to be his first coup. Involving a dark, Nietzschean worldview, it was almost the opposite of the cheerful Koonsian iconography people have grown accustomed to. Take two works from 1985: a cast-bronze scuba apparatus, which he called *Aqualung,* and a bronze *Lifeboat.* It's immediately obvious they aren't going to save anyone. Instead they'll take you down.

The "Equilibrium" works were exhibited in 1985 in Koons's first solo show, at International with Monument, a short-lived, artist-run gallery in the East Village. Dakis Joannou, a Greek collector, who would become an important champion of the artist's, was stunned when he saw the show. "I was so intrigued with the basketball piece, *One Ball Total Equilibrium Tank,*" he remembers. "I wanted to buy that piece." The now-iconic works of single or multiple basketballs in fish tanks had taken countless experiments and many phone calls to scientists, including Nobel Prize winner Dr. Richard P. Feynman, who encouraged Koons to work out the right proportion of distilled and saline water so that the basketballs would neither rise nor sink. Joannou asked to meet the artist. "He was serious," says Joannou. "He had depth. He had vision. He had an enormous world of his own that he had not even started exploring yet." (Joannou scooped up the work for $2,700.)

The Whitney exhibition will have prime examples from the Koons hit parade, from his earliest works to his most recent, including stainless-steel objects from both the "Luxury and Degradation" series (a *Travel Bar,* the

Jim Beam–J. B. Turner Train, etc.) and the "Statuary" series, which featured Koons's most critically admired work, *Rabbit,* 1986. This mirror-polished, enigmatic, silver stainless-steel bunny is the piece that won over previously unconvinced curators, art historians, and critics, who saw it as a dazzling contemporary update of a broad range of iconography, from Playboy bunnies to Brancusi's soaring forms.

But Koons aspires to appeal not just to the cognoscenti. Nowhere was this more obvious than in his "Banality" series, created mostly in traditional porcelain and wood in workshops in Italy and Germany in the late eighties. The works are a virtual populist paradise that runs the gamut from St. John the Baptist to an all-gold-and-white Michael Jackson, cradling his pet monkey. The springboard for the work was found common objects and popular souvenirs, to which Koons then brought his art wand. Plenty of people checked out these artworks at the Sonnabend Gallery, where the artist had finally found a home. Soon there would be even more signs that he might one day reach his goal, which he once described rather immodestly as wanting to create the art equivalent of what the Beatles had done.

Koons always captures the Zeitgeist, for better or for worse, so there is a perfect logic to the "Made in Heaven" series, which he exhibited at Sonnabend in the fall of 1991, a period in which sex went from under the counter to center stage because of AIDS. What Koons did was the heterosexual equivalent of Robert Mapplethorpe's taboo-busting images of men having sex together—in fact, Koons's paintings and sculptures, created out of wood, marble, glass, and canvases photomechanically printed with oil inks, include some of the most graphic sexual imagery ever produced in Western art that went public. It's impossible to imagine this work without its leading lady, Ilona Staller, better known as La Cicciolina (translated as the "little dumpling"), an only-in-Italy personage, whom Koons met after he saw her picture in a magazine as a model. Almost immediately they got up close and personal. The Hungarian-born Staller—a former porn star/erotic-video icon/politician—has so far been Koons's only human readymade, and, being human, she had issues.

The paintings Koons created of the two of them feature penetration, both anal and vaginal, and liberal amounts of semen. Discussing one of the most no-holes-barred pictures, Koons says, "What I really like about it are the pimples on Ilona's ass. The confidence to reveal one's ass like that. That's like my reference to Courbet's *The Origin of the World.*" And he's not kidding.

For a while their life imitated art, and vice versa. The couple fell in love and, after a wedding in Budapest and about a year in Munich, where Koons oversaw production of his "Made in Heaven" project, they came back to New York. "My dad said that he thought it was crazy, but he was very accepting," recalls Koons. Dad wasn't the only one who thought it was loony.

Not surprisingly, the "Made in Heaven" exhibition was extremely popular with a curious public and hungry media, but it was basically a bomb with the art establishment, many of whose members thought that Koons had committed career suicide. Selldorf remembers how shocking the work seemed at the time. "One time I was all alone in the studio and three of the gigantic 'penetration' paintings were there," she says. "I was staring at these paintings thinking, Holy Mother of God!" It was no picnic to sell the work, which had been expensive to produce, and it didn't help that the recession of the early nineties had people in a panic. Sonnabend was having trouble keeping up with Koons's needs, and something that had previously seemed unimaginable happened: Koons and Sonnabend parted ways. Antonio Homem, who ran the gallery with Ileana Sonnabend for some forty years until Sonnabend's death, and who now owns it, remembers, "It was a very difficult moment. Even though Ileana and [her husband] Michael had a huge collection, they always lived from one day to the other. . . . The great financial problem for us was to fabricate all the 'Made in Heaven' pieces beforehand, which were very expensive to produce. Jeff wanted all of the editions to be made right from the beginning. I explained to him that we were unable to continue. He felt that this was a betrayal and that we didn't believe in him, and therefore didn't want to finance his work. He took it very badly. We had no wish to betray him. It was very sad for all of us."

Today this work is finally getting its due. Happily, Koons couldn't destroy as much of it as he tried to—because it was so well constructed. (The Whitney will include some of it—with the usual not-for-minors warning.)

"'Made in Heaven' is just mind-blowing," says Dan Colen, one of the most talented artists of the generation that came after Koons. "It was a borderless, boundaryless body of work. There was no separation between the artist's life and his work. What he did is beyond Duchamp, beyond Warhol, beyond the readymade." Some might say it was also beyond reason and beyond the market, but this is not a guy who compromises his art, ever. Homem sums it up: "Jeff would throw me out of the window for his art, but he would throw himself out the window with me, as well, without a second thought. He is the most romantic artist I ever met."

By now the head-spinning details of the Koons-Staller affair are art-world legend. In a nutshell, Staller wanted to keep her X-rated porn-star job, and Koons wanted her to stick to their marriage vows. To make matters more complicated, the couple had a son, Ludwig, in October 1992. After Maria Callas–worthy drama, Staller blindsided Koons by outsmarting one of the bodyguards whom Koons had hired to watch her, and she left for Rome with Ludwig. Koons spent more than a decade and millions of dollars trying to get his son back, to no avail. He would fly to Rome to see Ludwig, but once he was there the visits would usually fall through. He was basically shut out of his son's life. So he poured his emotions into his "Celebration" series, begun in 1993, as a way to tell his son just how much his father was missing him. A massive sculpture of a wide-eyed *Cat on a Clothesline*. A painting of *Building Blocks*. A sculpture of a giant stainless-steel gold *Hanging Heart* suspended by magenta stainless-steel ribbons. A monumental stainless-steel *Balloon Dog*, or modern-day Trojan horse. The simplicity of these works, and others like them, belies the complexity of executing them according to Koons's high expectations and uncompromising standards. The production costs of the art and the legal costs of trying to bring back Ludwig nearly bankrupted the artist.

Eventually Koons started to rebuild his life. "A friend told me, 'Jeff, look, it's over,'" he recalls. "'You did everything you can. Stop this, and pull yourself together and get on with your life.' I lost everything." He never gave up on Ludwig, who is now twenty-one, and to try to help other children, he got involved with the International Centre for Missing & Exploited Children, and together they later formed the Koons Family Institute on International Law & Policy. At a certain point Koons was reunited with his daughter Shannon, who'd been born when Koons was in college and put up for adoption; they now have a close relationship. In 2002 he married Justine Wheeler, an artist and former assistant in his studio. Today pictures of their own kids along with those of Ludwig and Shannon dot the Koons households.

At the height of his crisis Koons's funding was depleted, and over time he had to let go of more than seventy assistants. Furthermore, in 1999, the IRS filed a three-million-dollar tax lien. On many days Koons, his studio manager McCraw, and Wheeler, who was then becoming closer to the artist, had the studio to themselves. Their strategy for saving "Celebration" ultimately worked. "One big problem at the beginning was that Jeff would start making a work without really having a clear idea of how he could complete it," explains Homem. "Problems would occur in which everything would stop. Although his pieces still take years to make, fortunately there is less of that." Eventually, thanks to dogged belief, a new model of working (not to mention forces of nature like Gagosian and Sonnabend), and a lot of problem solving, the "Celebration" works slowly began to see the light of day.

A fundamental problem with the "Celebration" series was that the fabricating processes and the technology had not caught up with Koons's visions. These evolving technologies are so sophisticated and so much a part of the work that the Whitney devotes an entire chapter to them, written by Michelle Kuo, the editor of *Artforum,* in the catalogue for the show. Reading about the CT scans, structured-light scanning, volumetric data, customized software, and personalization of fabrication technologies, I started to understand why all those people are needed in Koons's studio. Most days there are 128 of them going at it, some doing just what Michelangelo's assistants did, such as mixing colors, while others seem to be doing lab work for advanced degrees in radiology.

Such a huge operation, combined with the achievement of perfection in the work, helps to explain why Koons's art costs so much to produce, and also what Koons has to do to pull it off. Barbara Kruger, the artist whose unsentimental pronouncements have been cutting to the chase about the art world for decades, says "Oh boy" when I call to discuss Koons, whom she has known since they both were starting out in New York. She needed to think about it and later wrote me: "Jeff is like the man who fell to earth, who, in this grotesque time of art flippage and speculative mania, is either the icing on the cake or some kind of Piketty-esque harbinger of the return of Brecht's 'making strange.' Or a glitteringly bent version of that alienated vision. He brings the cake and lets them eat it." Kruger's reference to Thomas Piketty, the French economist whose book on the current chasm between the very rich and the very poor has become a cultural touchstone, is part of the whole picture; this social reality is what one can't help thinking about when one hears about the prices of contemporary art today, especially the sums that Koons's works are fetching. The odd thing, as many who know Koons, including Kruger, will say, is that money doesn't interest him. He has three very personal luxuries: his home in New York City, the farm, and his collection of older art, which includes Magrittes, Courbets, and Manets. The farm, now expanded from forty acres to approximately eight hundred, is almost a Koonsian artwork. The buildings are painted in heritage red, yellow, and white in the full-on tradition of the area. In the main house, historic wallpapers, the patterns shifting from room to room, give the feeling of a kaleidoscope. But this farm is very much a private retreat for the family.

In Koons's public life there is no showy "I am rich" stuff. Money is mostly a means to an end for him to create his art. What he does need is wealthy patrons. Rothkopf, whose retrospective is blessedly clear-eyed, puts it this way: "If it is going to cost several million dollars to produce new work, he has got to martial the resources from wealthy patrons to produce this thing. He has to convince extremely wealthy people, via art dealers, to buy into the dream of this perfect object."

While Koons has continued to explore popular imagery—such as the Hulk and Popeye (whose spinach he equates with art's transformative power)—he has also been producing other work in the last few years, both paintings and sculptures, which obviously draw on his love of antiquity and classical art. For last year's knockout show, "Gazing Ball," at the David Zwirner Gallery—the announcement of which temporarily caused the art-world gossips to venture that he was leaving Gagosian, which wasn't true—he collaborated with the Louvre's plaster workshop, outside of Paris, the Staatliche Museen's Gipsformerei, in Berlin, and others. An expert in stone and casting at the Metropolitan Museum helped formulate the custom plaster that Koons used for the sculptures—a modern plaster as durable as marble. Each work had an electric blue gazing ball—those glass globes that were a Venetian staple in the thirteenth century and repopularized in Victorian times—placed at a strategic spot.

Dr. Eric R. Kandel, a Nobel Prize–winning neuroscientist, was so impressed with the show that he e-mailed Koons afterward. I asked Kandel why. He explained, "I have been interested in the 'beholder's share,' an idea that came from the Viennese art historian Alois Riegl. It involves the concept that when a painter paints a painting or a sculptor makes a sculpture, it is not complete unless a beholder, a viewer, responds to it."

Kandel adds, "When you looked at the sculptures you saw yourself embedded in the gazing balls. Artists sometimes put mirrors in works, but they don't design the work so that you find yourself in the arms or chest of a statue, which is what Jeff did."

When I was visiting the artist and his family at their farm, and all of us—Jeff, Justine, and the kids—jumped into his Koonsmobile, a stretch van with a captain's chair for every child, he was the happiest I'd seen him in the thirty years since we first met. He told me, "One of the things that I'm most proud of is making work that lets viewers not feel intimidated by art, but feel that they can emotionally participate in it through their senses and their intellect and be fully engaged. And feel that they can get a foothold in it, to push themselves off of, and lift themselves up on." As we drove through small industrial communities that had definitely seen better days, Koons pointed out the ubiquitous garden ornaments in so many front yards—the gazing balls, the inflatable bunnies. It's a Jeff Koons world.

Vanity Fair, July 2014

Her Place in the Sun

I'll never forget how the night of the Oscars and the whole next day I was com-
pletely delirious from having seen Elizabeth Taylor on live television accepting the
gold statuette [for her performance in Butterfield 8, *1960] with the tracheotomy*
scar visible on her throat. . . . What Elizabeth Taylor offered to the camera was
a real woman who lives in the real world, who loves to eat and drink, and who
enjoys life.
　—Camille Paglia, 2007

There's something perfect about the mundane facts of how these photographs by Catherine Opie came to be. It wasn't a Hollywood agent, or an art dealer, or a celebrity, or a publisher, but Elizabeth Taylor's accountant—who also happened to be Opie's accountant—who made the introductions between the photographer and Taylor's trusted secretary, Tim Mendelson, that started the ball rolling for the photographs to be taken. Despite her stratospheric fame, Taylor was always deliciously regular in so many ways. She was also uncannily intuitive—this is abundantly clear in her extraordinarily authentic work as an actress—and so when Mendelson, who had met Opie by then, and had checked out her previous work thoroughly, told his boss all about the photographer and her wish to create a portrait of Taylor by photographing her home and her belongings, over time, it didn't take long for the actress to agree.

Looking back at that moment, Mendelson, who is now a trustee of the Elizabeth Taylor Trust, remembers, "Elizabeth was a genius at being Elizabeth Taylor. So she knew exactly what she was doing. I would over-explain things so often and she'd indulge me, but at some point she'd cut me off. I was ready to go on and on for an hour about Cathy's work, but Elizabeth just said, 'I don't need to hear any more. I get it. Just do it.'" But there was a poignancy behind this decision. Mendelson continues:

Elizabeth was so public in the world, but she was always so private in her home. She didn't ever want photographs to be done there. She was brought up in MGM. You had to have a separate life and she understood the importance of that. Normally she wouldn't have done this. But in hindsight it was pretty obvious she was close to the end of her life. We didn't want to believe it at the time. Nobody did. She was such a survivor and had pulled through so many times. But she must have understood the importance of what Cathy wanted to do. Thank goodness she was able to capture it all, at least before it all changed.

Even though Opie spent six months working at Taylor's house, at 700 Nimes Road in Bel Air, from January to June in 2011, and at the beginning Taylor was there upstairs in her bedroom, the two of them never met, because of the actress's ill health. Six weeks after Opie began to photograph at the house, Taylor went into the hospital and never made it back home. Although it was, of course, very sad, their not meeting wasn't a problem for Opie. "Here was one of the most photographed people on earth, who had been photographed by the greatest photographers over her lifetime," she explains. "I was never attempting or intending to do a portrait of her. I always wanted the home, and what surrounded her, to be the portrait. I was in the house photographing for three months before she passed away, and then I was there continually for another three months. I probably did about six thousand photographs. But I didn't go into the project anticipating Elizabeth's death, and the eventual transformation of her home."

Those are the facts behind *700 Nimes Road* by Catherine Opie. But I think larger forces, too, came into play. In a way, these two women couldn't be more opposite. For starters, Taylor had eight husbands—if you count the two marriages to Richard Burton—and Opie has a wife. Taylor was a clotheshorse who loved her fashion, be it the fancy couture made famous by designers especially for her or an off-the-rack schmatta; Opie has no interest in, or knowledge of, fashion, and pretty much wears the same uniform of jeans every day and night. The obvious differences go on and on. But it was their deeper affinities that account for why these photographs are such keepers. They have an honesty and a clarity and are haunting, touching, and telling.

Looking at the pictures, now gathered together in the book that's in your hands, and thinking about Opie's process, and Taylor's physical absence but constant emotional presence, the words I had in my head were from Emily Brontë's poem "Stars," written in 1845, a year before *Wuthering Heights:*

> *Thought followed thought—star followed star,*
> *Through boundless regions on;*
> *While one sweet influence, near and far,*
> *Thrilled through, and proved us one!*

In order to go at this documentary project, which might have seemed overwhelming, Opie wisely took it step by step. "I just tried to be quiet with everything," she recalls.

> *I was very slow and methodical with this body of work. I took it one day at a time, trying to unpack what was in front of me and do something with it that was poignant. I didn't want it to be one of those situations where everything ends up looking catalogued or archived. Of course, to a certain extent everything is archived, but I wanted to do something more, that hopefully embodies the person in some way, where the viewer feels a personal connection to her. Elizabeth loved her objects, whether they were her iconic jewels*

or the stuffed animals at the end of her bed. Thinking about her and trying to connect to the person, Elizabeth, through her objects, I tried to create a narrative more like a novel than a catalogue. I would watch the light for hours to get certain moments. The light was so important for the photographs to pull them off. You wanted to be able to feel the passing of time, and light does that in images and still lifes.

There is an obvious precedent for this body of work by Opie—and that is William Eggleston's perfect-pitch tour guide of Graceland, shot in 1983, about six years after Elvis died. Opie herself says that she had been thinking about Eggleston's pictures, especially his Elvis project, around the time that she became interested in doing something on Elizabeth Taylor. "I thought what a fantastic thing to do—make a portrait of someone through their home," she explains. In fact, Opie and Eggleston approach their subjects in ways that are poles apart. Although they both feature ordinary life, Eggleston has an eye for the surreal, and Opie is always looking for the humanness in what she photographs. Eggleston is outside of it; Opie is in it.

This is not the first time that Opie has touched upon territory that Eggleston has explored. His "Election Eve" images, created on the eve of the 1976 election, as he journeyed from Mississippi and in and around Plains, Georgia, are an unforgettable record of the American South at the brink of change—or not. Opie, in turn, journeyed to Washington, D.C., for her "Inauguration" project, which captures that historic day, on January, 20, 2009, when one million people gathered to witness the swearing in of Barack Obama, America's first black president. Of course, Robert Frank set the bar for turning-point documentary images about our nation in his classic 1950s book, *The Americans,* and also with his lesser-known coverage of the 1956 Democratic National Convention in Chicago. Then there are Garry

Winogrand's electric 1960 photographs of Richard Nixon's campaign rally in New York and the Democratic National Convention in Los Angeles during which John Kennedy ignited the dream that is still America to many. While each of these photographers has a distinct voice, and their works constitute a record of a distinct time, what connects them all is an ability to tap into our national psyche and the changes that are in the air.

Although it might seem a stretch to discuss Opie's Elizabeth Taylor work in this social/political context, in fact politics do have a genuine role here.

Taylor may have been a giant movie star, who lived a larger-than-life existence, but she was right there when it counted. I was privileged to know her. We had a lot of laughs as well as serious conversations. When I was doing a series of interviews with her a few years before she died, I asked her about the fact that she was the first person in Hollywood to really come forward in the fight against AIDS. "People told me not to get mixed up in it," she remembered.

> *They warned me that it was going to ruin my career. I said who gives a damn about careers when the people who we wouldn't have a career without are suffering, including the janitor. We've got to help them. If it weren't for homosexuals there would be no culture. So many of the great musicians, the great photographers, the great painters, the great writers were homosexual. Without their input it would be an entirely different, flat world. To see their heritage, what they had given the world, be desecrated with people saying, "It is probably what they deserve," or "It's God's way of weeding the dreadful people out," made me so irate. I felt the injustice of it.*

The vital, lonely stand, which the actress/activist took at such a crucial moment in the history of AIDS, was integral to the consciousness that Opie brought with her when she began her photographic project on Taylor. She says, "Being in the queer movement for so long and having been a member of ACT UP during the crisis years in the fight against AIDS, what happened when Elizabeth stood up to Ronald Reagan was a huge moment for many of us, and her continued leadership as a passionate advocate throughout her life was very meaningful to me."

But there were also powerful memories from Opie's earlier days as a child in Sandusky, Ohio. "My mom was in love with watching films on Sundays, and I was very into watching old movies," she explains.

So a lot of windy Sundays were spent with the three women who surrounded my life as a child in terms of film—Shirley Temple, Doris Day, and Elizabeth Taylor. Elizabeth was the most incredible one for me, even though her femininity frightened me a little bit. I've always been a tomboy and I didn't really know what to do with that kind of ultra-powerful femininity. It was very interesting being in Elizabeth's house and being one-on-one with so many of the objects that represented her fierce femininity.

If one looks carefully at the photographs, you can see that Opie included reflections of herself in some of them at various moments. Her presence in the images underscores their sense of intimacy and the feeling of how personal they really are, which is exactly the right tone for a portrait of Taylor through her possessions and home. As Mendelson says, "Elizabeth had an emotional connection to everything. To her these things were beautiful. She loved them. She appreciated the fact that she had them. She never took them for granted."

There's a wonderful story that Taylor was fond of telling about the time Burton took her into Bulgari in Rome to buy her something stunning. In what was known as "the money room," Johnny Bulgari toyed with them by flashing certain jewels but not actually producing them because he said the superstar couple, who at the time were filling the papers with headlines about the dramas that went on during the making of *Cleopatra,* couldn't afford these pieces. Burton, who had $100,000 to spend, got fed up and told Bulgari they wanted to see *everything*. Bulgari finally pulled out two breathtaking emerald necklaces, one bigger than the other. Taylor tried them both on and played with both of them. Then she told Burton she wanted the smaller piece. Her punch line to this anecdote was that Burton's dresser, who was along for the shopping expedition, said to the actor, "You just can't hardly get women like that no more." The point being that she knew what really mattered. Her materialism should never be confused for shallowness. Put in Elizabeth's words: "You can't cry on a diamond's shoulder, and diamonds won't keep you warm at night. But they're sure fun when the sun shines."

What's striking about Opie's imagery is its way of communicating how much Taylor cherished her stuff: the clothes in her closets, by a whole range of designers including Gianfranco Ferré, Dior, Zoran, Valentino, Halston, Ralph Rucci, and Versace; the bags by Louis Vuitton, Gucci, Fendi, Prada; the shoes by Chanel; the jewelry by Cartier, Bulgari, Van Cleef & Arpels, and JAR, all of it kept in special boxes; the Krupp diamond; the La Peregrina pearl; the Mike Todd diamond tiara; the ballet slippers she'd had as a child, saved by her mother; the Oscars she'd won for her work in pictures; her copy of *A Place in the Sun,* the film she starred in with Montgomery Clift; the paintings, including some she'd inherited from her father, an art dealer, and Andy Warhol's red portrait of her; the dozens of framed photographs of her with family and friends; her humanitarian awards; the pet cemetery where she buried her beloved animals, including Sugar, the Maltese; Sugar Ray Robinson's boxing gloves; the yellow chiffon wedding dress that she had worn the first time she married Burton. Opie does not create a hierarchy among the objects, which is true to how Taylor felt about them. All of it had meaning to Taylor, and all of it tells the story of her life. "I wanted the material that is already glamorous to hold its glamour in the everyday," says Opie. "I think it helped that I don't know that much about fashion or jewelry. I wasn't gaga over it. I didn't try to fluff it up. I wanted to capture a kind of democracy of glamour."

One of my favorite images is of a dog-eared remote-control manual on Taylor's bedside table. Opie has a soft spot for this photograph, too, because of its suggestion of just how human Taylor was. Opie laughs. "It says, Hey, I don't know how to work my TV and the remote so I better keep the manual next to the bedside table." Already in her 1964 biography, Taylor was emphatic about her belief in keeping it real. "I have never thought we should avoid what life dishes out to us," she wrote. "I believe people are like rocks, formed by the weather. We're formed by experience, by heartache, by grief, by mistakes, by guilt, by shame. I'm glad that in my life I have never cut short my emotions. The most awful thing of all is to be numb."

Perhaps that's why she wasn't a fan of having her portrait taken unless it was by someone she could relate to. "I always thought it was vain," she told me. "Having to smile when you feel like snarling. Turn to your left, turn to your right. There's something meretricious and superficial about having to look into the camera knowing you should look your best and try to look pretty." I am sure she would have loved Opie's photographs, which ask nothing of her beloved objects except to be themselves. That, of course, is a characteristic of Opie's photography in general, and part of its resounding power. One witnesses her acceptance throughout her work, from early portraits of transgender people to her fiercely honest self-portraits, from her portraits of fellow artists to her documentary work on a wide range of subjects, including surfers, high school football plays, and gay and lesbian communities. This is photography that doesn't look down on its subjects, and doesn't look up to them—but *at* them. Which is very rare. (A human dimension is also always present in Opie's landscape photography and her architectural studies.)

Toward the end of this book, you will notice a photograph of a blue room with wallpaper that looks like it has angel wings on it. Taylor was still in the hospital when she announced that she wanted one of the bedrooms in sky blue before she returned home. After meeting with her interior designers, Mendelson presented her with some options for wallpapers and fabrics and she touched the ones she wanted. Her team worked twenty-four hours a day to get everything ready. But Taylor never made it home. In Opie's photograph of the room, the feeling of emptiness is visceral. But so is the sense of order and peace. Mendelson is sure that Taylor was conscious that this would be the case when she made the decision to redecorate the room, that she had wanted them all to have a place that was peaceful and fresh and new, when all the madness was going on in the rest of the house as everything was being dismantled and taken apart after she died.

I asked Opie what was the hardest part of this project. She replied, "Watching the house transform and how quickly someone's life ends up being scattered." One of the most touching pictures in the book shows a white shopping bag. Soon it and others like it would be picked up in armored vehicles and dispatched to Christie's, their contents to be auctioned off, sent back out into the world, for new owners to get a kick out of. True to the end, was she. You see it all in Opie's photographs. As Mendelson says, "They tell us where she lived, what she lived with, how she loved, and who she was." Opie puts the flesh and blood back into the legend. Remember, this is a woman who at the height of her fame and of the world's obsession with her beauty said that all she saw in the mirror was a face that needed washing.

700 Nimes Road, 2015

Catherine Opie, *Bedside Table,* 2010–2011

Acknowledgments

This book could only have been realized with the efforts of many people and I would like to thank all those whose help and collaboration have made it possible.

My profound gratitude goes to Laurie Anderson for her beautiful foreword. Written from the heart, it is a warm and sensitive portrait of Ingrid. It truly captures her in a way that no one else could have done.

Thanks, above all, to Andrew Wylie, who embraced this project with enthusiasm. And my heartfelt appreciation to Rebecca Nagel, whose knowledge of Ingrid's writing was so valuable as I worked to shape the selection of these pieces.

My deepest thanks go to the remarkable photographers, designers, and artists who allowed us to reproduce their work in this book: Cindy Sherman, Jean Kallina, Julian Schnabel, Lee Friedlander, Bruce Weber, Francesco Clemente, Grillo Demo, Jeff Koons, Subhankar Banerjee, Rem Koolhaas, Ruben and Isabel Toledo, Robert Polidori, David Goldblatt, Brigitte Lacombe, Derrick Santini, Hedi Slimane, Annie Leibovitz, and Catherine Opie.

I would also like to thank all those individuals at museums, galleries, and foundations who provided invaluable help during this process: V&A Museum; Pericles Kolias, Janelle Reiring, and Helene Winer, Metro Pictures; Omar Ramos, Julian Schnabel Studio; John Broderick; Howard Greenberg; Jeffrey Frankel, Rebecca Herman, and Emily Lambert-Clements, Fraenkel Gallery; Verde Visconti, Prada; George Kocis, Staley-Wise Gallery; Penelope Phillips, Condé Nast International; Gregory Spencer, Art Partner; Matthew Richards, Little Bear, Inc.; Annelise Ream, Keith Haring Foundation; Muna Tseng and Cindy Lee, Estate of Tseng Kwong Chi; Chris Rawson, David Zwirner Gallery; Claartje van Dijk, International Center of Photography; Yana Rovner, Francesco Clemente Studio; Michael Shulman, Magnum Photos; David Strettell, Dashwood Books; Jeremy Higginbotham and Sander Manse, OMA; Stephen

Watt, Bob Adelman Books, Inc.; Peter MacGill and Kimberly Jones, Pace/ MacGill; Brittany Sanders, Robert Polidori Photography; Paul Kasmin and Mariska Nietzman, Paul Kasmin Gallery; Liza Essers and Bronwyn Nay, Goodman Gallery; Janet Johnson, Lacombe, Inc.; Ruth Bernstein, Viewpoint; Karen Mulligan, Annie Leibovitz Studio; Susan White, *Vanity Fair;* and Heather Rasmussen, Catherine Opie Studio.

And a very special thanks to those who were each so enormously generous with their time and insight: Joree Adilman, Robert Mapplethorpe Foundation; Julia Gruen, Keith Haring Foundation; Marin Lewis, Princeton University Art Museum; Gary McCraw, Jeff Koons Studio; Michael Stout and Mimi Thompson.

The book's interior was designed by Sam Shahid and Matt Kraus of Shahid and Company. I am enormously grateful to them for creating a beautiful book whose sensitive and thoughtful design is completely in tune with its content.

I would also like to thank Elaina Patton, who was the principal assistant on this project. Her intelligent and energetic collaboration was indispensable.

At Knopf, my brilliant editor Shelley Wanger has astutely guided this book through every step to publication. My deepest thanks go to her for her steadfast warmth, humor, support, and wise counsel. I also wish to acknowledge the important role that the talented Knopf team played in this publication: Brenna McDuffie, Kathy Hourigan, Andy Hughes, Peter Mendelsund, Roméo Enriquez, Kathleen Fridella. And an enormous thanks is due to Carol Carson for her gorgeous and absolutely perfect jacket design.

Special thanks go to my family for their love and support. And to Lindsay for always being there to listen.

My greatest thanks and deepest gratitude must go to Ingrid Sischy herself whose original and beautiful mind as well as her fierce search for the essential truth were always an inspiration.

Index

Page numbers in *italics* refer to illustrations.

Illustration Credits

489 Francesco Clemente, *Rene Ricard,* 2006. Oil on canvas, 60 x 30¼ inches. Courtesy of Clemente Studio.

492–493 Annie Leibovitz, *John Galliano, Saugerties, New York,* 2013. © Annie Leibovitz.

522–523 Annie Leibovitz, *Jeff Koons, New York City,* 2014. © Annie Leibovitz.

545 Catherine Opie, *Bedside Table,* 2010–2011. © Catherine Opie and Courtesy of Regen Projects, Los Angeles.

A Note About the Author

Ingrid Sischy was a South African–born American writer and art critic who focused on art, photography, fashion, film, and culture. She was the editor in chief of *Artforum* from 1980 to 1988, the editor in chief of *Interview* magazine from 1989 to 2008, a consulting editor at *The New Yorker* from 1988 to 1996, and a contributing editor to *Vanity Fair* from 1997 to 2015. She died in 2015.